UPDATED EDITION

FROM DAWN TO DUSK

MASTERING THE LIGHT IN LANDSCAPE PHOTOGRAPHY

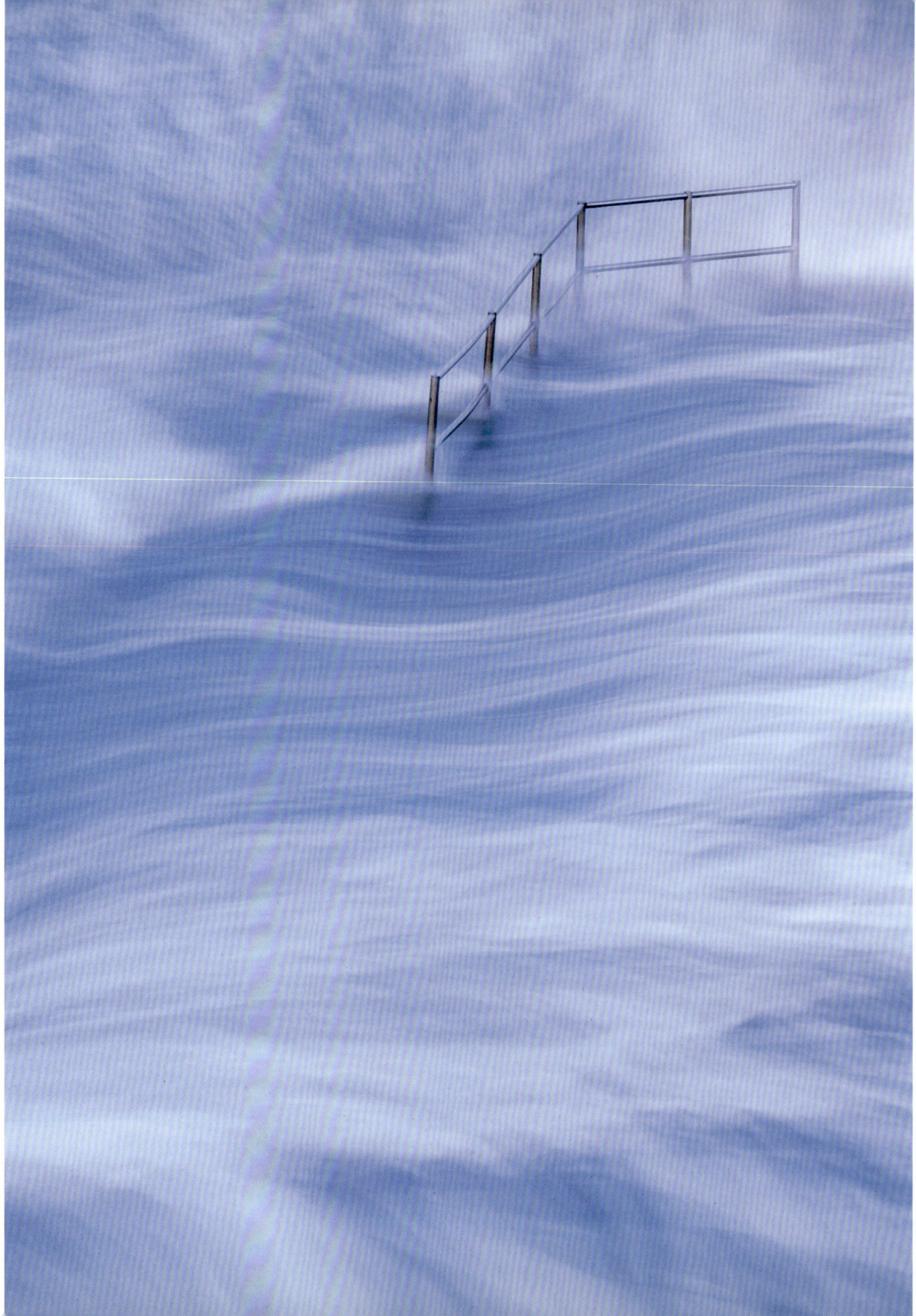

UPDATED EDITION

FROM DAWN TO DUSK

MASTERING THE LIGHT IN LANDSCAPE PHOTOGRAPHY

ROSS HODDINOTT & MARK BAUER

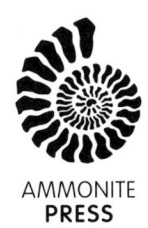

AMMONITE
PRESS

This edition published 2025 by
Ammonite Press
an imprint of Guild of Master Craftsman Publications Ltd
Castle Place, 166 High Street, Lewes, East Sussex, BN7 1XU, United Kingdom

First published 2018

ISBN 978-1-78145-494-7

Publisher: Jason Hook
Designer: Robin Shields
Editor: Rob Yarham

Color reproduction by GMC Reprographics
Printed and bound in China

◀ SEA POOL

There is no wrong time of day to take landscape images. Each passing
hour offers fresh and unique opportunities. For example, this atmospheric,
minimalist shot was taken late morning on a dull, overcast day. The
conditions perfectly suited the use of a neutral density (ND) filter and
a creatively long shutter speed to blur wave action.

Nikon Z7 II, 24–200mm (at 200mm), ISO 64, 2.5 sec. at f/11, 4-stop ND filter

CONTENTS

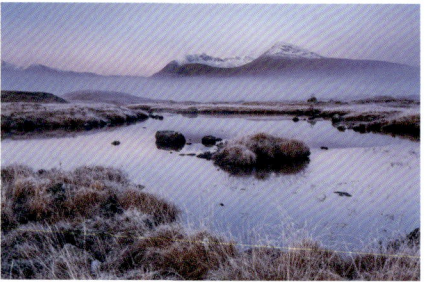

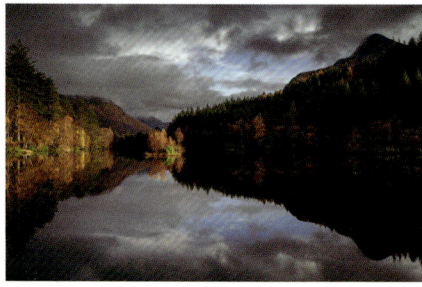

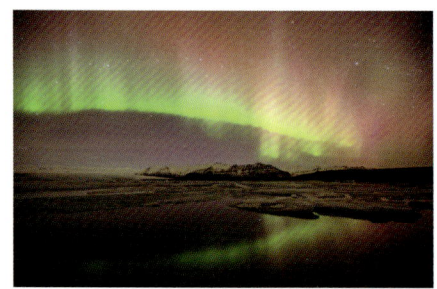

INTRODUCTION

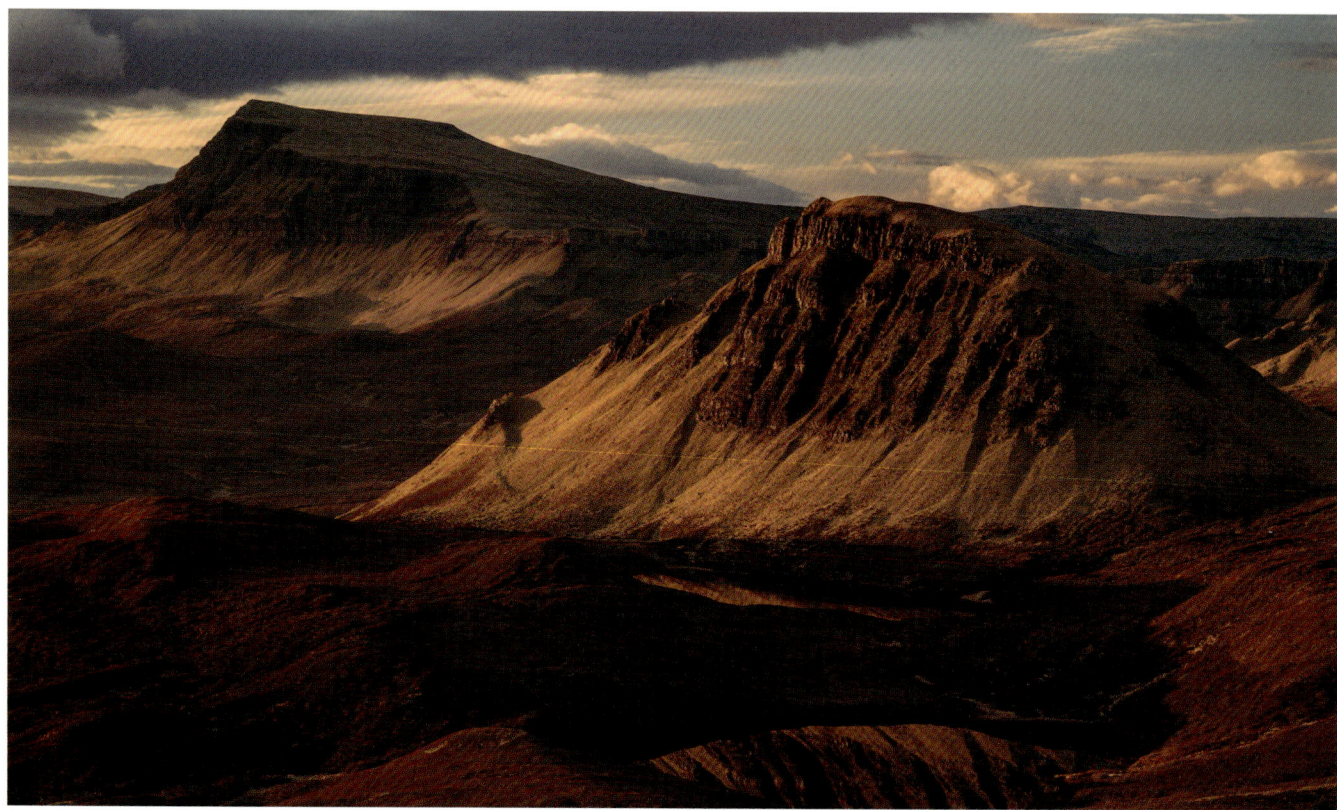

Dawn and dusk are truly magical times of the day. Natural light is soft and gentle, the color in the sky is vibrant, and there is a certain mood—arguably a peace or tranquility—about being outdoors at the beginning or at the end of the day. They are bewitching times, and are also among the most seductive and productive for landscape photography. Why is that? Well, landscape images require a number of ingredients to make them successful and stand out. Good technique and camera-handling skills are essential, while composition, creativity, and innovation are also key. However, perhaps the most important element of any landscape photograph is mood—and it is the light, time of day, season, weather, and general atmosphere that typically provide this.

Although dawn and dusk are well known to outdoor photographers for being excellent times to photograph scenery, they by no means have the monopoly. It is a myth that you can only capture compelling images at either end of the day, or in

▲ THE QUIRAING
Golden sunlight will shape the landscape, highlighting form and detail, and providing contrast and depth. To ensure you are in just the right place at the right time, planning and preparation are key. Motivation is important, too. Some of the best conditions are during unsociable hours, so be prepared to get up early or stay out late to capture the magical images you crave.

beautiful, golden sunlight. In truth, great landscape images can be captured throughout each day, and also during the darkness of night. Each and every passing hour possesses its own individual character and quality, providing fresh opportunities to any photographer willing to adapt their style and outlook to take advantage of this fact. This rather neatly brings us to why we decided to write *From Dawn to Dusk—Mastering the Light in Landscape Photography.*

Having already worked together to coauthor both *The Landscape Photography Workshop* and *The Art of Landscape Photography*, we felt we had not yet done justice to one key area. In our previous titles, we focused on camera skills, general technique, and esthetics, but we hadn't yet had a proper opportunity to fully explore the practical side of planning and timing shoots. In fact, this is an area often neglected in photography books and magazine articles. Publications tend to be so focused on providing advice on how to take the photo that they overlook the importance of putting yourself in the right place at just the right time to capture images with that all-important ingredient we mentioned earlier—mood.

PLANNING

This title aims to be different. Yes, we will still provide practical and expert guidance on camera equipment, core techniques, and framing—after all, we can't assume you already own our previous titles. However, this book will be more focused on just how you plan a shoot, and the photo opportunities that different times of the day, and night, provide. For example, we will show you how apps and other modern tools can help you plan your shoot remotely, enabling you to maximize your chances of success and minimize the risk of disappointing or mistimed visits. We will also look at the importance of scouting a viewpoint in advance, and pre-visualizing shots.

We dedicate progressive chapters to each time of the day. Beginning at dawn and leading you from morning to midday, to the afternoon, and through dusk. Each section will look at the benefits, challenges, and unique qualities of shooting at that particular time of day, and highlight suitable landscape types, styles of photography, and post-processing techniques to match.

And we don't stop once the sun has set. Despite the title, we continue into darkness, dedicating the final chapters to the "blue hour" and nighttime photography. Thanks to advances in digital technology, you don't need sunlight to capture correctly exposed images. The high ISO performance of modern sensors is so exceptional now that the camera can "see" far more than the human eye. As a result, photographers are able to capture extraordinary images of stars, moonlit scenery, and natural wonders—such as the Aurora Borealis—with relative ease. We will show you how.

In this book, we aim to take you on an enlightening, and hopefully inspirational, picture-taking journey, from dawn to dusk, and into darkness. With over 30 years' professional experience between us, we hope our hands-on guidance will have an instant impact on your photography, enhancing your landscape images, regardless of the time of day at which they are taken.

Thank you for joining us and we hope you enjoy it…

Ross Hoddinott and Mark Bauer

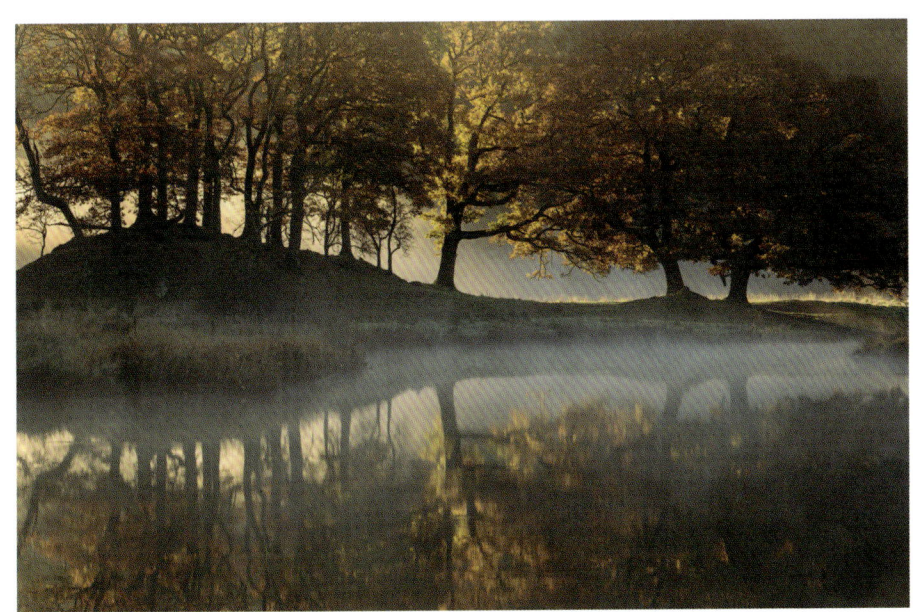

◄ AUTUMN REFLECTIONS
Dawn and dusk are often the optimum times of day to be out with your camera, photographing the landscape. The color, light, and mood are usually at their most photogenic, but don't think for a moment that these are the only times you can capture great images. Good landscape shots are possible at any time of the day (or night) providing you adopt the right approach.

PREPARATION
EQUIPMENT

⬤ ⬤ ⬤ ⬤ ⬤ ⬤

Great landscape images are captured as a result of the skill, creativity, and endeavor of the photographer. You do not need the latest, most expensive equipment to take great photos—today, it is possible to capture results using a camera phone. A camera is simply a tool for the job—the equipment that allows us to accurately capture the images we pre-visualize once we are on location. That said, our choice of equipment is still significant. It is important to use the type of camera that best suits your needs in terms of handling, size, weight, and performance.

Lens focal length is a key consideration. Wide-angle lenses will stretch and distort our perception of the landscape, while longer lenses will appear to foreshorten perspective—your lens choice will greatly shape how you capture the world.

It is important you carry the right accessories, too. Some physical filters remain essential tools for the job, and a landscape photographer's kit wouldn't be complete without a tripod. You will also need a good backpack to safely house your equipment and appropriate outdoor clothing.

So, before you head out on location for the day, let's briefly go through a checklist of the items of kit you will ideally need to accompany you for dawn to dusk photography…

▶ **THE BLACK MOUNT**
The evening before a dawn shoot, get into the habit of checking through your kit thoroughly to ensure you have everything you are likely to need, including a hat, gloves, and hand warmers during winter months. This is also an opportunity to check that all batteries are charged, and filters are spotlessly clean. Finally, make sure your tripod's quick-release plate is already attached to your camera, and that everything is in the right place, and quickly and easily accessible.

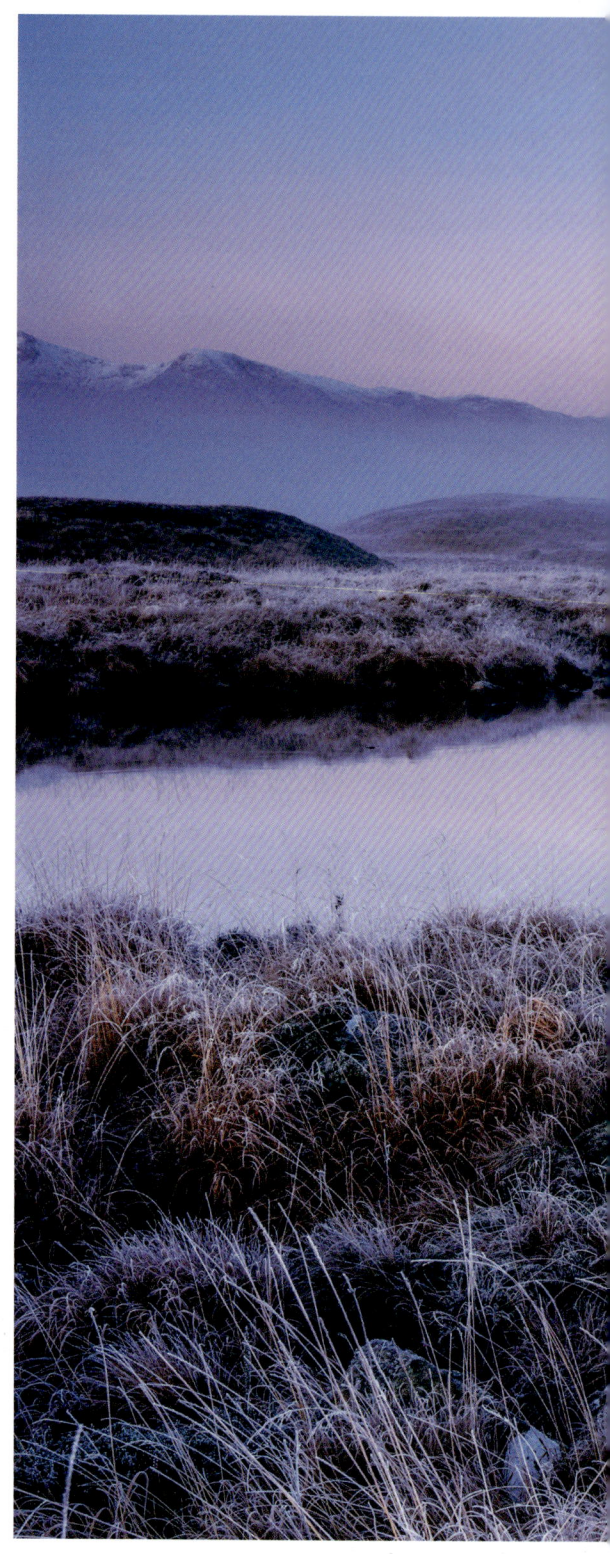

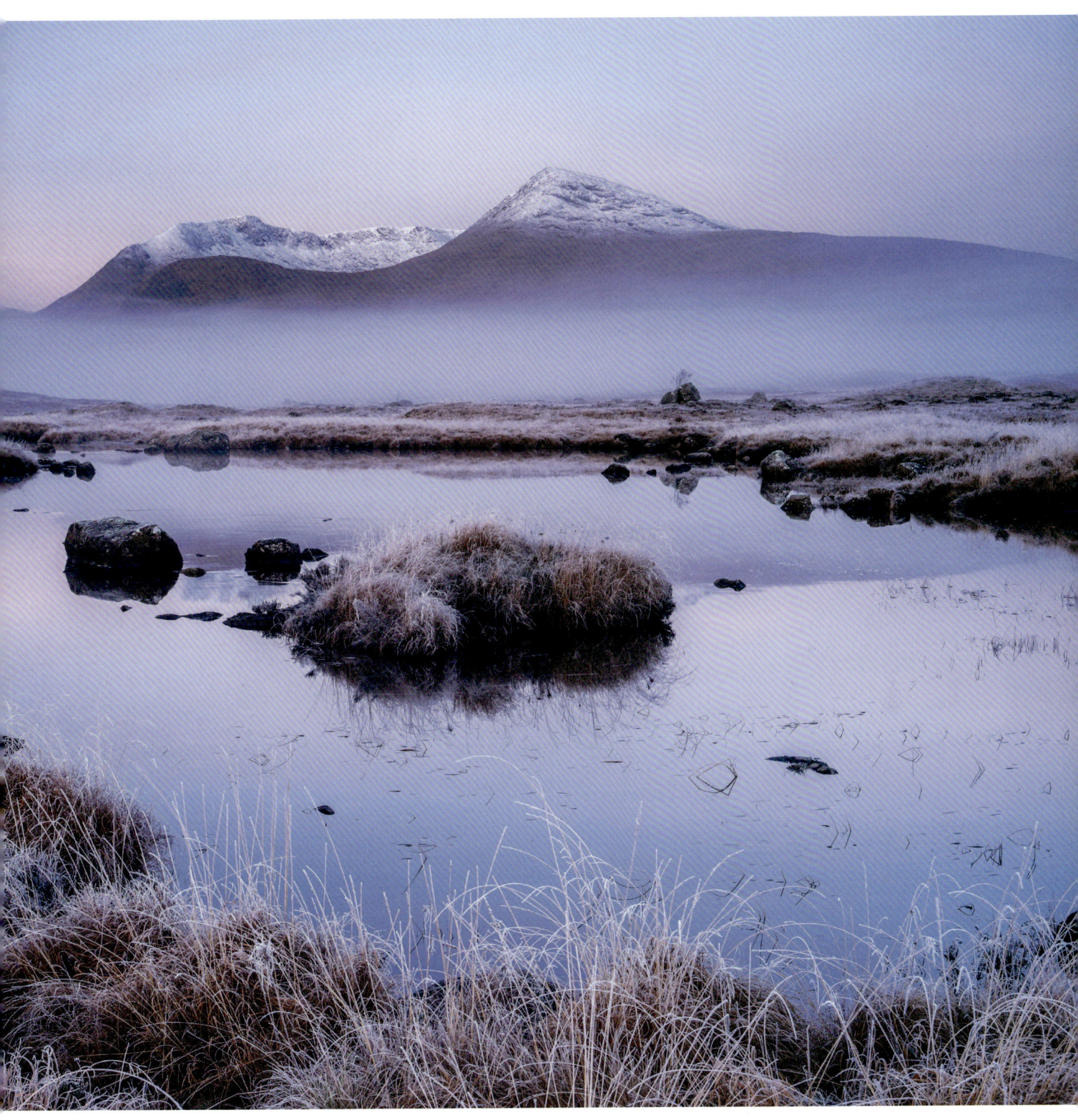

CAMERA TYPES

Great landscape images can be captured on almost any camera today. While you don't have to invest substantially, smartphones, compact cameras, and bridge cameras arguably lack the functionality, customization, and versatility you'll need for serious landscape photography. Therefore, most landscape enthusiasts will invest in a mirrorless or digital single lens reflex (SLR) camera —both systems are easily expandable and compatible with a wide choice of interchangeable lenses and accessories. There is a wide range of camera models—sensor size, resolution, speed, capability, size, weight, and cost will help dictate your choice.

DIGITAL SLRS

Digital SLR cameras remain the most popular type for landscape photography. SLRs have a mechanical mirror system and pentaprism designed to direct light from the lens to an optical viewfinder. When you trigger the shutter, the mirror assembly swings upward, the aperture narrows to the f-stop selected, and the shutter opens to allow sufficient light to pass through the lens and expose the sensor. This whole process can take just a fraction of a second, and some models are remarkably fast, with the ability to capture up to 12 to 14 frames per second (fps). SLRs in one form or another have been popular for generations. They are versatile— being suited to a wide range of photography genres—and boast superb ergonomics, image quality, rapid AF, and creative control. They are highly customizable, being compatible with a wide range of interchangeable lenses, filters, and accessories. This provides them with almost endless creative potential.

Until recently, digital SLR cameras were the most popular choice for landscape photography, but mirrorless cameras have now greatly superseded them. That doesn't necessarily mean their output is significantly better, but other aspects of a mirrorless camera's design and operation are superior. Many of the leading camera brands are not continuing to produce or support digital SLRs, and, ultimately, they will become obsolete. However, for the time being they remain a great option and increasingly affordable as prices tumble due to the migration to mirrorless.

MIRRORLESS CAMERAS

The main difference between a digital SLR and a mirrorless camera lies in the mechanism they use to capture light. While a digital SLR employs a mirror to reflect light onto the image sensor, a mirrorless camera enables light to strike the sensor directly, resulting in a quieter and quicker process. A preview of the image is sent to the camera's electronic viewfinder (EVF) and rear screen. By discarding the bulky reflex mirror and prism mechanism, cameras can be a lighter, more streamlined and portable construction. Mirrorless cameras use contrast-detection autofocus systems, which tends to be more reliable and accurate than the phase detection systems typically used in a digital SLR. They also work better in low light and provide a real-time preview of depth of field and any exposure adjustments. High end mirrorless cameras tend to be faster too, shooting continuous bursts of up to 20fps in full resolution, and even faster rates in lower resolution modes. However—in practice—speed is rarely a big consideration when shooting landscapes. On the flipside, battery life still tends to be shorter on mirrorless cameras and—unlike a digital SLR—the sensor is totally exposed and therefore more prone to dust and dirt, although some mirrorless cameras are now constructed with a shutter curtain to help provide extra protection. Most mirrorless cameras boast in-body image stabilization (IBIS), aiding sharpness

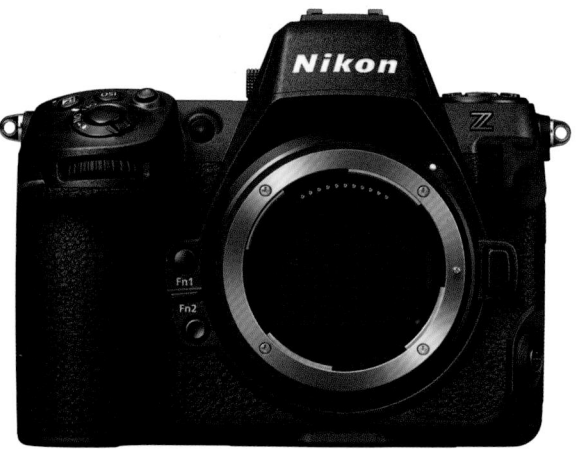

◀ FULL-FRAME NIKON DIGITAL SLR
Full-frame mirrorless cameras are more costly, but larger sensors boast more pixels, better resolution, and higher image quality. Sensors with a larger surface area enable the light receptors or "photosites" to gather light from a wider area and this improves low light performance, reduces noise, and provides better dynamic range—perfect for landscape photography.

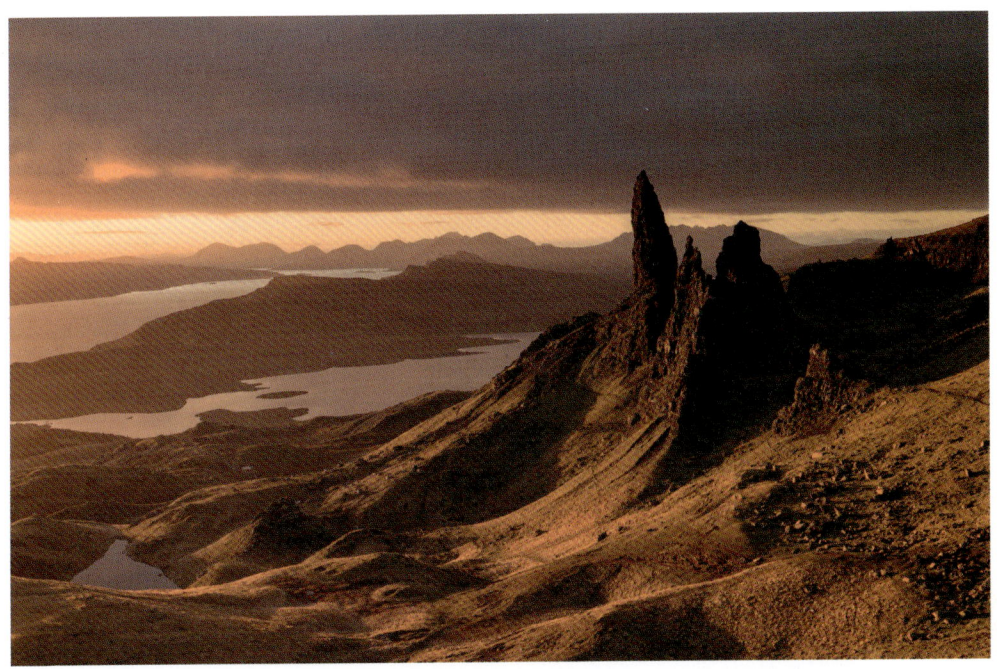

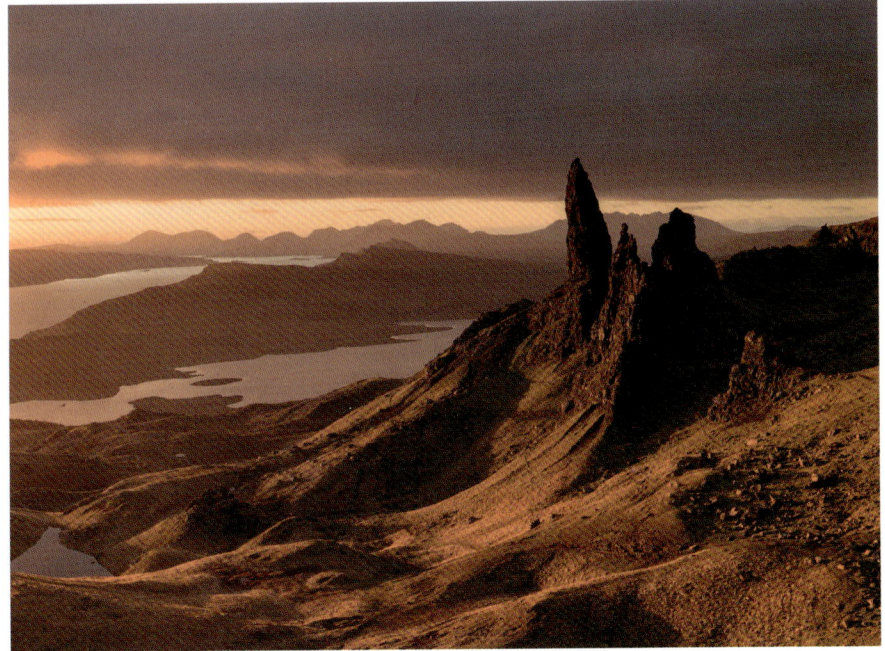

▲ ASPECT RATIO
Most mirrorless and digital SLR cameras have a native 3:2 aspect ratio (top). However, Micro Four Thirds cameras have a slightly squarer 4:3 ratio (above). This comparison helps illustrate the difference. Aspect ratio can have a significant influence on composition and balance. Many modern cameras allow you to adjust aspect ratio in-camera, while it can also be altered post-capture through cropping (see pages 78–81).

of handheld images without the need to have image-stabilized optics. While both digital SLR and mirrorless cameras have their unique strengths and selling points, overall, mirrorless cameras have the edge. However, ultimately sensor size and resolution holds the key to image quality rather than the type of camera.

SENSOR SIZE

The sensor is a piece of hardware inside the camera that captures and converts light and color into signals to create an image. Mirrorless and digital SLR cameras tend to be either full-frame or cropped-type. This refers to the physical size of the sensor, not the number of pixels. Full-frame models employ a chip that is approximately the same size as a traditional 35mm film frame (36 × 24mm), while cropped type cameras adopt a smaller sensor—typically in the region of 25.1 × 16.7mm. The smaller size of a cropped sensor effectively multiplies the focal length of the lens. This multiplication factor can range from 1.3× to 1.6× depending on the manufacturer and chip size and needs to be applied to calculate the camera's 35mm equivalent focal length. For example, a 24mm wide-angle lens effectively becomes 36mm when attached to a cropped-type camera with a 1.5× multiplication factor. To achieve the exact same wide-angle characteristics and field of view of 24mm on a cropped-sensor camera, you would need to attach a 16mm lens instead. Most camera brands have a lens range designed for cropped-type cameras to compensate. While full-frame and APS-C size sensors remain the most popular chip sizes, smaller and larger sensors can be found in other camera types. One of the most common is Micro Four Thirds—also known as MFT, M4/3, or M43—which is the longest-running mirrorless system. Founded by Panasonic and Olympus (now OM Systems), MFT sensors have an imaging area of 17.3 × 13mm and a crop factor of 2×. The system provides a smaller and more compact alternative to full-frame bodies. They also produce a slightly squarer native aspect ratio compared to other cameras.

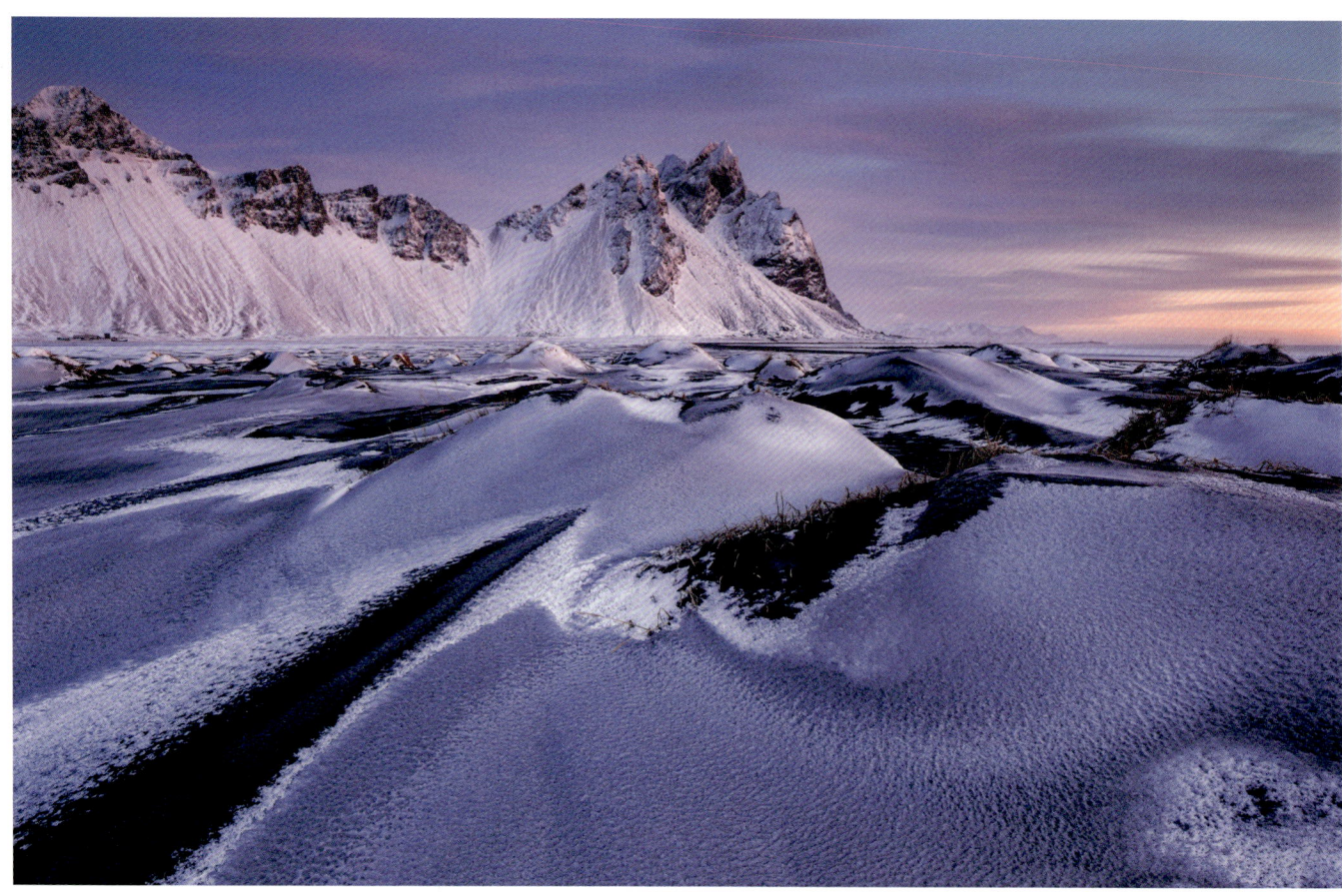

FOCUS ON...
DIGITAL MEDIUM-FORMAT

A camera with a sensor exceeding 36 × 24mm (full-frame) is said to be medium-format, and Fujifilm, Hasselblad, and Phase One are among the brands producing cameras of this type. They are specialist and can be costly, but, thanks to the sensor's large physical size, the camera is able to produce unparalleled image quality, with high-resolution files upward of 100 megapixels. Cameras can capture smoother tonal transitions, minimal noise, exceptional dynamic range, and unrivaled detail. However, an effect of using a larger sensor is reduced depth of field, as photographers must employ longer focal lengths to retain the same field of view. Therefore, technique, focusing, and camera-handling skills need to be flawless—there is little leeway for error. Medium-format cameras offer optimum quality, but their bulkier design and higher price tags limit their appeal and popularity.

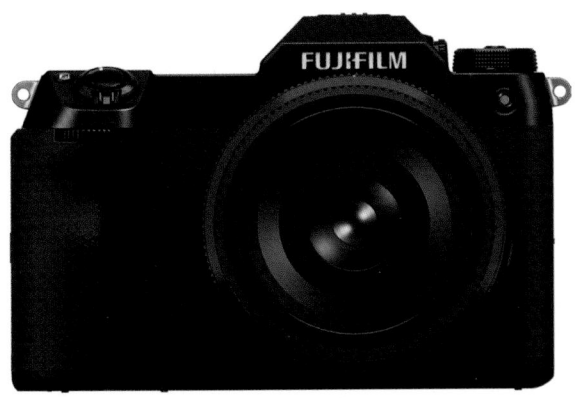

▲ FUJIFILM GFX100S II CAMERA

EXPOSURE MODES

Cameras have a choice of exposure modes, each of which provides different levels of control. Although many models have a range of pre-programmed Picture, Scene, or Subject modes—including a Landscape mode—we recommend ignoring all of these in preference for the "core four" modes, below, which offer a greater degree of creative control.

Programmed Auto Mode (P)

This is a fully automatic mode, in which the camera selects both aperture and shutter speed. While it is a reliable enough mode for achieving correctly exposed results, the camera is in complete control of the exposure equation. It can only guess at the result you wish to achieve and therefore is best used only for snaps and test shots.

Shutter Priority Mode (S or Tv)

This is a semi-automatic mode, in which the photographer selects the desired shutter speed and the camera sets the corresponding f-stop required to achieve a correctly exposed result (within the limits of the available light). It is a mode that is popular for action and wildlife photography, but is far less suited to landscapes.

Aperture Priority Mode (A or Av)

This is the mode most widely recommended for landscape photography. Using this mode, the photographer selects the aperture they require, while the camera sets the appropriate shutter length. Crucially, this mode gives photographers complete control over the extent of depth of field.

Manual (M)

In this mode, the photographer sets both aperture and shutter speed manually. Using this mode requires more input, but you are able to quickly override the camera's recommended settings. The camera still meters the scene and the recommended exposure is displayed via the exposure indicator—it is up to your discretion whether to apply the suggested exposure or ignore it.

◄ TRAVELING LIGHT

When hiking long distances and climbing hillsides to reach remote locations, you will feel the benefits of smaller, lighter mirrorless systems. The reduced weight is also of benefit when traveling, as many airlines have weight restrictions on hand luggage.

LENS CHOICE

Whether you invest in a mirrorless or digital SLR camera, you are using an expansive system of compatible lenses and accessories, ensuring your camera's versatility and capabilities have no limits. The biggest advantage of an interchangeable lens system is the ability to choose from a wide range of focal lengths to suit different shooting scenarios and to produce different results. You are not restricted or bound to a certain focal range as is the case with a compact, bridge, or smartphone camera. Ideally, you should always carry a range of focal lengths to provide creative choice and versatility while on location. Here we offer a brief overview of the most popular options for landscape work.

WIDE-ANGLE LENS

Arguably, this is the most essential lens type for a landscape enthusiast. Generally speaking, any focal length below "standard" (see right) is considered wide-angle and these lenses are the mainstay for many landscape photographers. Their extensive angle of view allows photographers to capture big vistas and include compelling foreground interest (see page 58).

Ultra wide-angles have the ability to distort perspective—stretching the relationship between near and far. This effect can create results with enhanced depth and visual impact. Such lenses allow you to exaggerate the scale of nearby objects, making them appear more imposing. They possess an inherently large depth of field and a wide-angle zoom—in the region of 14–30mm (on 35mm/full-frame or equivalent)—is among the most useful and popular focal ranges for landscapes. Not all scenes will suit a wide-angle approach, though.

STANDARD LENS

A standard lens is one that has a focal length roughly equivalent to the diagonal measurement of the sensor. On a full-frame camera this is approximately 43mm. However, a focal length of 50mm has long been considered as "standard." It is often regarded as a rather uninteresting focal length, being not dissimilar to the angle of view of the human eye. This lens displays minimal distortion and produces very natural-looking landscapes. It is a good choice when you wish to avoid foreground objects dominating the frame or wish to keep the emphasis on background elements.

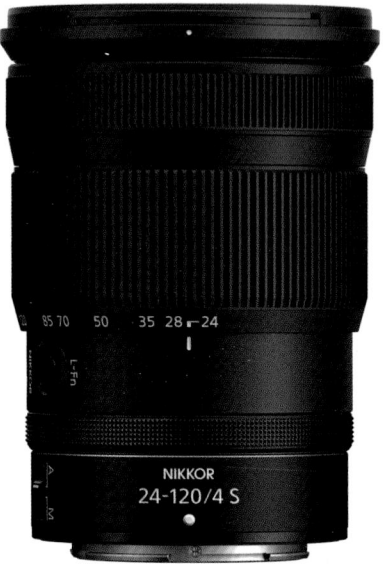

▲ WIDE-ANGLE ZOOM LENS
So, the big question is: what is the most useful combination of lenses to carry in your kit bag for a day out shooting? Most landscape photographers would conclude that something in the region of a 16–35mm, 24–70mm, and 70–200mm (or 35mm/full-frame equivalent) is the most logical selection. Combined, they cover a comprehensive and versatile range, suited to most shooting scenarios. However, you might prefer to buy one zoom lens covering a larger focal range to reduce both cost and the weight of what you need to carry. A zoom in the region of 24–120mm can prove a good choice.

Prime standard lenses are fast, lightweight, and relatively cheap. However, in truth, this is not a focal length you are likely to use regularly for landscape photography. For this reason, we advise investing in a good standard zoom instead—24–70mm (on 35mm/full-frame or equivalent). This should prove a more versatile option for dawn-to-dusk photography.

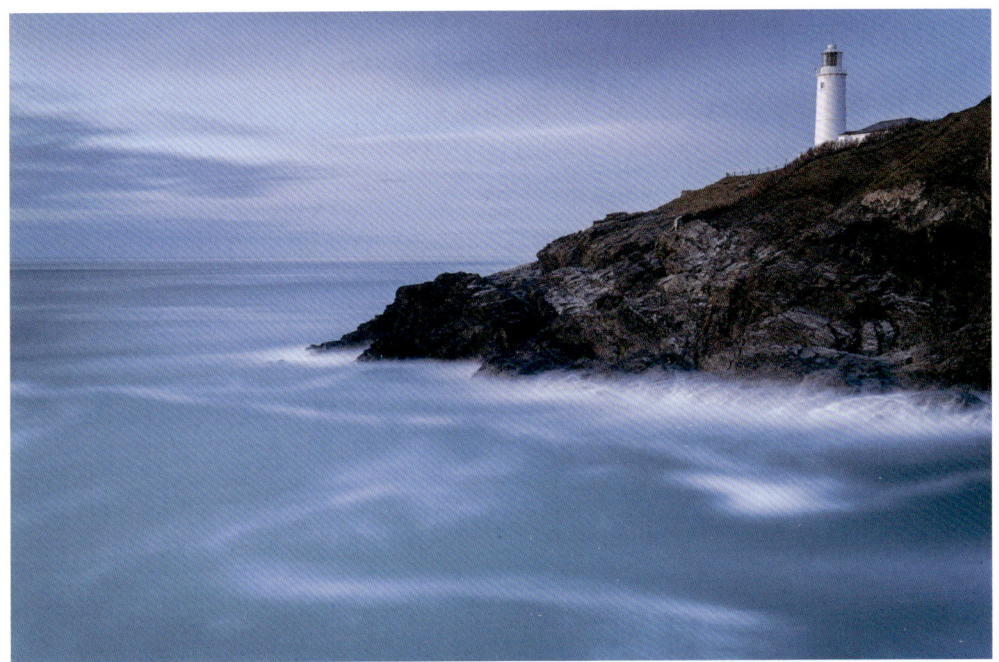

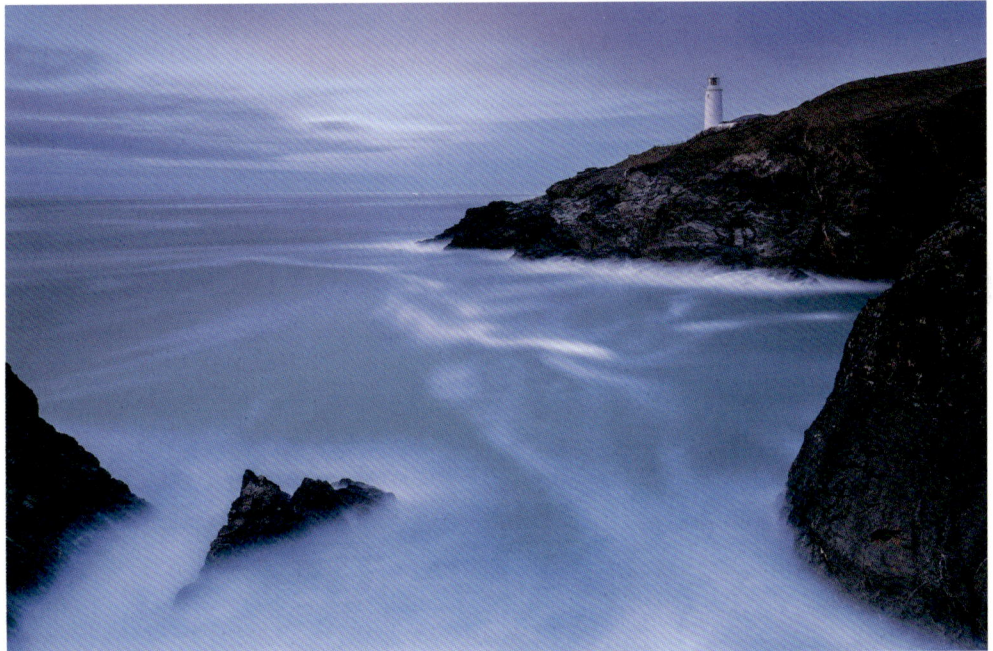

▲ FOCAL LENGTH COMPARISON

This comparison helps illustrate the shift in perspective, emphasis, and depth created by switching from a 50mm standard lens (top) to a 28mm wide-angle lens.

Top: Nikon D810, 50mm, ISO 100, 3 min. at f/11
Bottom: Nikon D810, 17–35mm (at 28mm), ISO 100, 3 min. at f/11

SHORT TELEPHOTO LENS

Longer focal lengths are severely underused in landscape photography, but a short-to-medium telephoto lens will prove a great addition to your camera bag. Any length longer than 50mm is considered to be telephoto, magnifying subjects, and making them appear larger in the frame. The relationship between subject and focal length is geometric—assuming the same subject-to-camera distance, doubling the focal length will also double the size of the subject in the frame. A characteristic of longer lenses is the way in which they appear to foreshorten perspective, and so they are a great choice for placing emphasis on background subjects or for isolating key points of interest within the landscape—such as a building, tree, or mountain range. Longer lengths will help highlight layers within the landscape and exaggerate atmospheric conditions, such as mist and fog. A tele-zoom in the region of 70–200mm is a popular choice among landscape photographers.

LENS JARGON
Image stabilization

Image stabilization (or vibration reduction) is lens technology designed to compensate for the photographer's movement. It employs internal motion sensors, or gyroscopes, to work in inverse relation to the lens's movement to eliminate camera shake and maximize image quality. Landscape photographers will often use a tripod, making stabilization unnecessary. In fact, if you are using a tripod, it is best to switch image stabilization off to conserve battery life. Most mirrorless cameras now boast in-body image stabilization (IBIS).

▼ FORESHORTENED PERSPECTIVE
Landscape photographers can rely too heavily on ultra wide-angle lenses today, but this can place too much weight on foreground objects. A medium-length telephoto lens will help place emphasis on elements placed farther away.

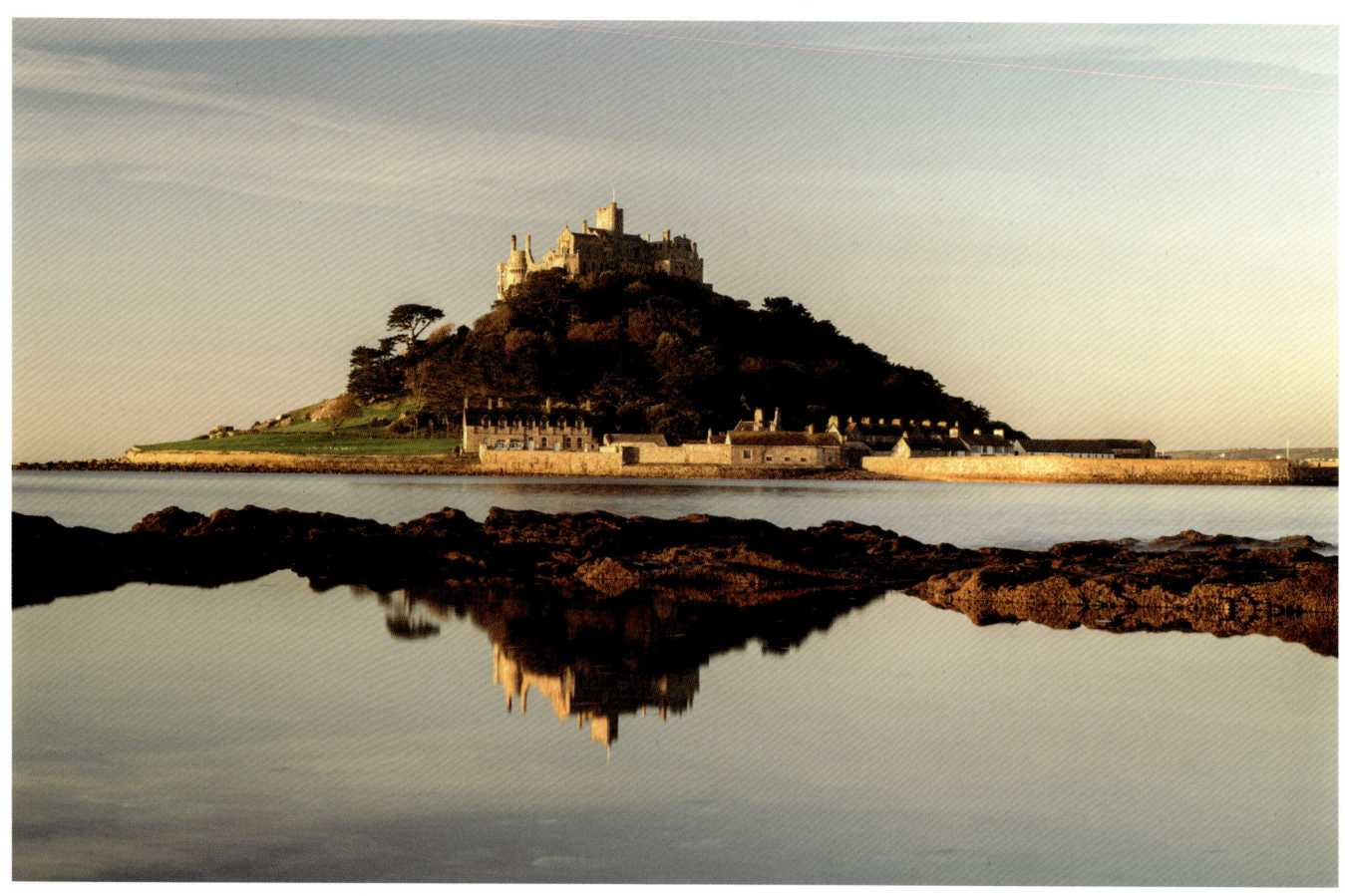

Lens speed

This simply refers to the lens's maximum (or fastest) aperture, which is typically in the region of f/2.8 or f/4. Lenses with a large maximum aperture can gather more light, which can aid focusing and composition in low light. However, lens speed is less relevant for daytime landscapes, with photographers often prioritizing a smaller aperture to generate sufficient depth of field. A fast lens can be advantageous for nighttime photography.

Zoom versus prime lenses

There are two types of lens—zoom and prime. Zooms—with a variable focal length—are the most popular lens type today, being more versatile and reducing the frequency with which you have to physically switch lens. They also conserve space in your camera bag, as you need fewer lenses to cover the same range. They allow photographers to be more spontaneous, too. A prime lens is one with a fixed focal length that cannot be altered. Optically, they tend to be high quality and—due to their simpler construction—are often fast and compact. Both zoom and prime lenses have their place in your kit bag.

Angle of view

This is the measurement in degrees of the amount of a scene that can be captured by any given focal length. It is often a diagonal measurement across the image area. Short focal lengths have a wider angle of view, while telephoto lengths have a much narrower one. Simply speaking, the wider the angle of view, the more of the subject you can include within the frame.

Tilt-and-shift lens

This is a specialist lens type designed for perspective control. With conventional optics, the axis of the lens is fixed, perpendicular to the sensor plane, so a degree of convergence will occur if you point the lens up or down, while the focal plane is often different to the subject plane, limiting depth of field. Tilt-and-shift lenses are designed to overcome this by allowing photographers to alter the plane of focus to extend depth of field and correct distortion. These lenses have two types of movements—rotation of the lens (tilt) and movement of the lens parallel to the image plane (shift). They are suited to landscape and architectural photography, but their price tag limits their appeal. They are always prime lengths, but often have a spherical front element, restricting compatibility with filters. To a great degree, distortion and convergence can be corrected using photo-editing software.

FOCUS ON... LENS CARE

A lens is the eye of the camera, and so it is important to keep optics clean at all times. Dirty, marked, or scratched lenses will adversely affect image quality and resale price. A popular method of protecting the lens's vulnerable front element is to keep an ultraviolet (UV), skylight, or protective filter attached. These are clear and relatively inexpensive screw-in filters. UV filters absorb ultraviolet light to produce crisper results, while skylight filters are also tinted with a faint pink coloring to add slight warmth to shadows. However, their visual effect is minimal. Protective filters are exactly as you would expect—a clear piece of optical glass designed to do nothing more but protect the front of the lens. While we recommend you keep your valuable lenses protected in this way, it is best to remove the protective filter prior to attaching a holder or any other filters. Once these are attached, the protective filter is redundant anyway—it is the system, or additional filters, that now provides the lens with protection. If you leave the protective filter in place, you increase the likelihood of vignetting (due to the added depth of the filter mount) and risk getting adapter rings and the protective filter stuck together. It is good practice to only have filters attached that are actively doing something. Use a good microfiber lens cloth to keep lenses and filters spotless, while dedicated, disposable lens wipes are handy for removing greasy fingerprints or sea spray.

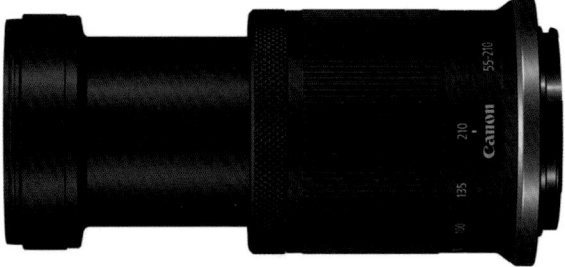

▲ **TELEPHOTO LENS**
A 70–200mm tele-zoom is a versatile focal range. There is rarely demand for fast optics when shooting landscapes. Therefore, a slightly slower, but lighter lens can be a more practical option if you are walking long distances with your kit.

FILTERS

A landscape photographer's kit bag wouldn't be complete without filters and a suitable filter system. Even in this digital age, when certain filter effects can be replicated using software, physical filters remain essential tools. In a wide range of circumstances, there is no substitute for filtering the light at the time you trigger the shutter, either for corrective or creative purposes. There is a vast choice of filter systems, sizes, and types. So, which filters do you need to equip yourself for a day's photography?

FILTER SYSTEMS

Camera filters are available in two types: slot-in or screw-in. Screw-in filters are circular and attach to the front of the lens via its filter thread—different lenses have different filter diameters. Slot-in filters are square or rectangular and attach to the lens using a compatible filter holder. A filter holder or bracket allows you to easily combine filters and is a necessity if you want to use graduated filters, as you need to be able to adjust their position to align them correctly.

There is a wide choice of filter systems, with Kase, LEE Filters, and Nisi among the most popular brands. Filter holders typically hold up to three slot-in-type filters, but are normally customizable, so you can add or remove slots to suit your own individual requirements. Two slots are usually all you require and it is best to keep holders as streamlined as possible, to minimize the risk of vignetting (darkening of the corners of the frame).

Systems are available in varying sizes—84/85mm and 100mm systems are the most popular. For most landscape photographers, a 100mm system is the best choice. While the holder and compatible filters are more expensive than smaller systems, the larger size makes it more versatile and compatible with extreme wide-angle lenses. LEE Filters' 100mm system is the preferred choice for many landscape enthusiasts and professionals. However, some lenses—particularly those constructed with a spherical front element—require a larger system or a specialist adapter. For example, the Nikon Z 14–24mm f/2.8 requires a bespoke system. Some filter providers offer a system match tool via their website where you can select your lens and the tool then identifies the filter, system, or adapter ring most suited.

Ultimately, your choice of filter system will be dictated by your budget and requirements. However, always buy the best you can afford. Filters are an important long-term investment that can have a profound influence on the look and quality of your landscape photographs.

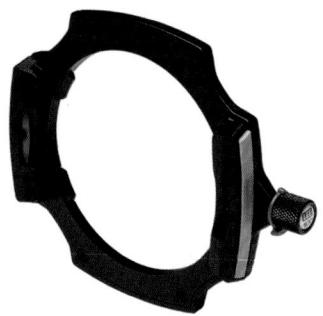

▲ LEE FILTERS 100MM SYSTEM
For most mirrorless or digital SLR users, a 100mm filter system is the best choice. A number of brands produce 100mm filters including Kase, LEE Filters, and Nisi. Filter systems attach via a compatible adapter ring, which screws onto the lens using its filter thread.

FILTER TYPES

Look online, and you will discover a vast and rather intimidating choice of filters. However, in practice, many are either gimmicky or unnecessary. In our view, there are just a handful of filters that you will genuinely need for landscape photography.

Neutral density filters

Neutral density (ND) filters have a neutral gray coating to absorb light and are a key creative tool. They are available as both slot-in and screw-in versions and in a range of densities—the higher the density, the more light they absorb and the more extreme their effect is.

Despite what we might immediately think, the landscape is full of movement, such as moving water, clouds, or foliage. ND filters allow photographers to intentionally prolong exposure length to creatively blur movement—doing so can imply a wonderful sense of motion, interest, and energy. They are available in a range of densities from one to 15 stops, but the most popular strength ND filters are three-, six-, and 10-stop versions. A stop is equivalent to a doubling or halving of an exposure value, so if you attach a three-stop ND, exposure length will effectively be doubled three times. To give you a quick example, let's say your unfiltered exposure time is 1/30 sec.—shutter speed will be extended to 1/4 sec. if you attached a three-stop solid ND. Using the same example, it would be lengthened to two seconds if you attached a six-stop filter or 30 sec. if you attached an extreme 10-stop ND filter. These values each represent a significant shift in exposure, which can radically alter the look, mood, and perception of the landscape. You just cannot replicate this type of natural movement in post-processing on the computer.

For lower-density filters, your camera's TTL (through-the-lens) metering should automatically compensate for the filter's strength in order to achieve correct exposure. However, when using extreme ND filters for middle-of-the-day photography (see pages 92–95) or minimalism (see page 96) you might need to calculate and then time your exposure manually. Although, theoretically, these filters are neutral, extreme NDs can possess a slight color cast, but this is easily corrected by adjusting the white balance in-camera or altering the image's color temperature during Raw conversion on the computer. Due to the length of exposure that ND filters require, a sturdy tripod is essential.

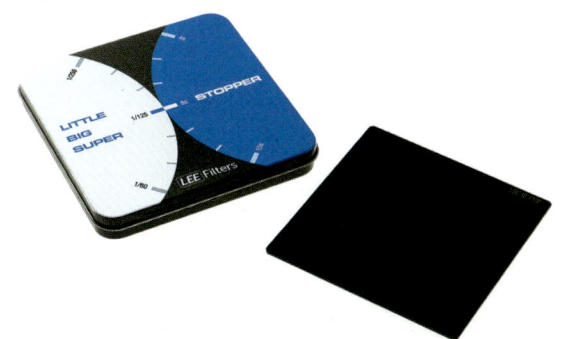

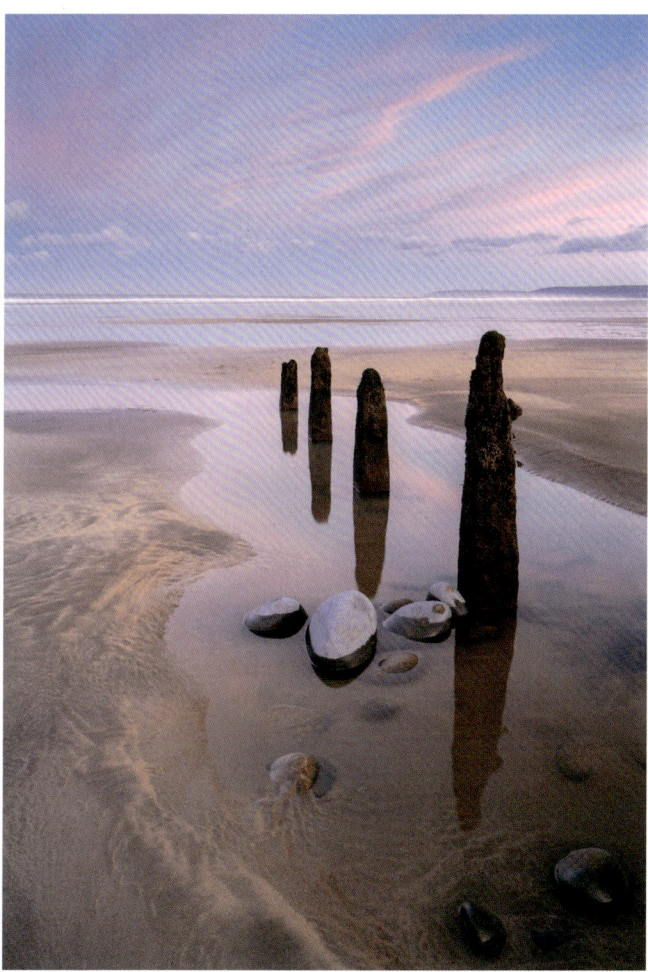

Thanks to a filter system, it is easy to combine filters. For example, when I took this photograph of a decaying groyne I used a solid ND filter to generate a creatively long exposure, and a two-stop medium-edged ND grad to balance the contrast between sky and sea.

▲ EXTREME ND FILTER
You can now also buy variable ND filters—circular filters where you can adjust the filter's density by rotating the front of the filter mount. However, for the most consistent and reliable performance and optimum image quality, opt for ND filters with a designated strength, such as LEE Filters' range of Stopper filters.

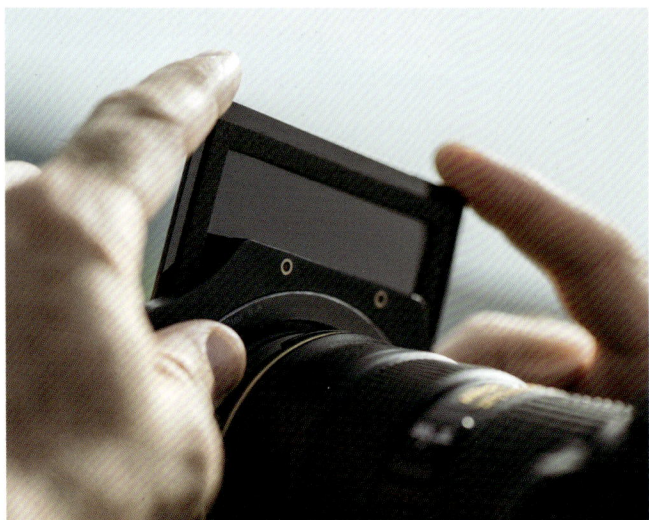

▲ LIGHT LEAKAGE
There is an enhanced risk of image-degrading light leakage when using higher density ND filters. To help prevent this, ensure the camera's eyepiece is covered (if using a digital SLR) and always position the filter closest to the lens, with its foam gasket positioned inward toward the camera to form a seal.

Graduated ND filters

Despite the excellent and improving dynamic range (a sensor's ability to capture shadow and highlight detail simultaneously) of modern cameras, they still need help coping with high-contrast scenes, particularly at dawn and dusk. The difference in brightness between the sky and darker foreground can be several stops, and—unaided—this can result in either underexposed foregrounds or overexposed highlights. There are a couple of ways to resolve the problem. One method is to use exposure blending (see page 60), while the other is to use filtration.

There are certain situations when blending is the best or only logical option, but there is something hugely satisfying about achieving the result you desire in-camera without the need to spend additional time on a computer post-processing later. Graduated ND filters are the only in-camera solution to successfully capturing high-contrast scenes. As with solid NDs, grads are available in a range of densities—typically one-, two-, and three-stop strengths. They are also available in a choice of soft-, medium-, hard-, or very hard-edged feathered areas.

Ideally, carry a choice of soft-, medium-, and hard-edged grads so you are equipped to deal with all types of landscape and shooting scenarios. Reverse grads are also available—aimed primarily at sunrise and sunset photography when the highest luminance is close to the horizon. Like hard grads, reverse grads feature a hard transition in the center of the filter, but then their density reduces toward the top of the filter to protect against skies growing too dark—or "over-graduated"—toward the top of the frame. For more information about using graduated filters, see pages 54–57.

Polarizing filters

Polarizers are typically circular filters that reduce glare and reflections within the landscape. By doing so, they restore natural color saturation, providing images with punch and vibrancy. It's not possible to replicate their effect in processing—you need to polarize the light in-camera. Arguably, they are the most useful filter for outdoor photography. They work by blocking polarized light—scattered and reflected wavelengths of light, traveling in only one direction—from entering the lens. Filters are constructed with a thin foil of polarizing material sandwiched between two pieces of optical glass. You then rotate the front of the filter mount to adjust the level of polarization. You can determine the point of

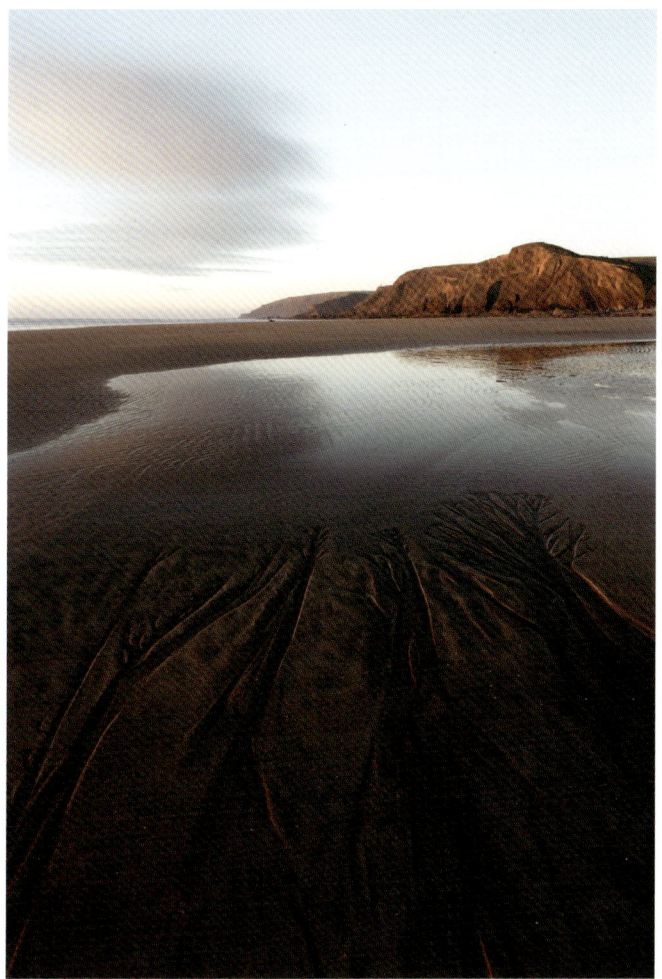
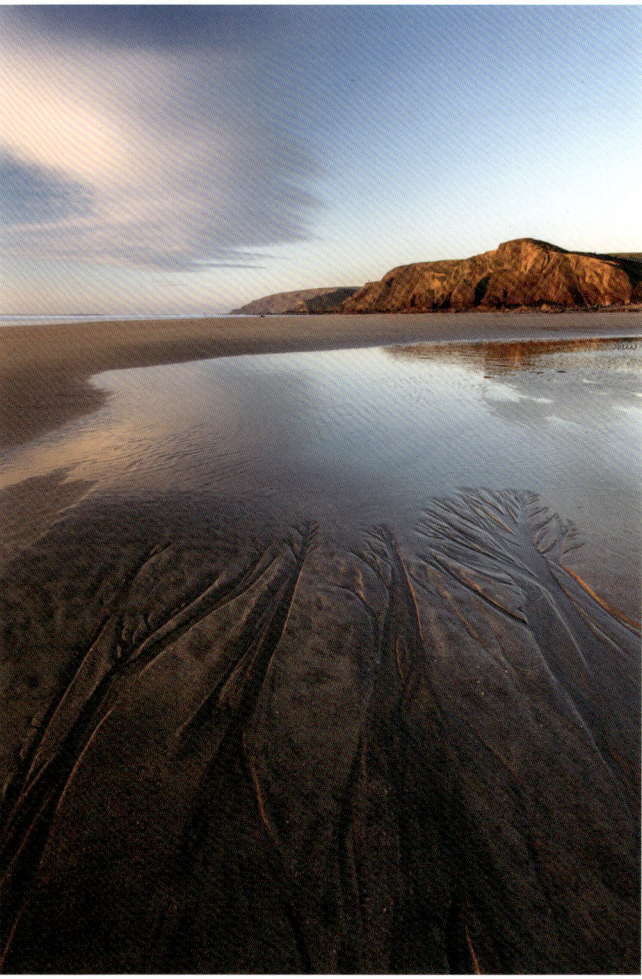

optimum contrast by rotating the filter until you achieve the most pronounced effect through the viewfinder or with live view. As you do so, you will notice reflections come and go, and the intensity of colors strengthen and fade. There is no golden rule as to how best to use a polarizer—simply rotate the filter until you achieve the effect you desire.

Polarizing filters provide the most pronounced effect when used at a 90-degree angle to the sun. Be careful not to over-polarize clear blue skies—when the sky can appear too dark and inky. Also, be aware of uneven polarization, when the effect is uneven across the sky—a problem ultra wide-angles are most prone to. If you notice over- or uneven polarization, simply reduce the level of polarization by rotating the mount. Polarizers have a filter factor of 4×, absorbing up to two stops of light, but TTL metering will compensate for this automatically.

▲ POLARIZER COMPARISON
Although polarizing filters are best known and used for their effect on blue skies, they are excellent for reducing reflections on water and wet foliage—see the effect of switching from shooting without (above left) to with a polarizer (above right). As a result, they are useful for shooting woodland interiors, and coastal scenes boasting wet rocks and reflective sand.

CAMERA SUPPORT

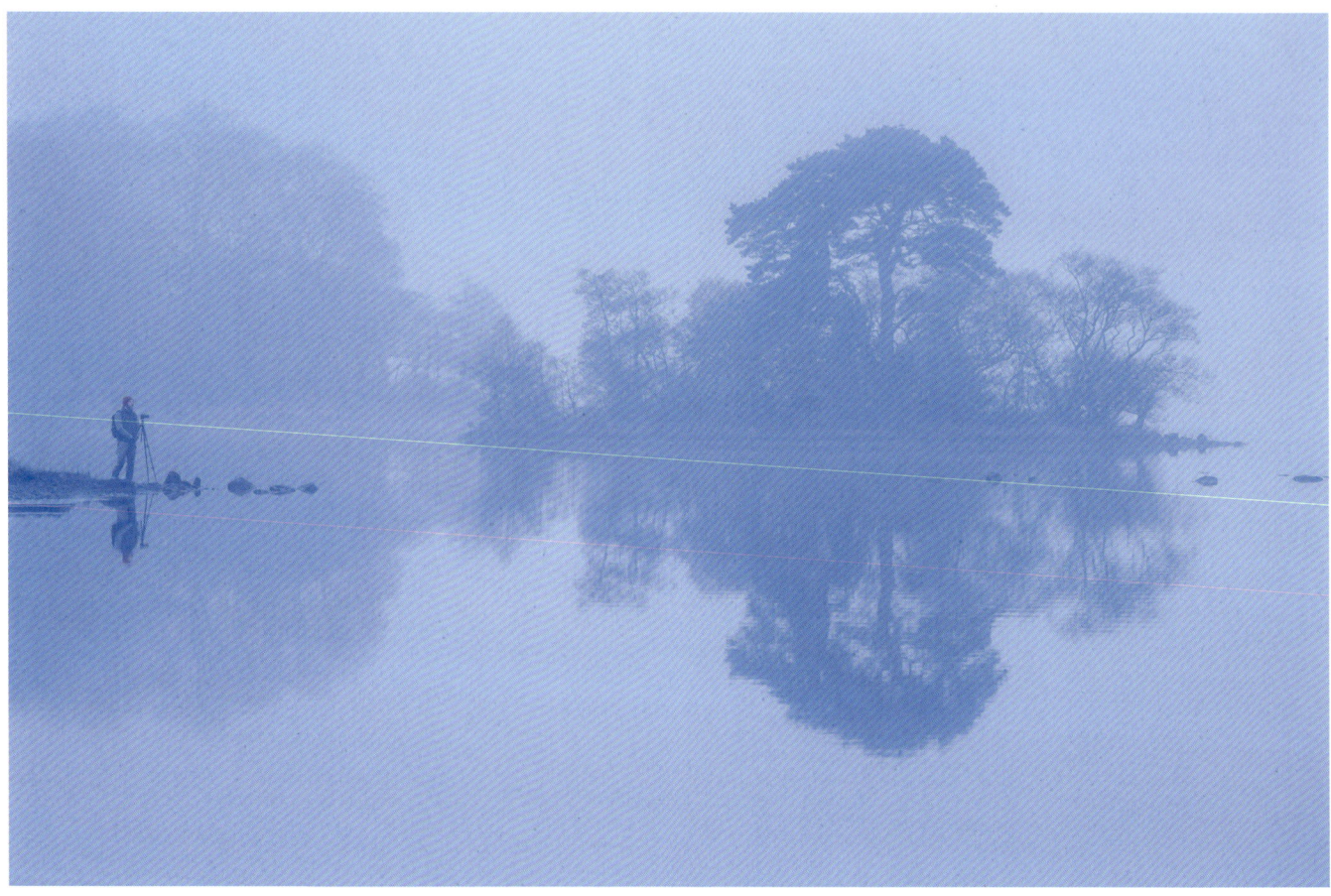

A tripod isn't a luxury item—it is essential for landscape photography. Using one provides stability and practically eliminates all risk of camera shake. However, a tripod offers more than just this. It slows you down, makes you think, and it is a great framing aid, helping you to fine-tune your composition. While shooting handheld (see page 74) can promote spontaneity and opportunism in certain shooting situations, our message is don't head out for a day's photography without a tripod.

LEGS

Modern digital cameras boast excellent high-ISO performance, allowing you to generate shorter exposure times in low light. This does not mean that you should dispense with using a tripod, however. While its primary role is to provide a stable platform,

▲ TRY BEFORE YOU BUY

When choosing your combination of legs and head, try before you buy. Go into a camera shop and ask their advice based on your requirements—try a variety of designs and set-ups. You can then get a true feeling for weight—is your set-up going to be sturdy enough, or too heavy to carry comfortably for long distances? Does the design suit your needs—do you find it easy to adjust the head precisely? Will the head support a load capacity at least equivalent to your heaviest camera and lens combination?

there are other key advantages to having your camera in a fixed position. A tripod helps you to fine-tune and perfect your composition over several frames, and also align graduated filters accurately. In addition, creatively long exposures are only possible with the aid of a tripod, and it is also easier to focus precisely when your camera is fixed in position.

FOCUS ON...
TRIPOD HEADS

The advantage of buying legs and head separately is that you can buy the style of head that best suits your needs and personal preference. It is an important choice—the wrong design will only slow you down and frustrate you. Ball-and-socket heads are popular among landscape photographers. They have an overriding locking control that allows you to smoothly rotate the camera around a sphere and then lock it securely into position. Depending on the sophistication of the head, they have additional controls to adjust tension and friction and also a panning lever.

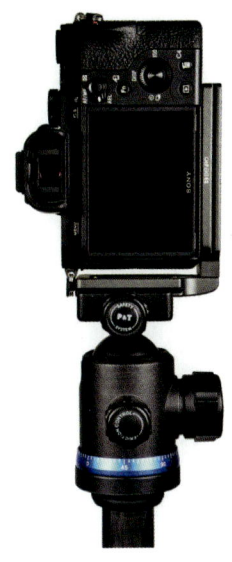

Three-way pan-and-tilt designs are also popular. These heads offer three individual axes of movement—left-to-right tilt, forward-to-back tilt, and horizontal panning. The best versions are geared, which—although more expensive—allow you to make precise, micro-adjustments to each control—as opposed to having to unlock, reposition, and then lock each lever, as you have to with a standard three-way head. Geared heads, like Benro's popular GD3WH, are a favorite among landscape enthusiasts.

Your camera attaches to the head using a quick-release plate (many are an Arca-Swiss type design), which screws onto the camera via the tripod bush. This then allows you to attach and remove your camera quickly and easily. Buy extra plates or brackets for each camera body, or for any lenses with a tripod collar—doing so will save you the fuss of removing a plate from one lens to attach it to another. A variation of a quick-release plate is the L-bracket. This design allows you to switch from horizontal to vertical orientation (or vice versa) quickly and without the need to recompose your shot. An L-bracket also allows you to keep the weight of the camera down the center axis of the tripod (rather than place it to one side), which can compromise stability with some designs.

You can buy a wide variety of supports, including monopods, Gorillapods, and amazingly compact and lightweight designs. Depending on circumstance, they all have their place. However, serious landscape photographers need to invest in a solid set of legs to cope with the demands of outdoor photography and to withstand all types of weather. Creative photographers will often employ slow shutter speeds, as a result of using a small aperture (to generate a large zone of focus), filtration, or shooting in low light or darkness. Bitingly sharp results are only possible with a sturdy tripod. Compact and lightweight legs will be adequate for short periods—when traveling, for example, when weight is a consideration. However, for day-to-day landscape photography, you will want a good set of legs.

All-in-one designs, in which the legs and head are fixed together, are generally best avoided. Instead, it is better to buy a good set of legs and then purchase a compatible head to create a bespoke combination that suits your exact requirements. Budget, weight, and maximum and minimum height are all things that will help determine your choice. Benro, Gitzo, Manfrotto, 3-Legged Thing, and Really Right Stuff are among the leading brands, and each provide a wide choice of designs. If budget allows, opt for a carbonfiber design, being lighter than aluminum, yet stiffer and stronger. You need legs that will extend to a height you are comfortable using. Ideally, it should do this without the need to extend the center column fully, as this can compromise stability.

ACCESSORIES

We've now looked at the most essential items of kit. However, there are a handful of key accessories that, while they may not be as obvious, will more than justify their place on your kit list and will aid your pursuit of the perfect landscape shot.

Camera backpack

To capture drama and mood you need to shoot in all weather conditions. To adequately protect your gear, invest in a good camera bag. A backpack will distribute the weight of your gear more evenly across your shoulders and back. Comfort, capacity, and cost are the

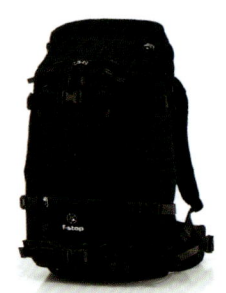

key things to consider. Look for a design made from weather- resistant material—or that has an internal all-weather cover. F-Stop Gear, Lowepro, and Shimoda are among the brands you should consider.

Remote release

Using a tripod doesn't completely guarantee that you'll be taking shake-free images. Physically pressing the shutter-release button can create camera movement that, although slight, can degrade critical sharpness. One solution is to simply trigger

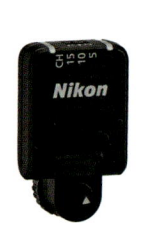
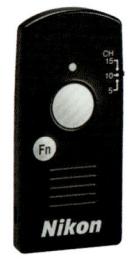

the shutter using your camera's built-in self-timer. However, this won't suffice when you need to carefully time your shot—to capture the light in just the right place, perhaps, or to photograph wave motion. Using a remote cable, or a wireless or infrared device, is a better option. There is a wide range of triggers available for you to choose from. Some are basic, with just a trigger button at the end of a cable, while others offer a high degree of functionality, with a backlit control panel and multiple timer and shutter functions. Cords and devices connect to the camera via its remote release terminal. They also enable you to lock open the shutter in Bulb mode in order to capture long, timed exposures.

Camera spirit-level

Camera spirit-levels, which are attached to the camera's hotshoe, are popular among landscape photographers to help them achieve a perfectly level horizon. They have a double-axis level and are particularly useful when capturing a sequence of frames

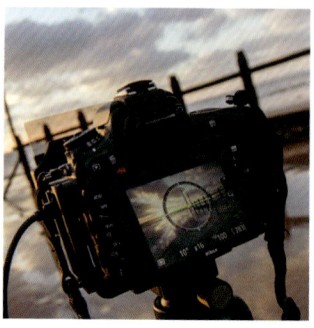

to later create a panoramic stitch. However, most modern cameras now possess a virtual horizon function—a digital leveling gauge that you can display on the scene via the camera's EVF or monitor.

Loupe

Light or glare reflecting off a digital SLR's screen can make live view focusing and composition difficult, and hinder assessment of images replayed on the back of the camera. A simple, but wonderfully effective, solution is to use a loupe. These are designed to block out the

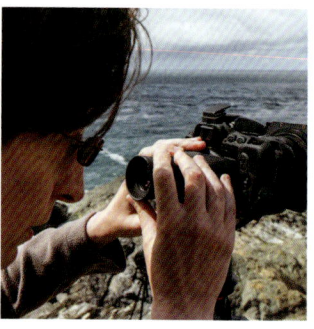

light to enable photographers to view the LCD screen properly. Most versions have a diopter so you can adjust it to your eyesight. Users often wear them around their neck on a lanyard so they are always readily accessible.

Head lamp

Although not strictly a camera accessory, a head lamp is an essential item for any outdoor photographer. You will often be walking to a viewpoint before sunrise, or returning after dark, and a flashlight is important to help you see safely where you are going. The major advantage of a head lamp is that it allows you to keep your hands free—perfect when trying to set up or pack away kit in the dark. For nighttime photography, a flashlight is essential for checking camera settings in darkness. Buy one that allows you to direct or pivot the lamp and that also has a red LED to preserve night-vision.

FOCUS ON...
OUTDOOR CLOTHING

You won't feel creative or have the motivation to wait for the best light if you are cold or wet. Therefore, appropriate outdoor clothing is arguably as essential as any other piece of camera kit. In wintry or windy weather, a good base layer is an essential item of clothing. It will help "wick" moisture away from your skin and keep your body warm and dry. Although costly, merino wool is a great natural fiber, being light but great for insulation.

Water- and wind-proof outdoor pants will provide comfort, will stretch, and offer protection against the weather. They use weatherproofing technologies and fabrics to deal with moisture, sweat, and heat to keep you comfortable—perfect if you need to trek a long way to capture an atmospheric scene.

A good, insulated jacket is important, particularly in winter. Down jackets are great for keeping you warm, containing a layer of synthetic down or feathers for added insulation. Montane, Paramo, Patagonia, and Rab are all worth considering. Insulated jackets are not a replacement for waterproof jackets, but work well underneath a waterproof layer.

Remember to wear proper walking socks in winter, too—look at those made by Brasher, Bridgedale, and SealSkinz. Always wear a hat in cold weather—doing so will help you to retain heat. Gloves are also important for photographers. They need to be warm, but also thin enough to allow you to adjust camera controls and attach filters without the need to take them off. Skiing and cycling gloves are often worth considering, depending on likely conditions.

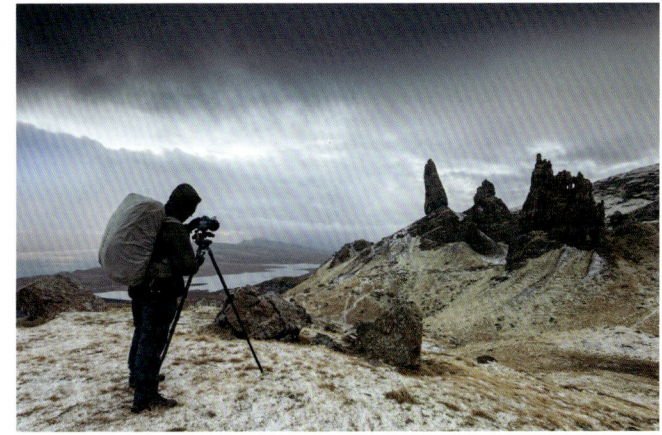

Lastly, invest in good walking boots. They need to be comfortable, warm, and waterproof, and they need to give your ankles adequate support when clambering over uneven surfaces. Brasher, Mammut, Meindl, Salomon, and Scarpa are brands with good reputations.

Smartphone

A smartphone can prove a useful, ever-present resource for landscape photographers. Not only can you use the camera to practice composition or to record your position (via GPS), but there is a wide range of apps available to help with navigation, planning (see page 34), weather, tide prediction, or for calculating exposure. The LEE Stopper App, PhotoPills, Space Weather Live, Sun Surveyor, Tide Charts (iOS), Tides Near Me (Android), and TPE (The Photographer's Ephemeris) are among the most popular apps.

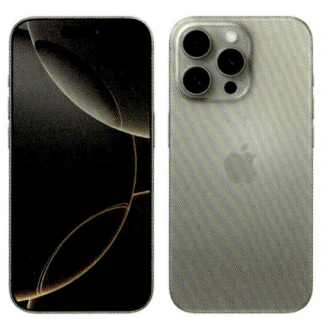

PREPARATION
PLANNING

● ● ● ● ● ●

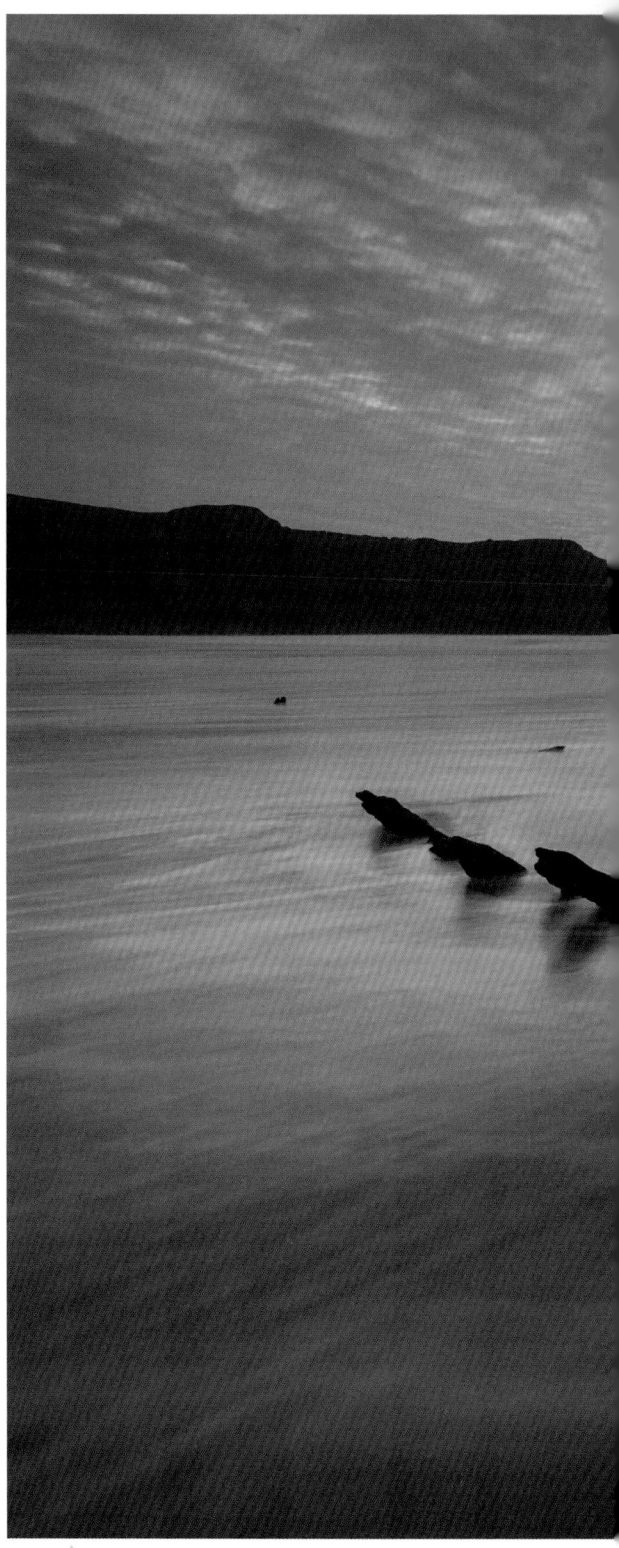

In any artistic endeavor, spontaneity can be a good thing—improvisation can result in heightened creativity. In landscape photography, too, heading out with no fixed plan, and simply reacting to what we see in front of us, can open our eyes to possibilities we may otherwise have missed and help us to create more original images. However, if we habitually avoided planning we would need an extraordinary amount of good luck in order to produce consistently good work.

The fact is that landscapes change enormously through the day, the year, and in different weather conditions. A location may look fabulous on a frosty morning in winter but quite unremarkable on a summer's evening. There is a huge variation in the height and position of the sun at different times of the year, which can completely transform a scene. On the coast, the tide height can be the difference between an untidy, cluttered foreground or dramatic ridges of rock with waves breaking between them. Without planning, the chances are that you'll simply end up in the wrong place at the wrong time.

In this chapter, we will look at the factors to consider when planning a shoot and the resources available to help you.

▶ **PLANNING**
For this shot to be successful, a number of factors had to coincide. Firstly, the sun had to be setting in the right position, just over the distant island (though it is obscured by low cloud); this gives the maximum chance of color. Secondly, the tide had to be exactly the right height at sunset, so that waves would wash around the boat wreck as it came in. Finally, there had to be enough cloud to catch the color of the setting sun. Getting exactly the right weather conditions is largely down to luck, but tide height and sunset position are easily researched.

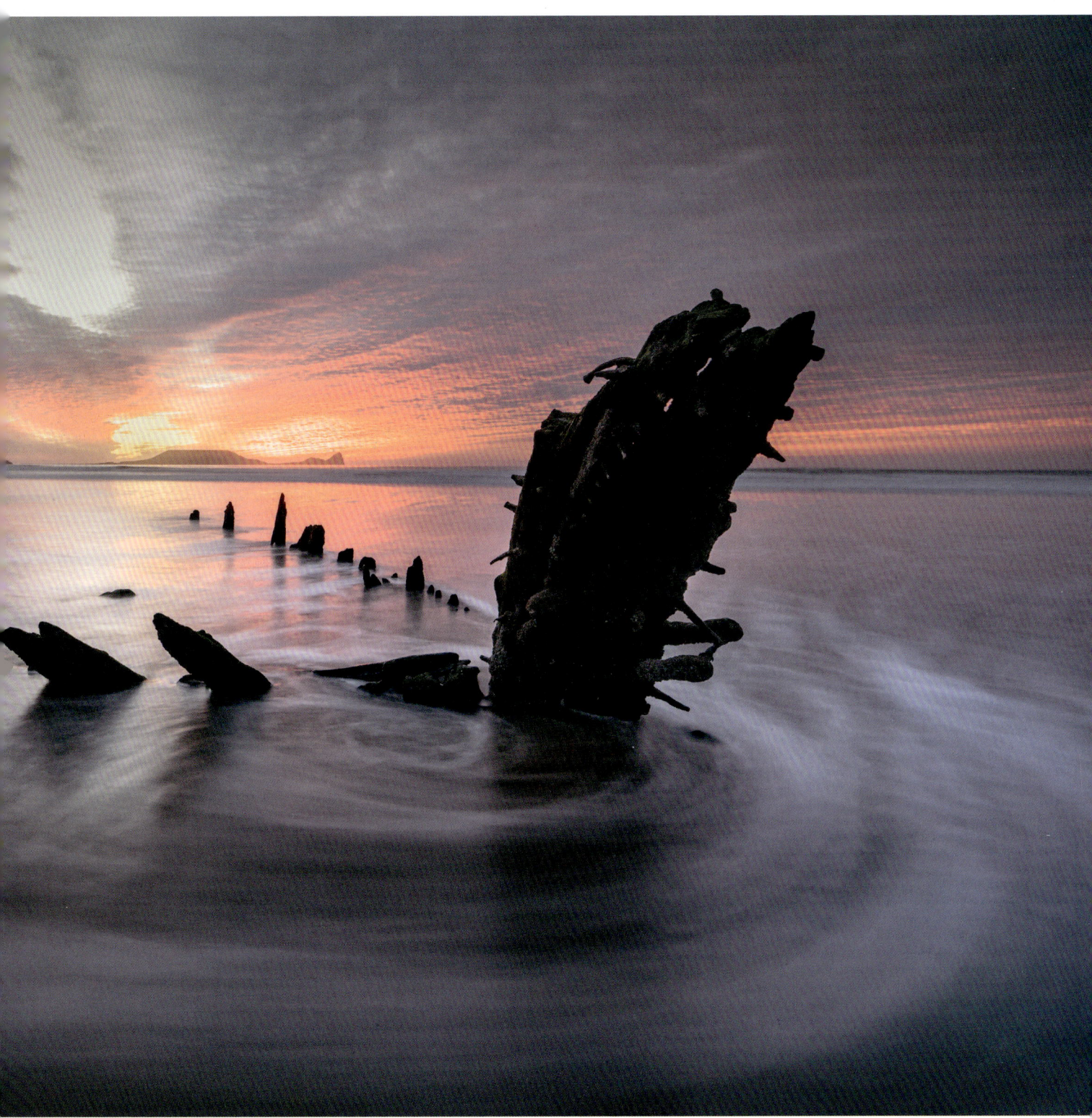

TIME OF YEAR

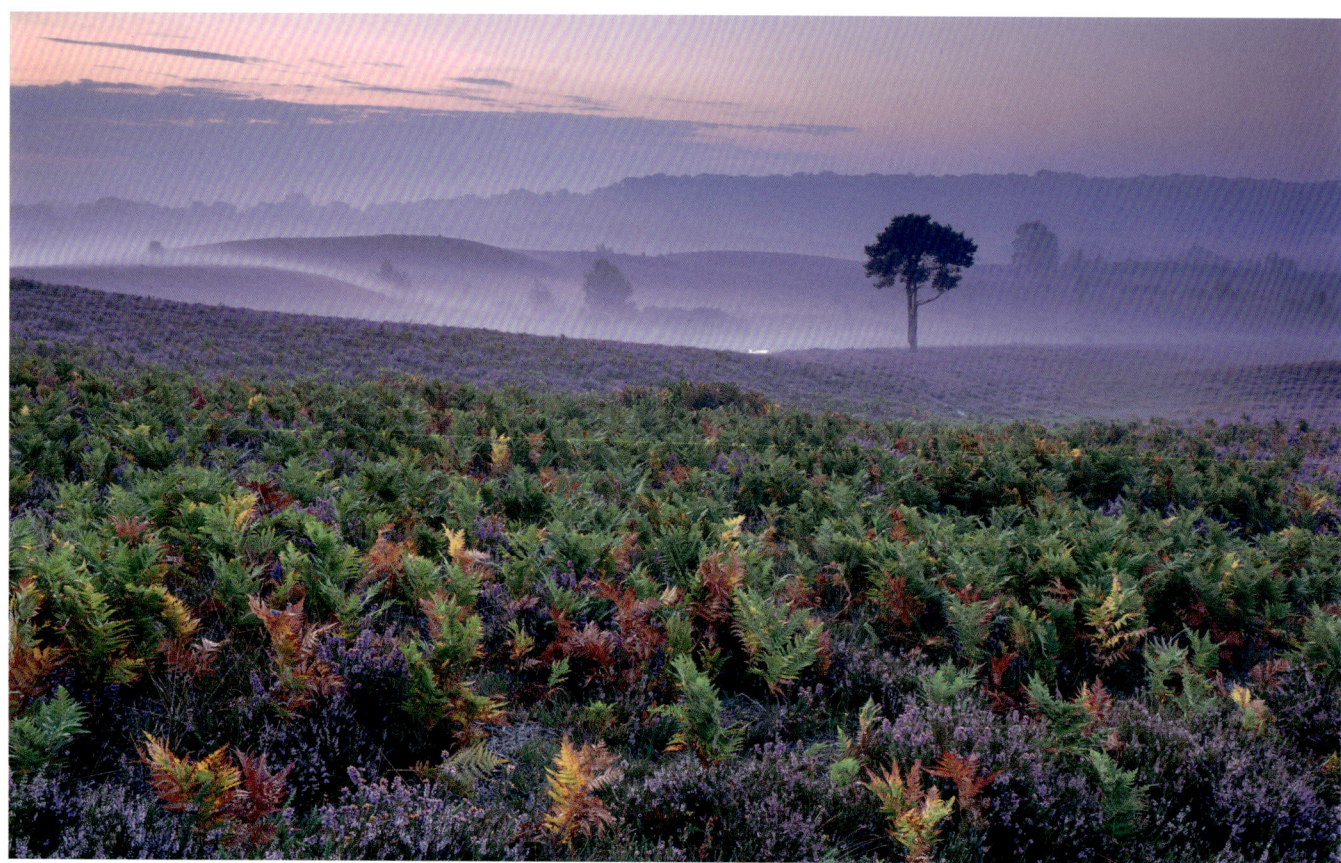

The landscape changes constantly throughout the year and any one viewpoint can look remarkably different from one season to the next. The position of the sun, the quality of light, and the prevailing weather all change, and they all have an enormous impact on the appearance of the landscape.

There are other fundamental changes through the seasons: foliage comes and goes and changes color, wild flowers appear and disappear, and water levels in rivers, ponds, and lakes rise and fall. On the coast, the difference is one of calm, tranquil water or angry, dramatic seas. All of this has implications for planning, in terms of both the types of landscape you choose to shoot at different times of year and also selecting individual viewpoints.

▲ HEATHER

The heather in this location is at its peak for little more than a week. To capture this scene with the mist in the background required good timing, careful planning, and an element of luck.

WINTER

Winter is the favorite season of many photographers. There is often a greater clarity of light on some winter days, as a result of less dust and pollen in the air. Trees are stripped bare of foliage, and the sun stays low in the sky, providing directional light throughout the day. Therefore, plan to shoot viewpoints where the shape and texture of the land are revealed. Keep a close eye on the weather forecast for snow or frost—these both simplify the landscape, so otherwise cluttered scenes become easier to shoot.

On the coast, storms can result in big waves crashing dramatically on the shore. When planning, check the wind direction as well as the tide height, and look for locations that suggest the battle between humans and the elements, such as lighthouses, harbors, and seafront locations. Do not take risks, however—shoot from a safe distance with a long lens and keep away from cliff tops, harbor walls, and so on.

SPRING

The landscape appears fresh and green as leaves appear on trees and, in some parts of the world, forest flowers bloom, including bluebells and wild garlic, so it's a great time of year to shoot woodland. It's also worth investigating agricultural land, as fields of some crops provide striking color. In mountainous areas, snow starts to melt, which means water levels in lakes and rivers rise and waterfalls are at their most dramatic. With the ground beginning to warm, but nights still cold, mist is common. Toward the end of the season, coastal cliff tops are often covered in flowers.

SUMMER

Summer isn't universally popular with landscape photographers—the light can be harsh and, with high levels of dust, pollen, and pollution in the air, clarity can be poor. To make up for this, however, wild flowers add interest in meadows, on cliff tops, and on farmland. Flowers can make a significant difference to a landscape, adding foreground interest or a focal point to locations that might have little interest at any other time of year.

In midsummer, other flowers, such as poppies, can transform featureless fields into a riot of color. These flowers do not appear annually in the same location, but flower when the seeds are disturbed—for example, when fields are plowed—so be prepared to spend time scouting farmland. In late summer, heather adds color to heathland. This time of year also coincides with cooler nights, so check the forecast for any indicators of mist when planning your trip.

When choosing summer locations, bear in mind that water levels inland will be low, especially toward the end of a dry season. Some streams disappear altogether and some locations therefore do not look their best.

FALL

This season is famous for golden colors, and so the obvious thing to do is head for woodland. When planning, check the weather forecast carefully—overcast days can actually be best, as the light is diffused. The dappled light of sunny days is attractive to the eye, but the contrast range can be difficult for cameras to cope with. The exceptions to this are when spotlighting picks out individual parts of a scene or where there is low backlighting at the beginning and end of the day, which casts dramatic shadows toward the camera and gives a warm glow to foliage. Along with spring, fall is the other time when misty mornings are common.

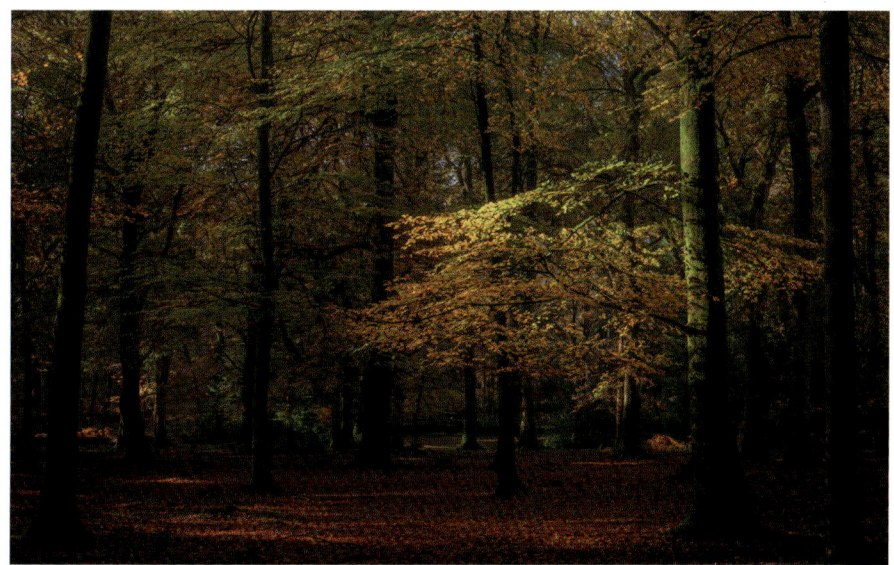

◀ WOODLAND
Fall is the time of year to focus on woodland. Light streaming through the branches has picked out the low canopy on the right-hand tree, helping to highlight it as a focal point in the scene.

WEATHER

Weather is one of the most important considerations when planning a shoot—but probably also the most difficult to predict. The weather strongly influences the mood of the landscape and quality of light and color temperature. The very shape of the landscape can seem to change, too, depending on the direction and intensity of the light, or as areas get hidden and revealed by light and shade when weather patterns change.

We need to consider a wide range of information when looking at weather forecasts. Perhaps the most important is cloud cover. Some cloud is useful to provide interest in the sky, and especially at sunrise and sunset when it can catch the color from the sun. Low cloud can look more dramatic, but high cloud will often catch pink tones a little better. It's impossible to give an "ideal" percentage for cloud cover, as so much depends on where the gaps are—and this is where luck comes into it. Some of the most dramatic conditions are in almost 100% cover, but where there just happens to be a small gap for the sun to shine through.

Clarity is also important. If you are relying on having a strong focal point in the background, you need it to be visible. Related to this is wind speed—still, warm days in the summer months tend to be hazy. Atmospheric haze isn't all bad news, however, as it can help to increase depth perception in photographs by creating aerial or atmospheric perspective, the effect where distant objects become lighter and less distinct. This can be exploited in locations such as ranges of mountains or hills. Wind speed is also important—it gives an indication of how changeable the weather may be and how likely gaps will appear in the cloud, creating the possibility of dramatic spot-lighting on the land below.

FORECASTS

Good weather forecasts will also provide a guide to the dew point and air pressure, which are important considerations as well. The dew point is the atmospheric temperature below which water droplets begin to condense and dew can form and can be used along with other indicators (see page 52) to predict the likelihood of a low-lying ground mist. If the air is still enough, mist is likely when the air temperature is less than 1°C above the dew point.

Air pressure can be important when planning coastal visits. Tide charts are based on a standard pressure of 1013 millibars (29.9inHg); a pressure of 1040 (30.7inHg) (high but not exceptional) would result in a sea level 12in. (30cm) lower than predicted.

FOCUS ON...
WHERE TO GO
With the weather playing such an important role in the look of the landscape, it's vital that you match the right location to the right conditions for your photography. There are no hard and fast rules, but here are some suggestions.

- **Calm and still**: Shoot near water and make the most of reflections. Inland, that means lakes, ponds, and slow-moving rivers. On the coast, choose "pretty" locations, such as harbors and sandy beaches.
- **Overcast**: Woodland is ideal in diffused light. Also try long-exposure coastal photography, especially if there is a strong, textured sky.
- **Broken cloud**: There's always the chance of spot-lighting, so hilly landscapes or anywhere with a strong focal point can provide good locations.
- **Snow**: A strong focal point is essential, as much of the landscape can be featureless. Trees and buildings are ideal.
- **Mist**: Lakes and rivers, especially if there are boats or other strong shapes in the mist. Fog lying in valleys is very photogenic, especially if there are tree tops or buildings rising above the mist, so look for high viewpoints looking down. Woodland is also good, with trees looming in the mist.
- **Sunshine and showers**: Almost anywhere! This is the favorite weather for many photographers as it often produces the most dramatic light when a shower clears and the sun shines through. Be on the lookout for rainbows and, if you see one, use a polarizer to make it stand out from its surroundings.

It's worth remembering that the most dramatic conditions are often produced on the edges of weather fronts, as one system is replaced by another. If this coincides with the naturally photogenic light at the beginning or end of the day, then the result can often be something very special.

FOCUS ON...
WEATHER APPS

With weather forecasts, the more local you can get the better, as weather can be surprisingly localized, especially in hilly or mountainous areas. For instance, in the United Kingdom, the Met Office and the BBC provide good local forecasts, with plenty of information, as well as smartphone apps, which can be dowloaded free.

Metcheck is another website which offers a wealth of information (www.metcheck.com) and Accuweather (www.accuweather.com; a smartphone app is available) also provides detailed local forecasts. The smartphone app WeatherPro has a good reputation for accuracy and Clear Outside is also very popular. A number of photographers rate the Norwegian meteorological office (www.yr.no) very highly regardless of whether they are based in Norway. For short-term forecasting, an app which uses satellite or radar to track weather patterns can be useful. There are many to choose from, including Accuweather (see above), which includes a radar feature.

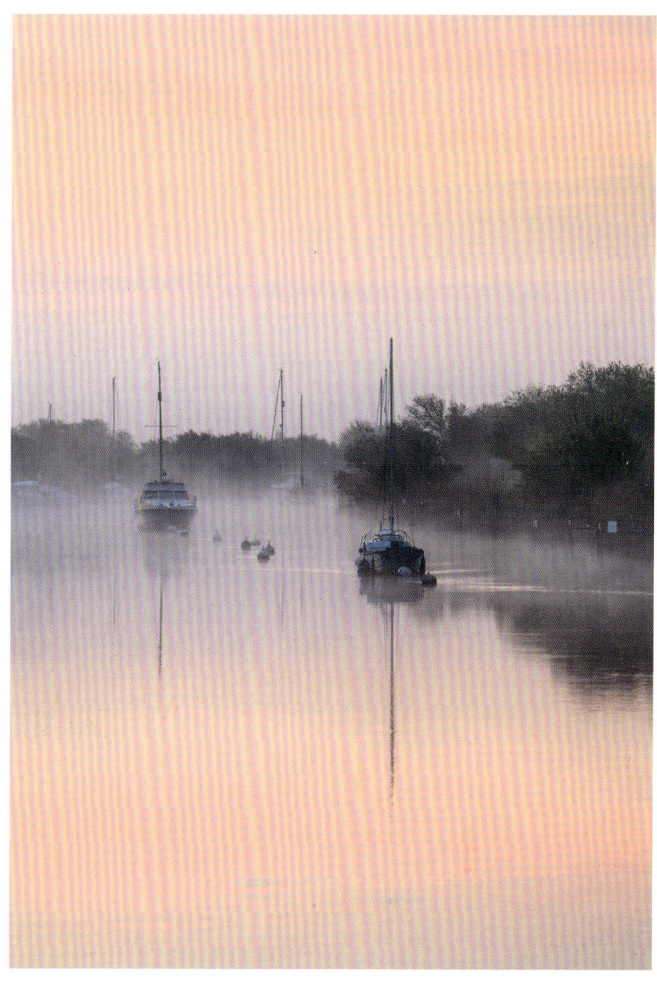

▲ REFLECTIONS
Calm, still mornings are ideal for shooting at lakes, ponds, and slow-moving rivers, where you can make the most of any reflections.

◄ SUNSHINE AND SHOWERS
Make sure you head out if the forecast is for sunshine and showers, as the chances are you will catch some really dramatic light, and, if you're lucky, even a rainbow! The best light is fleeting, so make sure you set up and are ready to shoot before the showers finish, otherwise, you risk missing the best light.

SUN

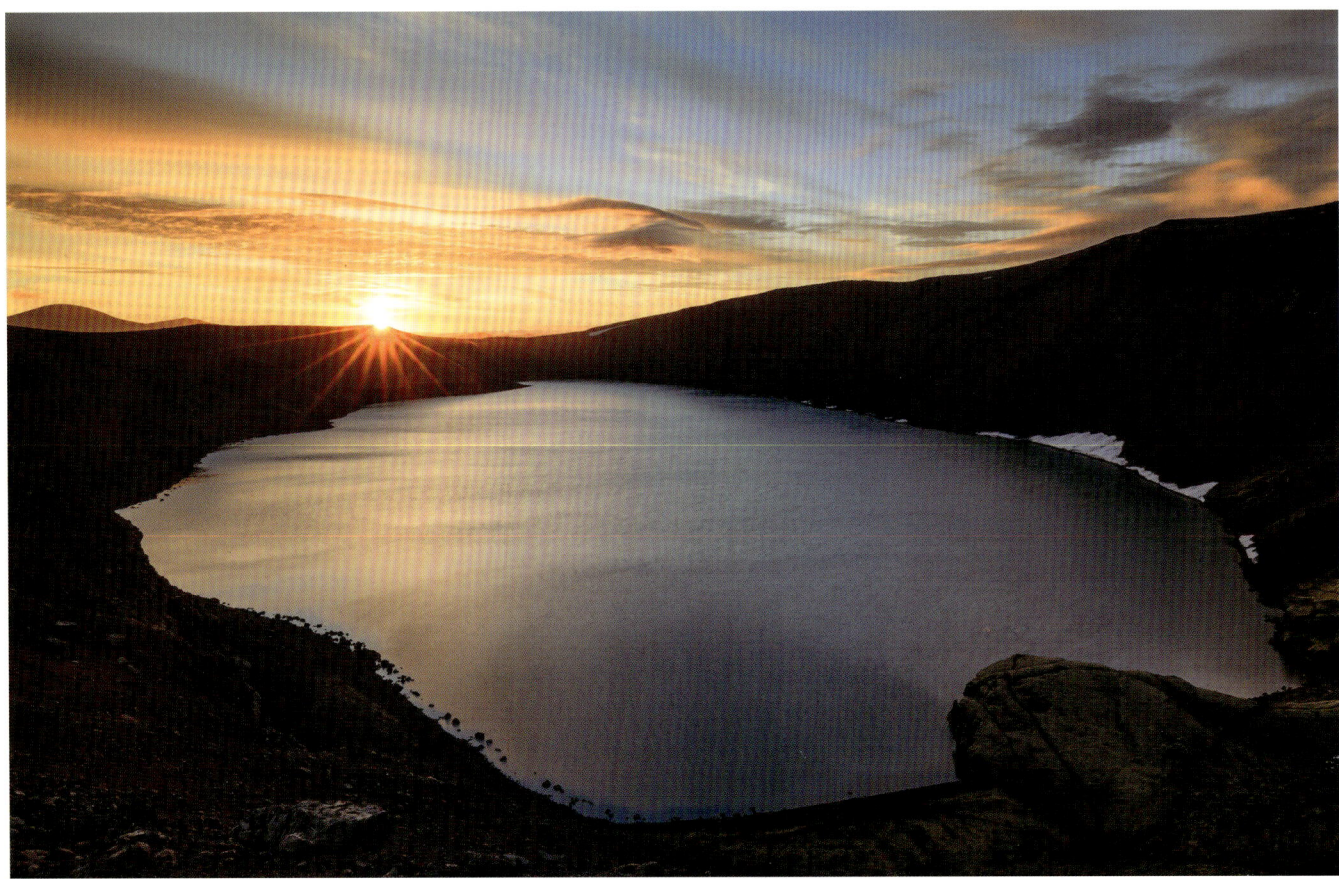

▲ CRATER

For this shot of an extinct volcano in Iceland, it was important to have the sun rising in the frame in a place where it would provide a counterpoint for the rock in the foreground. As the angle of sunrise varies enormously throughout the year in Iceland, this gave a window of just a few weeks in midsummer in which the shot was possible.

Most people will tell you that the sun rises in the east and sets in the west. While this is broadly true, it does not tell the whole story and we need to look at things in a little bit more detail.

In fact, as a result of the elliptical nature of the Earth's orbit around the sun and the fact that its axis is tilted, the sun only rises and sets due east and west on the equinoxes (which is true wherever you are in the world). In summer, it rises and sets in the north-east and north-west and in the south-east and south-west in winter. The difference is surprising—in the United Kingdom, for example, it's around a 75° difference between midsummer and midwinter. The sun is also higher in summer and reaches its highest point at a different time each day.

Geographical location also has an impact on where the sun rises and sets and the number of daylight hours—the further you are from the equator, the longer the days are in summer and the shorter they are in winter. For example, north of the Arctic circle and south of the Antarctic circle, the sun is visible for 24 hours for a time around the summer solstice.

This all has implications for planning. Some locations will only receive direct lighting in certain months—or weeks—of the year. Some compositions rely on the sun rising or setting in a particular spot—which it may do for only a couple of weeks in the year. Being aware of this and knowing how to find it out is an important skill for landscape photographers.

LIGHTING

On a day-to-day basis, being aware of how the sun's position and height affect the look of an image is important when planning shoots and choosing subjects. Side-lighting, probably the favorite type of lighting for most landscape photographers, reveals texture and helps to suggest depth in an image. The modeling effect it has means that you are able to place emphasis on the shape and form of the landscape—it's flattering to rural vistas and, if there are buildings in the landscape, it helps to lend them a three-dimensional quality.

Backlighting can be dramatic, with shadows racing toward the camera. Look for bold, graphic compositions, and seek out strong shapes to create silhouettes, especially if there is a colorful sky at sunrise or sunset.

Front-lighting can be flat—with shadows behind the subject, form and volume are not suggested. However, when the sun is low over the horizon, color saturation is naturally high, and subjects which feature strong, primary colors can look eye-catching. In these conditions, for instance, some rock formations can pick up flattering, warm color.

Overhead lighting is perhaps the trickiest to deal with. Contrast is high, shadows are harsh, and there is little textural relief on subject matter. However, on cloudy days, the light is more diffused and less harsh.

▼ CASTLE SILHOUETTE
Backlighting can produce dramatic results, especially if you seek out strong shapes to silhouette against color. Capturing this silhouette without the hill directly behind the castle, and with the shadows coming toward the camera through the mist, required careful planning—it was important to know where the sun was rising, and I also monitored the weather forecasts closely to try to coincide the shoot with a foggy morning.

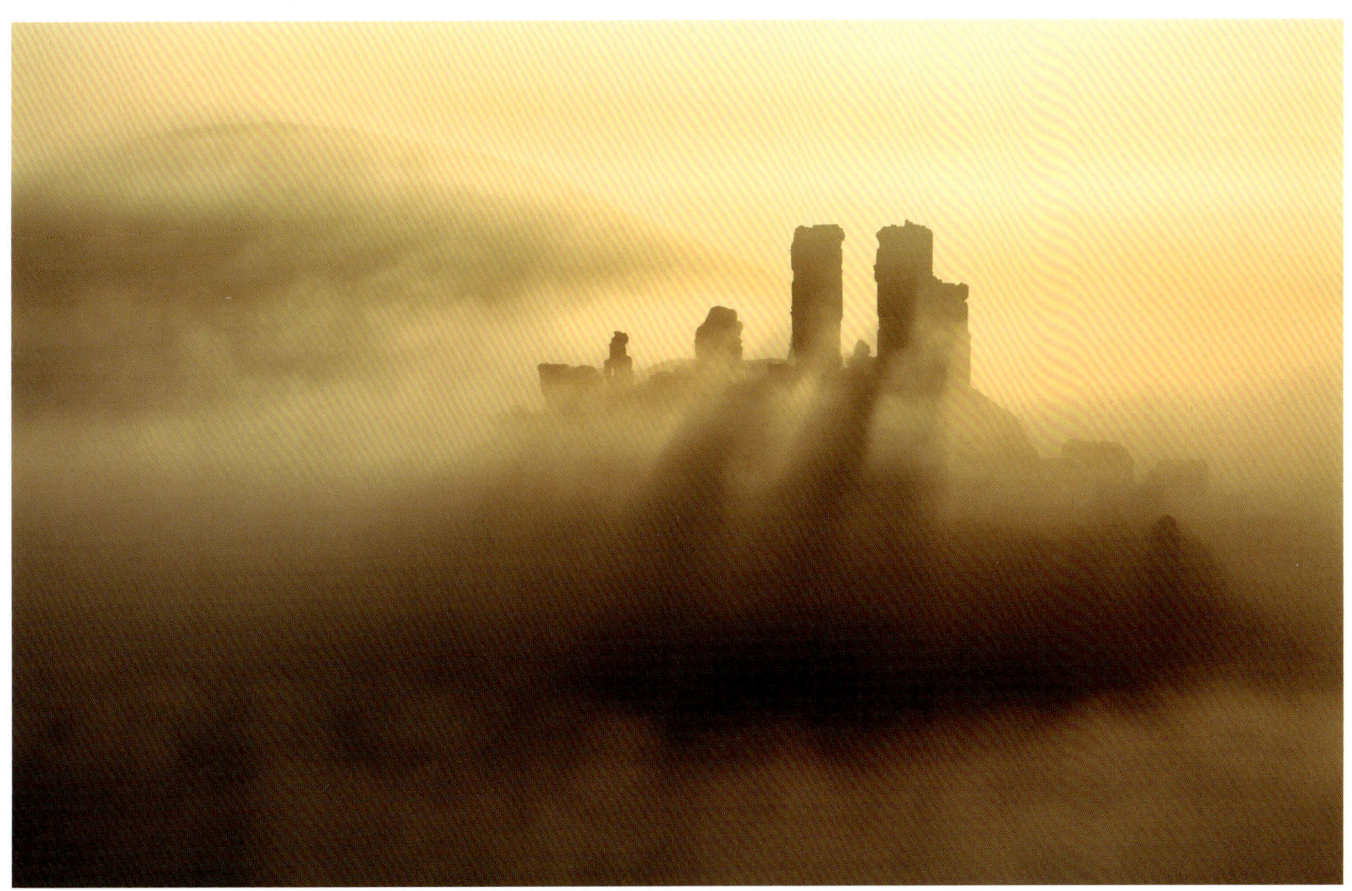

MAPS AND APPS

When planning a shoot, you will need to research the physical layout of your chosen location, which compositions are possible, and which light will suit the scene best—both in terms of the time of day and the time of year. For coastal locations, you should know the best tide height. It sounds obvious, but you will also need to choose a location in the first place.

When researching locations, your first port of call should probably be an internet image search. This will yield a number of shots; they may not all be of high quality, but should give you an overview of the area you are interested in. Make notes of likely-looking places and follow this up with a search through the larger stock libraries, and also see if social media turns up any useful images. There are also dedicated photography guide books, which provide incredibly detailed information including nearest parking, clear directions to viewpoints, and lots of example pictures. In the UK, the fotoVUE series of books is very popular (www.fotovue.com) as is the Long Valley Books series (www.longvalleybooks.com). Many individual photographers have also published ebook guides to different regions.

Once you have an idea of the compositional possibilities of a location, it's time to start looking at maps. Online maps such as Google Maps are excellent, especially if you use Satellite View, which allows you to identify geographical features—you should

therefore be able to work out the viewpoints from which shots were taken. However, you will want to go beyond this, as you don't just want to copy other photographers' images. Look for other features in the landscape which could make interesting foregrounds, and other potential viewpoints which may have been missed. It's also worth trying Street View, as this allows you to explore the area from ground level, which can be a great help for identifying potential compositions—although this won't be available in more remote locations.

While you're in Maps, you can add pins with map directions and obtain GPS coordinates for viewpoints. It's also worth identifying the nearest parking spots and obtaining their GPS coordinates to make life easier when you visit the location.

TIMING

Perhaps the most important part of online research is establishing the best times to visit your chosen location. Are there times of year or day when the light doesn't fall on your location? What time of day would suit it best?

There are several apps that work with Google Maps and show the angle of sunrise and sunset for any date, anywhere in the world, but the most popular is probably The Photographer's Ephemeris (TPE). This is available both as a free desktop version and a paid-for phone or tablet version. TPE gives a huge amount of information useful for the planning process—sunrise and sunset times and angles, moonrise and moonset times, the times of different phases of twilight, the angle of the sun throughout the day, and more.

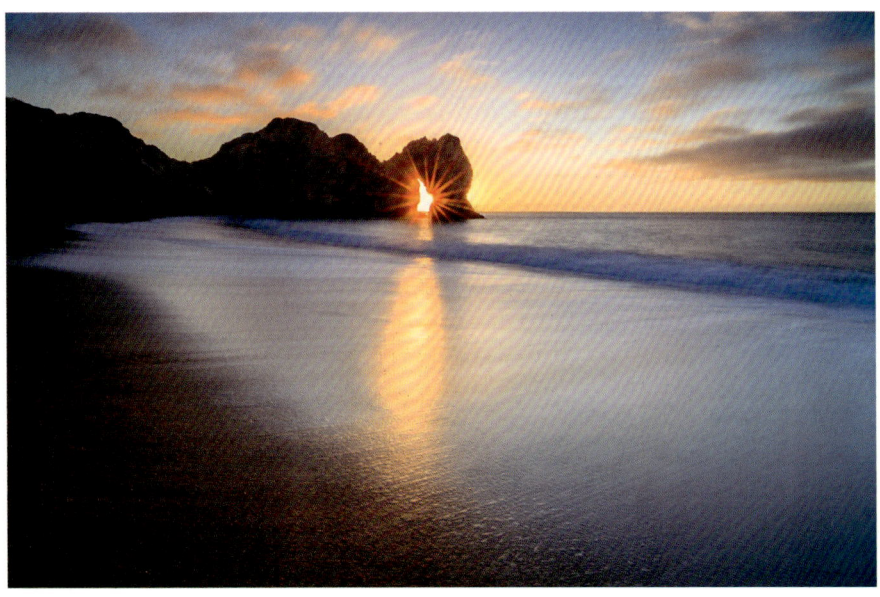

◄ ARCH
This composition of the sun rising through a rock arch in Dorset, England, is only possible for a few weeks in winter. Using TPE allowed me to predict the specific window when this shot would be possible.

For basic information about sunrise, sunset, moonrise, and moonset, you just need to search for a location and place a pin there. The amount of information and how to use it goes beyond the scope of these pages, but there are detailed tutorials on TPE's website (www.photoephemeris.com/tutorials/).

FOCUS ON...
USING MAPS

Before the advent of the internet and Google Maps, the only way to research locations before visiting them was to study printed maps, such as Ordnance Survey (OS) maps in the UK. Even with plenty of information being available online, there is still a case for using such maps. Once you understand them, you can pick out features in the landscape, such as valleys and hills, including their height and steepness of incline, and rights of way. The latter is very important, as trespassing is to be avoided for obvious reasons. You can also use maps to accurately pinpoint locations using grid references. A four-figure grid reference identifies a single kilometer square on a map and a six-figure grid reference identifies a hundred meter square within a single kilometer square. For detailed information on using the UK's OS maps, for instance, refer to their website (www.ordnancesurvey.co.uk). An Ordnance Survey app is also available for smartphones.

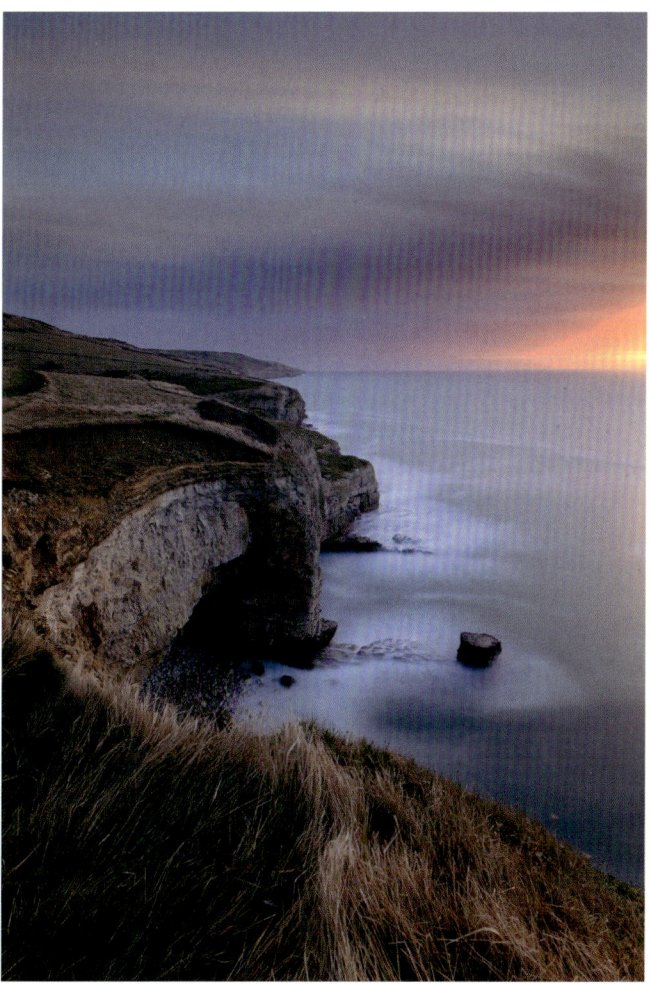

▲ CLIFFS
Online research using Google Maps revealed the photographic potential for this image. The Photographer's Ephemeris allowed me to work out the best time of year for shooting it.

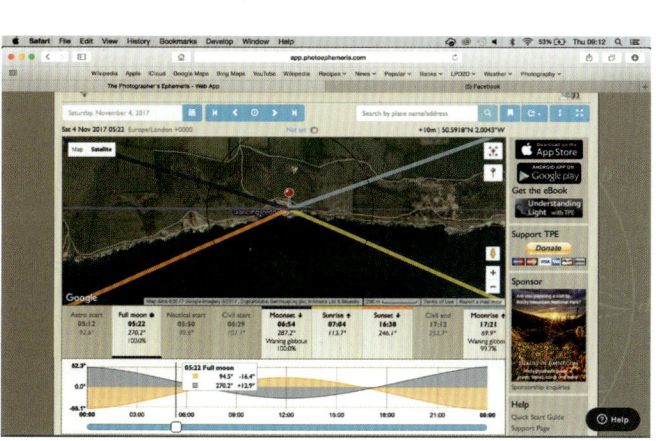

◄ THE PHOTOGRAPHER'S EPHEMERIS
This screenshot shows sunrise and sunset positions for a location on the south coast of England during winter.

SHOOTING THE COAST

The great thing about photography on the coast is that it never looks the same from one visit to the next. Changes in weather conditions will vary the mood, and different tide heights can completely change the character of a location. Over time, the forces of nature and coastal erosion can also change the basic geography of an area. While this means that it is difficult to tire of shooting coastal locations, it also means that careful planning is even more important when shooting by the sea than it is when shooting inland.

Tide height is probably the most important consideration when planning a coastal shoot. Depending on the location, tide height can vary by many feet—the world's biggest tidal range is an incredible 54ft (16.3m) in the Bay of Fundy, in Canada. Researching the tides is therefore crucial from both an esthetic and a safety point of view.

The "correct" tide height is, of course, location-specific, but we can make some generalizations. Sandy beaches often have maximum impact in an image at low tide—a wide beach stretching out in front of the camera encourages simple, minimalistic compositions. Whatever tide height suits a particular beach, shooting on a falling tide is preferable, as there is a greater chance that the sand will be clean and free of footprints.

Rocky beaches and bays can seem cluttered and confusing. The trick is to shoot them when the tide is low enough to reveal some interest, but high enough to cover distractions. Waves washing through channels in rocky ledges can also look very dramatic. Again, falling tides are preferable, as you won't find yourself retreating up the beach and there is less danger of getting a soaking if you misjudge an incoming wave. It's perhaps harder to generalize when talking about cliff-top views, but they often suit a higher tide as, again, there can be distracting clutter on the foreshore and it's easier to find a "neater" composition when the sea level is higher.

As well as doing online research for coastal shoots, it's really important to scout the location. Ideally, visit it at different tides or, if that isn't possible, visit at low tide and try to visualize how it will look at different tide heights. From a safety point of view, you should also check if you are likely to get cut off at high tide and make a note of exit routes for when the tide is coming in.

TIDE AND WEATHER

Calculating tide times and heights is relatively straightforward as there are many tide tables published both in book form and online. Two useful smartphone apps for worldwide tides are Tides Planner (www.imray.com/digital/imray-tides-planner/) and AyeTides (www.ayetides.com). Bear in mind, though, that although tide times can be calculated precisely, tide heights will be affected by air pressure, wind speed, and wind direction.

When it comes to the weather, there are not necessarily any ideal conditions: overcast days can be perfect for long exposures, stormy weather can produce dramatic light, and few

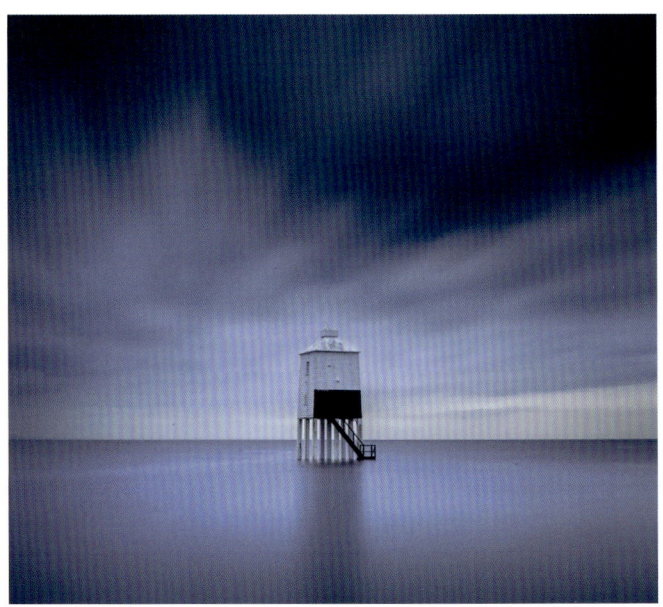

FOCUS ON...
PROTECTING YOUR KIT

The coast can be a harsh environment and you'll need to look after your equipment. A large wave or sea spray might splash your camera, lens, and filters. Protect your camera by using a rain cover or improvise your own. Check the front element or filters for spray and clean them using a good-quality cleaning fluid (a lens cloth alone will simply spread the spray around). When you get home, wipe down your kit with a damp cloth and rinse your tripod legs—otherwise, over time, the leg locks will corrode.

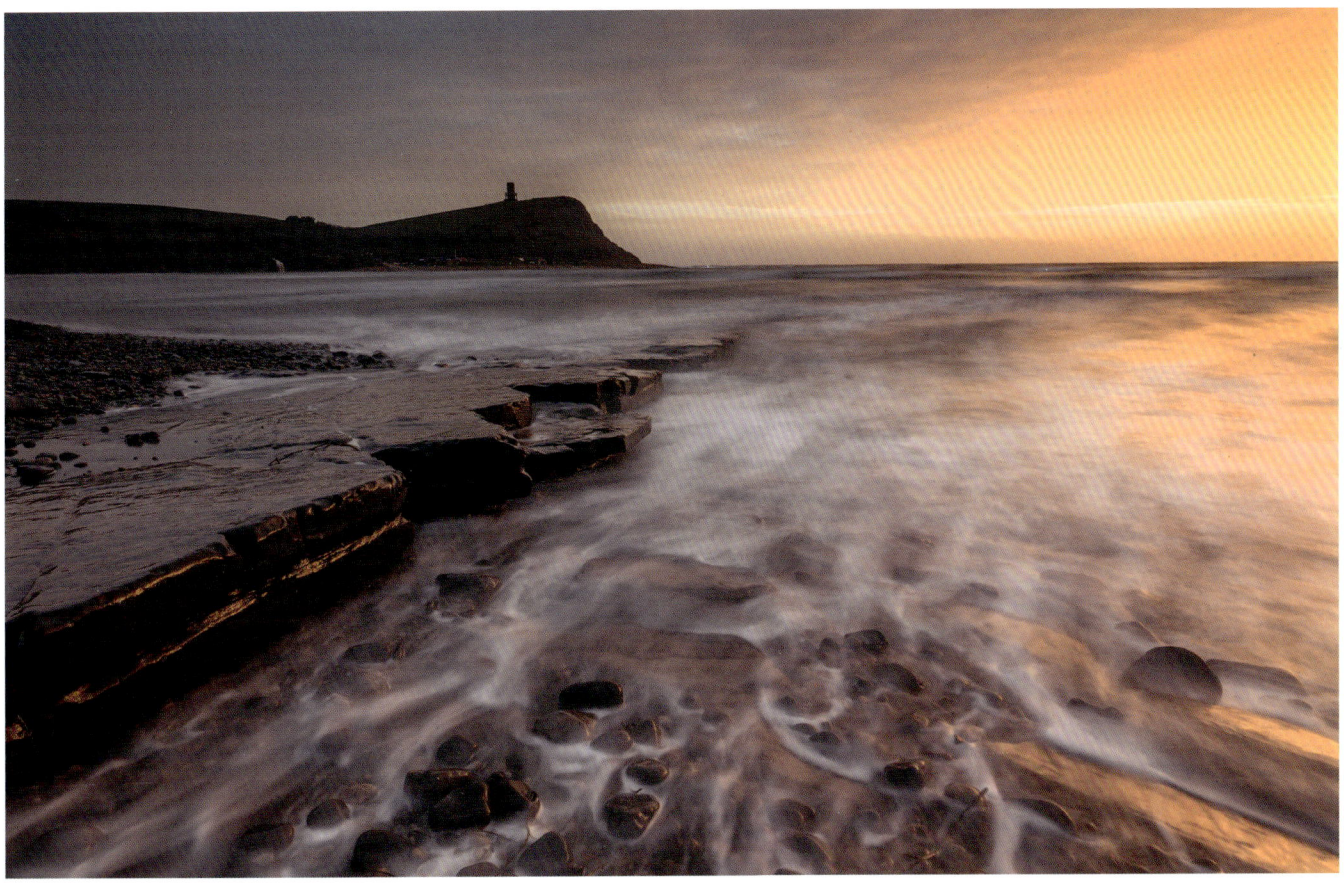

photographers can resist colorful sunsets and sunrises. Perhaps the most challenging conditions are cloudless blue skies, but even then, with the right choice of location and the right approach, successful images can be created.

When checking the weather forecast it is always worth looking at wind speed. This can have an impact on cliff-top views as gusts can blow foliage and cause it to blur. When shooting on the shoreline, if the wind is blowing toward the camera and wind speed is greater than around 15mph (24kph), this can result in sea spray coating your camera and lens or filters. As well as being potentially harmful to your equipment (see box opposite, far left), spray on your lens or filters will reduce image quality.

◄ LIGHTHOUSE
This old wooden lighthouse on a Somerset beach in the UK is an interesting sight, but so much more photogenic when the sea hides the clutter of the beach and simplifies the scene. A high spring tide is necessary for this, so research is needed.

▲ ROCKS
A mid-tide often suits rocky beaches, as it hides distracting clutter, while still allowing interesting features to remain visible—in this case, waves washing back out to sea through the rocks created interesting trails.

FOCUS ON...
SAFETY

It's important to know what's happening with the tides so that you don't get cut off when shooting on beaches. Also, keep an eye out for unexpectedly large waves. When you arrive on location, spend several minutes before you set up observing the waves—you may be surprised how far up the beach they run. Avoid standing at the base of cliffs. They are typically unstable, rock falls are common, and, from time to time, fatalities do happen. When shooting from the cliff top, it goes without saying that you should not stand too close to the edge.

SCOUTING

Online research and using maps to identify potential viewpoints are important parts of the planning process, but there is no substitute for actually visiting your chosen location and checking it out for real. Ideally, you should visit on more than one occasion, so that you become thoroughly familiar with the place. You can then plan your shoot from the starting viewpoint through to the finish, making sure you are always in the right place at the right time; both in terms of the light and, wherever appropriate, in terms of your personal safety.

When you visit the location, make sure you have a map with you, with your chosen viewpoints marked on it so that you can find them easily. If you obtained GPS coordinates from Google Maps, your smartphone can guide you to the exact position you identified. Check all of the viewpoints to make sure they work and see if there are any others you've missed. Take some test shots to try out various compositions and, if they're successful, use them as a reference when you return.

FOCAL POINTS

When scouting locations for viewpoints, it obviously helps if you know what to look for. So, what makes a good viewpoint? The first thing to look for is a strong focal point, such as a tree, building, or hill—which can be placed in a key part of the frame in order to give the eye somewhere to rest once it has explored the frame (see page 154). A good focal point will stand out from its surroundings by virtue of contrast, color, detail, and texture.

In order for a focal point to be successful, we need to direct the eye toward it. Keeping the composition simple and uncluttered is a good starting point—it's much harder for the eye to find the focal point if there's too much going on in the frame. Choosing

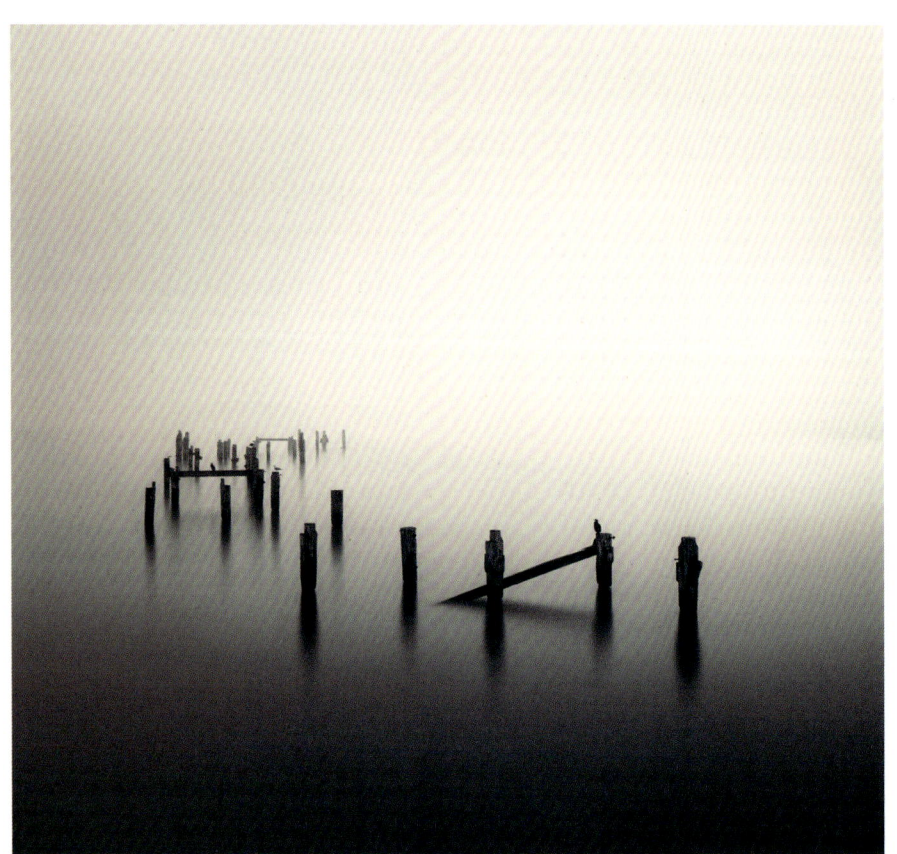

◄ PIER
It's possible to do a lot of online research on this decaying pier on the Dorset coast to find out its location, possible compositions, the angles of sunrise and sunset, and so on. However, online research is unlikely to reveal the fact that, for part of the year, it is partly obscured by a rather unphotogenic plastic pontoon, and that access to the viewpoint is restricted to certain times. Scouting the location and talking to locals is far more likely to help you gather this important information.

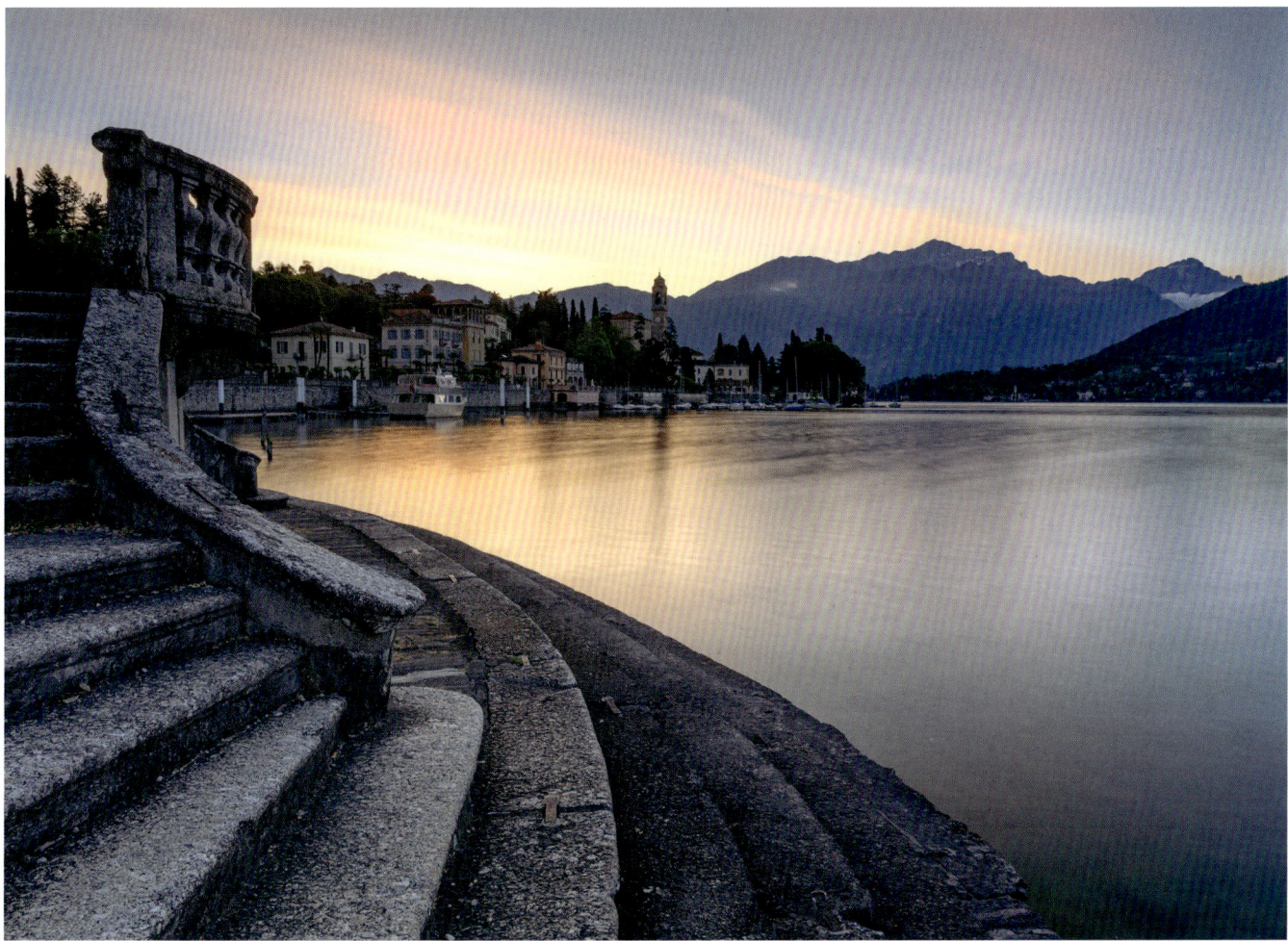

a suitable foreground and middle distance is also important. A well chosen foreground can lead the eye into the shot and subtly highlight the focal point—lines are useful for this, as the eye will tend to follow them. The middle distance can link foreground and background, tying them together to create harmony.

Not all scenes contain a natural focal point, and, if this is the case, you need to look for other ways of organizing a composition. Shapes can provide a sense of structure and cohesion, so seek them out, especially in rural landscapes, where there may not be strong individual features.

Layers, such as those created by ranges of mountains or hills, are also pleasing to the eye—they are naturally harmonious and generate a sense of rhythm in the landscape. The flattened perspective created by longer focal lengths can enhance the look, as can hazy or misty atmospheric conditions.

▲ STEPS

A combination of online research and scouting resulted in this image. I'd seen shots of the location, but not from this viewpoint and had predicted the sunrise using TPE. Visiting the location the previous day had revealed the potential for this composition.

When you are on location, you should take the opportunity to double-check how the light falls as well as the angle of sunrise and sunset. On location, this can be done using an augmented reality sun-position app, such as the one used in Photopills (www.photopills.com). This integrates with your smartphone's camera and superimposes an image of the sun, so you can see where it will be at any time of day. As with The Photographer's Ephemeris, you can also use the app to check the sun's position on any date.

CAMERA SET-UP

Modern digital cameras are complex pieces of equipment, with a plethora of settings to choose from. Before heading out on a shoot, it's therefore important to check that you have your settings optimized for landscape photography, especially if you also shoot other genres.

File formats

The two basic options are Raw and JPEG formats. JPEGs are processed in-camera—exactly how depends on what parameters you have set for contrast, color saturation, and so on—and therefore have less flexibility when it comes to post-processing. This is especially true when it comes to adjusting white balance and recovering shadow and highlight detail.

Raw files are essentially "digital negatives" which require processing in dedicated software such as Adobe Lightroom in order to create the final image. They contain a lot more information than JPEGs, including more tonal levels and a wider dynamic range. We would therefore recommend shooting Raw in order to maximize image quality. Some photographers like to shoot Raw and JPEG simultaneously, which allows them to have a straight out-of-camera image ready to email to others, or post on social media before they post-process the images from a shoot. If you really prefer shooting JPEGs, make sure you set the file quality to maximum.

Formatting cards

Before you leave, make sure there is sufficient space on your memory card(s) for the number of shots you are likely to take. If space is limited, format the card(s) in the camera, but first check that all the shots have been downloaded and backed up. Formatting cards rather than simply deleting images helps to prevent them from corrupting and is also quicker.

Setting up dual-card slots

Some cameras have dual-card slots, with several options for recording images, such as Raw files to one card and JPEGs to the other. The safest set-up, which protects against lost data, is to set the camera up to record Raw images to both cards simultaneously. This is sometimes called "back-up" mode, although different manufacturers use different terminology.

Exposure modes

The basic exposure modes available are Manual, Program, Aperture Priority, and Shutter Priority (see page 13). Some cameras also offer various "scene" modes, such as Landscape, Portrait, Sports, and so on.

Being in control of selecting the aperture is important, as this is fundamental to controlling depth of field, a key skill in landscape photography (see page 58). We therefore recommend shooting in either Manual or Aperture Priority mode. If shooting in Aperture Priority, if your image is under- or overexposed, simply changing aperture will not change the overall exposure, as the camera will adjust the shutter speed accordingly. To change exposure, you will need to use the exposure compensation facility. On many cameras, this is carried out by holding down the +/- button on the top plate and rotating the main control dial. Some cameras have a dedicated exposure compensation dial instead.

ISO

Unless there is a really good reason to do otherwise (for instance, light levels are extremely low and shutter speeds would become unworkably long), you should set the ISO to the lowest value in order to maximize image quality. Avoid setting Auto ISO as this tends to set the ISO to high levels in order to gain a fast enough shutter speed to allow handheld photography, therefore compromising image quality.

White balance

Many photographers like to shoot using the Daylight preset because, as with shooting daylight-balanced film, its response is predictable—warm tones when the color temperature of the ambient light is low, cool tones when it is high, and so on (see pages 148 and 151 for more information on color temperature). For landscape photography, Auto White Balance generally works very well, as the lighting conditions are straightforward. However, strong sunsets and sunrises can be rendered too cool, as the camera may assume the strong reds and oranges are a color cast and will "correct" them. In these situations, choosing a preset such as Cloudy may be better. Remember that whatever setting you choose, large adjustments can be made to the white balance of Raw images during post-processing.

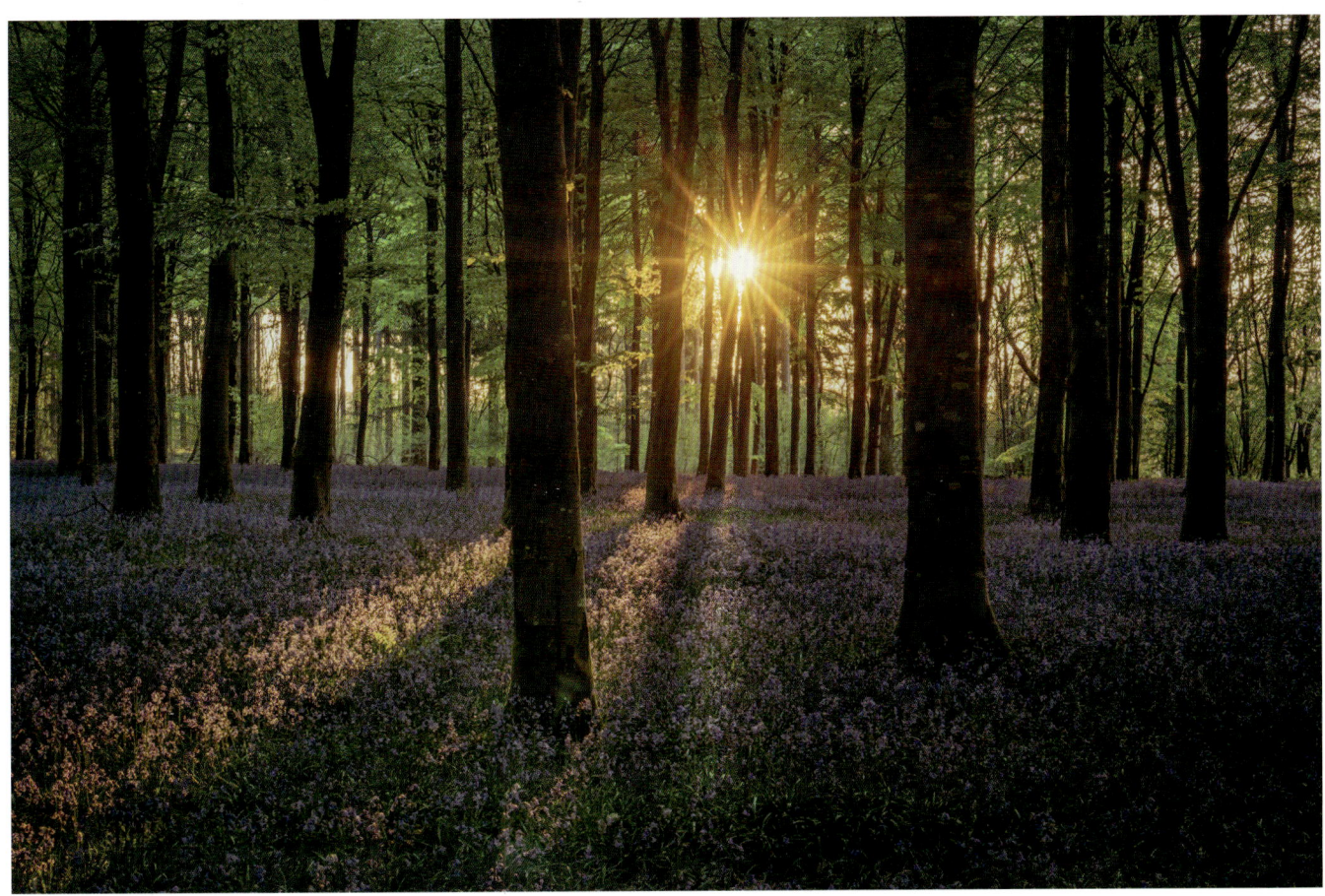

FOCUS ON...
COLOR SPACE

You have two color spaces to choose from in your settings: Adobe RGB and sRGB. Adobe RGB has the wider color gamut, so if shooting JPEG, it's best to use this. However, if shooting Raw, it does not matter, as Raw files do not have a color space—this is assigned during post-processing. The ProPhoto RGB profile features an even wider color gamut, but as it includes colors that cannot be reproduced it can be challenging to work with.

▲ **BLUEBELL WOOD**
Where there are bright highlights in the frame, such as in this shot, the highlight alert (see page 43) is a vital exposure guide as it shows the precise location of any blown highlights. In this case, the decision was taken to allow the sun itself to overexpose, as exposing for that extremely bright highlight would have resulted in severe underexposure of the rest of the scene; and in any case, with the naked eye, we would not expect to perceive any detail in such a bright object.

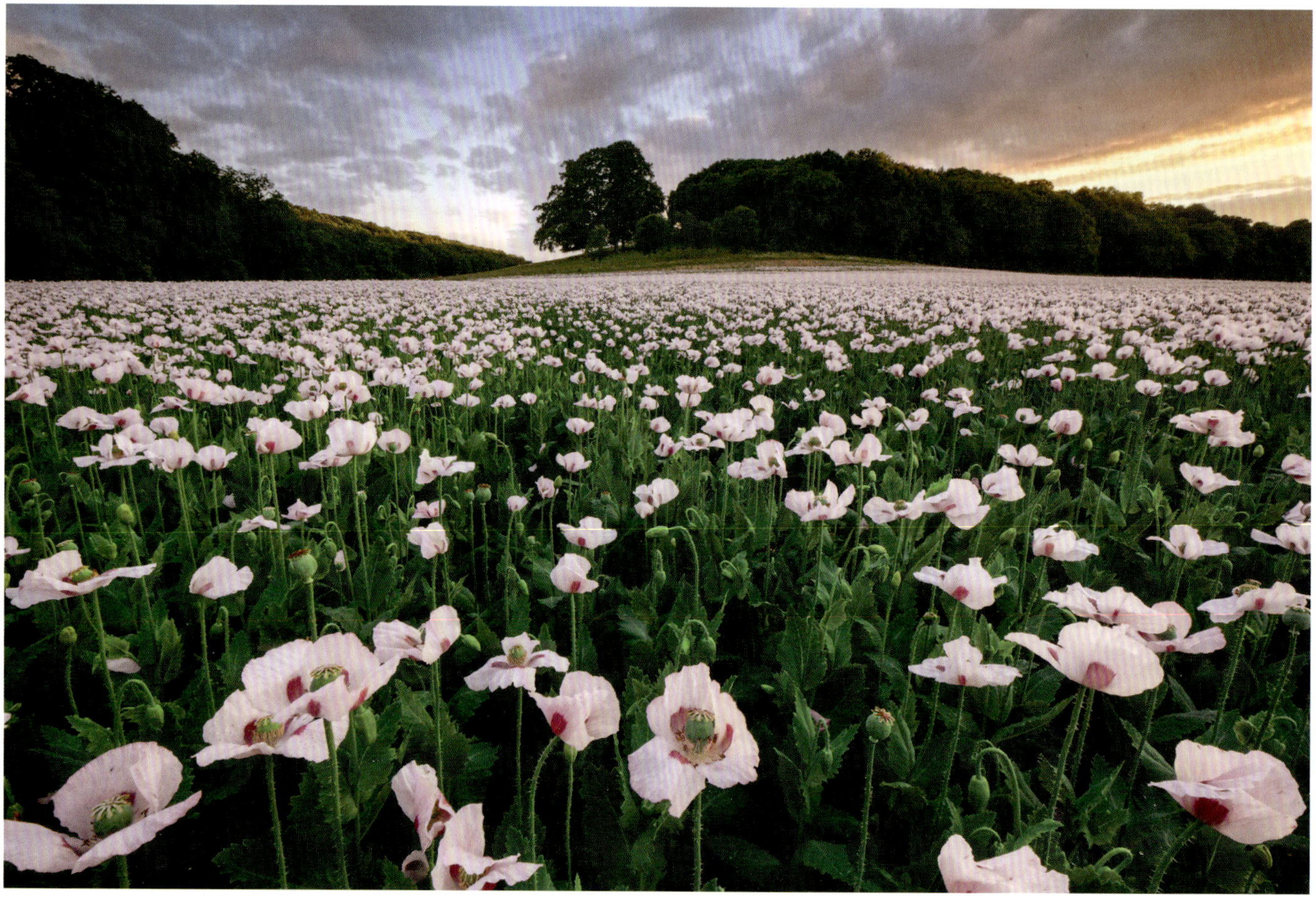

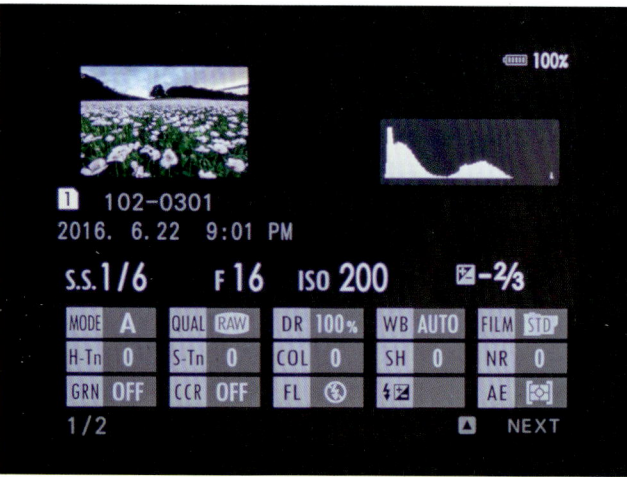

▲ FLOWERS

As depth of field is critical in landscape photography, the photographer, not the camera, needs to be in control of the aperture. When setting up your camera, you should therefore select either Manual or Aperture Priority as the exposure mode.

◄ HISTOGRAM

This image review screen from the camera features the histogram on the upper right, which shows the distribution of tones in the photograph above when it was taken.

Metering modes

Most cameras have a choice of three or four metering modes. Multi-segment metering takes readings from numerous parts of the frame and automatically compensates for challenging lighting conditions. Center-weighted metering biases (or "weights") the reading to a large central section of the frame. Spot metering takes a reading from a portion (2-3%) of the frame, and is useful if you want to isolate a mid-tone in the frame or take a reading from multiple areas and average them out. Partial metering is similar to spot metering but uses a larger portion of the frame.

Multi-segment metering is highly accurate in most situations and is probably best kept as your default setting. Before heading out for a shoot, check that you haven't left it on another mode. Whichever mode you select, remember that additional guidance is available in the live view and review histograms.

Drive mode

For landscape photography, the drive mode is best set to single shot. However, if shooting scenes where there is a peak moment—for example, seascapes with waves breaking over rocks—continuous shooting will give a range of shots to choose from. In very high-contrast scenes, it may be necessary to shoot a bracketed series and blend several shots in post-processing (see page 60). Some cameras have an auto-bracketing feature, which is recommended, as it avoids the possibility of moving the camera's position when adjusting exposure settings between shots.

Focusing

Whether you choose to use autofocus (AF) or manual focus (MF) really isn't that important, as AF on modern cameras is extremely accurate. What is far more important is knowing where in the scene you need to focus in order to get the depth of field that you require (see page 58). If you use AF, it's also important to know that it is locked in place and that the camera won't then re-focus, possibly incorrectly, when you press the shutter. Some photographers therefore like to use AF and then switch to manual focus before releasing the shutter. A better option is to set "back-button" focus in your camera's custom settings. This decouples the focus from the camera's shutter button and assigns it to one of the buttons on the back of the camera (some cameras have an AF-On button). Check your camera's manual for details of how to set this function.

Live view

Live view is a firmly established technology present on almost all modern digital cameras. It allows you to zoom in on specific parts of the scene for extremely accurate manual or automatic focusing. It is also possible to overlay useful information on the screen (and the viewfinder of mirrorless cameras), such as the live histogram, electronic level, and grid lines to aid composition. However, it is best to compose images with a clear screen or viewfinder, so there are no distractions and you don't accidentally include an unwanted part of the scene because it is obscured by the shooting data on the screen or viewfinder.

Image review

Image review is a key function of digital cameras, allowing you to check sharpness, depth of field, and exposure. As with live view, different information can be displayed, although not all of it by default, so look at the menu settings to see what is available. Histograms are vital for checking exposure, as they show the distribution of tones in the image—if the tones are pushed too far to the left of the histogram, this suggests underexposure, and too far to the right suggests overexposure. If the tones disappear off the end, this indicates that detail has been lost altogether. When this occurs, shadows or highlights are said to be "clipped."

Many cameras also offer a red-green-blue (RGB) histogram as an option, which allows you to check exposure in all three color channels for greater accuracy. Highlight alert is another function that you should enable. With this, overexposed highlights blink on the review image, providing a quick visual check for overexposure and also showing you exactly which highlights are blown. This is useful to know, as you may choose to allow any specular highlights to overexpose.

FOCUS ON...
PACKING FOR A SHOOT

As well as the obvious—camera body, lenses, and so on—make sure you pack your filters, adapter rings for all the lenses you're taking, remote release, rain cover, lens cloths, lens and filter cleaning fluid, spare batteries, a flashlight, map(s) of your location, warm and waterproof clothing if necessary, tools (such as allen keys) for adjusting tripods, as well as "gaffer" tape for emergency, on-the-spot repairs.

CHAPTER ONE
DAWN

● ● ● ● ● ●

There are three types of dawn—civil, nautical, and astronomical. Civil dawn—when the geometric center of the sun is 6° below the horizon in the morning—is what we are generally referring to when we think of dawn. It is that bewitching time before sunrise when we can begin to see light and color appearing in the sky.

This is when our cameras can "see" clearly again, and there is enough light for through-the-lens (TTL) metering systems to be able to achieve correct exposure unaided. At this time of day, shutter speeds tend to be lengthy due to the low levels of light, resulting in naturally long exposures. This can add further mood and atmosphere to images captured during the early morning.

Dawn can produce truly magical conditions for landscape photography, more than justifying the unsociably early start—early-morning sunlight can be vividly warm and dramatic. The period immediately after civil dawn is known as the "golden hour," and can be a productive, fulfilling, and exciting time for photographers.

Throughout this chapter, we will give you guidance and share hands-on experience to help you maximize the photo opportunities offered by this very special part of the day.

▶ DAWN COLOR
The light, color, and warmth at dawn can be intoxicating. The best skies often occur just as the sun breaks the horizon, so it is important to arrive early and be set up, ready, and waiting to capture the best of the dawn conditions.

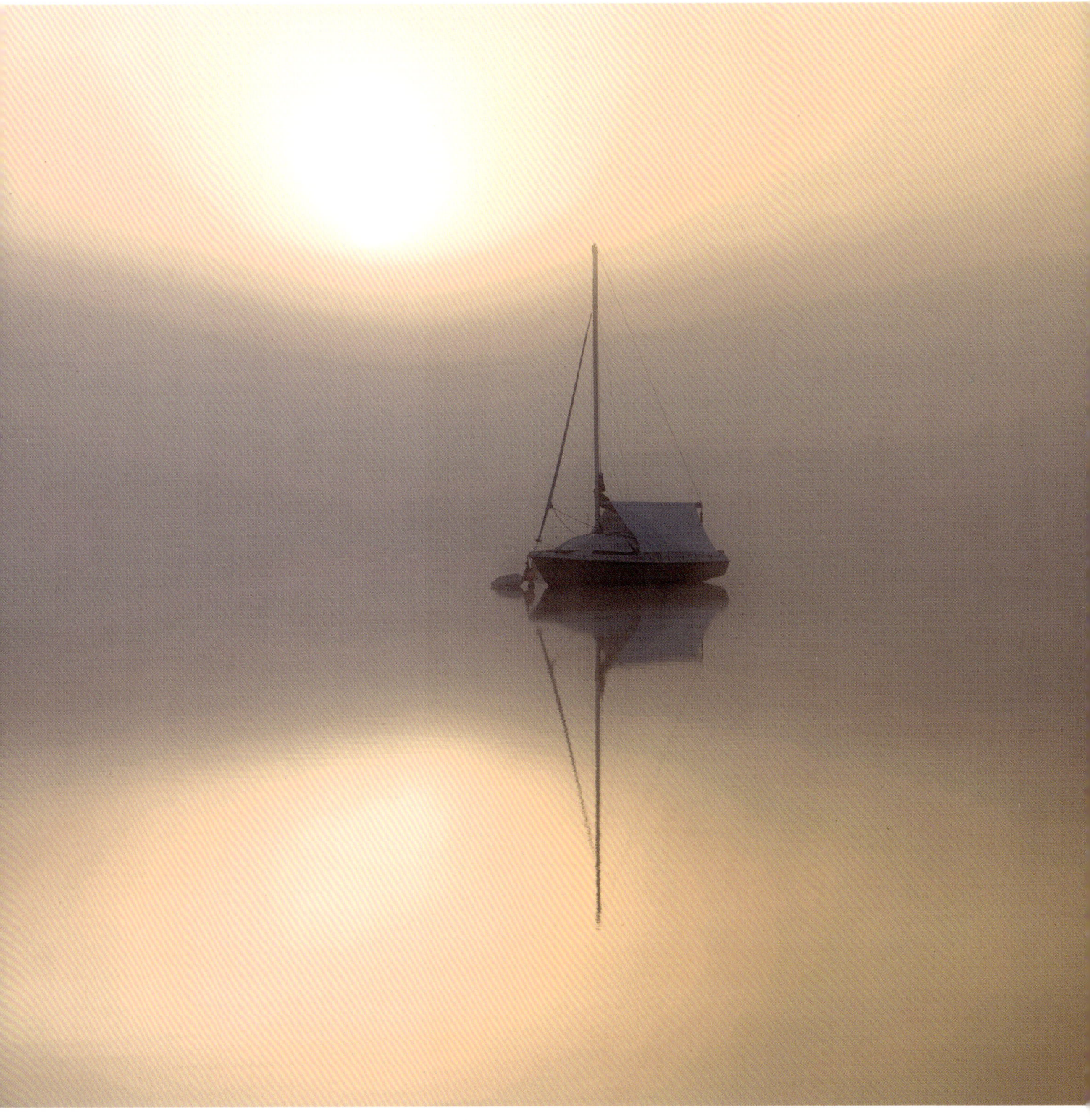

DAWN COLOR

Don't wait until the first rays of light strike the landscape to begin taking photos. The light before sunrise is subtle and beautifully diffused, while color in the sky can be warm and vivid. This is a surprisingly underused time of day, though. Many photographers will wait for the sun to appear above the horizon before they begin shooting, falsely believing you need direct, modeling light to strike and shape the landscape. This is a mistake. Color can form in the sky surprisingly early, many minutes before the sun actually appears. Therefore, get on location early—in semi-darkness—and make sure you arrive at your viewpoint as the pre-dawn color in the sky begins to glow.

Dawn skies can be colorful and dramatic. You will often see a graduation of warm tones close to the horizon, progressing and bleeding into cooler hues the higher you look. While the ambient light at dawn and dusk is similar, it tends to be cooler at daybreak. The air is often clearer—containing fewer particles—which tends to make dawn light appear cooler and bluer than at the opposite end of the day.

The contrast between a colorful and bright dawn sky and an unlit foreground can be significant—potentially several stops in light. This is likely to be beyond the capabilities of your camera's dynamic range, so be prepared to use a graduated ND filter (or blend exposures, see page 60) to achieve a correctly exposed result. One way to reduce the level of contrast between the sky and the darker landscape is to include a reflective subject in your foreground—for example, still water, wet sand, or snow.

FOCUS ON... COLOR

The glow in the sky close to where the sun is rising can understandably prove very seductive at dawn, but remember to also look behind you. The sky opposite the sun can take on a range of soft, pastel tones, providing a wonderful backdrop to landscape shots. Color can radiate all around the sky, bouncing and reflecting off cloud. This can provide unexpected opportunities in different directions, so be aware of this and glance up from your camera from time to time, to look around. While the color will be subtler and less intense, it can be just as photogenic, competing less with the landscape for attention. Therefore, be prepared to react to the conditions, adapting your composition—or adjusting your viewpoint quickly—to make the most of whatever nature provides.

▶ OTTER ISLAND
Skies can be extraordinarily colorful at dawn. Color like this doesn't last long and can only be captured successfully if you are already set up and waiting in anticipation.

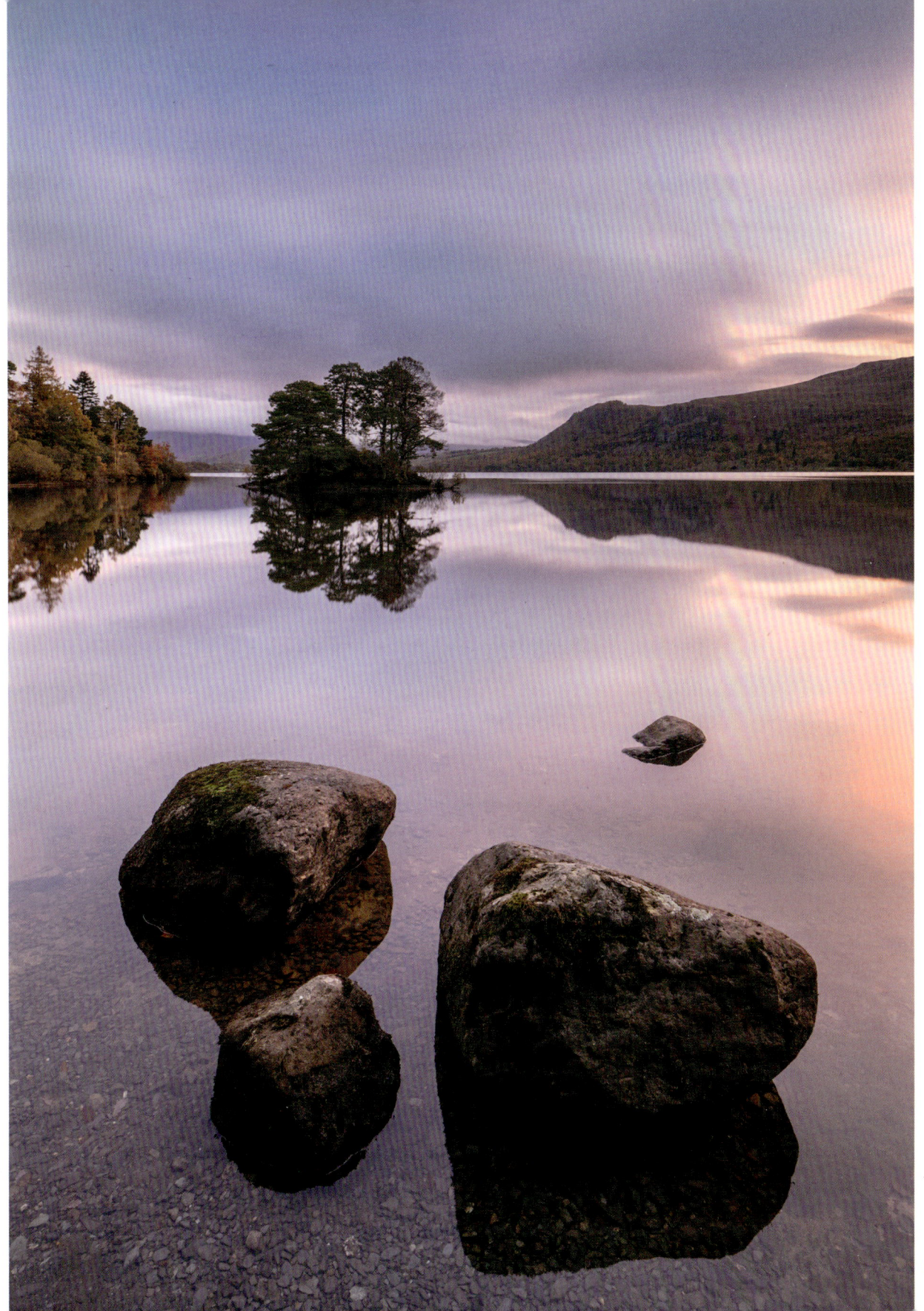

SETTING UP

At dawn, the light and conditions seem to alter faster than at any other time of the day. There is little leeway for error or indecision; the window of opportunity is short, so timing is important. This is where all your preparation begins to repay you. You should have calculated traveling time in advance, but still given yourself a few extra minutes to allow for any unforeseen circumstances or holdups. Having scouted the location beforehand (see page 38), you can make a beeline for your preferred viewpoint and set up quickly and efficiently, with no time wasted. Use a flashlight or head lamp to help guide you safely and set up your kit.

One of the trickiest aspects of low-light photography is focusing. Mirrorless cameras tend to be reliable even in poor light, but digital SLRs can struggle at dawn. If it is too dark for your camera's autofocusing system to precisely lock on to your focal point, shine your flashlight on a foreground object located at the distance you want to focus on within the frame. This should provide enough illumination for AF to work, or switch to manual focus if you feel this is a more reliable option.

Exposure times will be long at dawn. There is rarely a need to attach ND filters (see page 18) to creatively blur subject motion, as this will happen naturally—unless you select a large aperture, combined with a high ISO, to compensate. Your first exposures of the day might be over one minute in length, requiring you to switch to Bulb mode on some camera models, and time the exposure manually. Exposure length will quickly shorten, though, as the day gets lighter.

If you are shooting in Aperture Priority exposure mode (see page 13)—as we recommend—your camera will automatically adjust for the changing light. If you are shooting in Manual mode you must remember to continually adjust your shutter speed to compensate for the changing light. It should go without saying that a tripod is essential for stability when taking landscape photos at this time of day.

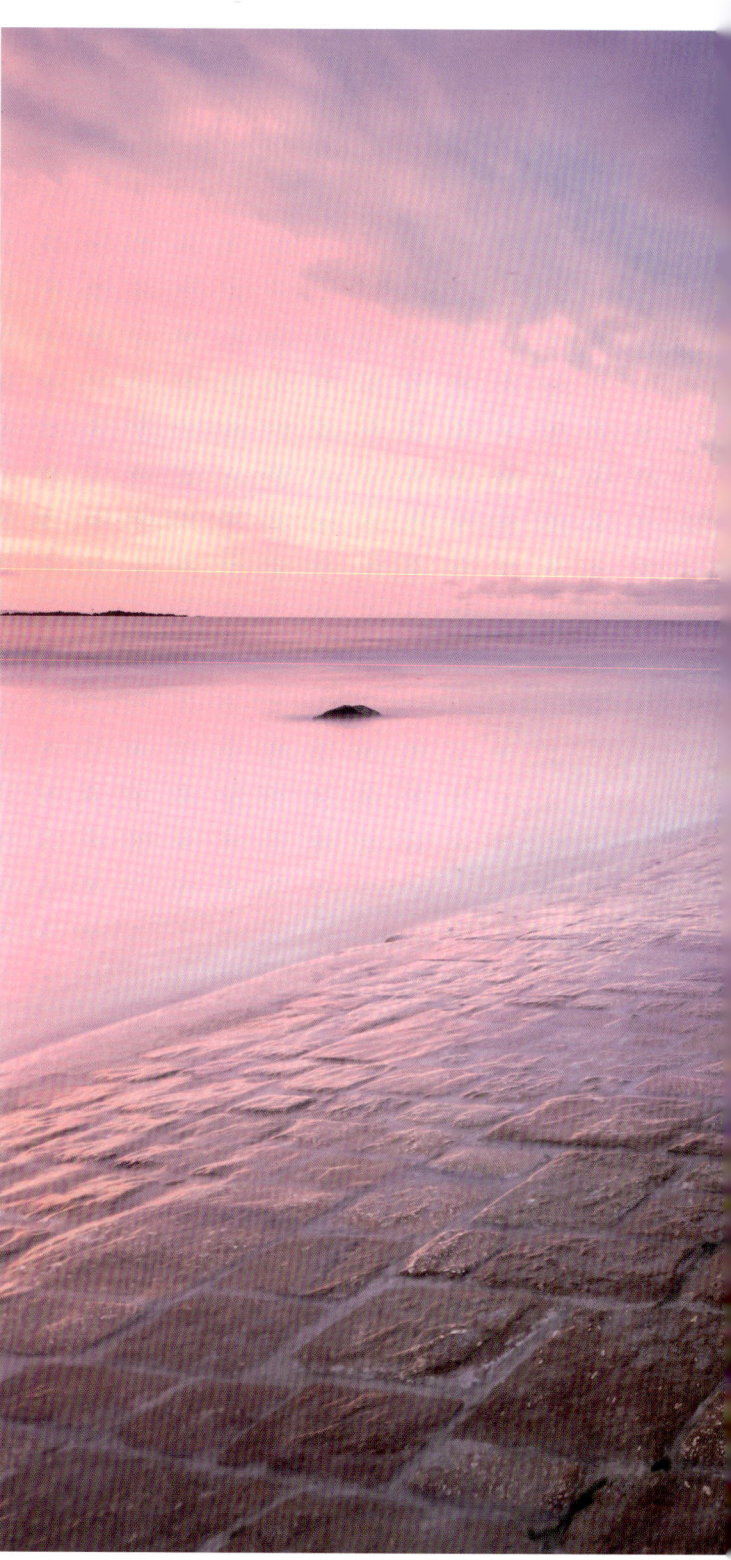

▶ **DAWN GLOW**
A big, colorful sky can be highly seductive and provide instant impact, but be careful it doesn't become the dominant force. Dawn color can be so vivid that it can overwhelm your subject and make compositions feel unbalanced. Subtle, pastel tones will often prove more pleasing and complimentary. The moral to the story is don't simply point your camera at the rising sun and most vivid color.

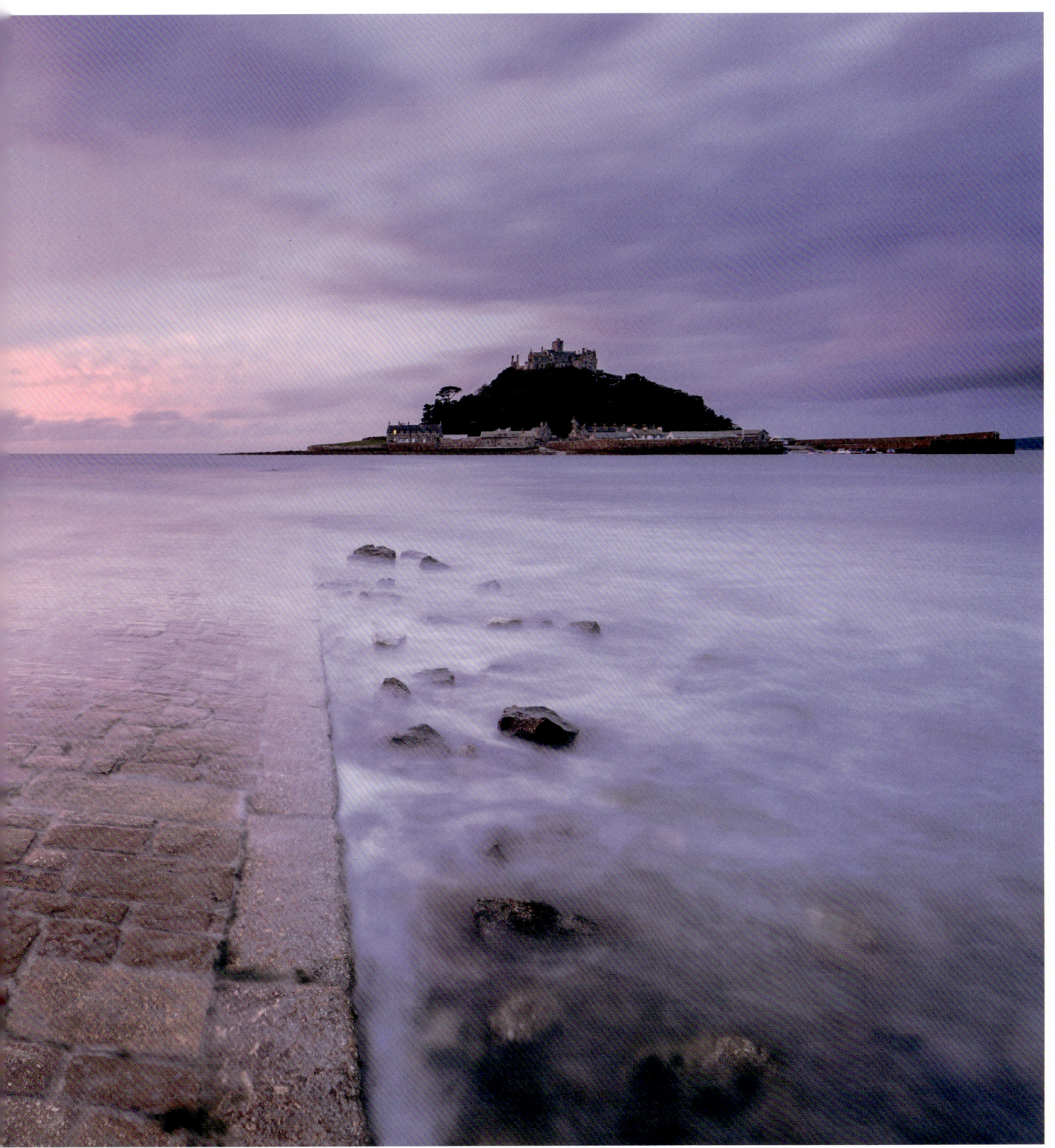

THE GOLDEN HOUR

As the sun appears above the horizon, the landscape will be flooded with rich, golden light—providing, of course, that low cloud doesn't block its path. Landscape photographers warmly refer to this time of day as the "magic hour" or "golden hour"—the brief period of time when the light is widely considered to be at its very best for scenic photography.

There are two golden hours: one is immediately following dawn, and the other is before sunset (see page 126). This is often defined as the period when the sun lies between 4° below the horizon and 6° above. "Golden hour" refers to the light's color and quality at this time of day, when the sun's low position provides warm sunlight. Don't take the "hour" too literally, though—the exact duration of golden light will vary depending on the time of year and your location—this period is rarely as long as an hour. If you search online, you will find golden hour calculators to help guide you.

So just why is the golden hour such a productive, fulfilling, and exciting time for landscape photography? Light is the photographer's language—it is the ingredient that allows us to convey the atmosphere, beauty, and character of a particular location—and the light is naturally soft and warm at this time of day, with the sun's low position in the sky revealing texture and providing depth. While we champion and outline the merits of shooting at various times of the day throughout this book, the golden hours remain the optimum times to capture landscape images.

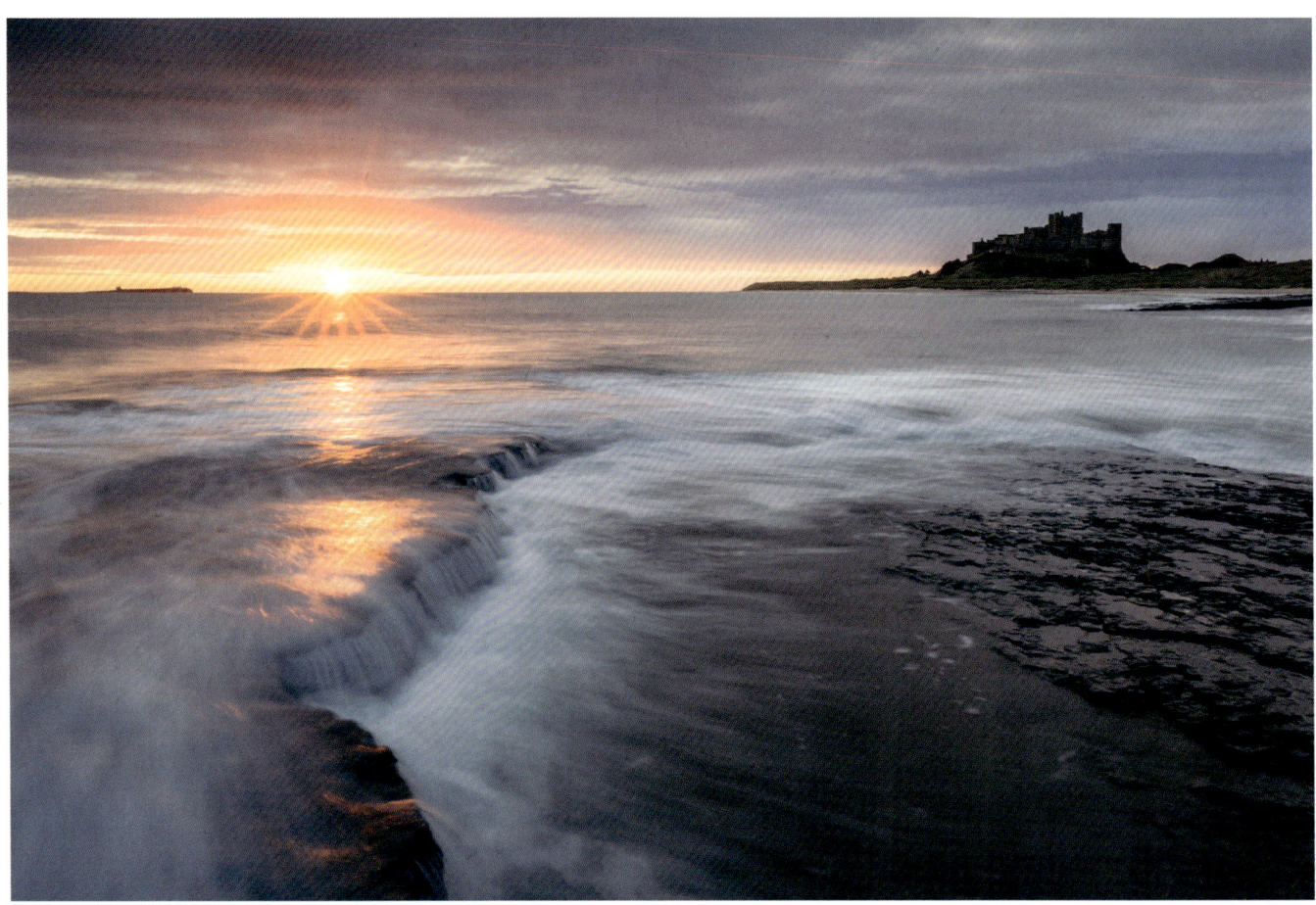

GOLDEN RULES

- Check the weather forecast the evening before. While you naturally don't want too much cloud cover, you equally don't want entirely clear skies. A degree of cloud will help add color, interest, and depth; cloudless skies tend to be boring.

- Get to your chosen viewpoint at least 45 minutes before golden light. This should give you sufficient time to find the best vantage point and set up.

- You can enhance the warmth of early morning sunlight through your choice of white balance (WB). A Cloudy WB preset can prove attractive for golden hour images—color temperature can be adjusted in-camera using the WB setting, or (if you shoot Raw) during post-processing.

- Use a tripod. Shutter speeds are typically slow at dawn, so a support will give you stability. You also need your camera in a fixed position if you intend to use ND grads (to balance the contrast between bright sky and darker foreground) or if you wish to take multiple shots to blend together or to create a panoramic stitch.

- Many digital cameras now have a built-in spirit-level or virtual horizon feature to help prevent wonky horizons—this can be particularly useful when shooting in low light. Alternatively, you can use an inexpensive hotshoe-mounted spirit-level.

WORK QUICKLY

Shooting at these times doesn't guarantee you will take great photos, but working in great light will certainly enhance your chances. Therefore, aim to shoot at this time as often as you can. Yet again, the window of opportunity is challengingly short, though. The pressure is always greater when shooting earlier in the day, as the light's quality is continually deteriorating as the minutes tick by and the sun gets higher. Typically, it is the first 30 minutes after sunrise that are the most precious. You will need to work relatively quickly, but don't rush or panic. Using an app (see page 35) to calculate the position of the sun in relation to your chosen viewpoint will help to ensure you are efficient with your time and set up in the best position.

Although the rising sun is very seductive and many photographers instinctively want to shoot directly toward it, I personally favor side-lighting at sunrise. Its ability to define and shape the landscape and also highlight certain features or landmarks is unrivaled. With the sun positioned at a right angle, this can also be a good moment to attach your polarizing filter (see page 114) and benefit from its effect.

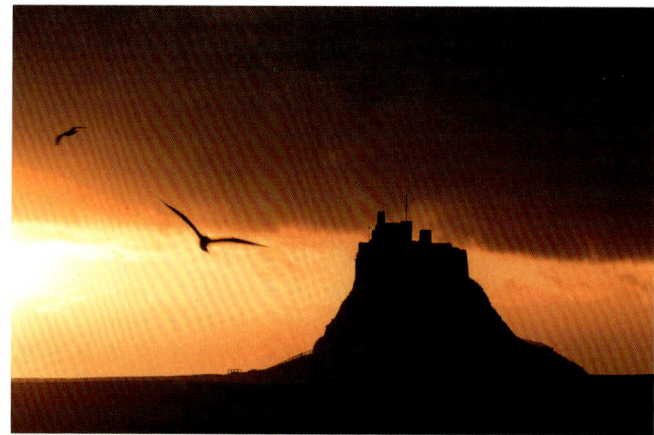

▲ CASTLE SILHOUETTE
Shooting toward the sun can produce very dramatic results at sunrise. The sky will often be full of warm, golden tones, and anything between you and the sunrise will be backlit or silhouetted. There is a danger of TTL metering being fooled into underexposure in such challenging light. Check histograms and apply positive exposure compensation if required. When shooting silhouettes (see page 147) it is best to opt for strong, instantly recognizable subjects or landmarks.

◀ STARBURST
While the sun is low in the sky, you might decide to include it within your composition as a point of interest. With the sun close to the horizon, its intensity will be reduced. A starburst or sunstar can add impact to shots incorporating the sun—to create one, select a small aperture, in the region of f/16 or f/22. Flare might be an issue with a wide-angle lens, but a lens hood will be of little help when shooting directly toward the sun. A degree of flare can prove attractive, but otherwise tidy up the image during post-processing on the computer using Cloning, Content-Aware, or Generative Fill tools.

MIST

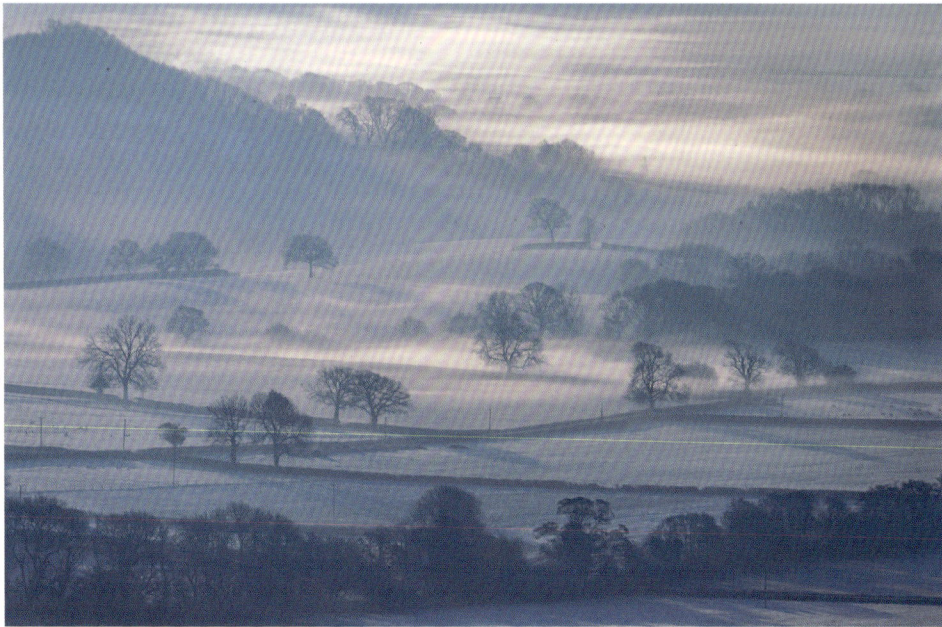

◄ THE VALE
Far-reaching, elevated vistas traditionally work well in misty conditions. Use a tele-zoom to isolate areas of beauty and interest. Keep a microfiber cloth close to hand to wipe away condensation from your lens.

An early alarm call can provide other rewards besides color and golden light. Mist can add wonderful diffusion and atmosphere to landscape shots. By reducing color and contrast, a thin veil of mist or fog can transform the look of the landscape. It effectively simplifies scenery, adding mystery and mood to your shots. Photogenic, low-lying mist is most likely to form overnight. Planning, preparation, and a tiny bit of luck are key to making the most of these magical conditions. However, early-morning mist can prove frustrating to photograph. Even with experience, it is impossible to predict precisely where and when mist will form and if it is too foggy—or not misty enough—you can return home frustrated and without any satisfactory images.

Fog consists of condensed, suspended water droplets, created when moist, warm air reaches its dew point. Basically, it is cloud on the ground. Fog is dense, reducing visibility to less than ½ mile (1km). Mist is thinner, impairing visibility less and is generally more attractive. There are several different types, including advection fog and evaporation fog, but probably the most appealing in terms of landscape photography is "radiation fog." This tends to form during clear, still nights when the ground is losing heat via radiation. The ground cools nearby air to saturation point,

resulting in mist forming. This type of mist will often remain attractively close to the ground, forming a thin, white layer at the bottom of valleys, over fields, and large bodies of water.

Mist is frustratingly unpredictable, though, and it can be tricky to anticipate when and where it will form and just how dense it will be. You will greatly increase your chances of capturing great misty images if you keep a close eye on the weather forecast. Look for clear, cool, and still conditions overnight, particularly during spring and fall when the temperature can drop steeply and there tends to be more moisture in the atmosphere. Precipation the day or so beforehand will increase your chances—high humidity (upward of 95%) will also help. Many weather apps will predict mist, but you can simply look for changes to predicted visibility in the forecast—if visibility drops from "excellent" or "very good" to "average" or "poor" overnight, it is often an indicator of mist or fog. This is your opportunity. Set your alarm early and arrive on location before daybreak.

LOCATION

The best conditions are often short-lived and confined to just before and after sunrise—mist will quickly evaporate as temperatures rise. To make the most of these magical but transient conditions, it is important to put yourself in the right place. Therefore, location choice is a big consideration. Although you can never be entirely sure where mist will form, or just how dense it will be, research or (better still) local knowledge and experience will help guide you. Elevated viewpoints, overlooking valleys, lakes, or the countryside, are normally the best option, allowing you to get above the mist and achieve good views below. A landscape with layers also works well—for example, a scene with far-reaching views of hills, mountains, or rolling countryside. Ideally, visit locations and viewpoints beforehand, so you are familiar with the potential they offer. As always, calculate the sun's position in advance (see page 35) so you are aware of the light's direction in relation to your chosen viewpoint.

Before daybreak, low-lying mist will appear naturally cool. However, Auto White Balance (AWB) will attempt to neutralize the lovely natural blue hues created by the time of day, so a Daylight WB setting is typically a better option, enabling you to capture, or even exaggerate, these tones. Once the sun has risen, early-morning sunlight will give mist natural warmth. The conditions will diffuse and reduce the sun's intensity, potentially allowing you to shoot in its direction. Doing so will allow you to capture incredibly atmospheric backlit images of the conditions.

Although wide-angle focal lengths are often favored for landscape photography, a telephoto length—in the region of 70–200mm—is often a better choice in misty weather. Longer focal lengths foreshorten perspective, exaggerating the mist's effect, and allowing you to isolate key points of interest within the landscape—a skeletal tree, church steeple, or landmark, perhaps. Misty landscapes are often accompanied by fairly clear, relatively uninteresting skies, so using a longer focal length will also help you keep the emphasis on the landscape, while restricting the amount of sky in the frame.

▼ RIVER BRATHEY
All types of landscape suit misty conditions, but typically scenes containing strong, obvious points of interest work well—for example, trees, a river, boats, buildings, or a recognizable landmark. The inclusion of a strong focal point will help cement your composition together.

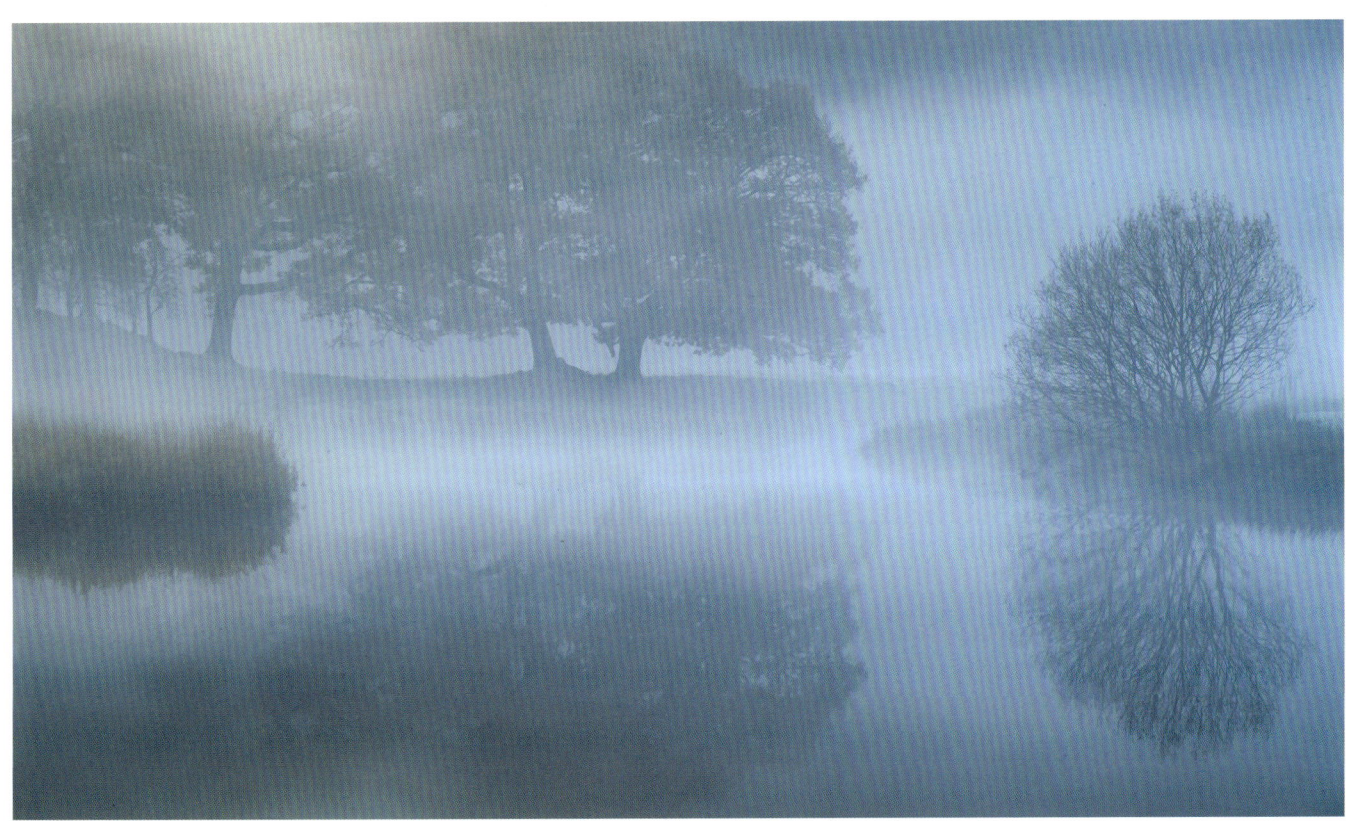

CORE TECHNIQUE
SELECTING THE CORRECT ND GRAD

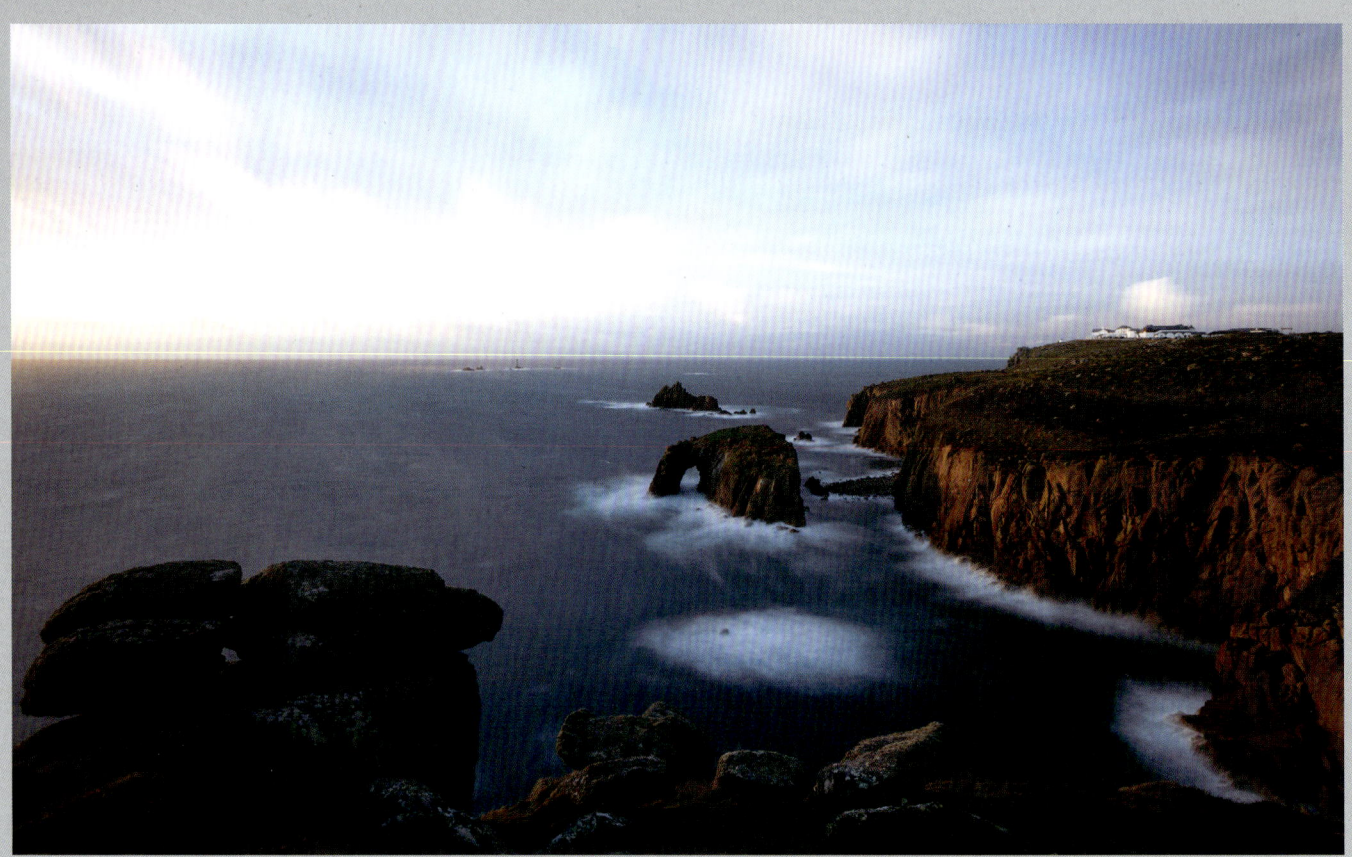

With the sun low in the sky, golden-hour light not only produces attractive warmth, but (potentially) a high degree of contrast. Skies are typically bright and colorful, yet the landscape below remains relatively dark and poorly or unevenly lit. High levels of contrast between a bright sky and darker foreground can pose a problem to digital cameras, extending beyond their dynamic range—their ability to capture detail in highlight and shadow areas simultaneously. As a result, achieving the correct exposure throughout the entire scene can be tricky—or even impossible—unaided. Cameras either tend to record detail in the foreground, but overexpose the sky, or they expose correctly for the bright sky, but then underexpose the landscape below. Although this exposure problem is most common at sunrise and sunset (see page 152), it is certainly not confined to these times. Therefore, it is important for a landscape photographer to understand how to balance the light in high-contrast landscapes. There are a couple of obvious solutions.

Graduated neutral density (ND) filters are designed to balance the light in high-contrast landscapes. They are half-clear, half-coated, with a feathered zone where the two halves meet. Grads are typically rectangular and attach via a dedicated, compatible filter holder or bracket. The idea is that—by sliding the filter up

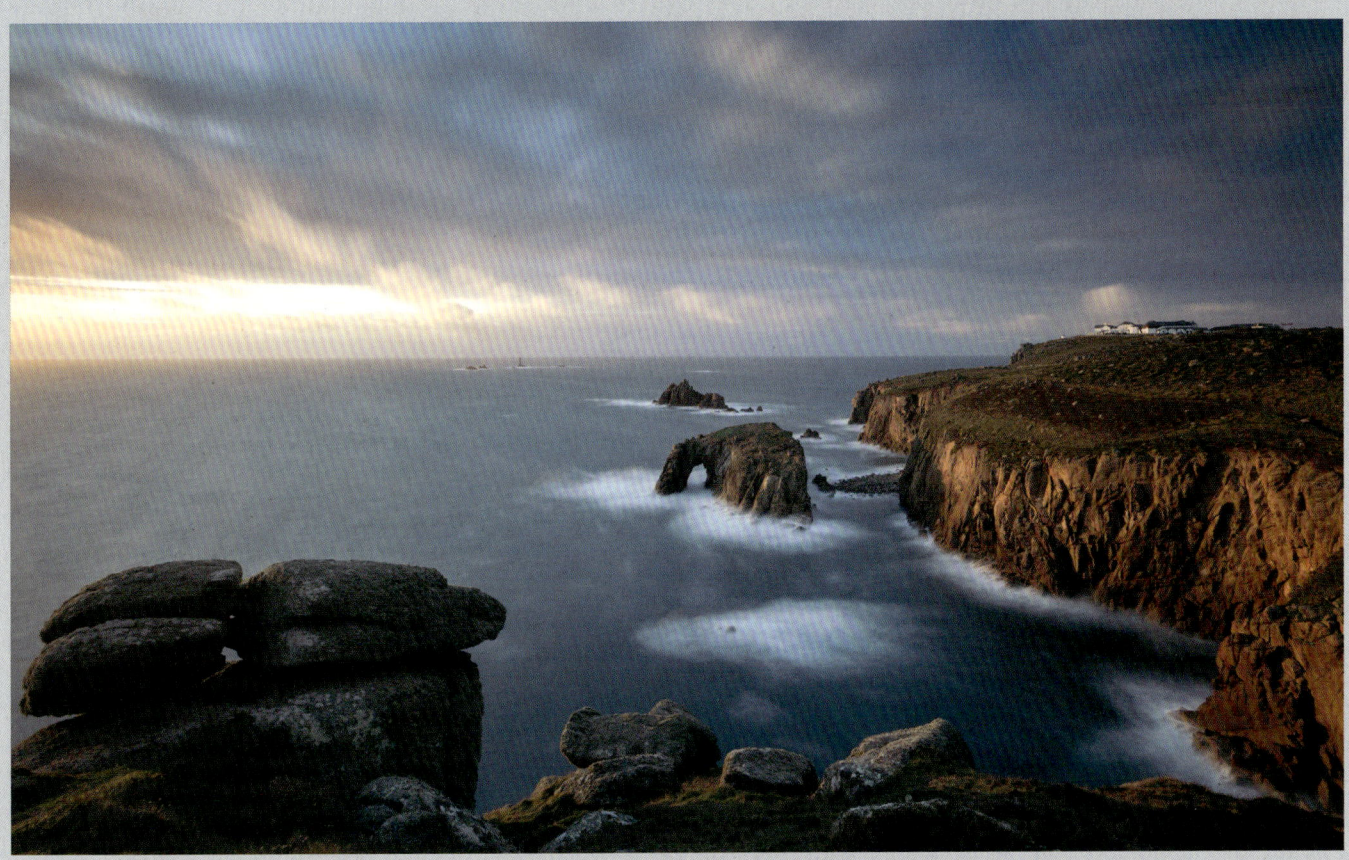

and down in the holder—you can carefully align the transitional zone with the horizon in your composition. The coated area absorbs—or holds back—the light in the sky, allowing you to balance the exposure across the frame. ND grads provide the only in-camera solution to shooting this type of high-contrast landscape, although there is also a post-processing answer, which requires taking multiple exposures and blending them together using software (see page 60).

Most landscape enthusiasts either already use grads or are at least aware of their role and purpose. However, grads only benefit your photography when applied correctly and appropriately.

◄▲ GRAD COMPARISON

Avoid using ND grads unnecessarily. Some landscape photographers attach grads through habit, but you only need one if there is sufficient contrast. The dynamic range of modern cameras is now so good that they are not always needed. Over-grading a scene will make skies look artificially dark, or record the foreground as unnaturally bright. The use of a grad shouldn't be detectable. In this instance (opposite), the sky was overexposed without a filter. I fitted a two-stop ND grad to balance the light within the scene, and capture a natural-looking result (above). I used a medium gradient filter to avoid darkening the cliff top and buildings at the right.

Over- or under-grading a scene can potentially ruin a shot. Grads are not only available in different densities, but different types of gradient, too. Therefore, it is important you are able to correctly calculate the strength of the grad you require (for any given situation), and also able to select the appropriate type.

STRENGTH

Graduated ND filters are commonly available in one-, two-, three-, and four-stop densities—although some filter brands also produce them in half-stop increments for added precision. The technically correct way to calculate the strength of the grad you need is to take a meter reading from the sky and then one from a mid-tone area in the foreground and work out the difference between the two. For example, if your reading from the sky is 1/500 sec. and the one from the foreground is 1/15 sec., the difference is five stops of light—remember: a stop is a doubling or halving of an exposure value. However, this doesn't mean you want to combine three- and two-stop grads to balance the light. Our eyes fully expect the sky to be brighter than the landscape, so if we evenly balance the light between the two, our shots would look unnatural. Instead,

you typically want to leave a two-stop difference between the sky and foreground to retain a natural-looking balance. Therefore, in this instance, a three-stop grad would almost certainly be the best option. If the difference was four stops of light, try using a two-stop graduated ND, and so on. When the level of contrast is less than three stops, your camera should be able to achieve correct exposure throughout the scene without the aid of filters.

Modern cameras have excellent dynamic range so the use of grads isn't always so essential today. Software, such as Adobe Lightroom, boast excellent masking tools that allow photographers to quickly and precisely select the sky in a photo to make it lighter or darker—or you could use a linear gradient tool. Therefore, if you slightly miscalculate grad strength you can easily rectify this during post-processing. However, it is important to underline that digital tools are not a replacement for physical filters. A digital grad will only work if you recorded highlight detail in the sky in the first place. If a sky is overexposed and highlights lost, digital solutions will not be able to retrieve any of the lost detail. Therefore, physical grads remain a vital accessory for many landscape photographers.

▲ **LEE FILTERS**
A set of medium ND grads is a popular choice among landscape photographers, with their feathered transition being suited to many landscape types.

▶ **VESTRAHORN**
If your budget allows, carry a choice of ND grads—of varying strength and gradient type—to cope with different lighting and scenery. In this instance, I selected a soft graduated ND to avoid the filter artificially darkening the mountain peaks poking up above the horizon.

FOCUS ON...
TYPES OF ND GRAD

ND grads are not only available in different densities, but various gradients, too. Once you have calculated the strength of grad you need for the light, you need to consider what type of gradient will suit the scene best. Graduated filters are available with soft, medium, hard, and very hard transitional zones. A soft grad will gently blend the exposure between sky and foreground when the skyline isn't defined or is very uneven—for example, a mountainous scene or a woodland interior. The soft transition helps prevent the grad from being detectable in areas where it overlaps parts of the landscape. A medium grad is less soft, but the transitional zone still isn't too abrupt. Therefore, it is well suited to landscapes where elements, such as trees, rooftops, and hills protrude into the skyline. A medium grad will hold back the sky effectively, without over-darkening these objects—making it a favorite among many landscape enthusiasts. Hard-edged grads are perfect for landscapes boasting very straight, uninterrupted horizons, like views out to sea. They are designed so that almost the full strength of their density is spread over the entire coated area of the filter. This gives them greater, more precise control over exposure in the sky. They can also be aligned more easily and more accurately. However, they are also less forgiving if you misalign them. Finally, very hard ND grads are now available, with barely any feathered zone. They are very abrupt and unforgiving if misused. Again, they are suited to very sharp, defined horizon lines, or when using focal lengths upward of 100mm, when transitions appear to grow progressively softer. They are also popular among users of cameras with a smaller sensor size, as the graduated part of a filter is effectively softer when the size of the sensor is smaller. Therefore, a very hard grad on a camera with a smaller sensor effectively performs like a hard grad on a large-sensor camera, while a hard grad is equal to a medium grad, and so on.

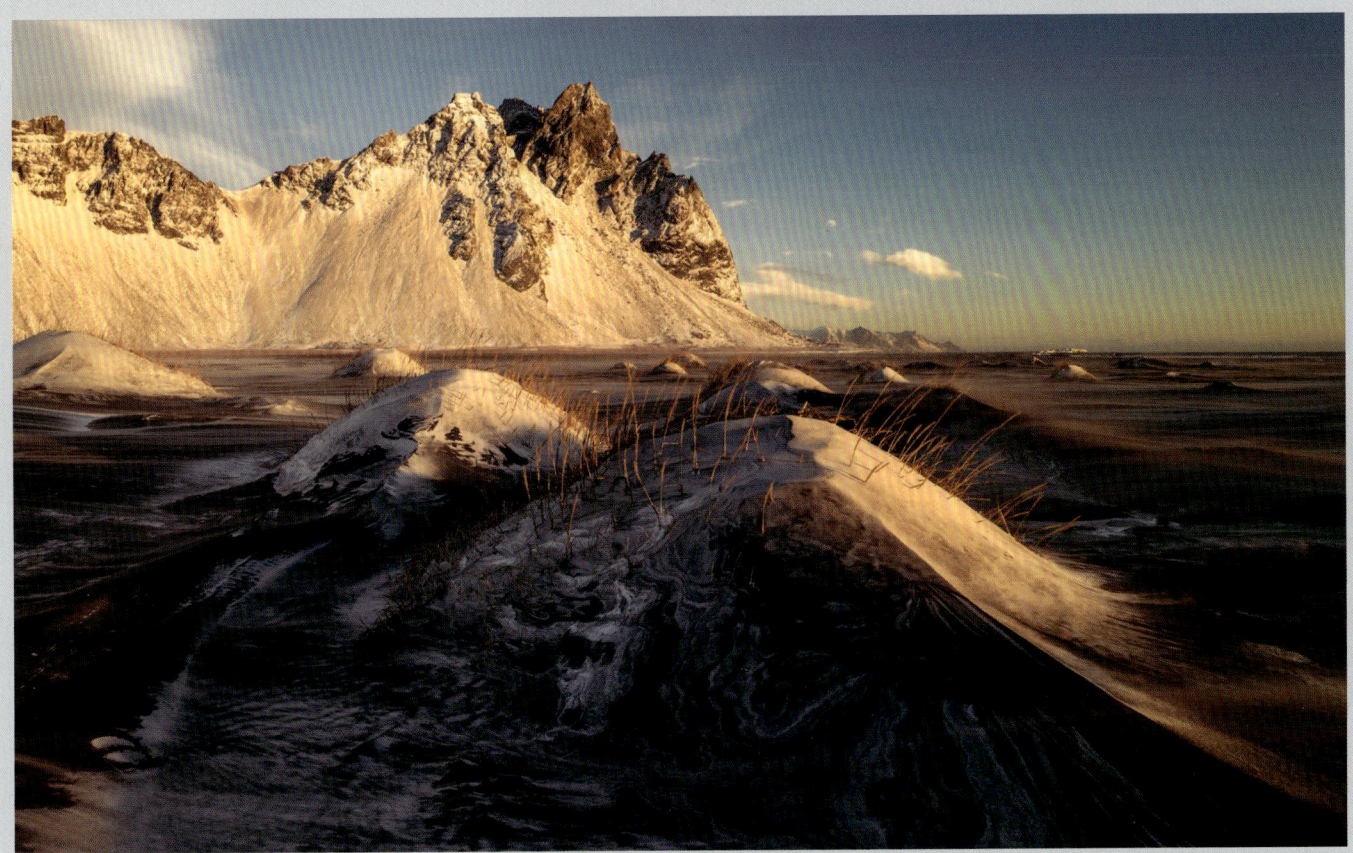

COMPOSITION
FOREGROUND INTEREST

The idea of composition is to arrange the elements within the scene in the most visually stimulating and pleasing way to communicate your ideas and vision. It is an age-old art form. Deciding what to include or exclude, your shooting angle, and focal length are all big decisions that will greatly influence the final image. Creating balance and harmony is your goal.

Even when the light conditions are magical, you should be just as diligent and creative with your composition—working hard to create the most compelling frame possible. However, with the quality of light quickly deteriorating as the sun rises higher, it is important that you can identify the best composition as swiftly as possible during your dawn shoots.

Good use of foreground interest is often an effective way of creating strong, three-dimensional-looking landscapes—this is useful advice for composition at any time of the day, not just at dawn. By implying depth you can make your images appear more lifelike. Foreground interest should provide an effective entry point into your photo, which the viewer's eye quickly identifies and follows. Almost anything can provide foreground interest, if it is appropriate and complements the scene overall. Rocks and boulders, tree roots, wavy sand patterns, reflections, reeds, fallen leaves, and wild flowers are just a small selection of popular foreground subjects. Your foreground subject should add balance to your composition and ideally a degree of scale and context too, yet it shouldn't dominate or overwhelm the image space. Your foreground needs to form a link with the middle distance and view beyond, or your composition will appear unbalanced.

LOW VIEWPOINT

When using foreground as a compositional aid, landscape photographers are often advised to opt for a low viewpoint. This, combined with a wide-angle perspective, can produce very dynamic, striking results. However, simply getting wide and close to your foreground does not guarantee a good composition. When using foreground interest, you often need to take great care and think carefully about the camera's height, orientation, and the relationship between foreground and background. If you get too low, not only can you make foreground objects appear too dominant in the frame, but you sacrifice separation between nearby objects and those in the middle or far distance. Equally, if you position your camera too high, you can create too much empty, boring space in the middle distance. Therefore, attention to detail and overall balance is key when including foreground interest. A successful foreground should complement the background—while the foreground, middle distance, and background need to work together in a logical and cohesive way.

FOCUS ON...
DEPTH OF FIELD

When including foreground interest in your shots, you will normally want everything to be in acceptable focus from the front to the back of your image. To achieve such a wide zone of focus, you will need a large depth of field.

Although both focal length and camera-to-subject distance can influence depth of field, aperture size is the overriding control. A large f-number or f-stop (f/2.8 or f/4), produces a shallow zone of focus, while a small f-stop (f/16 or f/22) will generate extensive depth of field. For most landscape images—particularly those featuring foreground interest—photographers should prioritize the use of a small aperture. By using Aperture Priority or Manual exposure mode, photographers can have full creative control over depth of field. Wide-angle lenses boast an inherently large depth of field, making them a popular choice for capturing images that are sharp from front to back. When including foreground, you should also think carefully about where in the frame you place your point of focus—consider double-distance focusing or calculating the hyperfocal distance (see page 112).

If you can't generate sufficient sharpness in-camera using a large aperture, consider focus-stacking (see page 134) and blending the images together in post-processing to extend the depth of field.

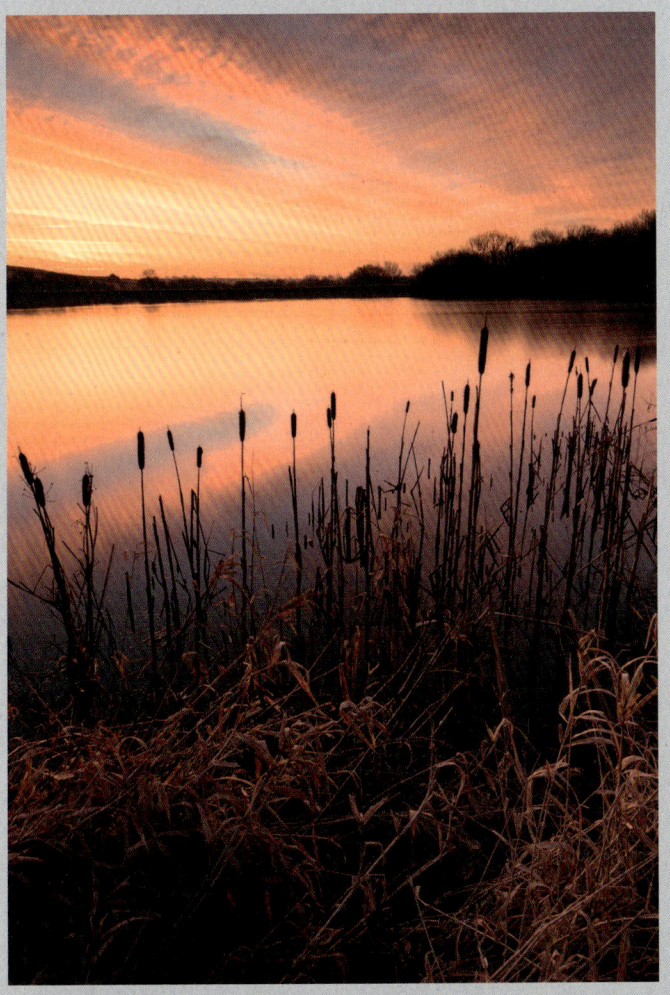

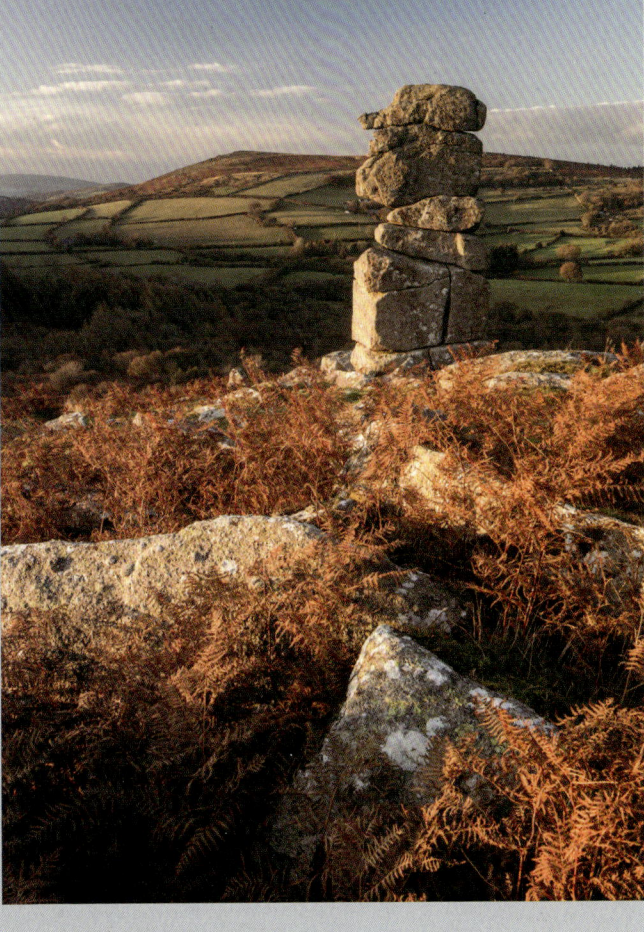

▲ **RUSHES**
Bulrushes created appropriate foreground interest in this early-morning view of a local lake. By opting for a small aperture of f/16 and super-wide focal length, I was able to generate extensive depth of field.

▲ **ROCK STACK**
When trying to identify a suitable foreground subject, pay attention to its shape, size, texture, and orientation. For example, angled objects can prove particularly effective, subtly directing attention into the frame. In this instance, the foreground rocks and golden bracken provide an entry point to the composition and help direct the eye through the image from the front to the back.

POST-PROCESSING STEP-BY-STEP
EXPOSURE BLENDING

With the sun low in the sky, photographers often have to contend with a high level of contrast during early-morning shoots. As discussed previously in this chapter, the difference in light between the sky and the land can be equal to several stops. When the contrast within a scene is too much for your camera's dynamic range to capture, you could use a graduated ND filter (see pages 54–57) to balance the light. However, this is not always the most practical solution. For example, when photographing a scene with a cliff, mountain, or landmark poking up and interrupting the skyline, a grad will artificially darken these areas, too. A much better solution is to exposure blend.

The principle of blending or merging is similar to high-dynamic range (HDR) photography, requiring you to take two (or more) photographs of the same scene using different exposures—

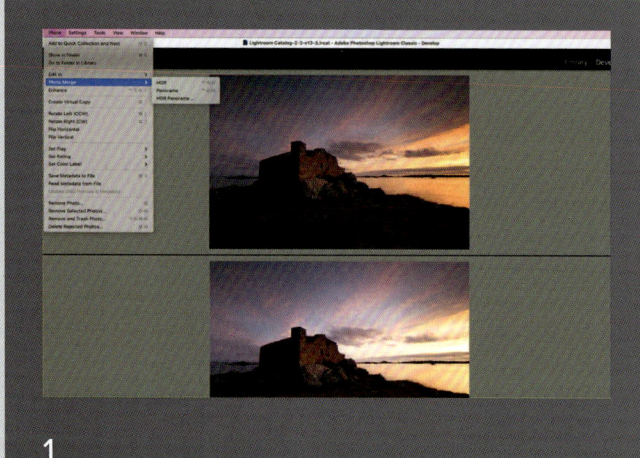

1

HDR techniques are a good way to retain detail in both the highlight and shadows areas of a high-contrast scene. Having captured two or more bracketed files—which between them contain all the data you require to produce one correctly exposed result—you now need to merge them using software. There are various plug-ins you can use to blend files, but Lightroom's own HDR Merge feature does an excellent job. Simply select the files you wish to merge and click Photo>Photo Merge>HDR.

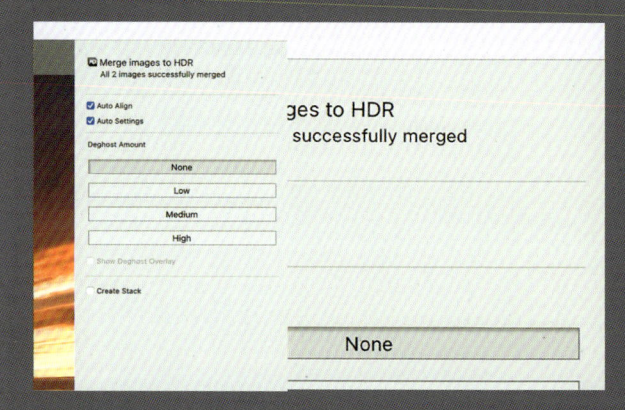

2

The HDR Merge window will open, providing Lightroom's preview of the blended exposure. There are very few settings you can adjust, as Lightroom aims to produce a natural looking HDR result which you can then process via the Develop module as you would any other file. The Auto Align and Auto Settings boxes are checked by default and the Deghost Amount set to None—if you alter these, Lightroom will remember changes and automatically apply them again when you next merge files.

typically one exposed correctly for the sky, and one for the foreground. Compositions need to be identical for the most seamless blend, so use a tripod when capturing your shots. You can alter exposure value manually between each frame, or use your camera's auto exposure bracketing facility.

Once you've captured your different exposures, you can blend them together during post-processing. Most photo-editing software has a facility to do this and using Layer Masks in Photoshop is a popular method. However, the HDR Merge option in Adobe Lightroom makes the process particularly fast and easy.

While a high level of contrast is most likely during the golden hours, knowing how to merge exposures can benefit your photography throughout daylight hours.

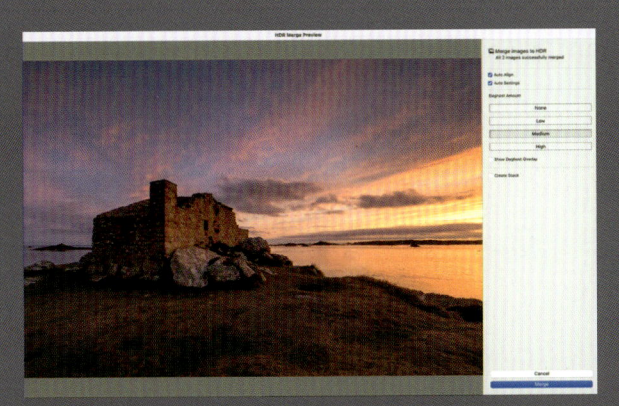

3
While Auto Settings often do a very good job, uncheck this box if you want total control over the look of the final image. If there was no movement between shots, keep Deghost Amount set to None. If there was movement between frames—for example, cloud motion or wind-blown foliage, set the Deghost Amount to Low, Medium, or High. This can be a matter of trial and error, selecting whichever setting produces the best result. In this instance, a Medium amount of deghosting worked best.

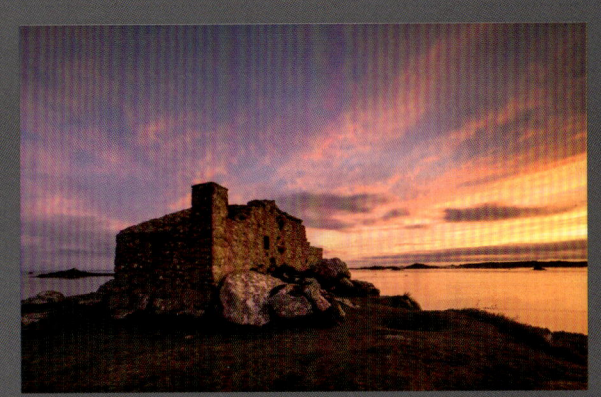

4
Once happy, go ahead and click the Merge button in the bottom right corner of the dialog box. Lightroom will merge the files and save them as a DNG (Digital Negative) file with the suffix -HDR added to the file name. You will be returned to the module where you started. Your new HDR file should be treated as a starting point—effectively, you've created a new Raw file that you can now edit in the Develop Module to achieve the look you desire.

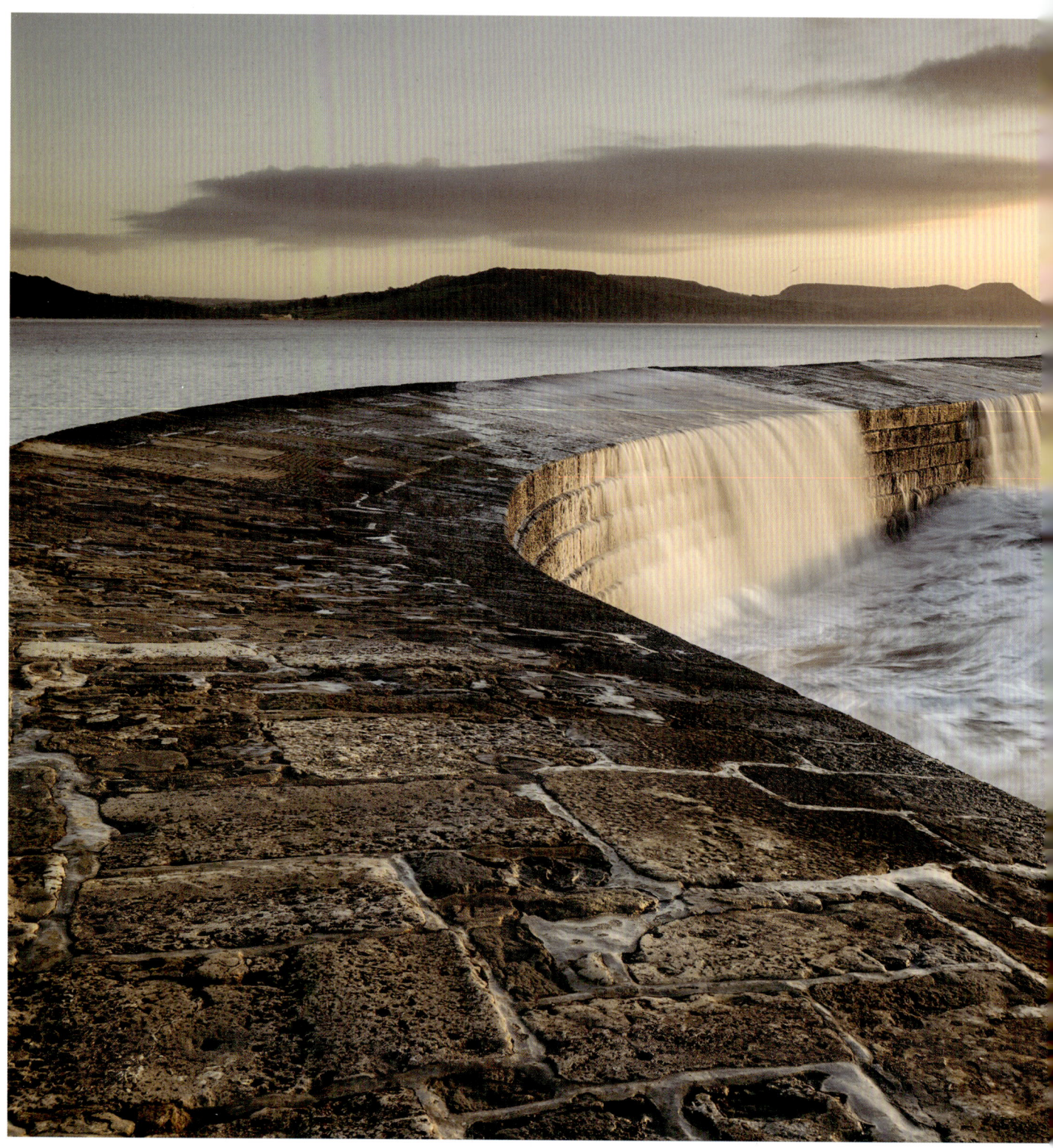

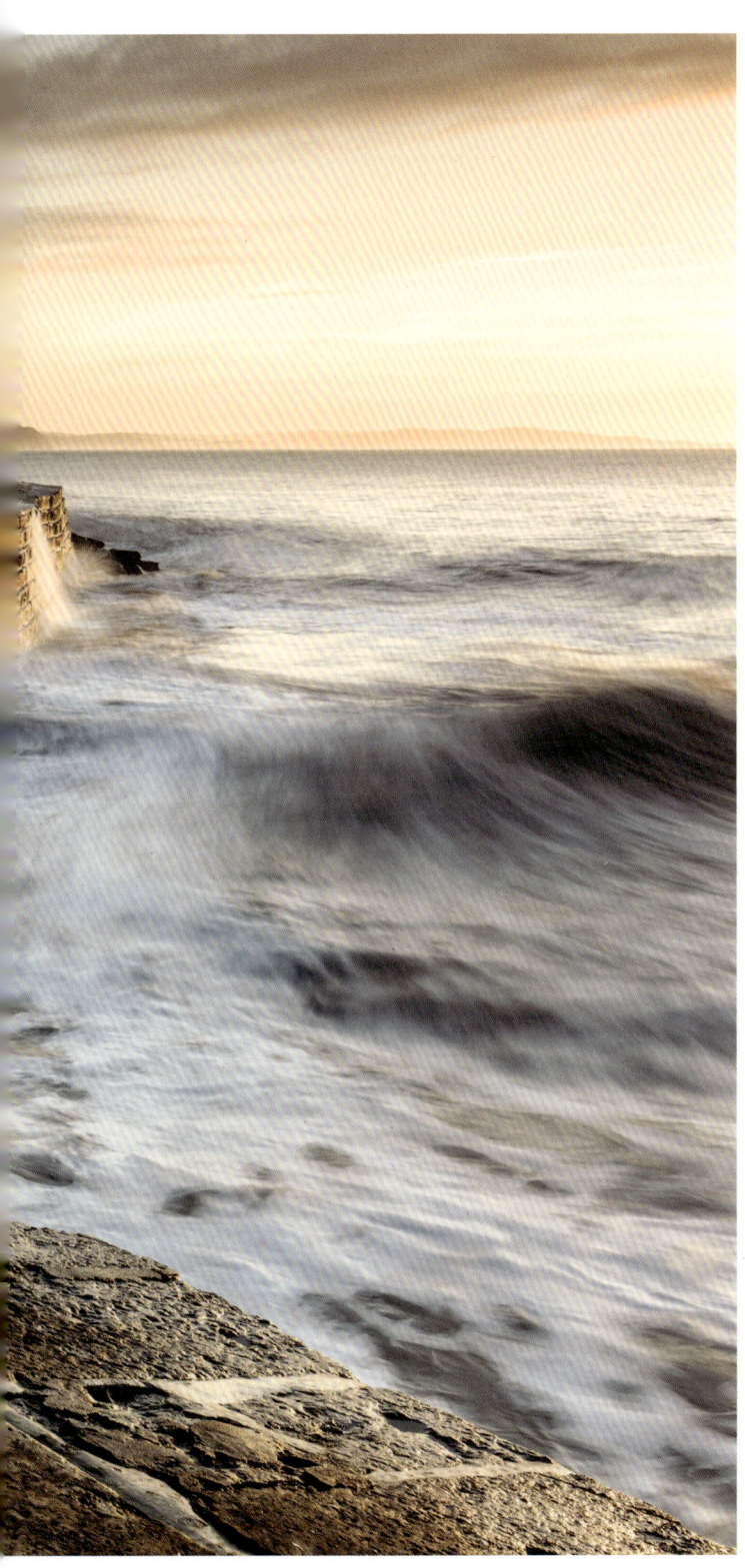

FINAL SHOT

Photographer **Ross Hoddinott**
Location **The Cobb, Lyme Regis, Dorset, United Kingdom**
Time and date **8.32 a.m., January 28**
Camera **Nikon D810**
Lens **AF-S Nikkor 17–35mm f/2.8D IF (at 30mm)**
Filtration **3-stop medium ND grad, 3-stop ND**
Exposure **ISO 100, 0.6 sec. at f/16**

THE STORY

"Like most good landscapes this shot is all about timing and being in the right place at the right time. Through previous experience and planning, I knew this location worked best at dawn and that the sun would bathe the harbor wall in golden sidelight during the winter months. This location is a two-hour drive from my home, so I set my alarm for 4.30 a.m., crept out of the house (thankfully without waking the kids!), and arrived soon after 7 a.m. The forecast looked promising and I purposely timed my visit to coincide with high water. In semidarkness, I walked along the top of The Cobb until I reached a spot where I could capture the sweep of the harbor. I carefully composed my shot so the edge of wall provided a strong lead-in line from the bottom right corner of the frame. I opted for a low, waist-height viewpoint to place emphasis on the stonework, which provided obvious foreground interest. To generate front-to-back sharpness, I selected an aperture of f/16 and focused approximately one third of the way into the frame. I used an ND grad to hold back exposure in the bright morning sky. I wanted to imply a degree of motion, but didn't wish to entirely flatten the movement of the water by using an exposure that was too long. Therefore, I selected a three-stop solid ND filter, which extended the shutter speed to just under one second. Then I waited… waited for just the right wave to crash over the breakwater. Although the large waves crashing all around made me a little nervous, I thankfully escaped with dry feet. The rich golden light didn't last long, but I had my shot and the early start proved worthwhile. Time for breakfast!"

CHAPTER TWO
MORNING

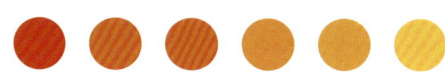

As the sun gradually rises higher in the sky, the light changes. Yes, it loses some of its natural warmth and softness, but it can still be photogenic—every stage of the day offers genuine and unique opportunities. When you can't simply rely on the light's color and quality for impact you have to work harder on composition and creativity to generate appeal… and that is not a bad thing.

As there is more light available than at dawn, shooting handheld becomes possible—this can promote freedom and spontaneity. Of course, you don't always have to shoot the "big picture." Photographers such as Hans Strand, Mark Littlejohn, and Guy Tal have helped popularize the "intimate" landscape. Abstracting the landscape can create quite compelling results and successful images rely more on the vision and perception of the photographer instead of the light's quality.

Learning to take good photographs at different times of the day will also help you learn more about light and how it shapes the landscape, and how it influences color, contrast, and perceived depth. In this way you can quickly grow into a more able and versatile photographer.

▶ **CASTLE BY THE LOCH**
The light's quality is not only affected by the time of day, but by the time of year and your geographic location as well. In winter, the sun remains lower in the sky for longer, producing rich morning light for longer. This photograph was taken just before 10 a.m., on a still winter's morning. Although this might not be a time of day many photographers would consider suitable for landscape photography, the low, dark cloud and spotlighting combine to produce an attractive and dramatic result.

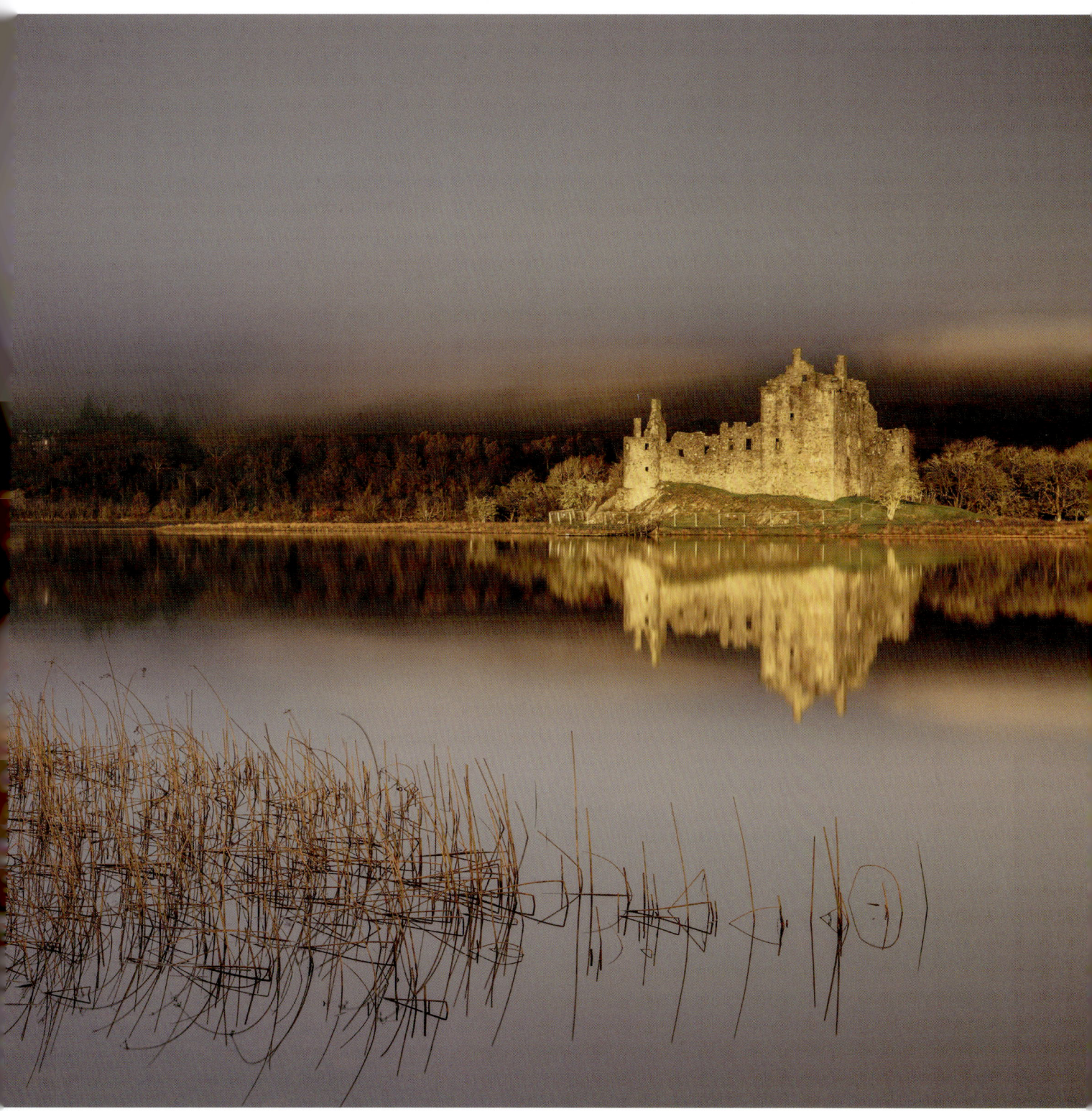

FINDING OPPORTUNITIES

There is no such thing as a bad time of day to take photos. However, as the light changes, you do need to adapt and think more about subject choice and landscape type. As the sun climbs higher in the sky, in theory, the quality of the light is deteriorating—the landscape is becoming more brightly lit and contrast is increasing. In these conditions, shadows can become inky black, obscuring detail, while highlights can begin to wash out, and so the light can appear harsh and unattractive. However, while this might not be desirable for some scenes, it can be suited to others. It is the photographer's job to match the right light or conditions to the right scene.

As landscape photographers, we would be foolish to restrict ourselves to golden-hour photography only—the windows of opportunity are too short, unreliable, and sometimes just not convenient. Instead, recognize and embrace the qualities and opportunities that morning light provides. In practice, the light in the early part of the morning often remains very good—particularly during the winter months, when the sun's arc is shallower, providing attractive lighting for longer periods. In the morning, the sun is still low enough to cast noticeable shadows and remains naturally warm, yet high enough to highlight photogenic shape and form within the landscape. Mist, frost, and heavy dew can linger for hours, adding atmosphere and beauty to photographs taken throughout the morning. Yet the light is typically more predictable and far-reaching than at sunrise, with the sun now high enough to be unaffected by significant features within the landscape—mountain peaks, hills, buildings, and cliff tops no longer obscure light from striking key parts of your scene as they can do when the sun is very low in the sky.

EXPERIMENT

With the light's quality and color being less influential at this time of day, you need to switch the emphasis to other factors to generate impact in your images. Good composition is always important, but when the light or conditions are less magical, even greater weight is placed on the way you arrange and frame the landscape. Take time to really consider your composition. With the light now more constant and less changeable, there is rarely any pressure or the need to panic. Photographers are often guilty of rushing when the light is at its best and quickly changing, and this can result in silly errors being made. The consistency of morning light gives photographers the time and ability to really study a scene to identify the best viewpoint and fine-tune composition. You have the luxury and time to experiment more with focal length, technique, viewpoint, and perspective, and compare how these things affect depth and visual balance. Exploit this opportunity—experiment and be innovative.

While light has a huge influence on the landscape, the sun is not always shining. Depending on where you live, the sun may regularly be obscured by cloud cover. When it is, the importance of taking photos at any particular time of day becomes less relevant. On overcast days, light is low in contrast and often attractively diffused. While this won't suit all scenes, the coast and woodland in particular are landscape types that photograph very well when there is a lack of strong, directional light.

▶ **WINTER WONDERS**
Snow needs to be virgin in landscape photographs, yet as the hours pass, it can begin to melt and is quickly ruined by footprints. You need to reach your viewpoint early—during the morning—while the wintry scenery still looks pristine and the light remains attractive.

▶ **THE OLD MAN**
Don't be hasty, and pack up too soon after your dawn shoot. This photo was taken at around 9.30 a.m., long after the best golden light and color had faded. Yet this was one of my favorite images from my morning's shoot—the light play on the background mountains and dark storm clouds combined to produce a lovely atmosphere. I could have easily missed the shot had I packed up and returned to my car immediately after my dawn shoot.

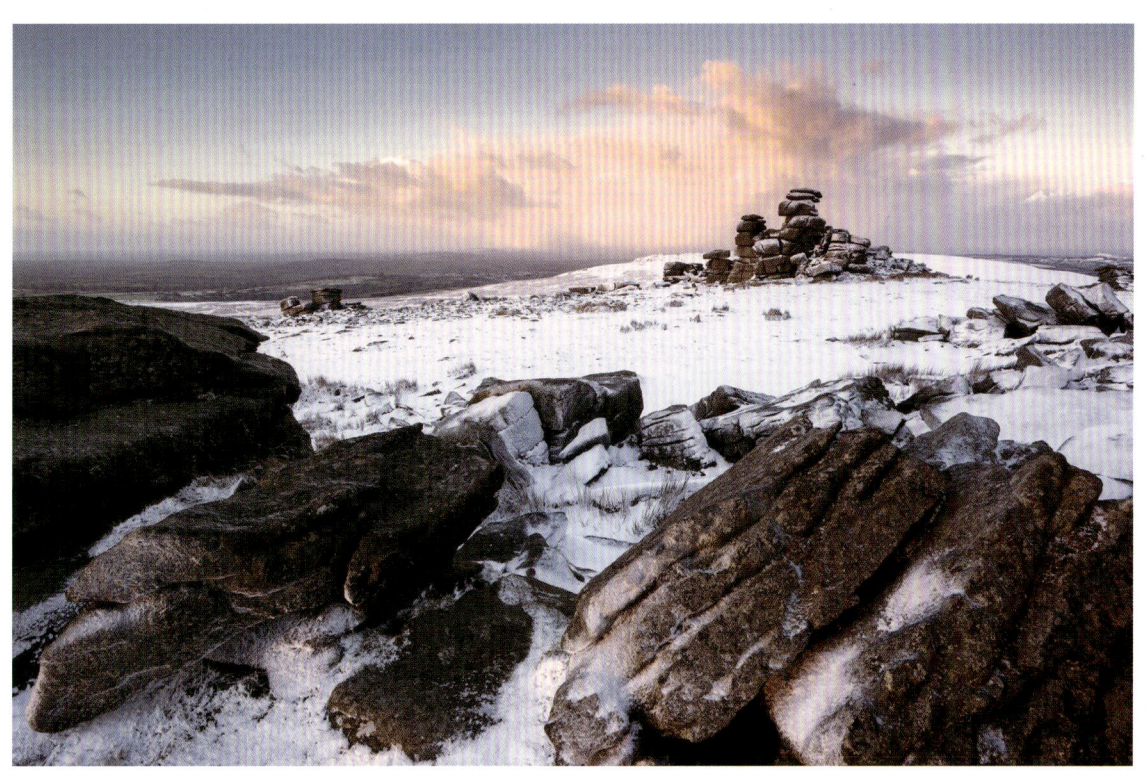

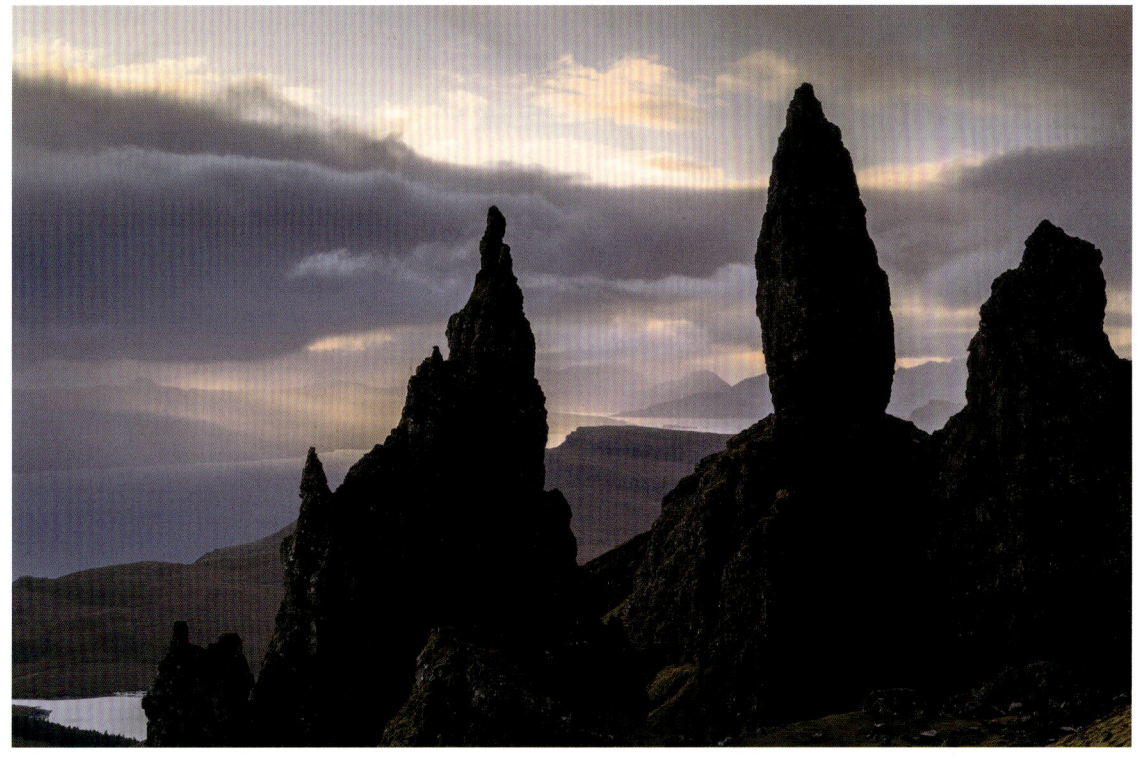

WOODLAND INTERIORS

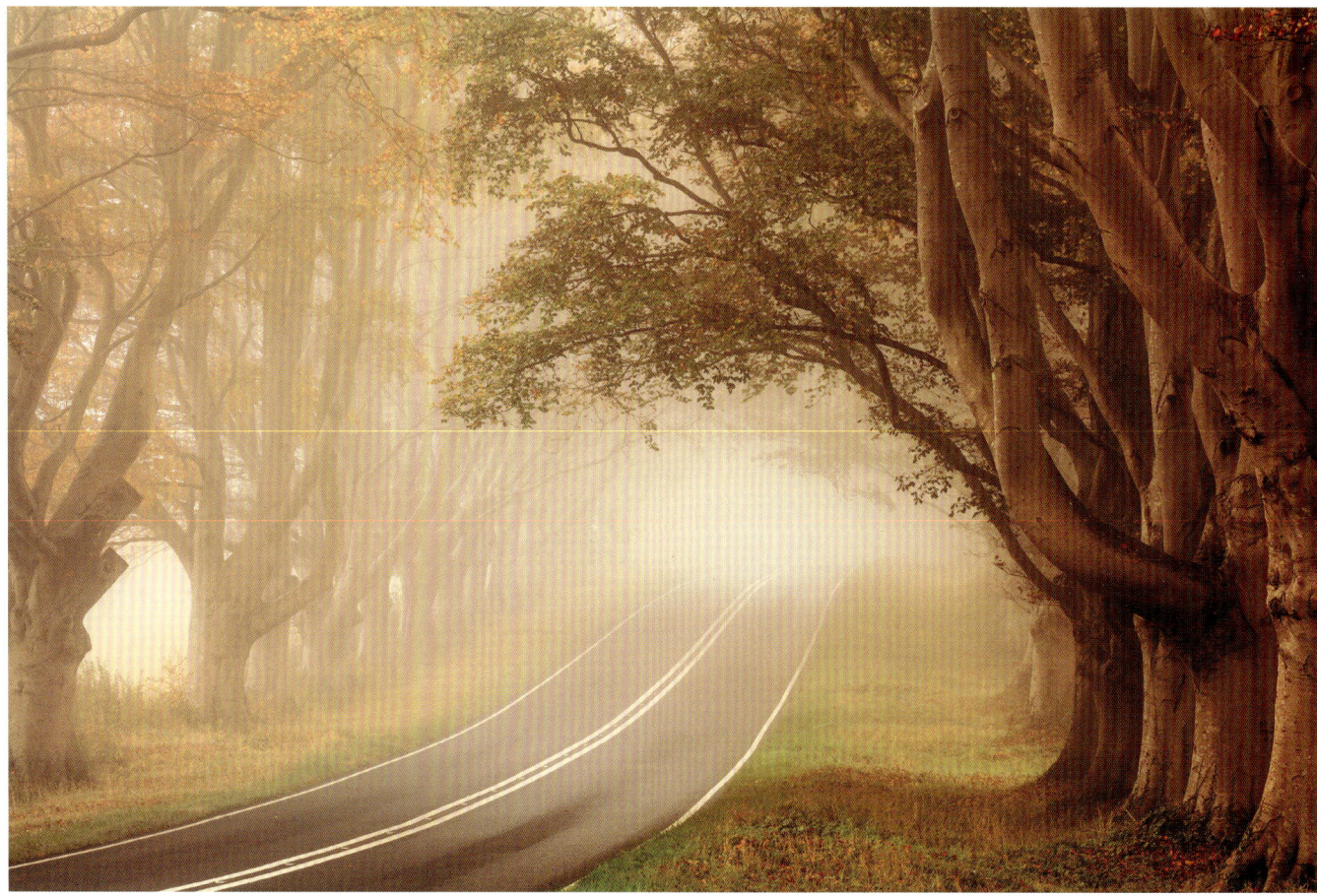

Most landscape photographers would admit to being instinctively drawn to trees and woodland. Forests can be magical, ever-changing places. Trunks, branches, and leaves distort and diffuse sunlight, while it is an environment full of strong shapes, textures, and colors. It is unsurprising that it is such a popular subject. However, woodland is arguably among the trickiest types of landscape to photograph successfully. Woodland interiors are busy, chaotic environments, so identifying compositions with balance, order, and direction is often a big challenge. Mood, timing, light, and composition are all key ingredients to capturing compelling images of trees.

Good woodland interiors can be shot throughout the day, but morning is arguably the best time. The sun's lower position will attractively backlight foliage and bleed between thick, tall,

▲ TREE AVENUE
Fall color can be one of nature's most impressive spectacles. An overcast, foggy morning can prove an ideal time to visit woodland, as the lack of contrast makes it easier to capture vibrant color. To add subtle warmth to your shots, select your camera's Cloudy or Shade white balance preset.

and gnarled trunks, highlighting their form and irregular shape. Another benefit of the sun being lower in the sky is the length of shadows—the long shadows of trees cast on the woodland floor can provide depth and also create obvious lead-in lines in wide-angle compositions. In the morning, any lingering mist or fog will help simplify woodland scenery and provide better separation between foreground and background elements. Morning mist will undoubtedly add mood and mystery to forest scenes and also help disguise the clutter of messy, unmanaged areas of woodland. When morning mist and light combine, conditions can grow magical and moody, with the water particles in the atmosphere highlighting light rays filtering through the branches.

By mid- to late morning, the sun's higher position is less suited to woodland photography. The dappled light might look attractive and appealing to our eyes, but the higher level of contrast can exceed the camera's dynamic range, and achieving the correct exposure can be difficult. Highlights will begin to blow and shadow detail will be lost. Generally speaking, it is best to avoid shooting woodland interiors when the light is strong and overhead. Instead, overcast light is better. While it might be less dramatic, a bright, cloudy day provides very attractive, consistent, and manageable light. Cloud cover acts like a giant soft-box, producing diffused light that enables photographers to capture authentic color and woodland detail. A polarizer (see page 114) is a must-have accessory for woodland photography. Simply rotate the filter until glare reflecting from foliage and fallen leaves disappears and natural color saturation is restored.

TIMING

Timing is significant—not just the time of the day, but the time of the year as well. In the winter, woodland can look a little bare and lifeless. However, come spring, foliage will be a vibrant lime green, while many woodland floors are carpeted with spring flowers. In fall, the foliage turns a wonderful palette of warm tones. Woodland is at its colorful best for just a short period, and this varies from year to year, and from region to region. Monitor local woodland and, as colors intensify and reach their best, visit regularly with your camera.

Compositionally, longer focal lengths are often well suited to forest photography, allowing you to isolate small sections of woodland to create simpler, more concise compositions. A telephoto zoom lens in the region of 70–200mm is often a good choice. Longer focal lengths also make it easier to exclude the sky—or large, empty gaps in the leaf canopy—which will often prove distracting and ugly. However, a wide-angle lens is useful when you wish to convey more depth, or include a key foreground object. To create some order and help to direct the eye through the scene, look to include a winding path, road, river, or fallen tree in your composition. This will not only provide some structure to the image, but also an implied feeling of depth.

Woodland is a very popular environment for a more intimate style of landscape photography, while the lines, shapes, and color of trees combine with more creative approaches, like intentional camera movement (ICM), infrared photography (see page 90), and the use of in-camera multiple exposure.

FOCUS ON...
INTENTIONAL CAMERA MOVEMENT

This is an ideal time of day to practice more experimental or innovative approaches. With the light being more predictable and less dramatic and changeable, you risk nothing by trying new things or by capturing the landscape in a less conventional way. More impressionistic styles of landscape photography will always prove subjective—none more so than intentional camera movement (ICM). This technique requires the photographer to intentionally move the camera during the exposure to blur the subject. Doing so can create energy, motion, and flow. Results can look painterly and individual. A shutter speed in the region of ½ sec. is often a good starting point, but experiment with exposure length and the speed with which you pan the camera. You can shoot handheld (see page 74), but for more predictable results, use a tripod. For smooth, flowing results, begin moving the camera just prior to releasing the shutter and then continue the motion until the shutter closes again. Vertical and horizontal panning is most popular for landscapes, but irregular movements or even rotation can yield striking, impressionistic results, where subject detail is obscured by motion, but still remains recognizable. It's a style best combined with landscapes containing strong shapes, lines, colors, or contrast—for example, the regimental, upright structure of trees.

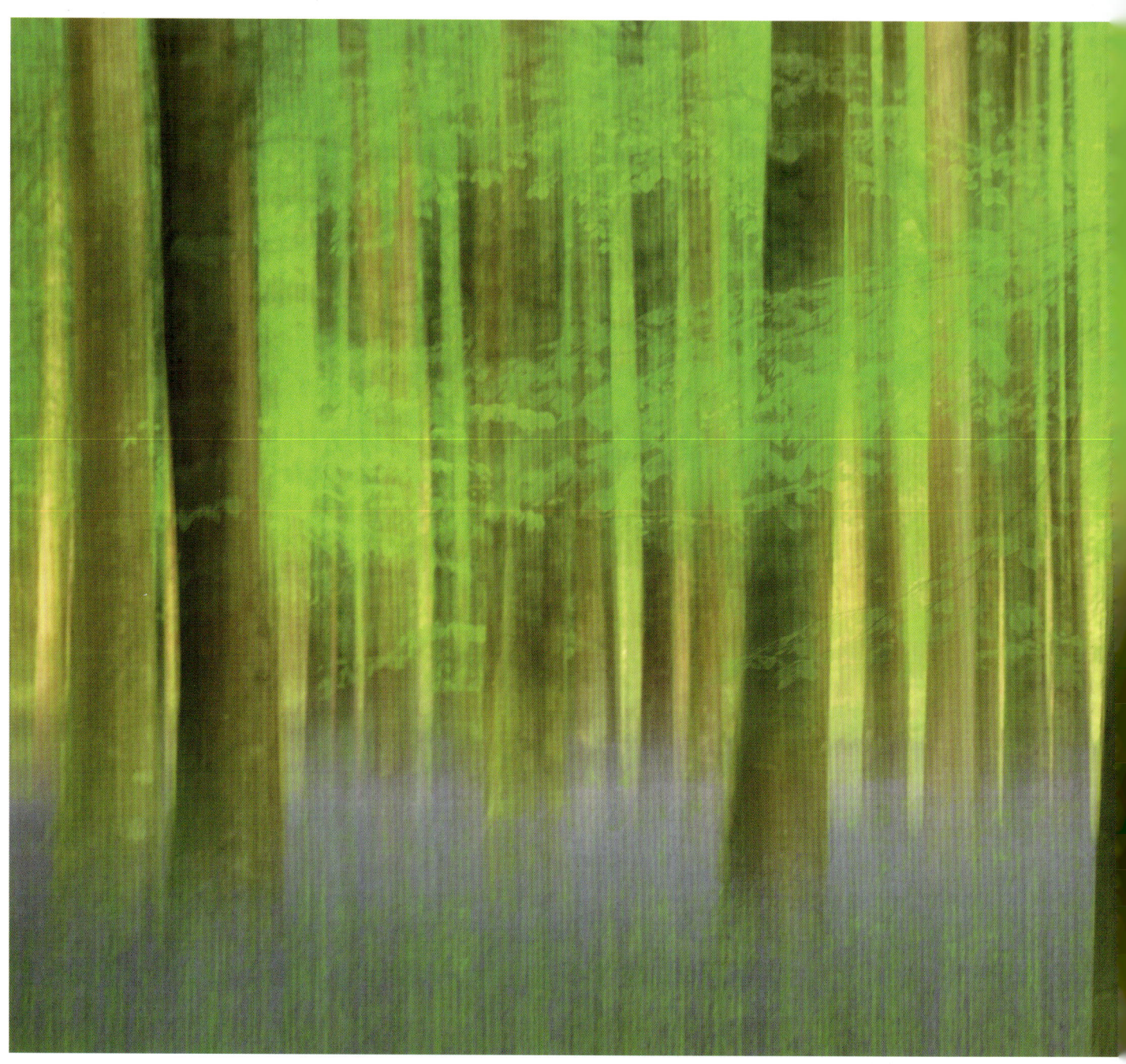

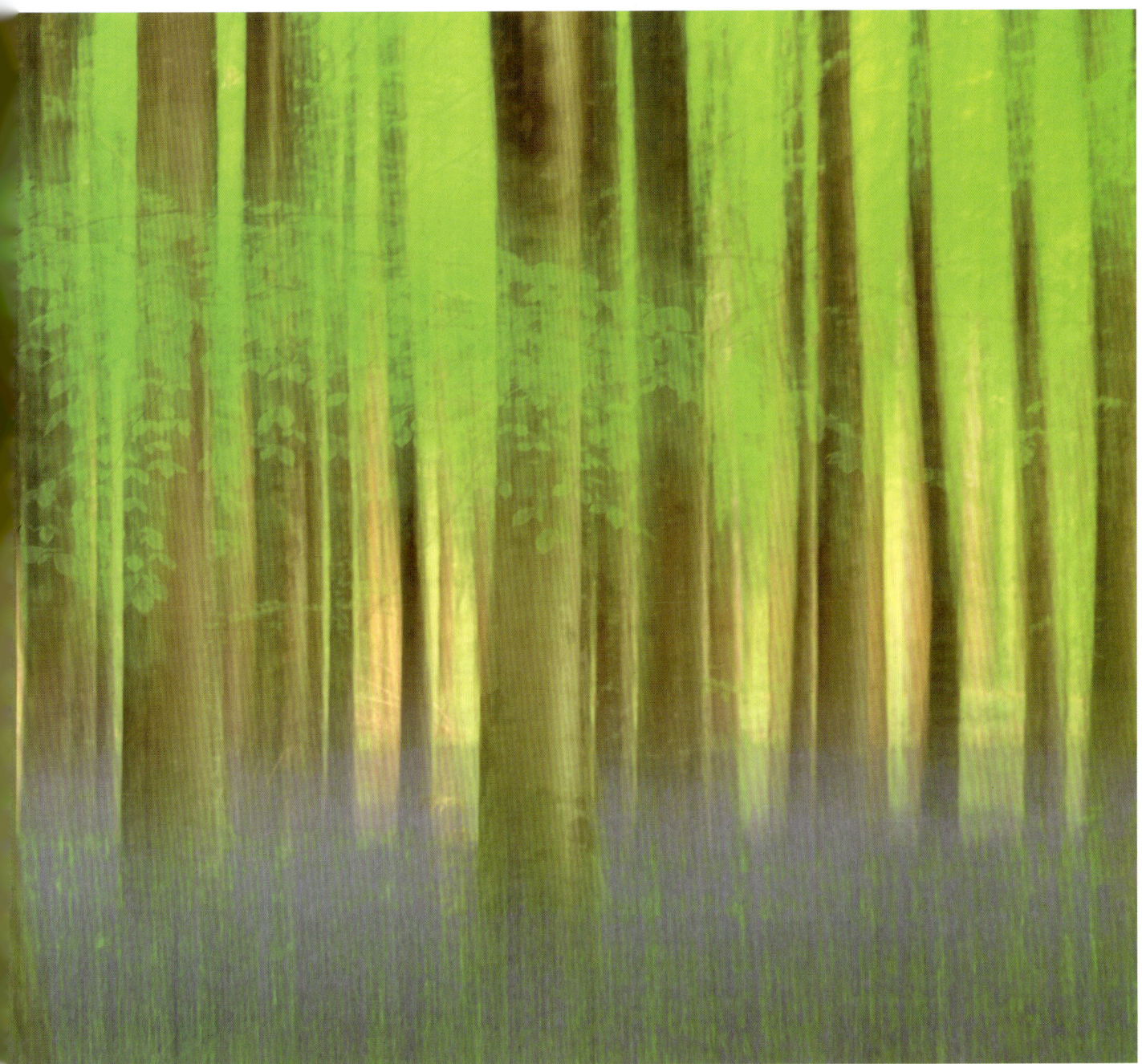

▲ TREE IMPRESSIONS

Intentional camera movement is a very hit-and-miss technique, so experiment and play. A vertical or horizontal motion is the most common way to pan the camera, but diagonal, circular, or back-and-forth motions can prove equally effective. Try rotating the camera or using a random, irregular motion—less conventional actions can sometimes provide the most painterly and eye-catching results. You will need to shoot multiple frames to achieve a result that you are satisfied with. No two images will ever be the same.

INTIMATE LANDSCAPES

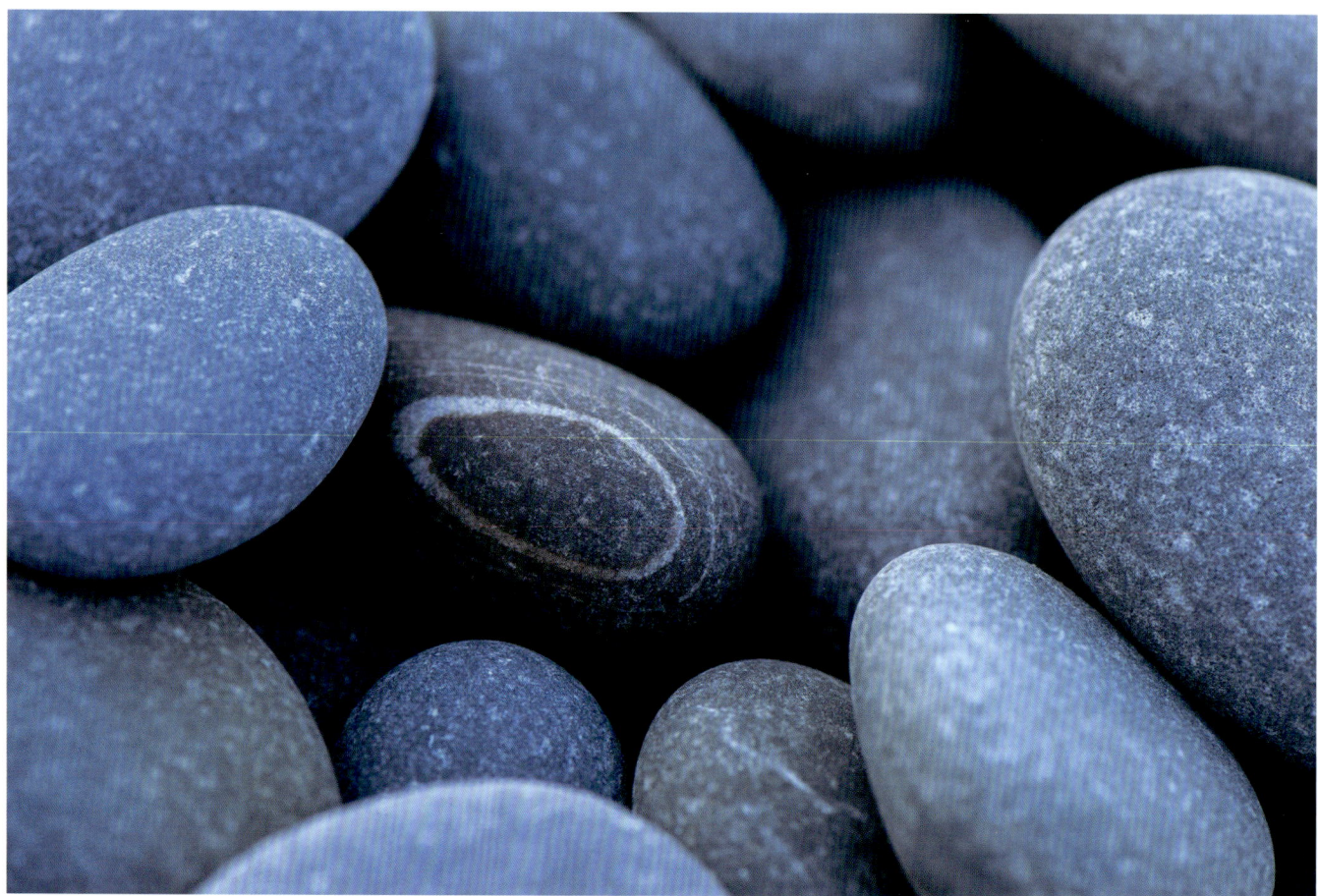

You need to remind yourself to look beyond traditional wide-angle views and big sweeping vistas, and study the detail within the landscape—the so-called "intimate landscape." Although a less mainstream form of photography, it is a fascinating and interpretive way of highlighting the finer details all around us. This style represents a very graphic, simple approach, where shape, form, and detail are paramount, and the light's quality or direction is less important. Wide-angle lenses are normally best replaced by a short telephoto or macro lens—focal lengths ideal for isolating key details, textures, structures, or natural harmony.

Its inclusion in this particular chapter isn't intended to imply that this is a style of photography that should only be confined to morning. However, morning is as good a time as any to broaden your horizons and photograph intimate—or miniature—landscape

▲ CORNISH PEBBLES
A narrower angle of view suits intimate landscape images. However, depth of field will be more limited when using longer focal lengths. If you require front-to-back sharpness, opt for a small aperture or consider focus-stacking (see page 134). Alternatively, manipulate the shallow zone of focus for creative effect, or to help direct the viewer's eye to your point of focus.

images. With large vistas, you are encompassing a wide area, but often with no great emphasis. In contrast, with intimate landscape shots, you typically isolate just a few elements, highlighting a small, predefined area. The photographer is aiming to bring just one or two elements together in an interesting and engaging way.

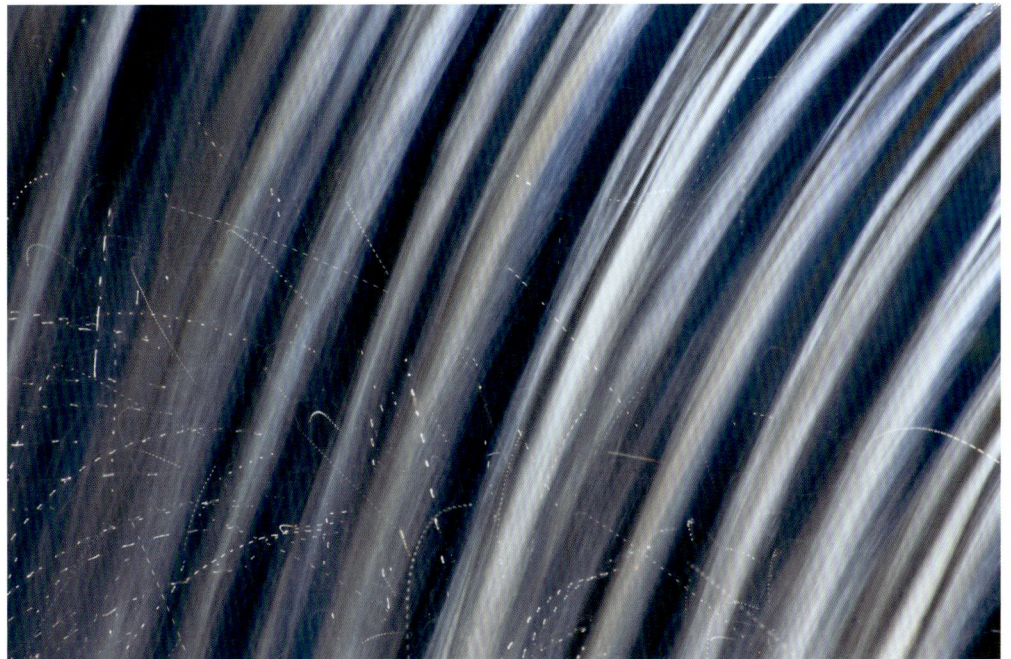

◀ **WEIR ABSTRACT**
This style of photography is an exercise in removing the extraneous and retaining the essential. You need time to think through the compositional possibilities—to problem-solve. Expect your composition to evolve over several frames. To do this effectively, ideally your camera needs to be fixed in position. A tripod proved an essential aid when I took this image of water rushing over a little weir on a morning's stroll along a local canal. It took me several frames before I captured the backlit spray—jumping around in front of the weir, creating lines and patterns—just as I had visualized.

GET CREATIVE

In intimate landscapes, the sky is normally excluded from the frame. This might seem alien and counterintuitive, but who says you have to always follow convention and include the sky in your shots? There is an argument that the sky limits compositional options and helps the viewer too easily and quickly identify the place and time of day, making the shot too familiar and accessible. However, maybe we shouldn't always make it so easy for viewers to define and digest our photographs? For more memorable, unique, and unconventional results, abstracting or obscuring our subject in some way can produce far more intriguing and unforgettable images. There is certainly nothing wrong with letting the viewer's imagination do some work for a change.

You will either love or hate this style of photography. Images are typically less obvious or immediately striking—they are subtle and suggest or imply, rather than scream out at you. As you don't need spectacular skies or light for smaller-scale shots, landscape photographers are freed from the (over-) reliance of shooting at dawn or dusk. Low-contrast light is often preferable—so even if the weather is dull, foggy, or wet, you can work regardless. Avoid harsh light, though, as strong contrast masks fine detail.

So what scenes or subjects combine best with this more intimate approach? Almost anything, in truth. Form is primary, content is irrelevant. Moorland, coast, and woodland are among the best places to depict the intimate landscape. Take time to study your environment. Look for repetition, patterns, shapes, rough textures, and strong or flowing lines. Look for subjects that work harmoniously together—maybe they echo one another's shape, or there is eye-catching juxtaposition between textured and smooth objects, or light and shade. Compositions will rarely jump out at you—they are less obvious and harder to identify. However, you are far more likely to return from a shoot with a unique image—something that is becoming increasingly hard to do in an age where iconic locations are so well photographed (and often from a similar viewpoint). When you work on a smaller scale, you will almost certainly capture an image nobody has seen before—it is much more of a personal statement.

CORE TECHNIQUE
HANDHELD LANDSCAPES

With light now being more plentiful—and shutter speeds growing naturally faster—the use of a tripod becomes a choice, rather than a necessity. Working without a tripod can be a liberating experience, and it can help to promote a spontaneous reaction to the prevailing light or conditions. We are in no way suggesting you discard your tripod—we are both big advocates of using a support whenever practical and the overall benefits are unquestionable. However, there is an argument for dispensing with a camera support from time to time, just to restore creative freedom, and to promote instinct and a sense of fun.

Unless you wish to intentionally create motion blur for creative effect (see pages 69 and 92), you will need to ensure you are using a shutter speed that is fast enough to eliminate camera movement. The longer the lens, the greater the risk of shake. A good rule of thumb is to shoot at a minimum of 1/60 sec., or a shutter speed that matches or exceeds the focal length of the lens—for example, if you are using a 200mm lens, select a shutter speed of least 1/200 sec. Ensure image stabilization (on either the camera or the lens) is switched on. If shutter speed remains impractically slow, don't be afraid to increase ISO sensitivity. Even at an ISO of 1600 or higher, noise remains low with modern cameras—and a sharp but noisier image is still better than a blurry, noise-free file.

LARGER APERTURES

Of course, there is another way you can generate a faster exposure—you can open up the aperture. As landscape photographers, we are tuned to select a small aperture to provide a large zone of focus. However, it is never a good idea to become formulaic in your approach. Employing a shallow depth of field for landscapes might be considered unconventional, but, when appropriate, the results can be compelling. Primarily, a shallow zone of focus will help your subject stand out sharply from surroundings that are attractively drifting into soft focus. With depth of field so limited, you need to focus with care and precision—there is little leeway for error. A shallow depth of field can really help you to direct the viewer's eye to just where you want. Often, you will want out of focus areas to remain defined and recognizable, and an aperture in the region of f/5.6 can be

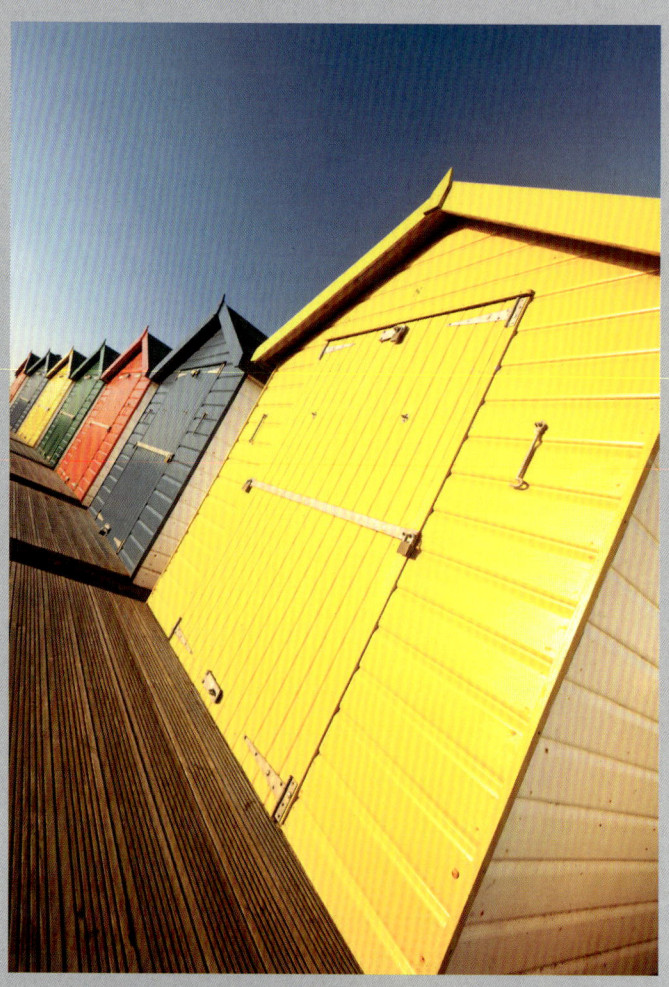

▲ BEACH HUTS
When was the last time you took a handheld landscape photograph? You can react to changing light or conditions more instinctively, while the freedom of working without a tripod will have you exploring different angles and mixing up your choice of camera settings.

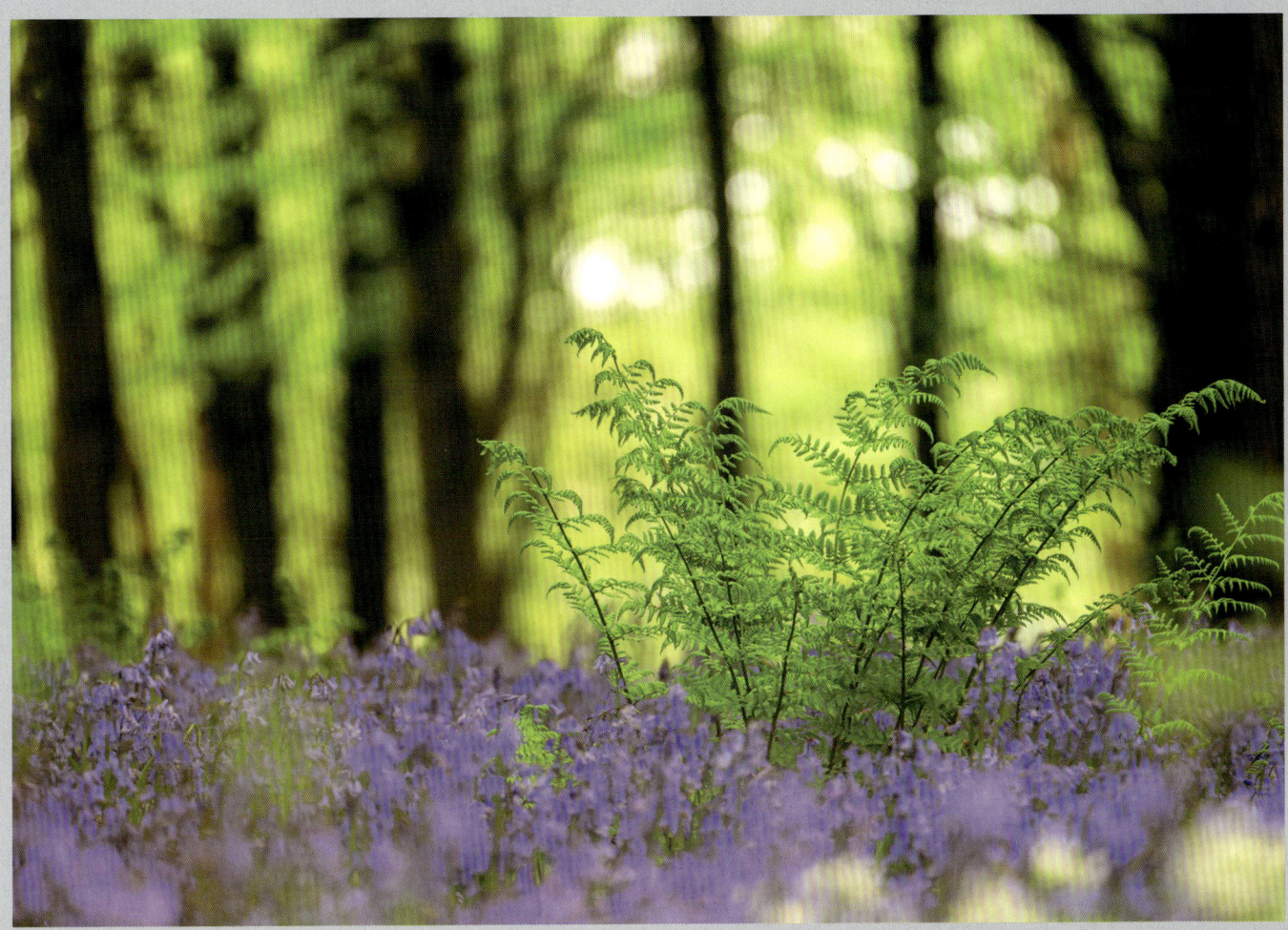

▲ FERN AND BLUEBELLS

Using a shallow depth of field will help you place emphasis on a certain point or subject. In this instance, the combination of long focal length and large aperture created a shallow zone of focus that proved more esthetically pleasing and intimate than if had I captured everything sharply from front to back.

a good starting point, providing a pleasing contrast between soft and sharp areas.

Exploit the added freedom of shooting handheld and really explore angles. For example, shoot from low down or high up—composing images via your camera's articulated LCD monitor to make it more comfortable shooting from awkward angles. Try all types of perspective that you wouldn't attempt with a tripod. Shooting handheld can help you quickly alter composition to identify the best viewpoint, focal length, or camera height. This can be advantageous in "busy" environments, such as woodland.

COMPOSITION
USING FRAMES WITHIN FRAMES

There are lots of different compositional tricks, tips, and rules you can apply to your landscapes to enhance their impact, interest, and depth. None of these depend on the time of day—they should be applied to any appropriate scene, whether it is morning, noon, or night. The rule of thirds (see page 154) and lead-in lines (see page 116) are popular methods of conveying a sense of depth in a still image, but there are other ways to do this. Another neat method of creating depth is to include a framing device—natural or artificial.

A picture frame separates the picture from the surrounding clutter and distractions, and effectively isolates the image so that our focus is concentrated on it. The same principle can be applied to landscape composition. Including a "frame within a frame" can place visual weight on your subject. Doing so also creates layers, which help to convey added depth. It is a visual trick you will see portrait, wedding, and reportage photographers use time and again. By using objects such as archways, doorways, mirrors, and windows, photographers can add intimacy or an almost voyeuristic feel to shots. Artificial objects can be used to frame the landscape, too, but there is no shortage of frames and borders occurring naturally within nature. Trees, overhanging branches, reeds, caves, rainbows, reflections, ledges, and light and shade are just some examples of the things that landscape photographers use to frame the landscape beyond.

Not only will a frame help draw your eye further into the image space, but it can also add context and intrigue. A frame can add structure and help tell a story, while it can also work to obscure unsightly elements within your scene. A barrier between the subject and the outside of the shot should help retain the viewer's eye for longer. However, due to the amount of depth you are recording within the frame, it is normally best to prioritize a small aperture to generate a large zone of focus.

PARTIAL FRAMING
Despite what you may automatically think, your frame doesn't need to go around all four sides like a traditional photo frame.

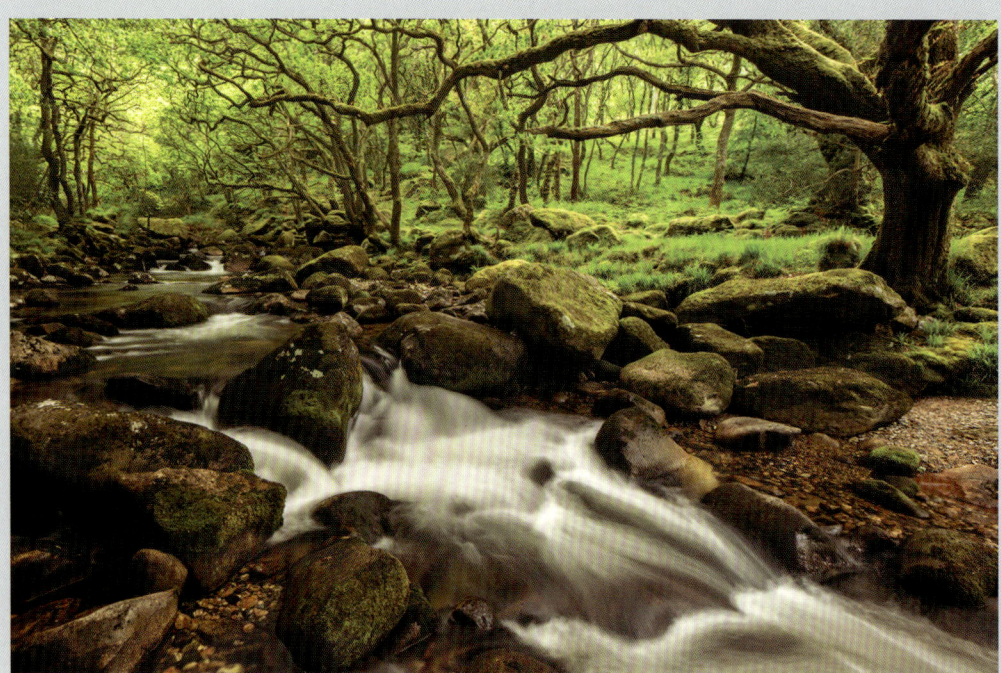

◄ FRAMED
In this instance, the inclusion of the tree at the right—with branches overhanging and framing the top of the image—helps focus attention on the river and stop the viewer's eye wandering off.

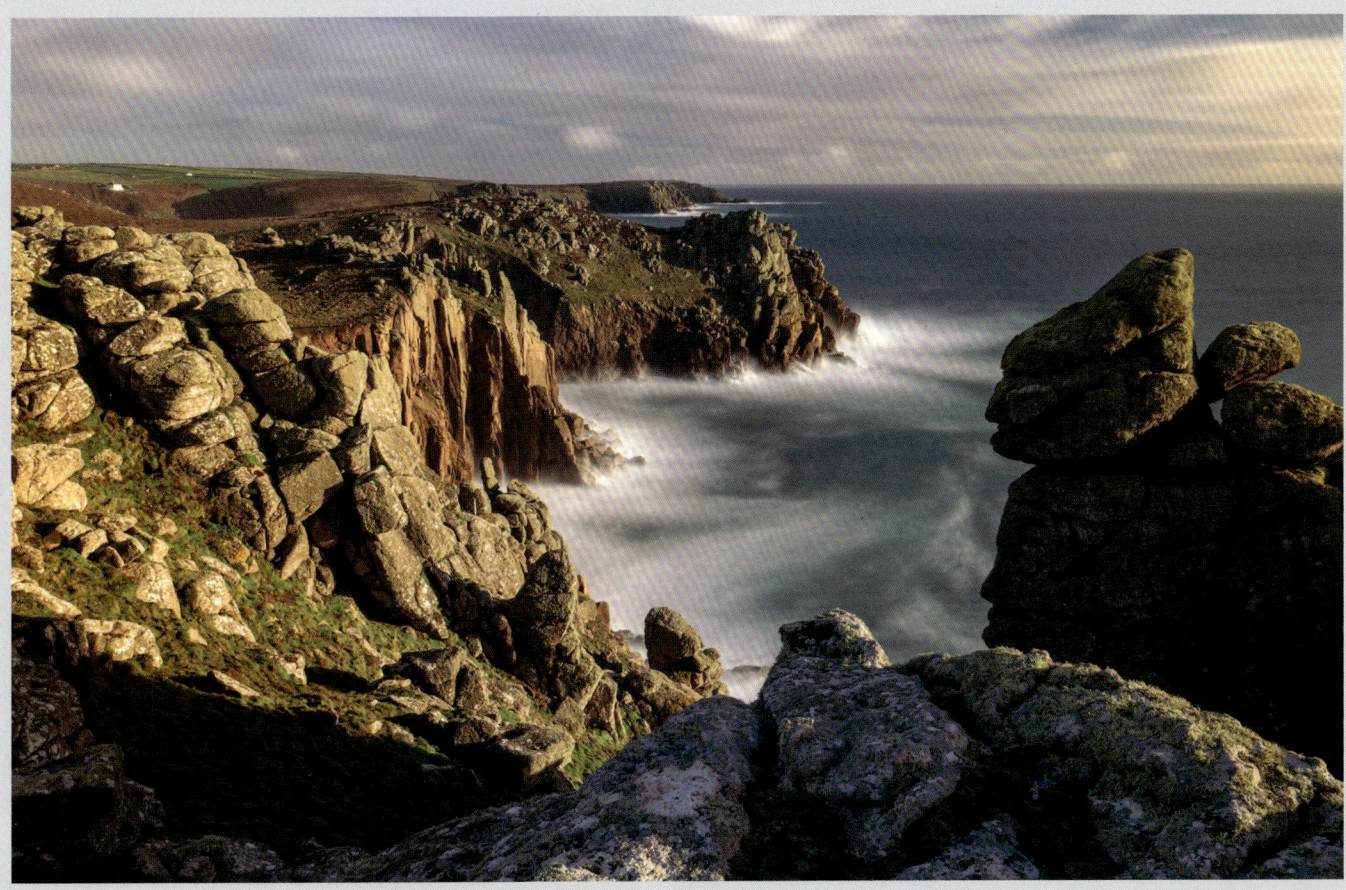

In fact, a four-sided frame can look too heavy and cumbersome in a landscape shot, obscuring too much from view and diluting awe and the feeling of a big, open space. Instead, it is more common to include a partial or incomplete frame—a one-, two-, or three-sided frame can prove every bit as effective. For example, overhanging branches will help prevent the viewer's eye from drifting up and out of the top of the image; while a rocky ledge in your foreground can create a strong frame for the scene beyond. Even cloud can act as a frame, encouraging your eye inward. You do need to apply the technique with care, though. Without due consideration, a frame within a frame can make a composition feel cramped, or even cluttered. Equally, including a frame will only add interest to an already interesting scene—it will not miraculously transform a mediocre one.

Using a shallow zone of focus can also create an implied frame. Grass, flowers, or foliage—thrown deliberately out of focus using a large aperture, long lens, or low viewpoint—can create what is sometimes referred to as a "dirty frame." Including attractive

▲ ROCKY FOREGROUND

In this instance, the rocky foreground and rock pillar on the right of the composition create an effective partial frame. They add an extra layer to the composition, which helps imply depth and channels the eye inward toward the sea and distant headland.

bokeh in the foreground can produce a soft (and creative) border for the main subject beyond. Shooting "through" leaves and grasses will create this effect. To generate the shallow depth of field required for this approach, opt for a large aperture—in the region of f/4—and focus precisely on your subject.

Once you recognize how effectively a frame can add depth and visual interest and intrigue to a landscape shot, you will begin consciously searching them out and using them to place clearer focus on your main subject.

POST-PROCESSING STEP-BY-STEP
CROPPING AND ASPECT RATIO

The landscape is hugely diverse and varied, so it is completely unrealistic to expect it to always suit the standard aspect ratio of your camera. Aspect ratio is the term used to describe the dimensions of an image, by comparing its width and height and expressing them in ratio form. A 3:2 aspect ratio is the full-frame standard, but Micro Four Thirds cameras have popularized a slightly squarer 4:3 format. Most cameras allow you to adjust the aspect ratio of the files you capture, providing a range of popular dimensions to select from. This can aid framing and help unleash creativity. However, many photographers prefer to crop their images during post-processing, rather than in-camera, as this gives you more time and opportunity to select just the right size of frame for the subject.

Cropping is perhaps the most basic step in post-processing, but arguably it can have the greatest impact on your shots. It can play a key role in the compositional process, allowing you to alter the balance and harmony of your photos. You can crop images to place more emphasis on your main subject or reduce the prominence of other elements. You can crop images to exclude distracting features close to the edge of the frame that perhaps you overlooked when you originally took the photo.

We wouldn't recommend you severely crop your photos—discarding too many pixels will affect image quality. And cropping should not be considered a solution for lazy compositions—you still need to arrange the elements in a balanced, harmonious way in-camera. However, cropping can really enhance your shots and frees you from being restricted by your camera's native aspect ratio, which is unlikely to suit every scene you photograph.

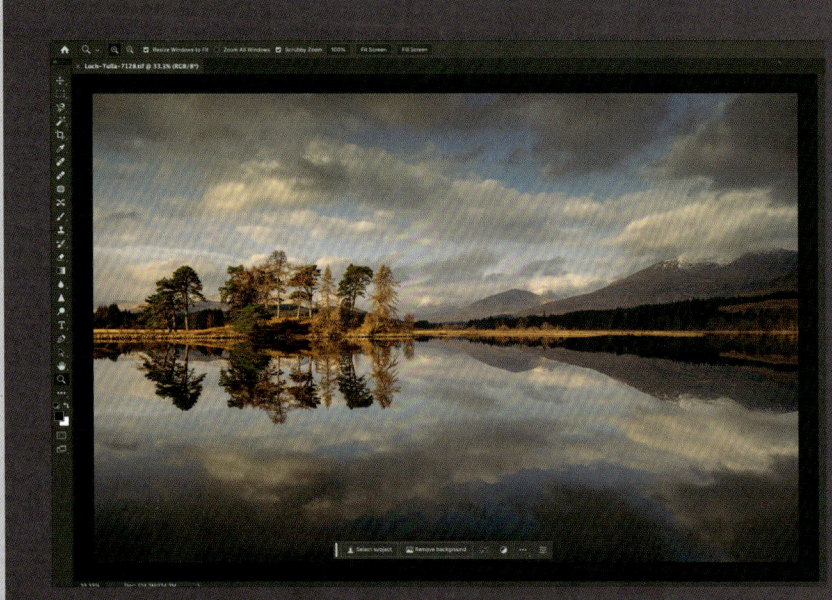

1

Even the most basic editing suite will have a crop tool. Using Photoshop, open your image and click the Crop Tool icon in the Tools Palette. Photoshop automatically overlays a crop box around your shot, with handles in each corner as well as at the top, bottom, left, and right. You can now click and drag the handles to resize and reshape the crop box.

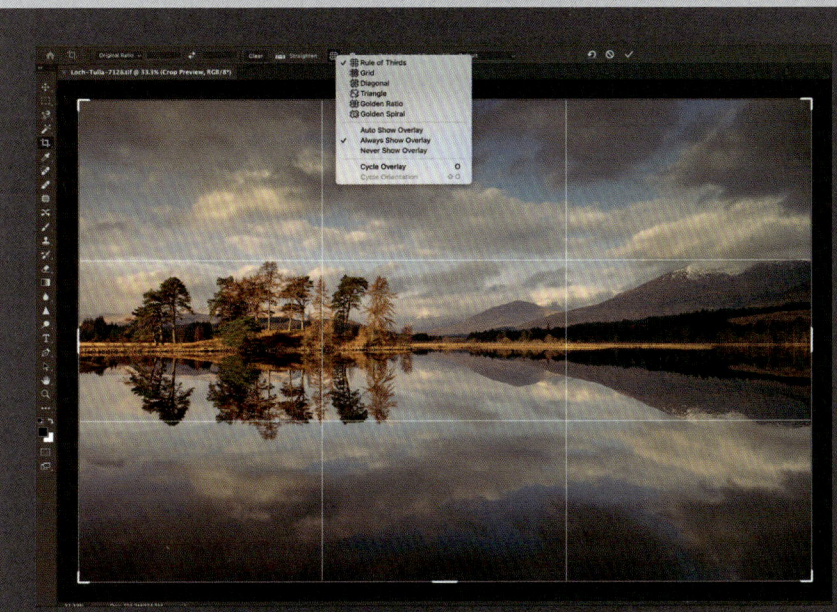

2

By default, Photoshop overlays a rule of thirds grid to aid composition. However, if you click the Overlay icon in the Options bar, you can alter this and choose from a range of useful overlays. Alternatively, to quickly cycle through the different overlay options, press the letter O. Photoshop darkens the area outside the box to help you preview how the image will look once cropped.

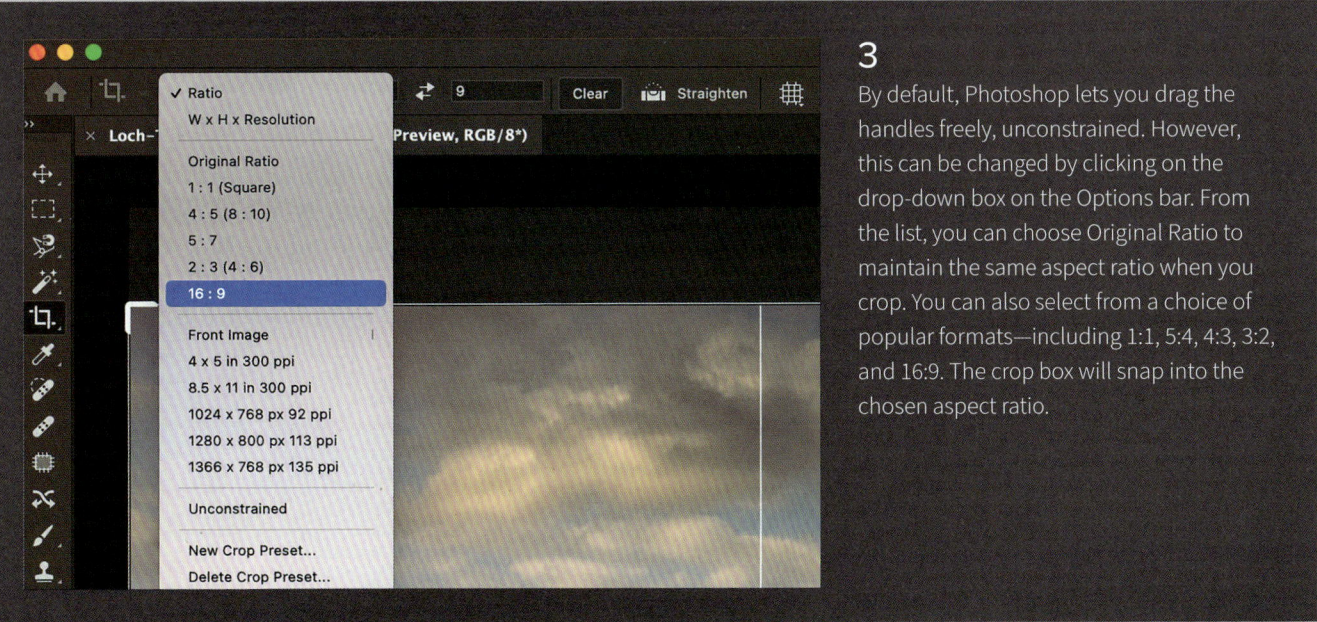

3

By default, Photoshop lets you drag the handles freely, unconstrained. However, this can be changed by clicking on the drop-down box on the Options bar. From the list, you can choose Original Ratio to maintain the same aspect ratio when you crop. You can also select from a choice of popular formats—including 1:1, 5:4, 4:3, 3:2, and 16:9. The crop box will snap into the chosen aspect ratio.

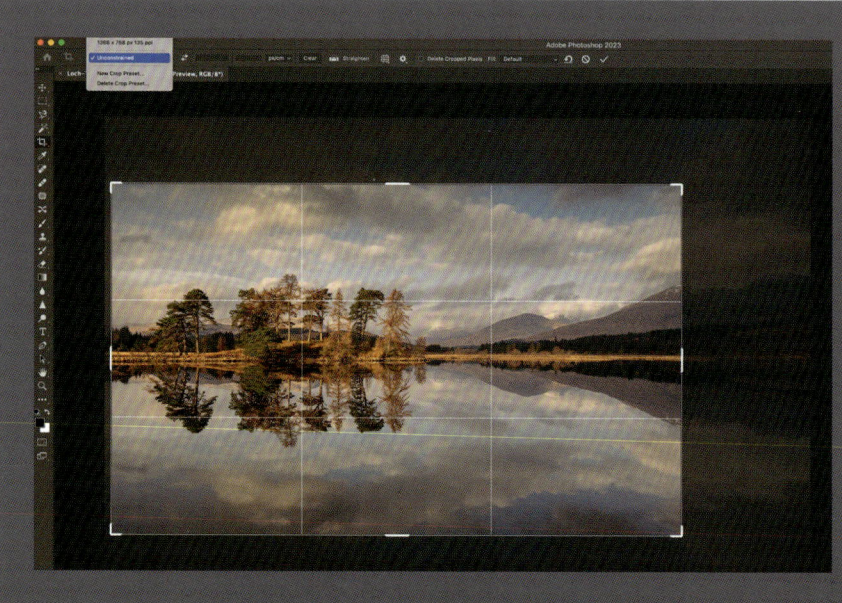

4

You can also create your own custom aspect ratio by simply entering the values you desire in the width and height boxes directly to the right of the Aspect Ratio box. If you wish to switch from horizontal to vertical format (or vice versa), click the Rotate icon in the Options bar or click the letter X. You can also select Unconstrained from the drop-down box and adjust the crop handles to quickly crop your file to whatever size you wish.

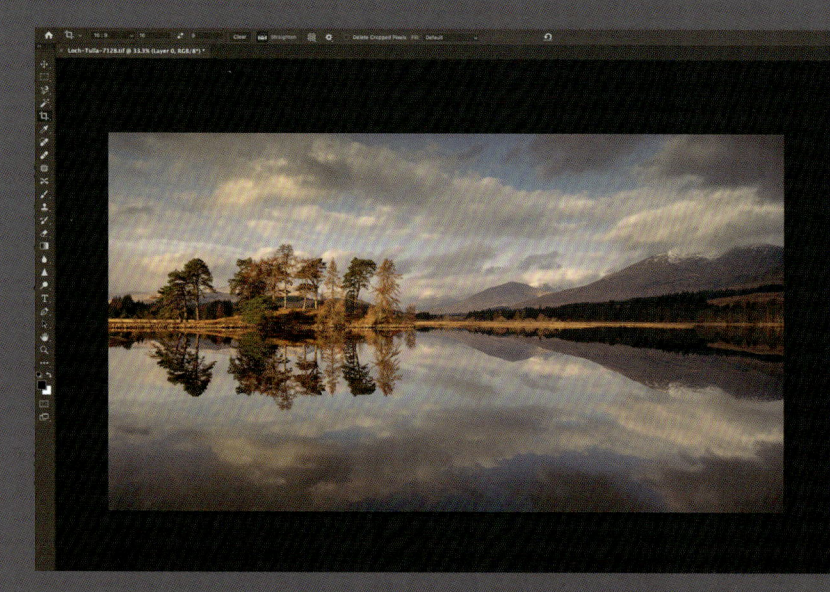

5

In this instance, I felt a narrower, more panoramic aspect ratio suited this scene better than my camera's standard 3:2 ratio, so I opted for 16:9. To apply the crop, click Enter or Return. By keeping the Delete Cropped Pixels option unchecked in the Options Bar, Photoshop will simply hide the pixels cropped, allowing you to re-edit your crop should you wish to do so.

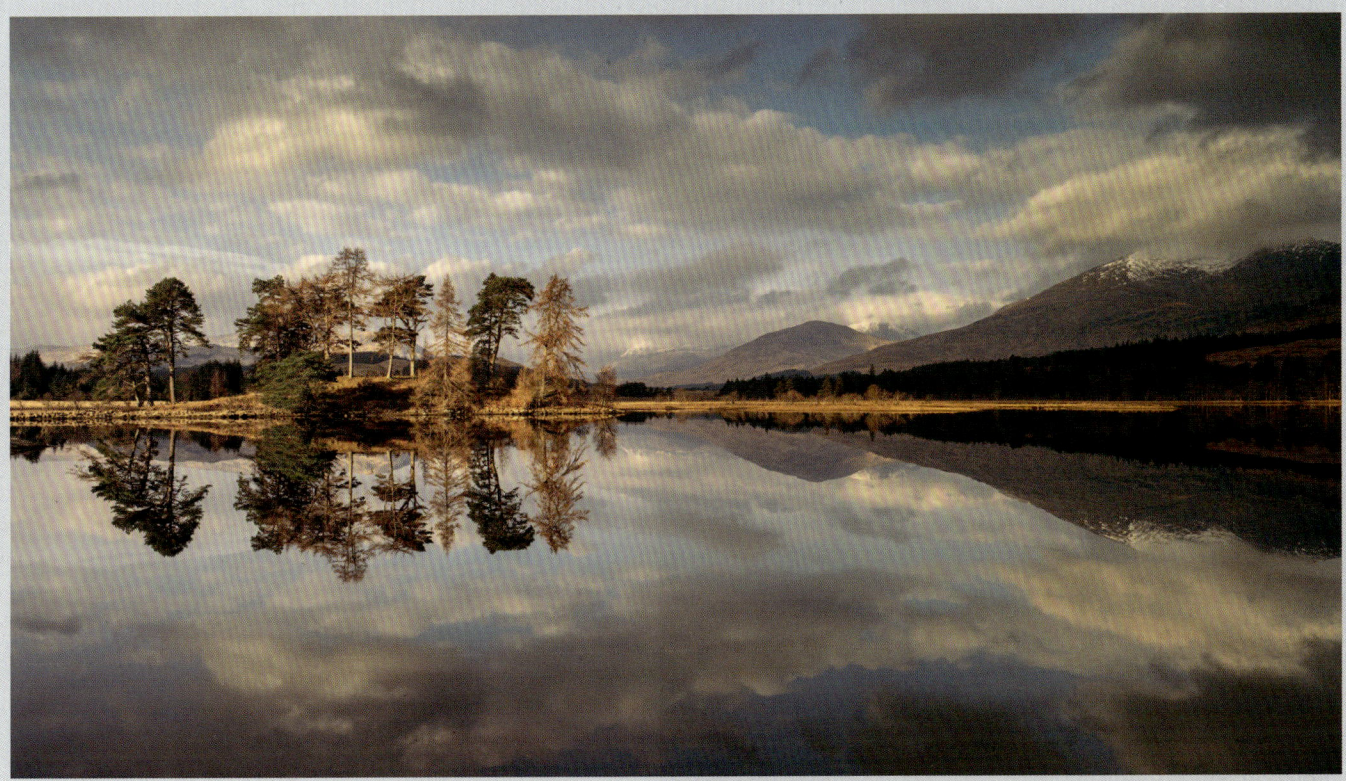

ALTERNATIVE FORMATS

Aside from the most popular 3:2 and 4:3 ratios, less elongated formats such as 5:4 and 6:7 have always been popular with landscape photographers. Squarer formats make it easier to exploit and emphasize foreground subjects. A square 1:1 aspect ratio won't suit every scene, but can be very striking and lends itself to symmetrical and minimalist compositions. A panoramic 3:1 format is another popular option for landscapes. The "letterbox" format helps photographers capture wide, sweeping vistas and suits mountainous scenes in particular. However, for optimum image quality it is better to create a stitched panorama (see pages 138–141) from multiple frames, rather than simply make a crop from a single file. Of course, you don't have to limit yourself to the standard, popular aspect ratios—you can opt for a custom crop and select whatever format suits the scene best.

TIP

If you need to straighten your image, click on the Straighten Tool on the Options Bar and drag the leveling line across whatever you want to be straight (either vertically or horizontally) and then release your mouse button to apply your action.

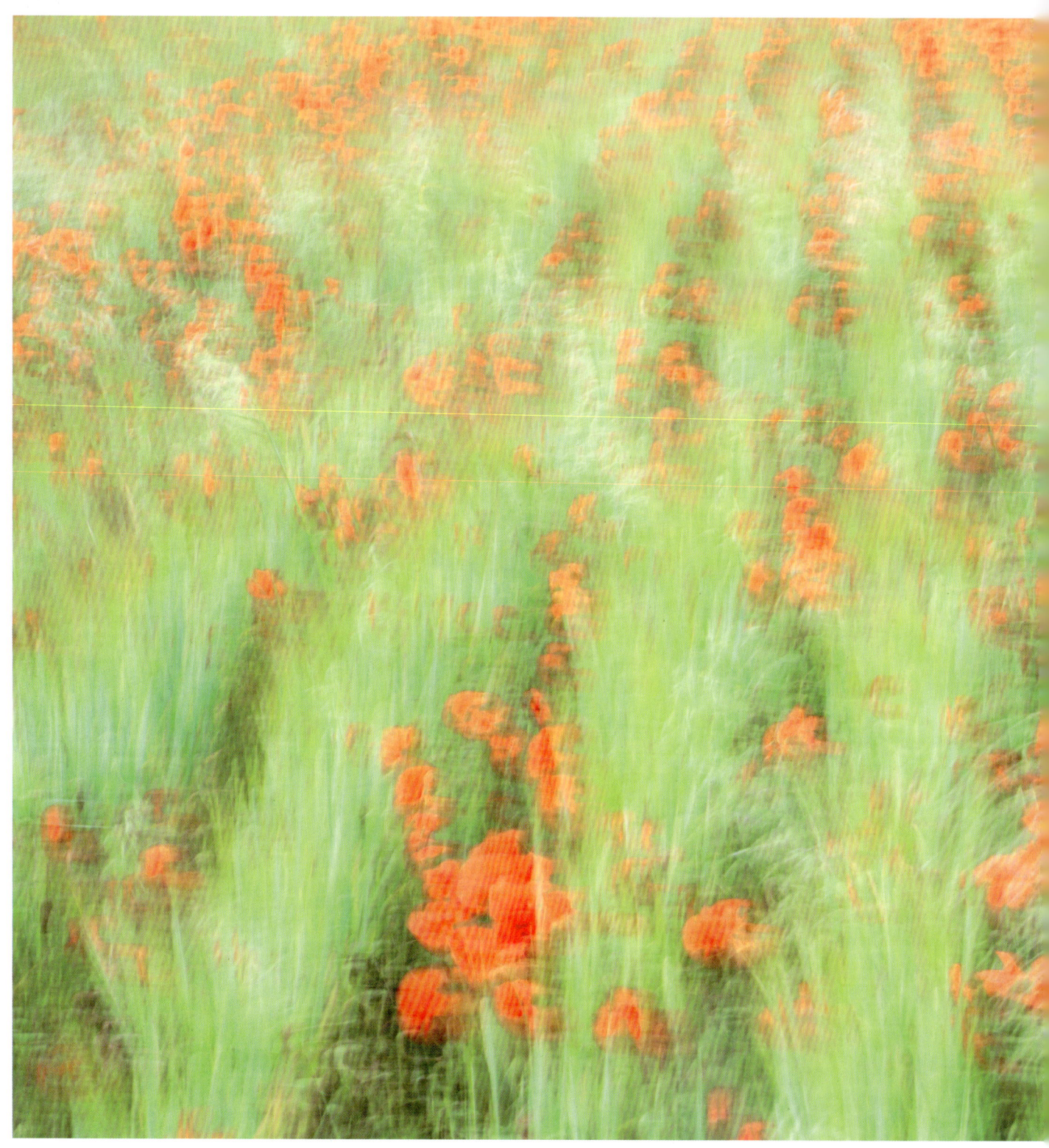

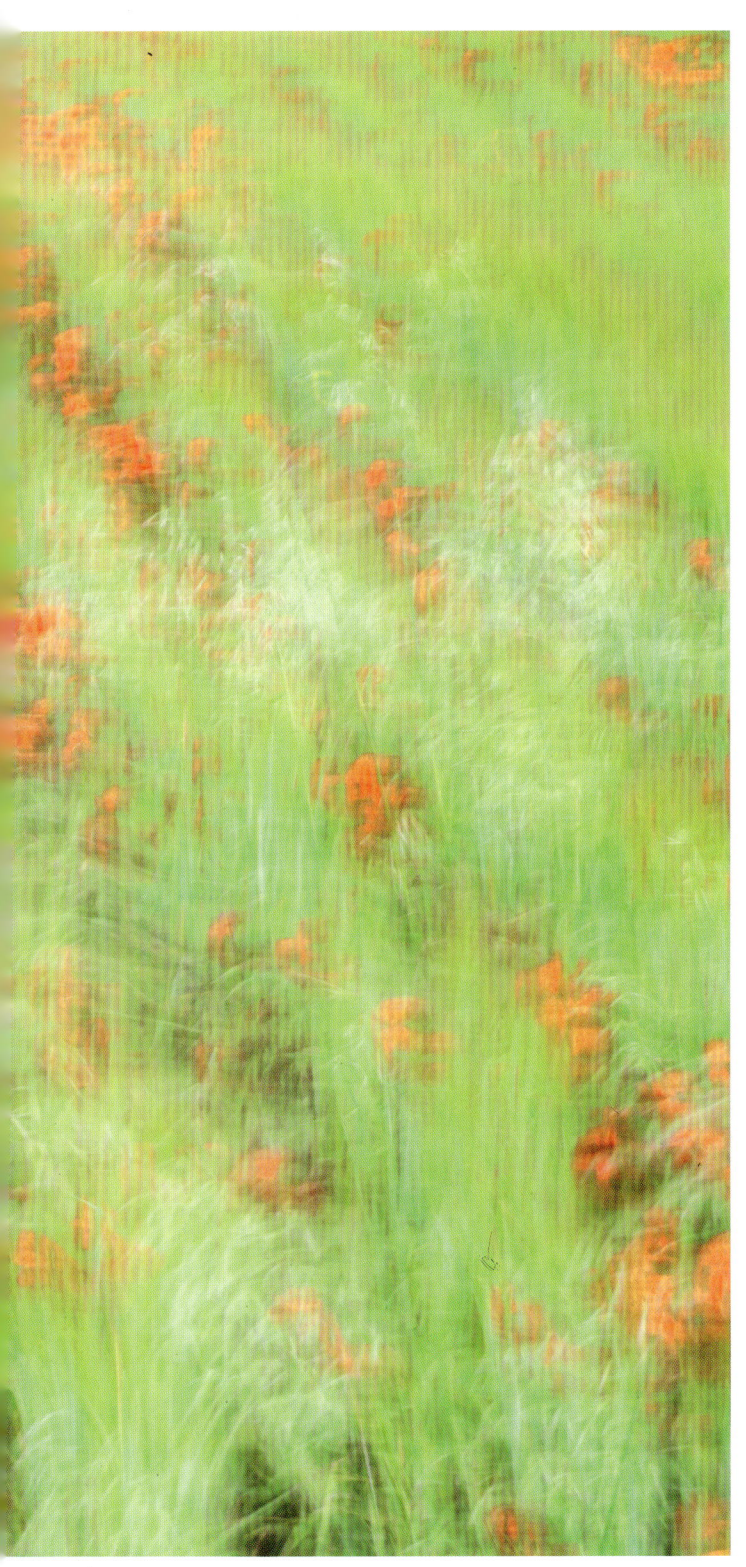

FINAL SHOT

Photographer **Ross Hoddinott**
Location **West Pentire, Cornwall, United Kingdom**
Time and date **11.03 a.m., June 16**
Camera **Nikon Z8**
Lens **Nikkor Z 24–120mm f/4 S (at 84mm)**
Filtration **None**
Exposure **ISO 64, 1/3 sec. at f/22**

THE STORY

"I'm always looking for ways to capture a scene or subject creatively or less conventionally. On this summer's morning, the overcast light was not very inspiring. However, I knew that the even, low-contrast light would help my camera record punchy, accurate colors. This field of poppies made an obvious subject, but the breezy conditions were proving a challenge. Therefore, rather than fight the windy weather, I thought I'd embrace it instead. Shooting handheld for more freedom and adaptability, I decided to apply a degree of Intentional Camera Movement (ICM) to highlight and emphasize the poppies' motion and create a sense of flow and energy. I took several frames, experimenting with shutter length and the type of camera motion before I captured a result that I was finally happy with. I later cropped the image slightly to tidy up the composition but retained my camera's 3:2 aspect ratio. I also increased contrast slightly to give the shot a bit more punch—as is often required with this style of landscape."

CHAPTER THREE
MIDDAY

Most photographers would probably agree that the light in the middle of the day is the most challenging for landscape photography. With the sun directly overhead, high in the sky, the strong contrast and harsh shadows provide little textural relief or modeling of objects. The light can also be hazy, with more dust and pollution in the atmosphere than at other times, especially on hot, still summer days.

However, it's worth pointing out that there are some photographic opportunities at this time of day that shouldn't be overlooked. Certainly, in the winter months, the sun stays low in the sky and it's possible to get moody shots at any time, but even at the height of summer it would be a mistake to write off the middle of the day altogether.

As with all landscape photography, the key to shooting successful images is choosing the right subject and waiting for the moment when the light falls in the right way. Clouds can diffuse harsh sunlight, and on days when the cloud is moving quickly, covering and then revealing the sun, there can be dramatic light on parts of the landscape.

In this chapter we cover the subjects and lighting you should look for and the approaches that are most likely to succeed.

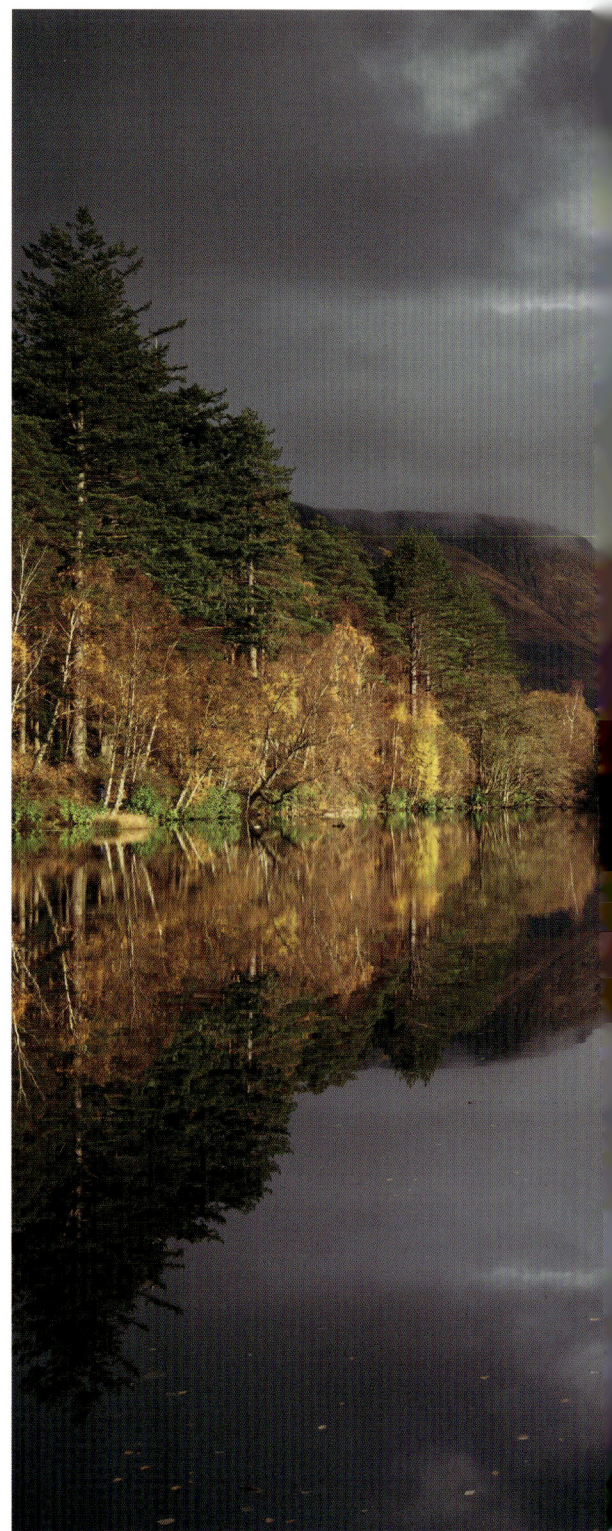

▶ **SCOTTISH LOCHAN**
Shooting just after midday in fall, I waited until there was interesting cloud filling the top of the frame and then watched for the sun to be partially covered. Not only was the harsh light subtly diffused, but there was also spotlighting key parts of the scene.

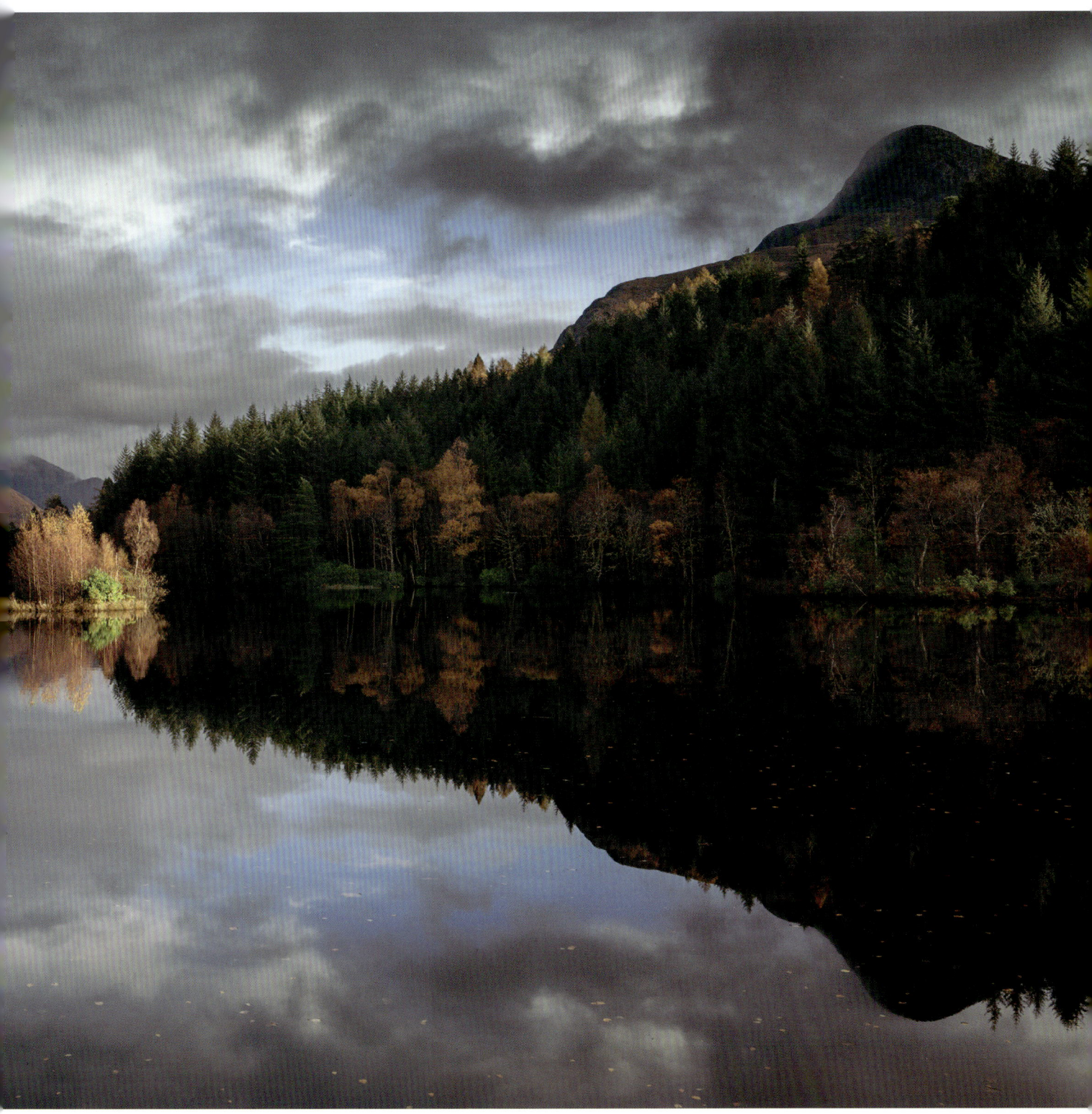

WORKING IN MONOCHROME

When the light is what would normally be considered unphotogenic, one of the most effective approaches is to shoot black-and-white images. A scene that might appear too contrasty and where the color is bleached out can actually look quite dramatic in monochrome. Overcast conditions can also benefit from the mono treatment—cloud patterns and textures can be interesting and pushing up the contrast in post-processing can produce eye-catching results.

The first step in creating a successful monochrome image is choosing a suitable subject. Without the distraction of color, the emphasis is firmly placed on form, tone, and texture. Simple, bold compositions work well—seek out strong lines and angles, such as paths, fences, boats, and structured subjects. With harsh shadows, the interplay of light and shade can also can be used as the basis for a wider composition, or for a more abstract study.

Scenes that contain a full range of tones, from deep shadows to bright highlights—which is often the case in the middle of the day—usually convert well, as do scenes with layered cloud and "textured" skies. Thinking in terms of tone, rather than color, can cause problems, however, and you have to be aware of how colors will translate to grayscale. For example, red and green can look very similar when converted to shades of gray.

This can have important implications for composition. Separating planes and key elements in the frame is fundamental to a successful composition—without proper separation, the perception of depth can be reduced. Tonal separation in a black-and-white image is harder to achieve, so physical separation therefore increases in importance. Seek out viewpoints which give a good degree of separation between foreground and background subjects, preventing key points of interest in the image from merging together.

FOCUS ON...
VISUALIZING BLACK AND WHITE IMAGES

Not everyone finds it easy to visualize how a color scene will translate to a monochrome image. Most cameras have a monochrome picture style—this won't affect the Raw image, which will still be recorded in color, but the live view image and the JPEG that is created for image review will be displayed in monochrome. This is a quick and easy way to check whether an image has potential for monochrome, although remember that it won't tell the whole story, as post-processing techniques, including digital filters, can enhance and change the contrast and tonal relationships in an image.

FOCUS ON...
MIDDAY COLOR

Black and white isn't to everyone's taste. If this is true for you, remember that there is also potential for color photography in the middle of the day. Wait for cloud cover to diffuse the harsh sunlight, or use a polarizer to saturate color, especially if you are shooting more abstract compositions based on the angles of structures. Shooting woodland can also work well, especially in the softer light of an overcast day.

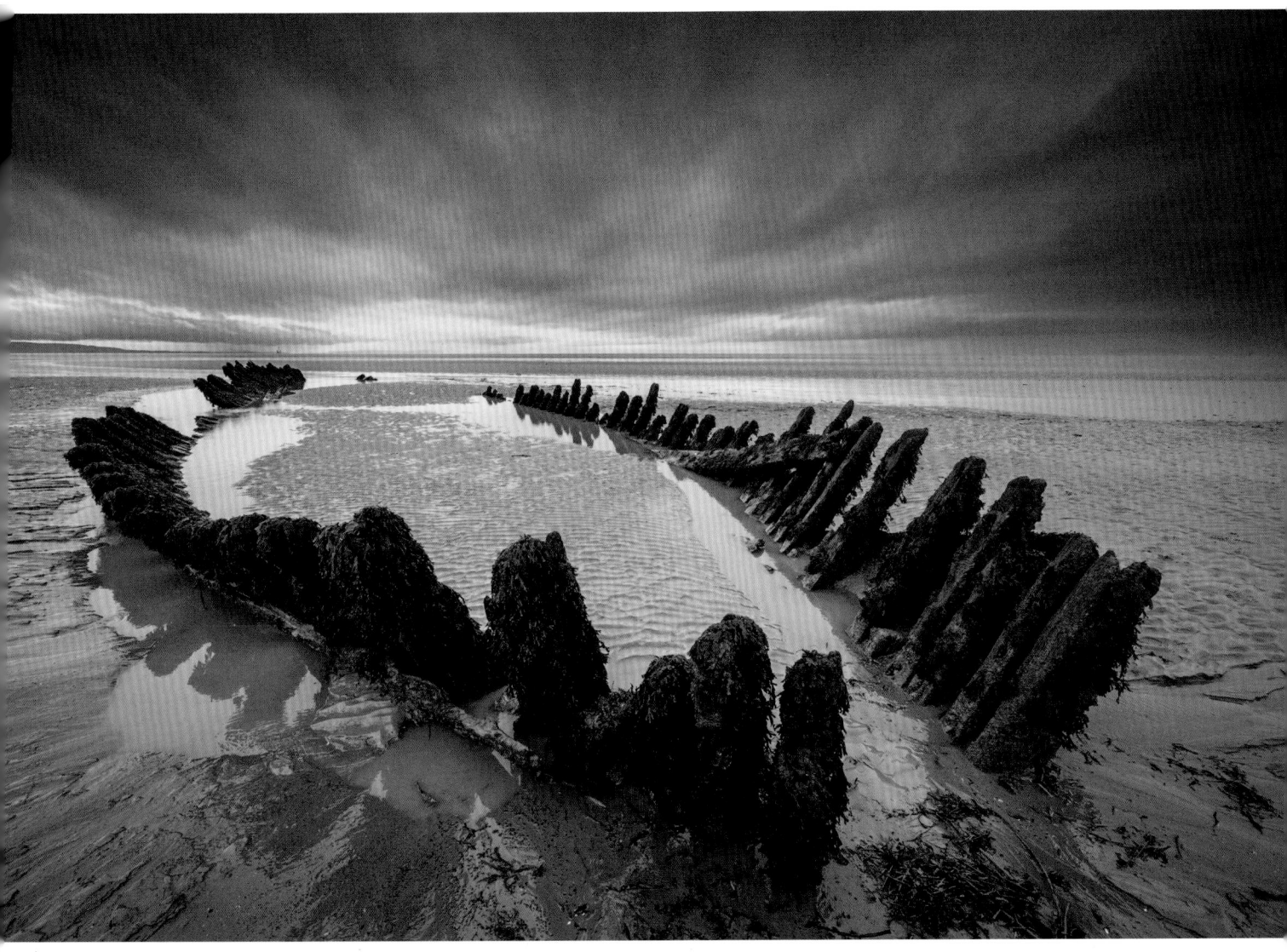

▲ **BOAT WRECK**
Shot in harsh light during the middle of the day, this monochrome capture places the focus on the bold shapes of the composition, as well as the texture of the sand and the posts of the wreck. An overcast sky helped to reduce the contrast in the scene.

DIFFUSED LIGHT

Although harsh light often suits monochrome, there are occasions when it is just too contrasty. If possible, you should wait for some cloud—even a small amount will help—to diffuse the light. On blustery days, there is often the chance of spotlighting on the landscape as the clouds are blown around, covering and then revealing the sun. If you compose a scene with a strong focal point there is always the chance that the focal point will become spotlit. This requires patience and you may be waiting for a long time—and sometimes in vain—but when it works, the results are worth it. You don't have to restrict yourself to monochrome in these conditions—this sort of dramatic spotlighting works equally well in color.

Traditionally, black-and-white film photographers would use color filters to enhance contrast within a scene and to change tonal relationships. These sorts of effects are probably best recreated during post-processing, although some in-camera filtration can still be useful. Polarized skies can look dramatic when the image is converted to monochrome and reducing glare off non-metallic surfaces will also improve the native contrast of the image.

Graduated filters can also be useful, to darken and add punch to textured skies, and neutral density filters will extend shutter speeds, allowing you to experiment with creative blur when there is movement in the scene (see pages 92–97).

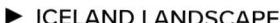

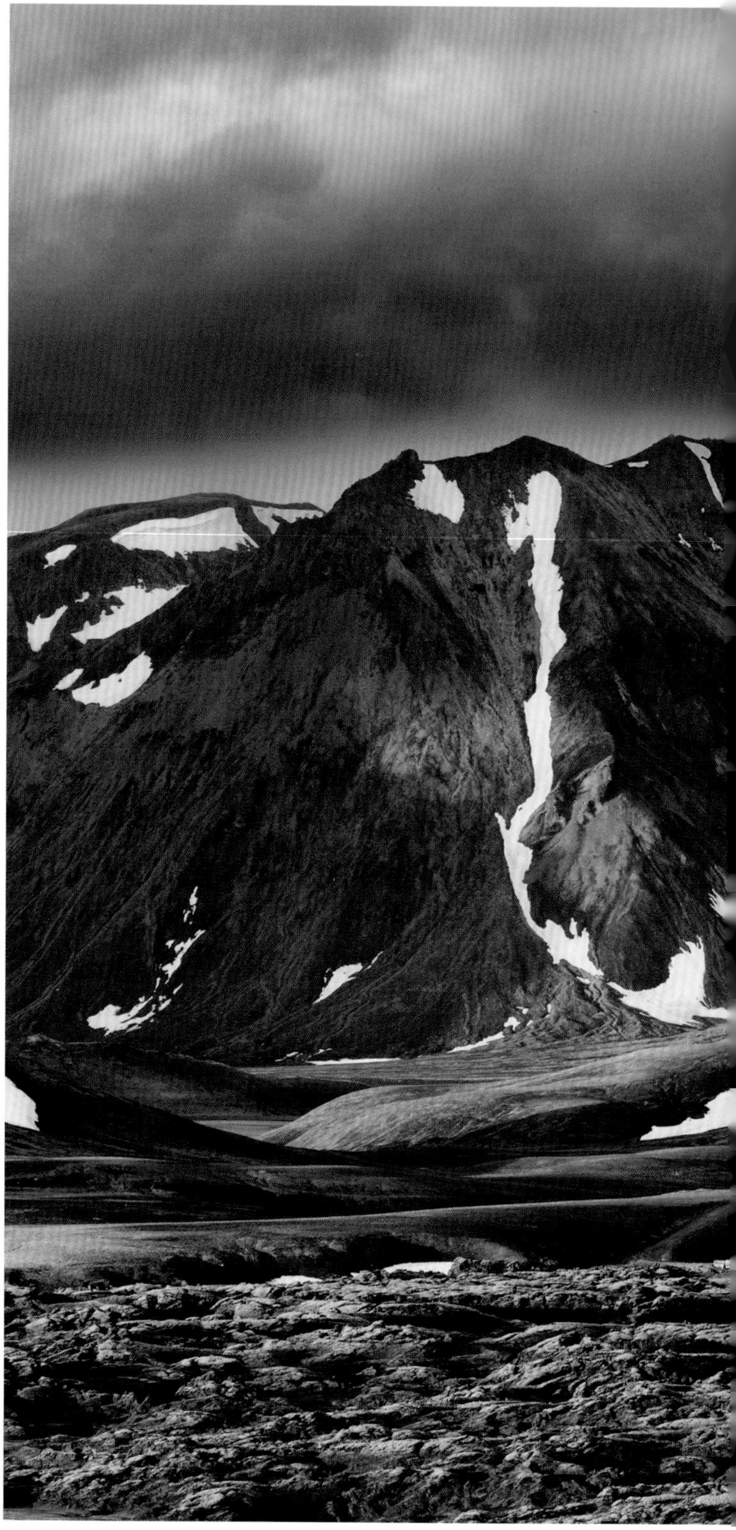

▶ ICELAND LANDSCAPE
Scenes with textured skies convert well to black and white. Although it was possible to capture the full range of tones without using a graduated filter, a "digital grad" was applied in processing to enhance the sky by darkening it and increasing contrast.

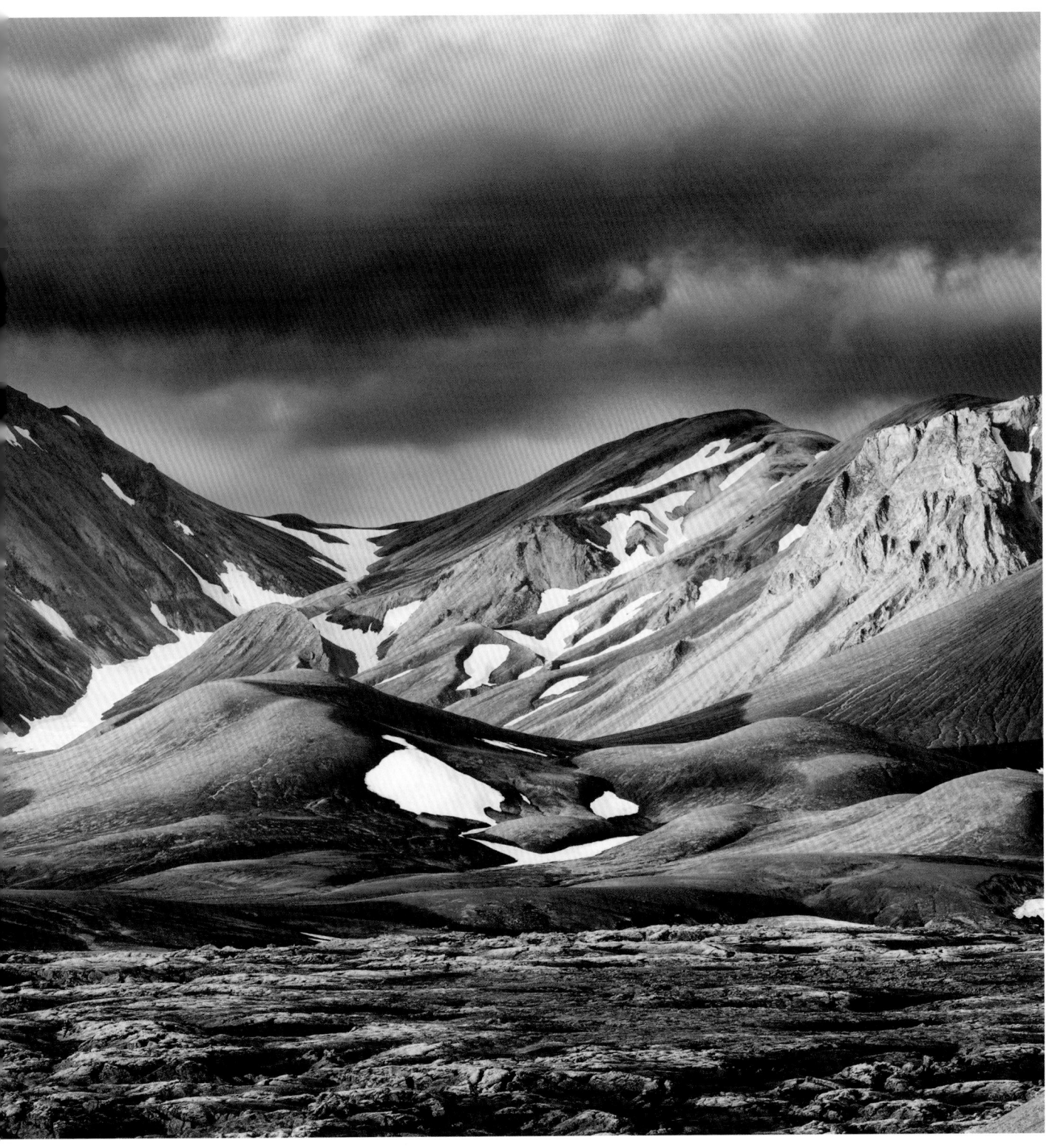

INFRARED

One technique that is especially suited to shooting in the middle of the day is infrared photography. This works particularly well during the summer months, when there is a lot of green foliage in the landscape. Done well, infrared landscapes—especially in monochrome—have a haunting, other-worldly look, with black skies and pale leaves on trees.

There are basically two routes to digital infrared photography: one is to use an infrared filter, such as the Hoya R72, which blocks out visible light and only allows infrared light through, and the other is to have a camera body modified, so that it only records infrared light. Using a filter is the cheaper option, but the disadvantage is that IR filters are opaque, so you have to compose the shot before fitting the filter, and exposure times can become very long. Focusing can also be slightly out on DSLRs, although not mirrorless cameras, which use the imaging sensor for focusing, rather than a separate AF sensor. Finally, it won't work well with all cameras—some models, even with the filter in place, just aren't sensitive to infrared light—they are, after all, specifically designed not to be. So this is worth researching before splashing out on a new filter.

Modifying a camera body is more expensive, but there are advantages: the camera's IR-blocking filter (the "hot mirror") is removed and replaced with a filter that blocks visible light but not infrared light. Therefore, you don't need to put a filter on the lens, and exposures are of normal length. Also, as part of the conversion process, the focus will be re-calibrated on DSLRs, so you do not need to make any changes to your focusing technique.

Filters of different strengths are available for the conversion, depending on whether you favor shooting color, monochrome, or a mixture of both. The most versatile choice is a 720 nanometer filter, as this works well for mono, but also allows the possibility of color photography.

THE INFRARED "LOOK"

Infrared images have a very distinctive "look". Objects that reflect a lot of infrared light, such as foliage, will be rendered very pale, whereas blue skies and water, which reflect very little infrared light, will record as very dark tones—almost black. For this reason, trees are very popular subjects, especially if they are underneath a blue sky with lots of white cloud for contrast. The infrared look can be very eerie, so churchyards, old buildings, and things like follies or monuments in overgrown gardens can also work effectively.

It's also important to step away from the big vista occasionally and not ignore smaller details—for example, windows with ivy growing around them can make interesting subjects, as can headstones in overgrown corners of churchyards. With monochrome images, a little texture in the composition adds depth and interest.

As with all landscape photography, the correct lighting conditions have a huge influence on the result. With there being more infrared radiation in the middle of the day in bright, sunny conditions, this is an ideal time to get out and about with your infrared camera or filter.

FOCUS ON...
COLOR INFRARED

Color infrared is sometimes known as "false color" as the camera does not see color in the same way as the human eye. Done subtly, false color can be very effective, having the appearance of a toned monochrome print. During post-processing, most photographers like to swap the blue and red channels, using the Channel Mixer in Photoshop—this renders skies blue rather than red. First, select Red as the output channel and set red to 0% and blue to 100%. Then select Blue as the output channel, and set blue to 0% and red to 100%. The colors still give the picture an air of mystery, but are less disturbing than having a red sky.

FOCUS ON...
BLACK AND WHITE INFRARED

To convert infrared pictures to mono, you can treat them as you would any other mono conversion (see pages 98–101). However, good results can also be obtained simply by desaturating the image (in Lightroom, pull the Saturation slider to 0). You may need to boost contrast, which can be done by using the Blacks and Whites sliders to stretch the tones across the full range of the histogram, as well as by using contrast tools such as the Contrast and Dehaze sliders. A little digital dodging and burning may be necessary to lighten and darken specific areas. To recreate the look of infrared film, add simulated grain, and to recreate the "glow" of infrared film, just drag the Clarity slider to the left.

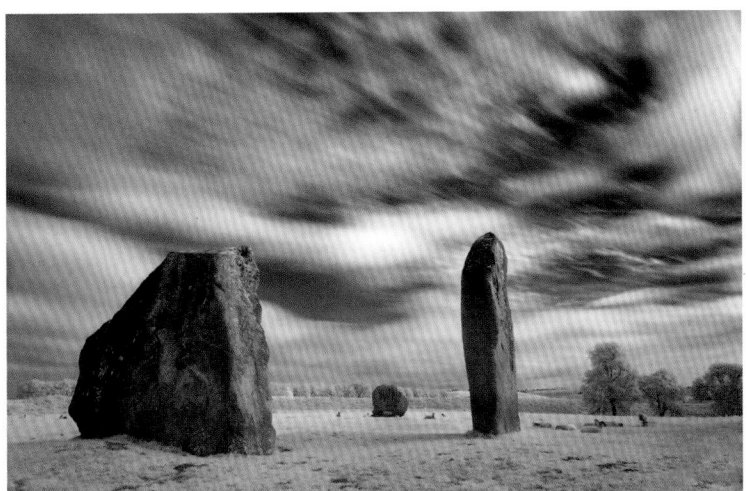

◄ STANDING STONES

Black and white infrared is characterized by black skies and pale foliage. Because of its rather spooky appearance, subjects such as this ancient stone monument work well. You don't necessarily need an infrared-converted camera for good results—this was shot with an unconverted camera and an infrared filter.

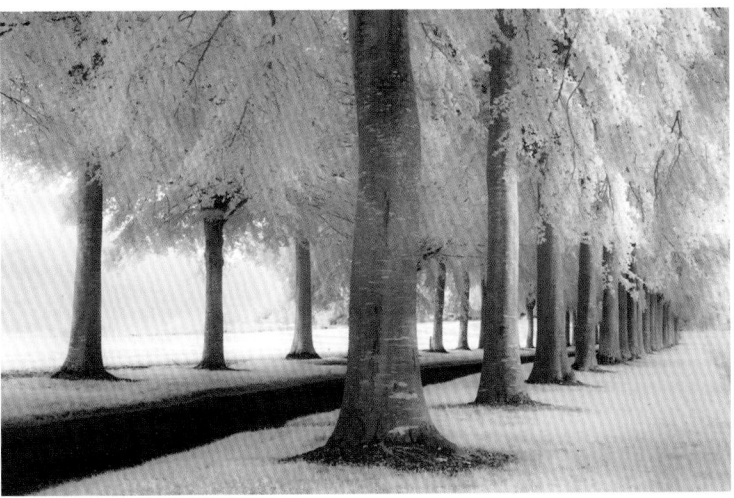

◄ TREE-LINED ROAD

Trees are very popular subjects for infrared, as the leaves are recorded as very pale tones.

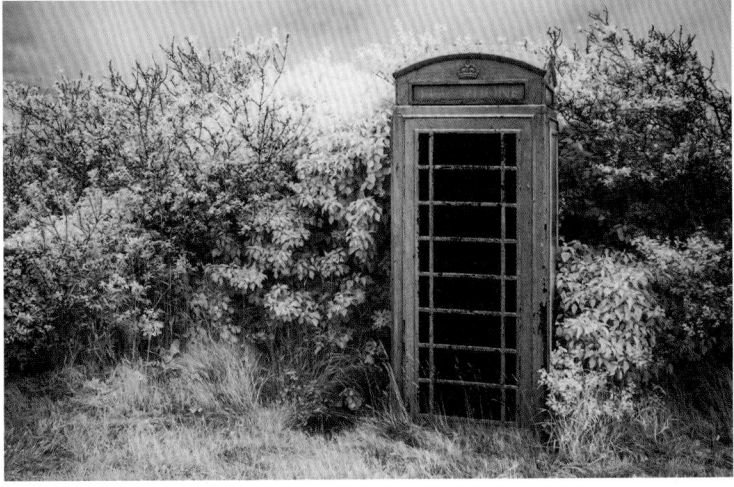

◄ TELEPHONE BOX

You don't need wide-open views. Some of the best infrared images are detail studies, such as this scruffy phone box, surrounded by overgrown foliage.

CORE TECHNIQUE
EXTREME ND FILTERS

If you want to capture moody pictures during the day, you don't need to restrict yourself to shooting in black and white. Using "extreme" neutral density (ND) filters to extend shutter speeds and creatively blur moving elements in the frame—such as water, clouds, crops, or foliage—is another way of creating atmosphere when the light is less than ideal. Long exposure images are often converted to monochrome, but they can look just as good in color.

Any filter that has six or more stops of density would be considered "extreme" but for shooting in the middle of the day you'll probably need a filter of at least 10 stops—this should allow you to generate exposures of one minute or more. These filters produce particularly good results in overcast conditions, especially when there is some layering in the sky, but can be used effectively in all sorts of light. If you are including the sky, it is best if there is some cloud.

Water is probably the most popular subject for long-exposure photography and a variety of effects can be created. With seascapes, water can be recorded as an ethereal mist (depending on the length of exposure and size of waves) or with calmer seas and longer exposures it can appear completely smooth and glassy. When shooting waterfalls, however, it's often worth using less extreme NDs—if the movement is blurred too much, the water can lose its texture altogether, and the image can have less impact.

Fields of crops or long grass and leaves on trees also have potential for long exposure photographs. You'll need to shoot on a windy day, so that there is a reasonable amount of movement and then experiment with different shutter speeds for different effects. As a general rule, you should avoid exposures that are too short as this can look as if you've simply made a mistake—there needs to be enough motion blur in your subject for it to look like a deliberate choice. With enough movement, an impressionistic effect can be created.

Clouds really add mood to a long-exposure landscape. Drifting clouds during a long exposure can take on the appearance of brushstrokes. Exactly how the clouds appear in your shot depends on the speed and direction of their movement and the length of exposure. The most dramatic effects are when the clouds are moving toward the camera and fan out toward the corners of the frame. One thing to be aware of, however, is that keeping the shutter open for too long can result in clouds losing all definition and the sky being recorded as a blanket gray or white.

FOCUS ON...
LONG EXPOSURE NOISE REDUCTION

Long exposures can suffer from noise, usually in the form of brightly colored "hot pixels." Most cameras have a Long Exposure Noise Reduction setting in their menu. When this is activated, after the shutter closes, the camera takes a "dark frame" of the same exposure time and then uses the information in this to map out the noise in the original image. This usually works well, but it effectively doubles the length of your exposure, which is not always practical. It's worth experimenting with your camera to see how badly long exposures are affected by noise and if you feel you need to activate Long Exposure Noise Reduction.

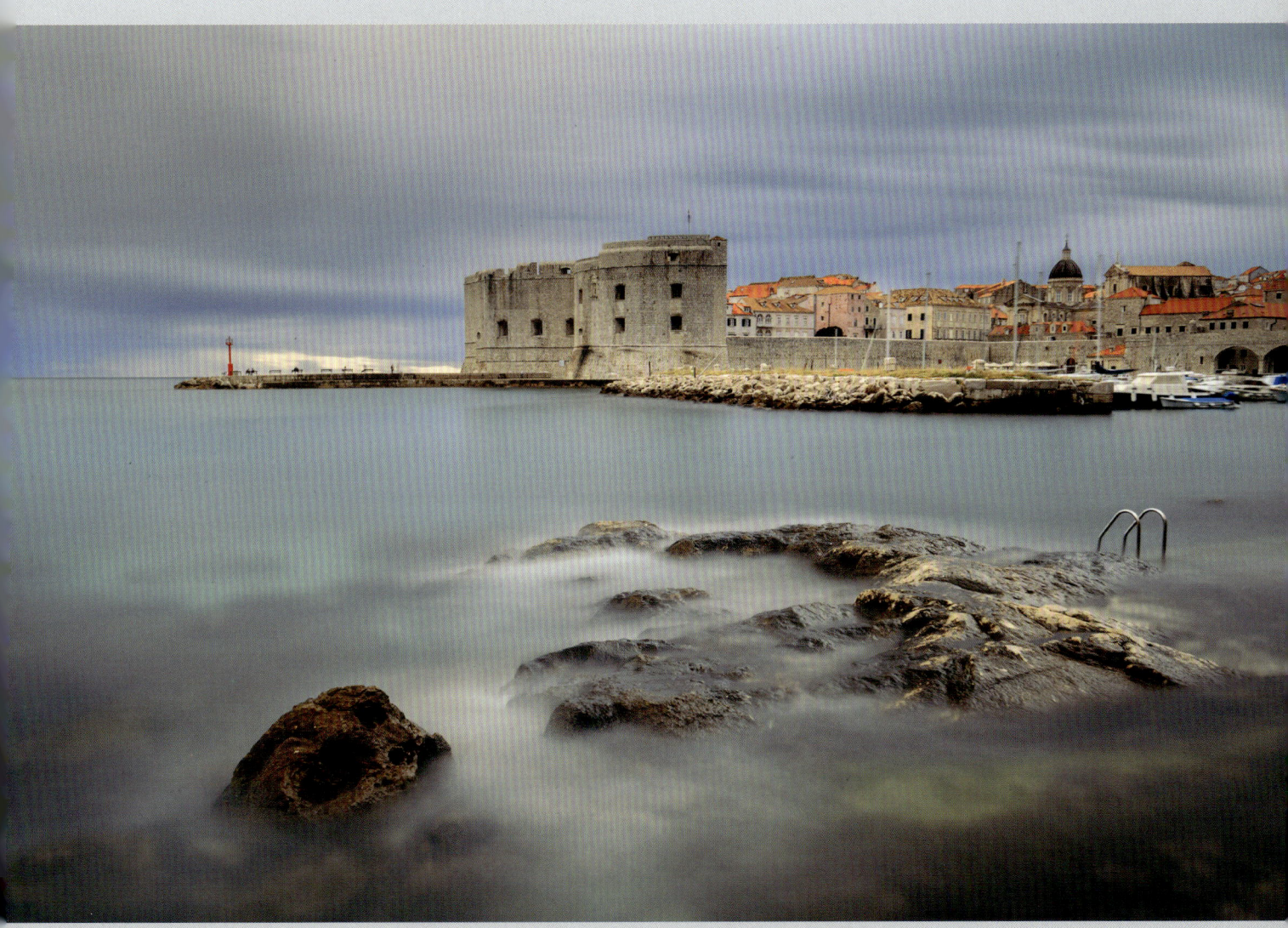

▲ CALM HARBOR
Long exposures on calm seas will record the surface of the water as smooth and glassy, and moving clouds will take on the appearance of brushstrokes.

TECHNIQUES

Working with extreme NDs is not difficult, but it does require a little practice and you will need to bear a few points in mind. First, anything denser than a six-stop ND is extremely dark and you will not be able to see through an optical viewfinder on an SLR. Live view and the EVFs of most mirrorless cameras will "see" through the filter in reasonable light, but in low-light situations it may be that you need to compose, focus, and adjust other filters such as polarizers and grads before fitting the ND. The extremely dark filter can confuse the camera's AF system, so use manual focus or back-button focus (see page 153) to ensure that focus remains locked on your subject.

Your camera's through-the-lens (TTL) metering may not be able to meter accurately through such a dark filter. If this is the case, take a test shot without the filter to determine correct exposure and then extrapolate this to account for the ND—double the exposure for every stop of filtration added. Although these calculations are not difficult, most manufacturers provide a "cheat sheet" with their filters so you can quickly and easily convert exposures. There are also various phone apps available.

If the exposure time exceeds your camera's longest shutter speed (usually 30 seconds) you will need to switch to Bulb mode. This allows you to lock the shutter open for as long as you like. Using a remote release when doing this means that you avoid the risk of camera shake.

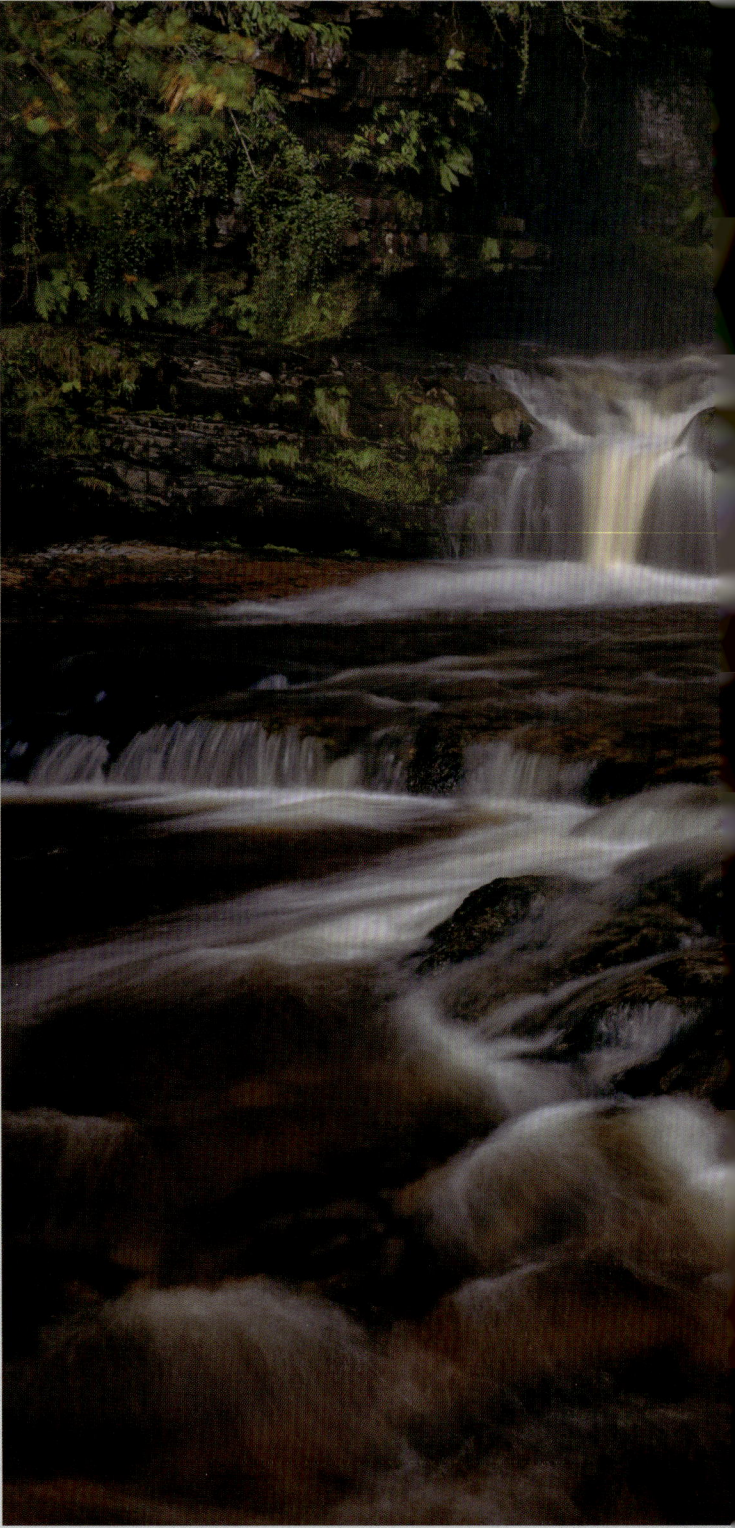

▶ **WATERFALL**
With fast-moving water, it is often better to avoid extremely long exposures in order to maintain some texture in the water.

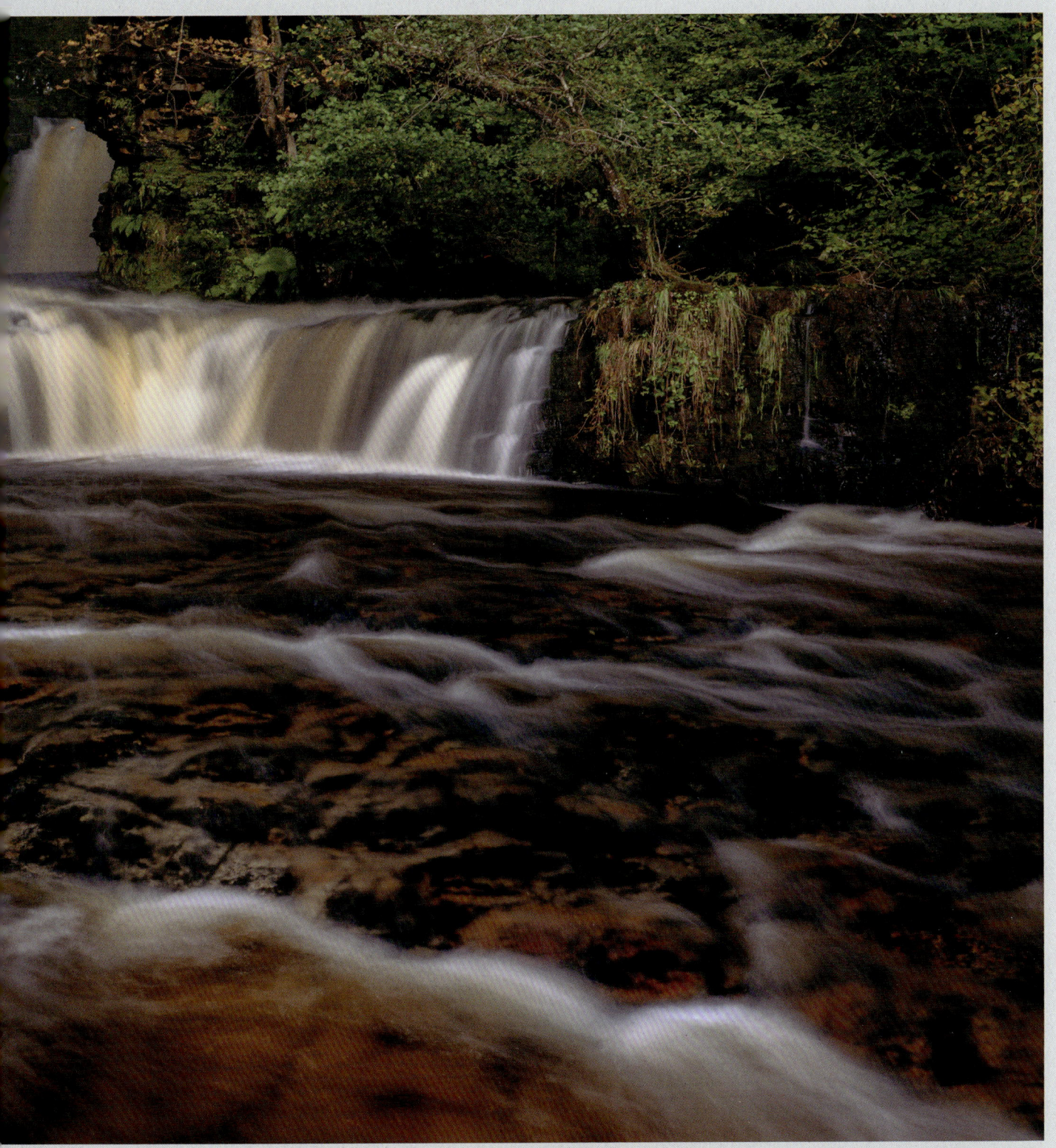

COMPOSITION
MINIMALISM

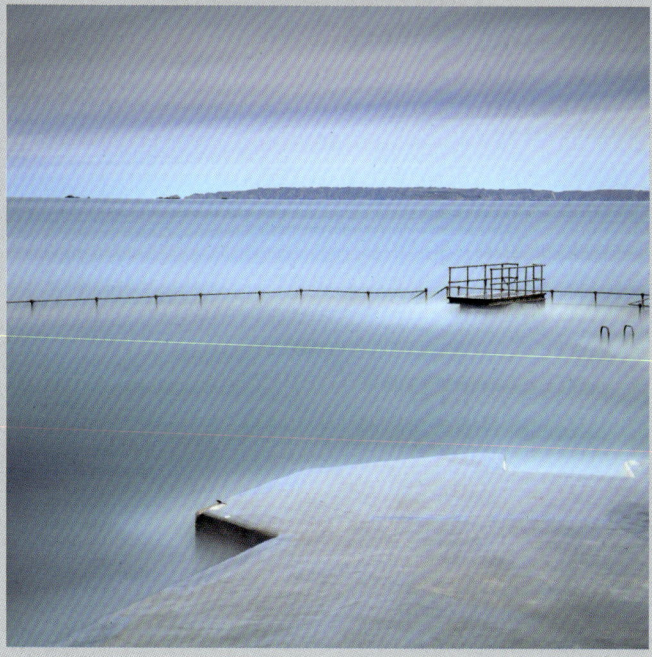

▲ SEA POOL
At high tide, the sea overtops this bathing pool in the Channel Islands, leaving only the railings and a few other features visible, which makes it a natural subject for a minimalist study. A long exposure simplifies the scene by reducing the waves to a misty texture. The square format was chosen to crop out some distractions on the edges of the frame, but its graphic qualities are naturally suited to minimalist images.

"Keep it as simple as possible" is advice that is often given with regard to composition. And it's generally excellent advice—a classic mistake of inexperienced landscape photographers is using a wide-angle lens and trying to get as much in the frame as possible. The result is often a photograph which contains so much information that the viewer is overwhelmed and the photograph's message is lost. However, by keeping any extraneous elements out of the composition, the viewer's attention is placed firmly on the key elements, which makes it much easier to communicate what it was that drew you to the scene.

Taking things a step further is the formal artistic style of minimalism. The philosophy behind minimalism is the belief that "less is more" and it involves reducing a composition to its bare essentials. Minimalist images feature clean, simple lines and shapes, and emphasize negative space (the space around the subject), which in some cases becomes the subject of the composition itself.

You'd think that it would be easy to adopt a minimalist approach—surely, all you have to do is make sure you don't have too much in the frame? However, there's more to minimalism than you might think. Subject choice is important. Graphic shapes and lines work well, so seek out subjects that feature them. These are likely to be artificial structures, such as piers, jetties, and groynes in coastal scenes, or isolated buildings in rural locations, but natural objects such as trees or hilltops are also possibilities. Long exposures are effective, as they naturally simplify scenes by smoothing the texture of water and skies.

FRAMING

Precise framing is even more important in minimalism because there needs to be the correct balance between the subject and negative space. If you have just a single subject, it is surprising how many options there are for placing it. Following convention, you might choose the "rule of thirds" or "golden section" intersections (see page 154), for instance, but bold placement can be very effective. Centering the subject is not uncommon in stripped-down compositions, especially if there are converging lines leading to it, and placing the subject at the edges or corners of the frame is also an option if it is pointing into the negative space.

The negative space has as important a role as the main subject, so ideally this should form an interesting shape and be consistent in tone and texture. Minimalism should apply to all aspects of the image, including color, so select a restricted color gamut or monochrome conversion.

▶ SEA DEFENSES
These zig zag groynes on a beach in Norfolk point to the open sea, making them a great choice for a minimalist composition. A 5-second exposure allowed the waves to wash around the posts, creating some texture for the negative space, and the raw file was converted to monochrome. Mono is a popular choice for minimalist images, especially when the range of colors might be distracting.

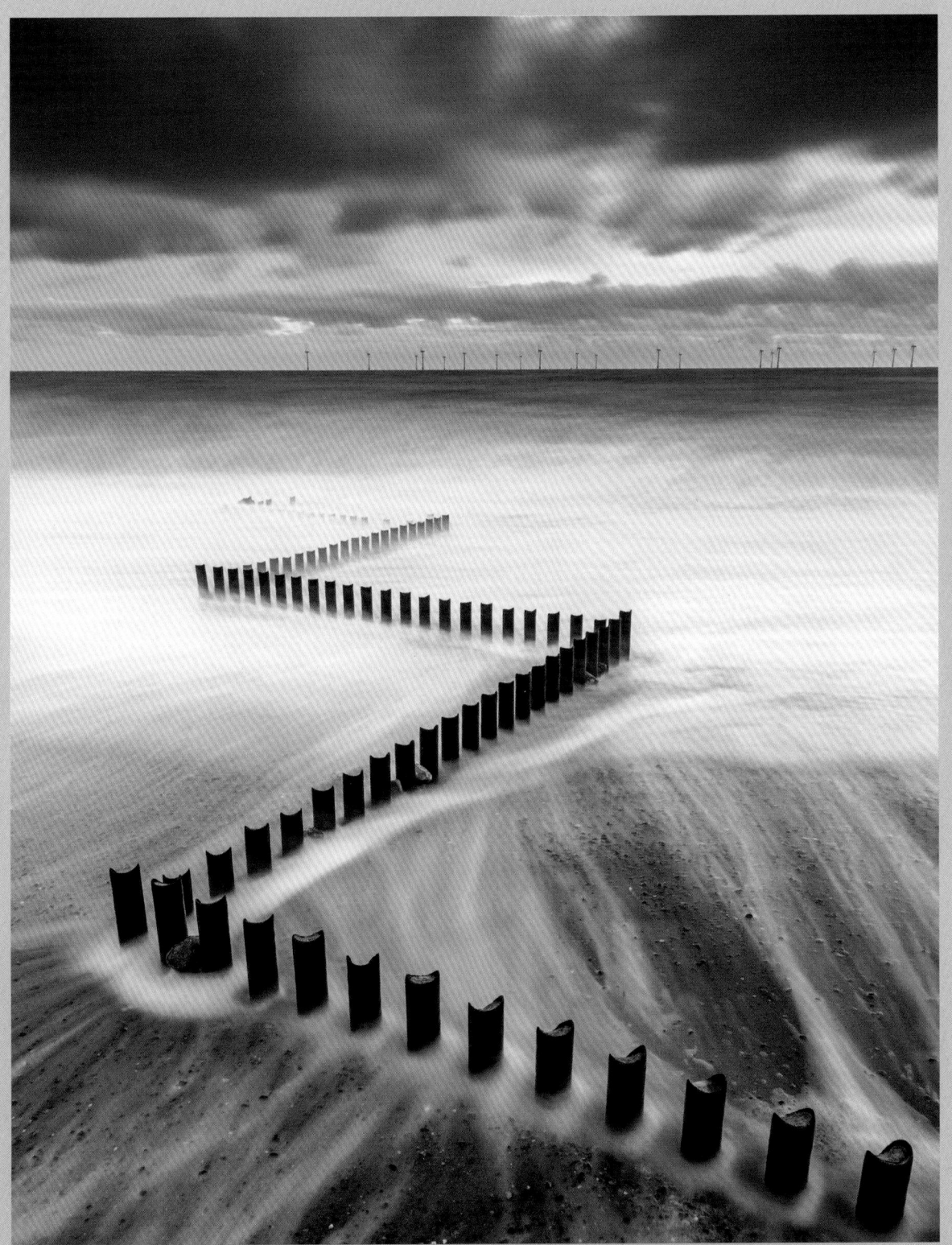

POST-PROCESSING STEP-BY-STEP
BLACK-AND-WHITE CONVERSIONS

Basic conversion to black and white is relatively straightforward using modern software, but there is a lot of control available, both with global and local adjustments, should you wish to take things further. The keys to a successful monochrome

conversion are selecting the right image and preparing the color original. Ideally, the first part will have been done at the exposure stage—the best results are usually from images which have been shot with the intention of converting them. They should exhibit

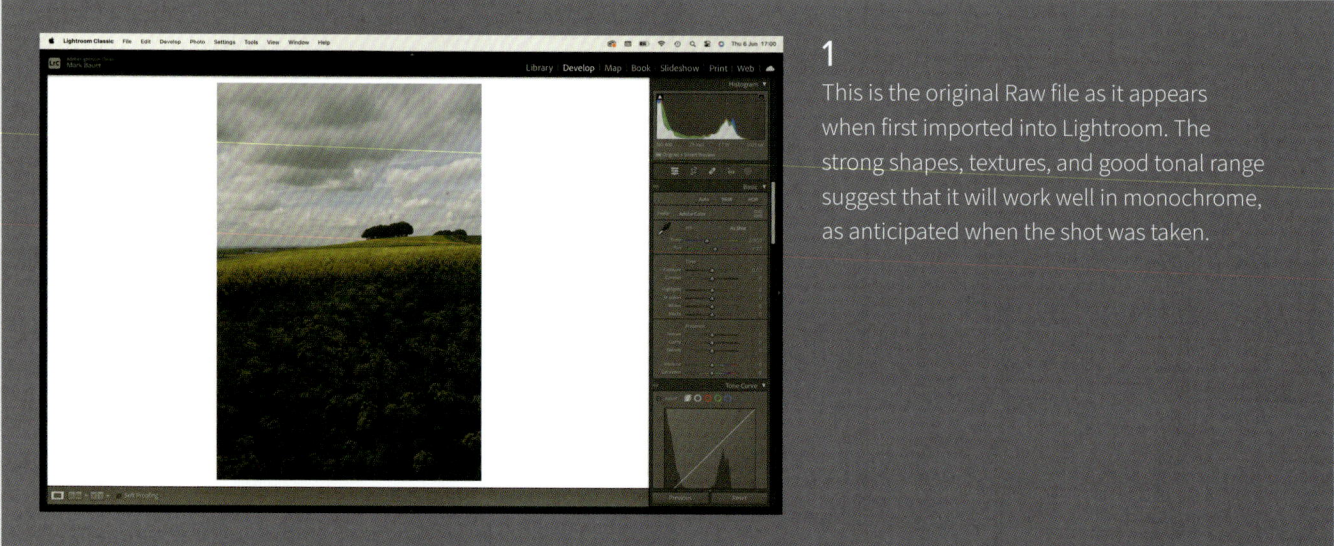

1
This is the original Raw file as it appears when first imported into Lightroom. The strong shapes, textures, and good tonal range suggest that it will work well in monochrome, as anticipated when the shot was taken.

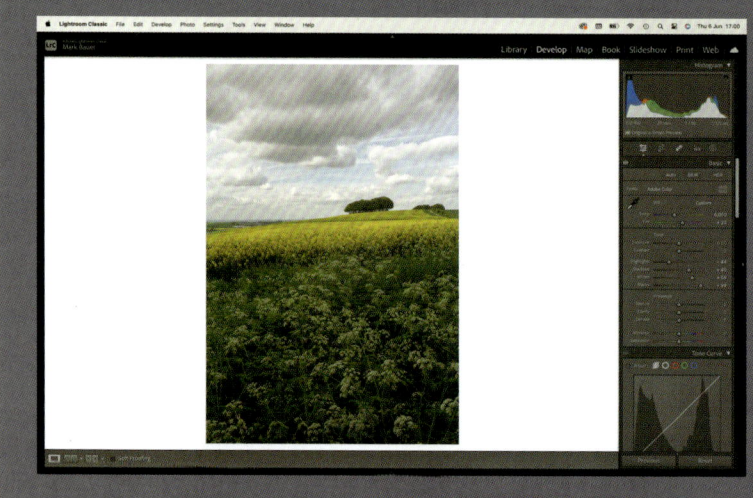

2
A neutral white balance was set by clicking with the eyedropper tool in the White Balance Panel on a mid-tone (you could also try using Auto White Balance). The tones were then stretched across the full width of the histogram, using the Blacks and Whites sliders, to make full use of the tonal range—this is also known as setting the black and white points. The black and white points were then fine-tuned using the Highlights and Shadows sliders.

good tonal contrast and make use of shape, line, and texture. Preparing the color image involves obtaining a neutral color rendition and enhancing the tonal range. The following step-by-step tutorial shows a range of techniques from a basic conversion to digital "dodging and burning" and local contrast enhancements. It uses Adobe Lightroom, which is one of the most popular Raw converters, but other applications are available with similar features.

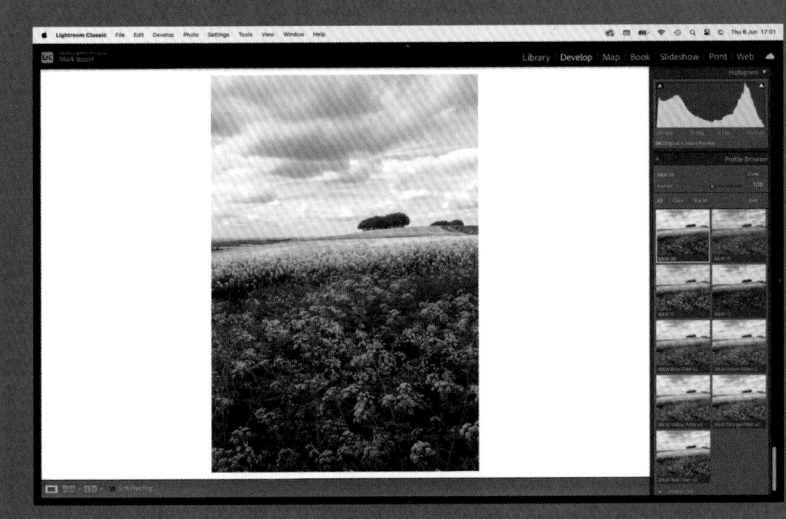

3

To convert to black and white, you can click the B&W button at the top of the Basic panel, but a better starting point is to choose a suitable profile. Click on Profile dropdown, then click Browse to open all the options. Experiment to see which profile looks best—in this case it was B&W 09. You can tweak the profile by adjusting the sliders in the Black & White Mix pane—these have a similar effect to the color filters used in black-and-white film photography.

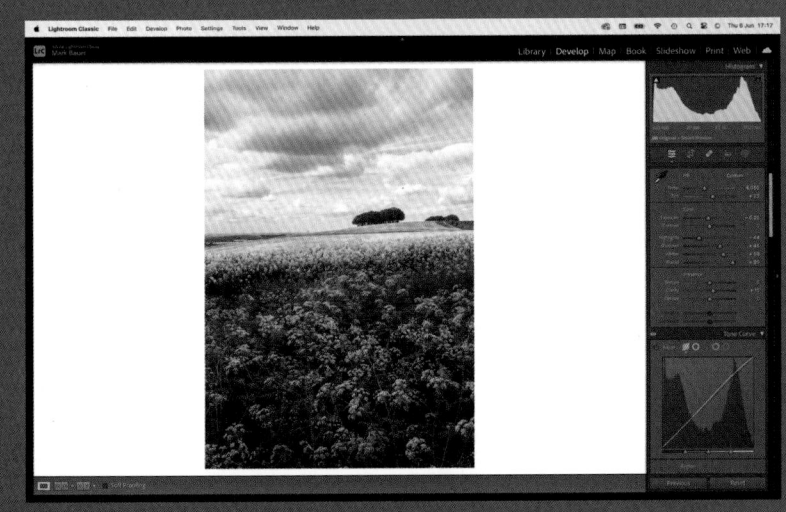

4

Global adjustments were made to enhance the contrast and texture of the image. These included a boost to Clarity, and adding an "S" curve to the tone curve. Pushing the Contrast Slider to the right would have a similar effect on the global contrast, but arguably offers slightly less fine control.

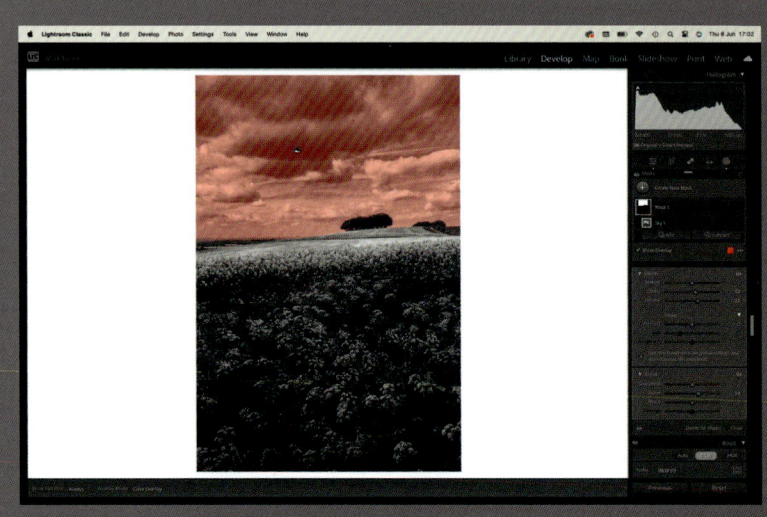

5

The local adjustments to this image are mainly aimed at bringing out the texture. The first is to enhance the strongly textured sky. The sky was selected using Select Sky from the masking tools. To reveal the texture in the clouds, Clarity and Contrast were increased, and Exposure and Highlights were pulled down.

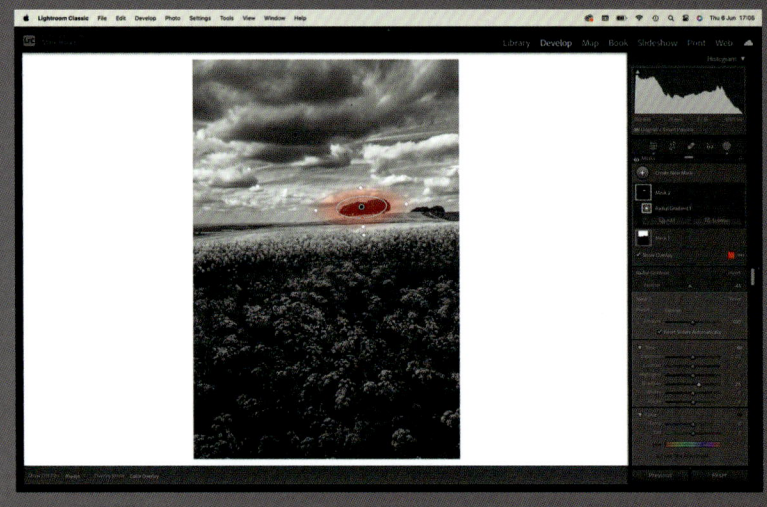

6

The clump of trees is a little on the dark side, with detail and texture hidden. For this adjustment, a rough selection of the trees was made using a Radial Gradient from the Masking tools, and Shadows were lifted slightly.

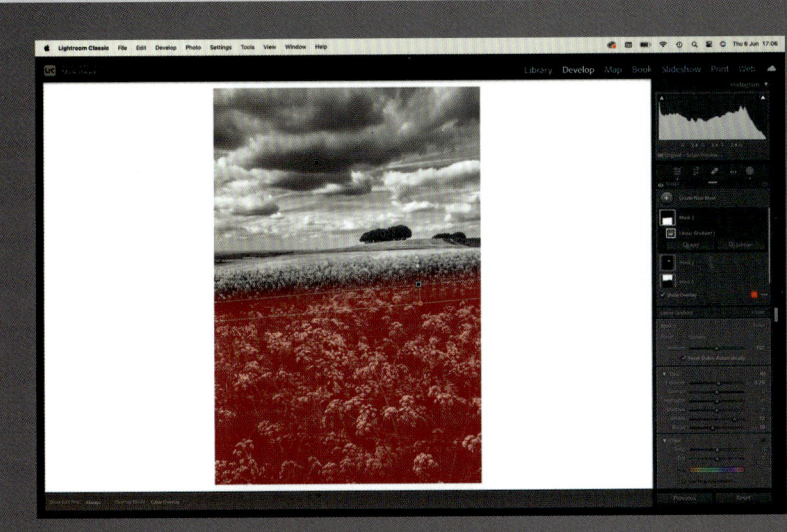

7

The sea plays a crucial role in this image, by providing tonal contrast to the dark shapes and textural contrast to the cliffs, rocks, and sky. This time, the Adjustment Brush was used to select areas of white water—remember if you get your selection wrong, you can undo it with the Erase brush. Clarity and Contrast were boosted to enhance the contrast with the rocks, and Highlights pulled down to maintain detail in the brighter areas.

FINAL IMAGE

The final image shows a full range of tones, from dark shadows to bright highlights, and the contrasting tones and textures help to show off the bold graphic shapes on which the composition is based.

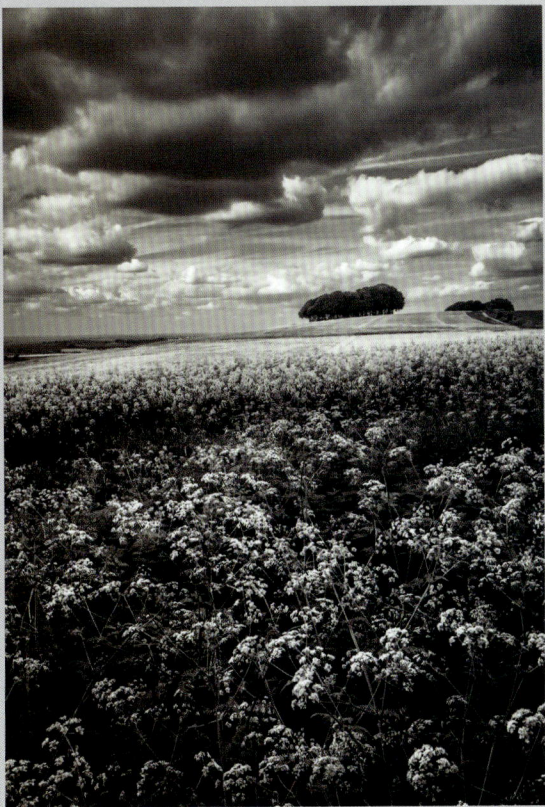

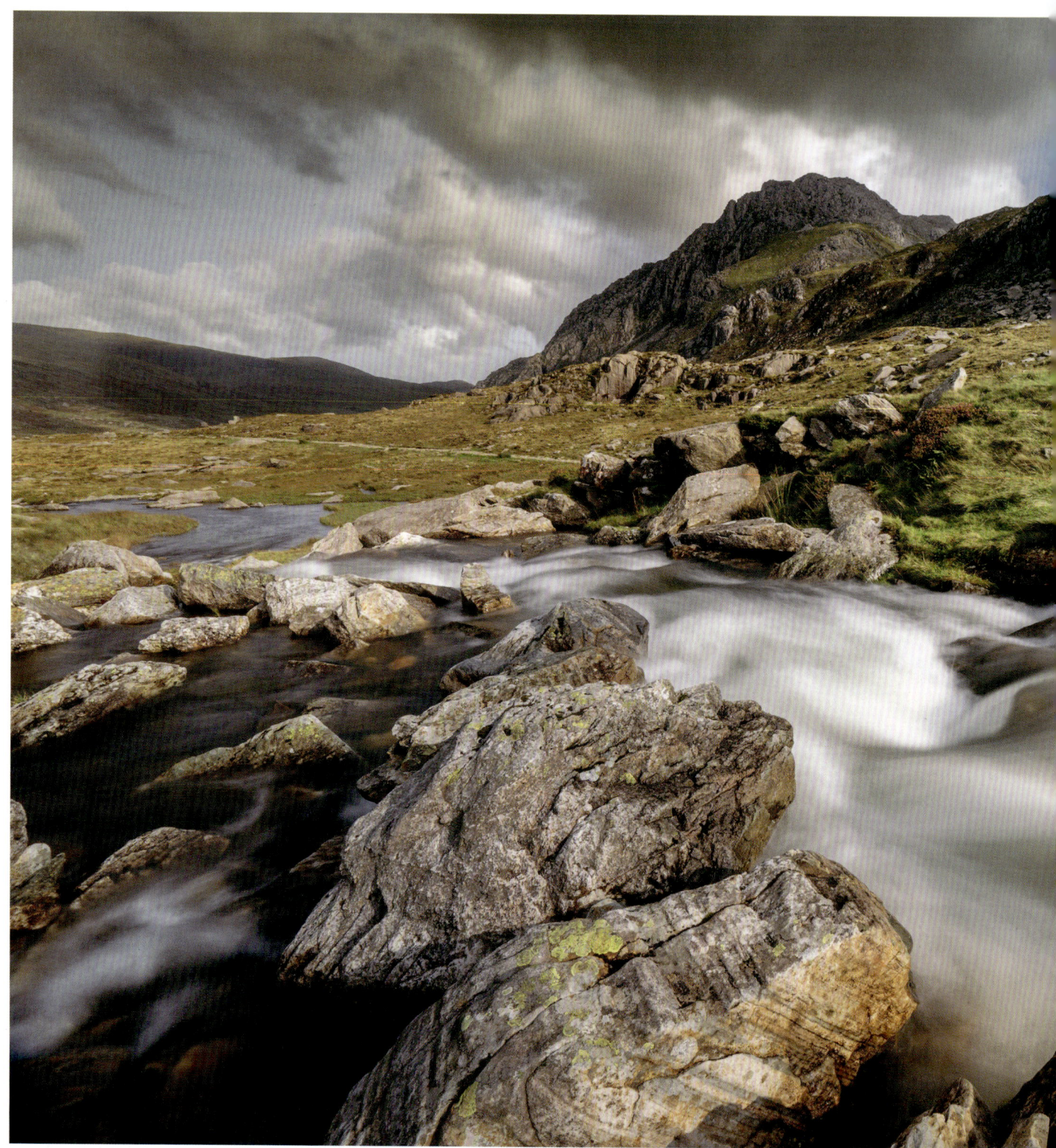

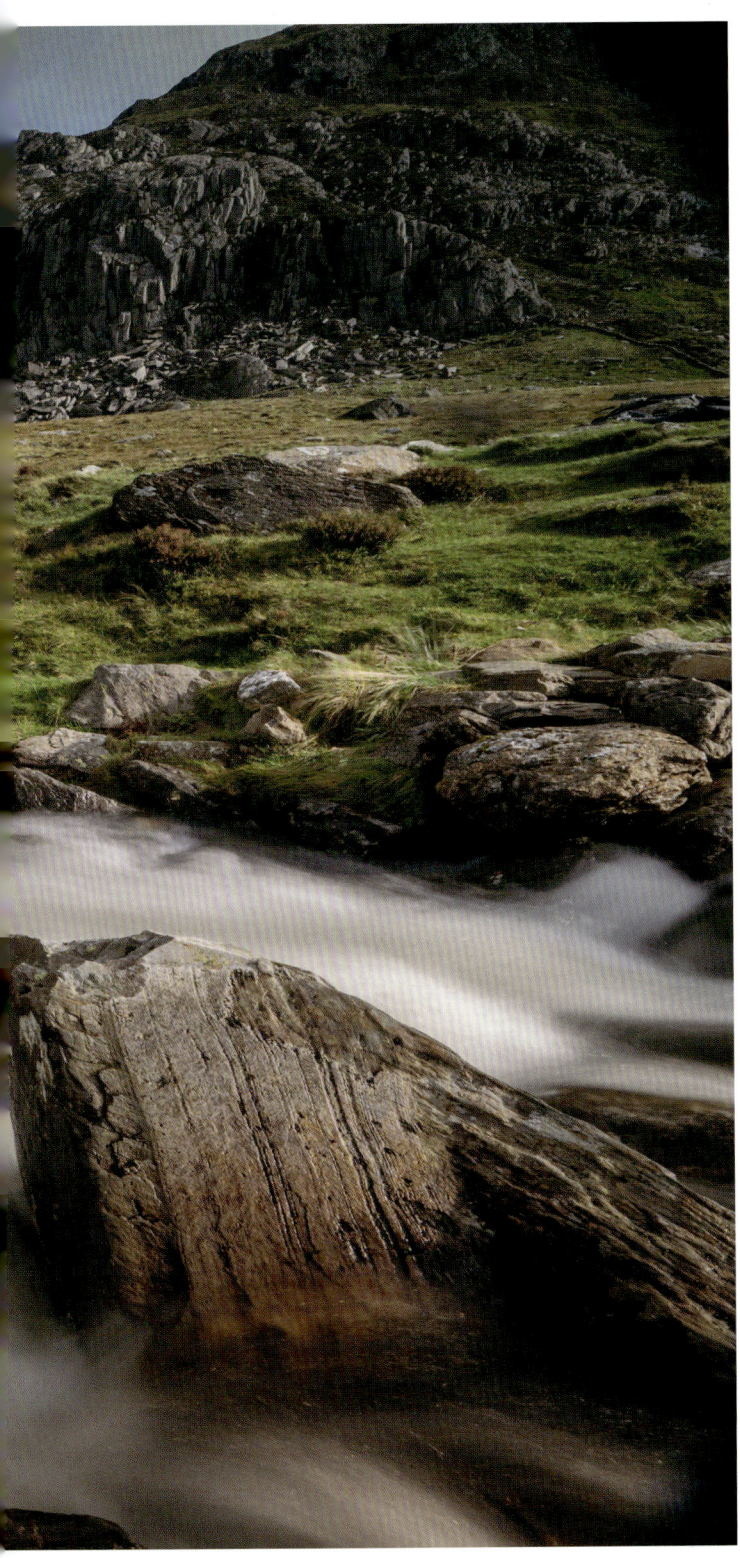

FINAL SHOT

Photographer **Mark Bauer**
Location **Cym Idwal, Eryri (Snowdonia), United Kingdom**
Time and date **1.30 p.m., September 25**
Camera **Nikon Z8**
Lens **Nikon 14–30mm f/4 (at 14mm)**
Filtration **Polarizer, 4-stop ND, 2-stop soft grad**
Exposure **ISO 64, 1.6 sec. at f/11**

THE STORY

"Cym Idwal is a dramatic valley formed by glacial erosion in Eryri (Snowdonia) National Park. It's a spectacular location, surrounded by high crags, with the lake of Llyn Idwal in its center and the imposing peak of Tryfan to the east. I saw the potential for a shot toward Tryfan, viewed from across a fast-flowing stream. The stream cascades over jagged rocks, which I thought would make an interesting foreground; the rocks could help to frame the distant view and direct the eye into the picture, and the rushing water, softened with a long exposure, could provide textural contrast with the harsh rock.

Setting the camera up proved a challenge, as it involved balancing on a wobbly rock close to the tumbling water. To compose the shot as desired, I also needed to shoot with my widest focal length of 14mm and frame very precisely. To obtain front-to-back sharpness, I employed the double-distance focusing method (see page 112). I wanted to retain some texture in the white water, so I decided that a shutter speed of between 1 and 2 seconds would give the desired effect and chose my filtration accordingly. After that, it was a case of waiting for the right light.

Lighting works slightly differently in mountainous locations. If you want some light on the landscape to reveal texture and form, the sun has to be relatively high in the sky to clear the peaks; in this instance, shooting in the middle of the day was an advantage. It was a blustery day, with clouds scudding across the sky, constantly covering and then revealing the sun and spotlighting different parts of the scene. When the light hit the foreground rocks and Tryfan at the same time, I released the shutter. Luckily, there was also some heavy cloud above the mountain, so that there is framing at the top as well as the bottom of the image."

CHAPTER FOUR
AFTERNOON

It can be tempting to take a break after lunch and get a little respite before the golden light returns later in the day, toward sunset. But the afternoon is a good time of day to explore, to experiment, and to capture color.

Color can be a powerful ingredient and high sun can enhance the color of water, foliage, and blue skies, providing photos with immediate impact. If you wish to add a splash of color to your landscapes, flowers are arguably the most obvious subjects to include. Throughout spring and summer they can be found in full bloom almost anywhere and can add depth, color, and scale to wider views.

While some photographers consciously avoid including artificial objects in their scenes, buildings and landmarks can provide key interest, scale, and a sense of place. Longer focal lengths are useful for isolating photogenic features like this within the landscape, so don't neglect or overlook your telephoto lens.

Employing different techniques can help compensate for the fact that the light is not quite at its best—enabling you to capture compelling landscape images at a time of day that many photographers still tend to overlook.

▶ BERWICK LIGHTHOUSE
In the afternoon, you can't rely on golden light for drama or impact. Instead, you need to focus on other ingredients, such as color, shape, form, structure, and creativity. You need to select subjects and scenes that suit the timing of your shoot. In this instance, the rainbow and the dark, moody sky framing the pier and lighthouse suited a creatively long exposure of 8 seconds—enough to smooth-out the water and sky. Capturing the lighthouse small in the frame helps produce a sense of size and place.

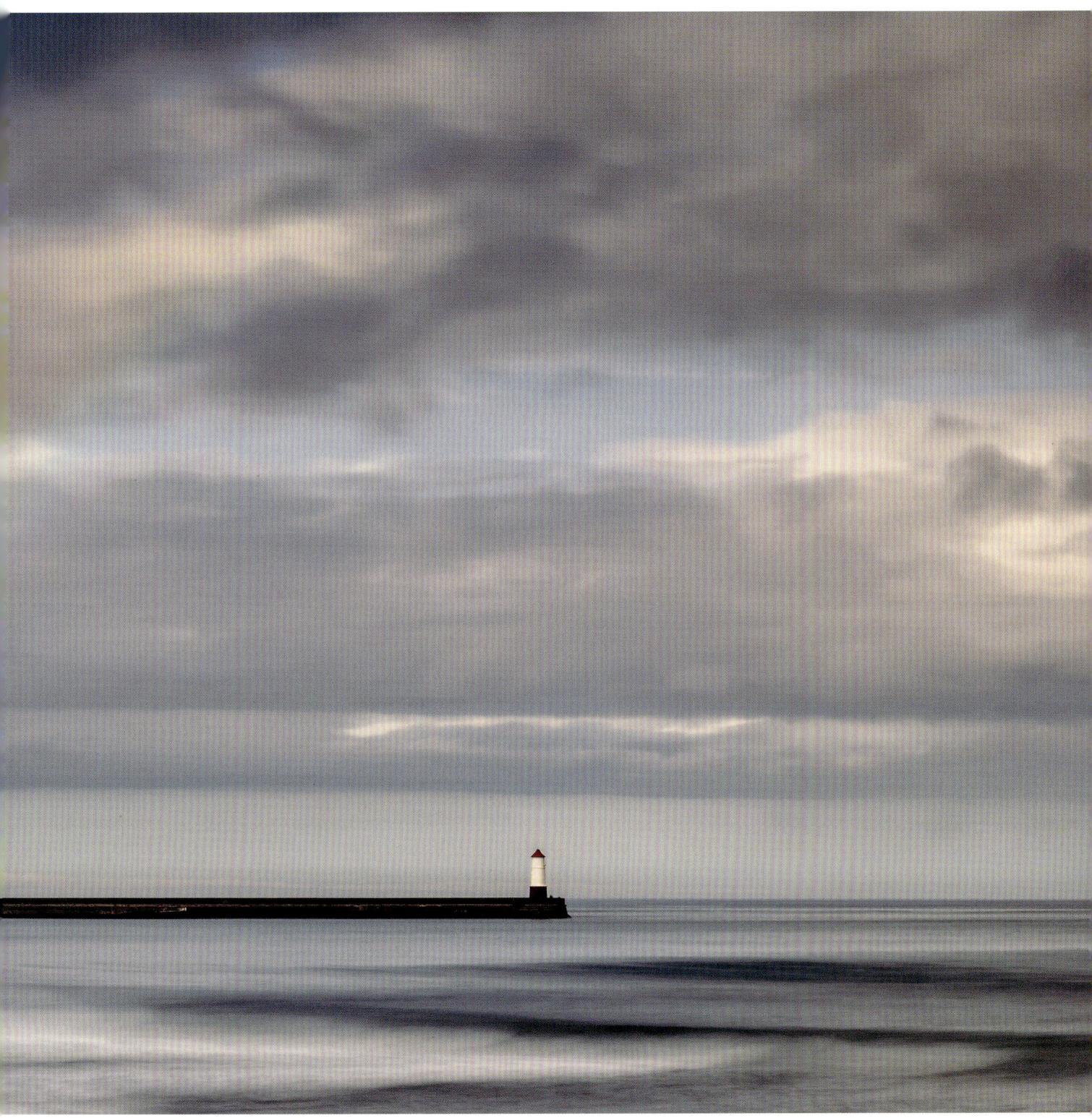

COLOR IMPACT

While the light is still improving, this is an ideal time to search out other ingredients that can generate interest and impact in your images. For example, the afternoon is well suited to capturing photos with an emphasis on color.

Don't underestimate the impact and influence of color. It can delight the eye, define form, and evoke emotion. A photographer's use of color can be striking or subtle, but its effect on the final image should only ever be a positive one. While it is possible to fine-tune color (see page 156) and contrast (see page 118) during post-processing, any adjustments should remain small and discrete. Color should always remain natural and authentic—not the result of aggressive or inappropriate use of the saturation or vibrancy sliders in Lightroom or Photoshop! Color impact should be a result of subject choice, timing, filtration, light, and viewpoint, and be captured in-camera when you press the shutter.

Different colors can create different moods and evoke different responses. Red is an advancing color that we instinctively associate with danger or excitement. No color demands more attention, and only a small splash of red can dominate a photograph. Blue is a more tranquil color, which we associate with skies, water, and coldness. It is fresh and calming, as is green, which is a color we often tend to closely associate with nature and vitality. Yellow is another strong, advancing color that is often considered happy and uplifting. The influence of color on the look and feel of our photographs is more significant than many realize.

COLOR WHEEL

There are no definitive rules as to how a photographer should or shouldn't use color in their shots. How you decide to employ, combine, or contrast colors is very much a personal and intuitive thing. At least some knowledge of color theory will prove helpful, though. By studying a color wheel, you will have a better understanding of which colors work together harmoniously and which are likely to conflict.

Arguably, the three most striking, commonly used color combinations in landscape photography are red/blue, red/green, and blue/orange, but other combinations can prove equally effective. Contrasting saturated, advancing colors against cooler, receding ones can create great color impact. Avoid color overwhelming your compositions, though—it should only ever enhance them. In other words, while color can provide an image

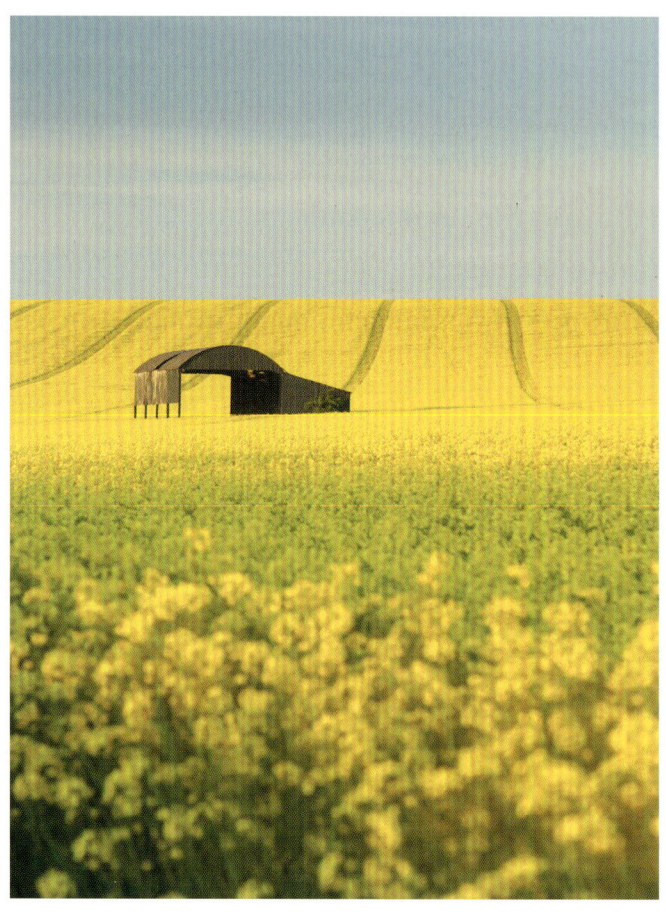

▲ **BARN AND CANOLA**
This is a simple composition of a dilapidated old Dutch barn, standing in the middle of a field in south west England. Had this been taken on a cloudy day, or at a time of year when the colorful crop of canola wasn't flowering, this shot wouldn't have worked. The photo relies almost solely on color for its impact—the bright yellow crop and blue sky combine to create an image that works.

with immediate impact, it won't disguise a poor shot. If the scene, viewpoint, or composition isn't strong in the first place, color will only give the image a brief and temporary reprieve. However, creative and appropriate use of color will unquestionably enhance a well-constructed landscape.

Several things can influence color. We know sunlight can be naturally warm or cold, while white balance (see page 40) can

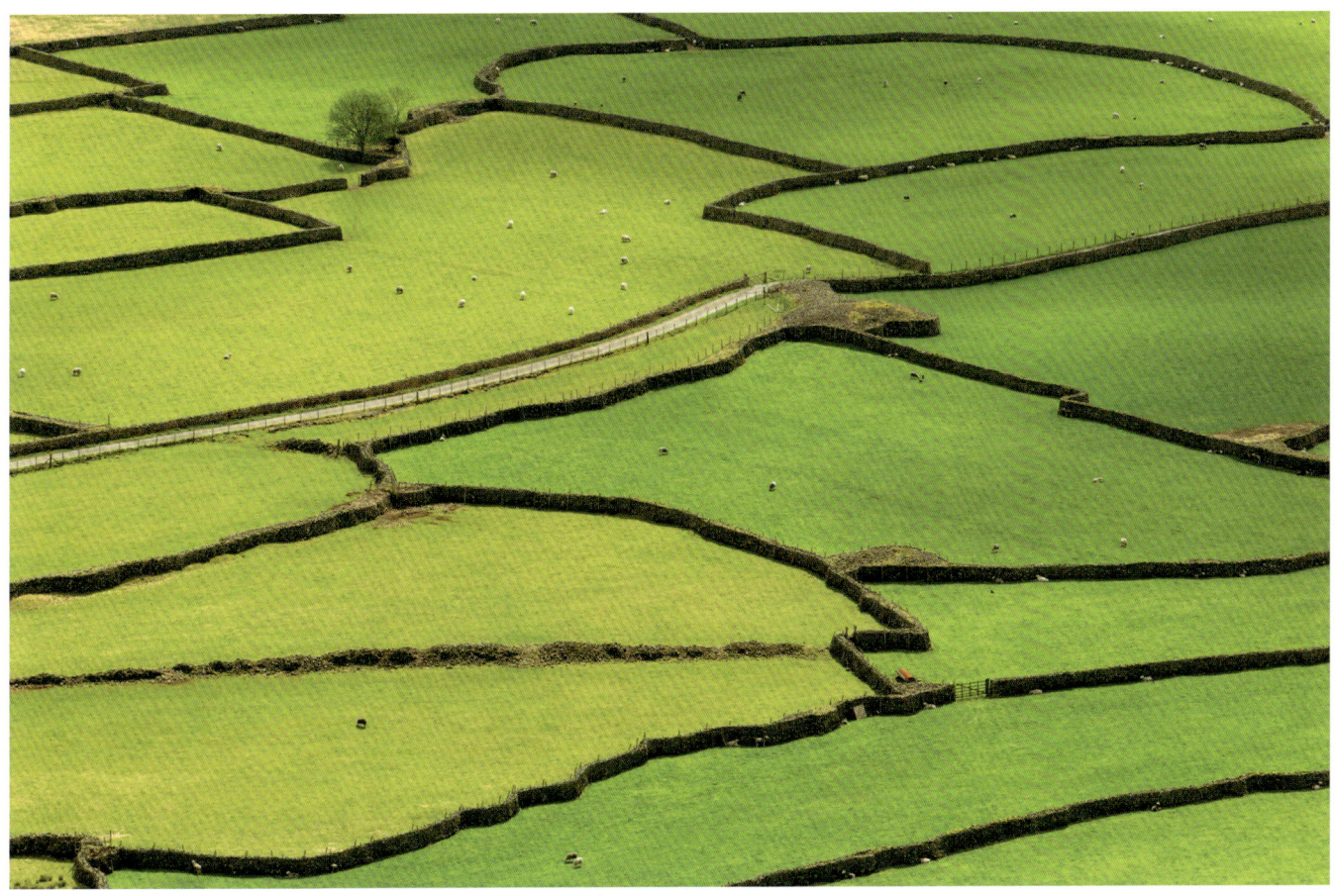

be used (or deliberately misused) to neutralize, enhance, or create a shift in the light's color temperature. Meanwhile, a polarizing filter can help boost natural color saturation within certain scenes.

However, the most likely source of color impact is provided by the scenery or subject matter itself—for example, the vibrancy of bright green spring foliage, colorful crops of flowering lavender, a long stretch of golden sand, richly painted buildings, or a patchwork of fields. Color impact can be created by including layer upon layer of frame-filling color, or from a single poppy standin out in a cornfield. When you say "color impact," most people immediately think of strong, vibrant, saturated colors. However, this will not always be desirable. Muted, pastel tones might seem less obvious, but can prove just as effective and as impactful.

▲ PATCHWORK FIELDS

When your aim is to achieve impact through the use of color, attaching a telephoto lens is a good option, allowing you to highlight shapes and isolate color within the landscape—for example, this patchwork of vibrant green fields in late spring.

LONG-LENS LANDSCAPES

When shooting landscapes, photographers have several key decisions to make. For example, which aperture will provide adequate depth of field? Which viewpoint offers the best perspective? And which filters should you use? However, one of the most important decisions regards focal length choice. Landscape photography has a close association with wide-angle lenses (see page 14). They are considered the mainstay of a landscape photographer's system due to their ability to capture big foregrounds and wide, sweeping vistas. However, the way they "stretch" perspective is not always desirable. This effect diminishes the size and importance of features within the landscape that are further away. For example, the size and dominance of hills and mountains will be vastly reduced should you opt to go wide, and this can produce images with less impact and sense of scale.

Telephoto lenses—upward of 100mm—are often overlooked among landscape enthusiasts. They can appear to foreshorten perspective, which helps a hilly or mountainous backdrop appear larger and more imposing, and so create landscapes with a different emphasis. Longer focal lengths are ideally suited to scenes where there is a lack of foreground interest, or where there are objects nearby that would be distracting or inappropriate. Placing emphasis on the landscape is also a way to obscure boring skies.

ISOLATING SUBJECTS

Telephotos are a great choice when you wish to isolate key points of interest within the landscape that would be "lost" if you opted to go wider. For example, a focal length in the region of 70–200mm is ideal for shooting rural scenes, allowing you to highlight shapely trees or place emphasis on interesting buildings and landmarks within the landscape. When doing this, it is normally best to avoid framing your subject too tightly. Instead, retain a degree of "breathing space" around the subject and capture it in context with its surroundings. For example, if you were photographing a church set within rolling countryside, consider placing it strategically on an intersecting third, but include enough of its surroundings to create a proper sense of place. The building should then act as a key point of interest and anchor the composition, without being so dominant that the eye never bothers to explore the rest of the frame. A telephoto zoom (as opposed to a prime lens) is a good choice as it allows you to quickly adjust focal length to fine-tune your composition.

Although perspective is an important term in landscape photography, telephotos do not actually compress it—as is so often described. Perspective is simply an effect of camera-to-subject distance (see page 136). While wide-angle lenses are credited with the ability to create depth, telephotos are good for highlighting interesting distant detail, repetition, and patterns within the landscape. They also help when you are seeking structure or simplicity within a chaotic environment. This is because they allow you to exclude unnecessary elements from your composition and instead focus on layers, shapes, and form.

Although telephotos provide less depth of field, the landscape you are shooting is more distant, so working with a shallower zone of focus rarely presents a problem. A mid-range aperture of f/8 or f/11 is normally a good choice for long-lens landscapes. Precise focusing is essential, though. Telephotos will exaggerate the effects of haze, fog, or mist, which can be a desirable effect.

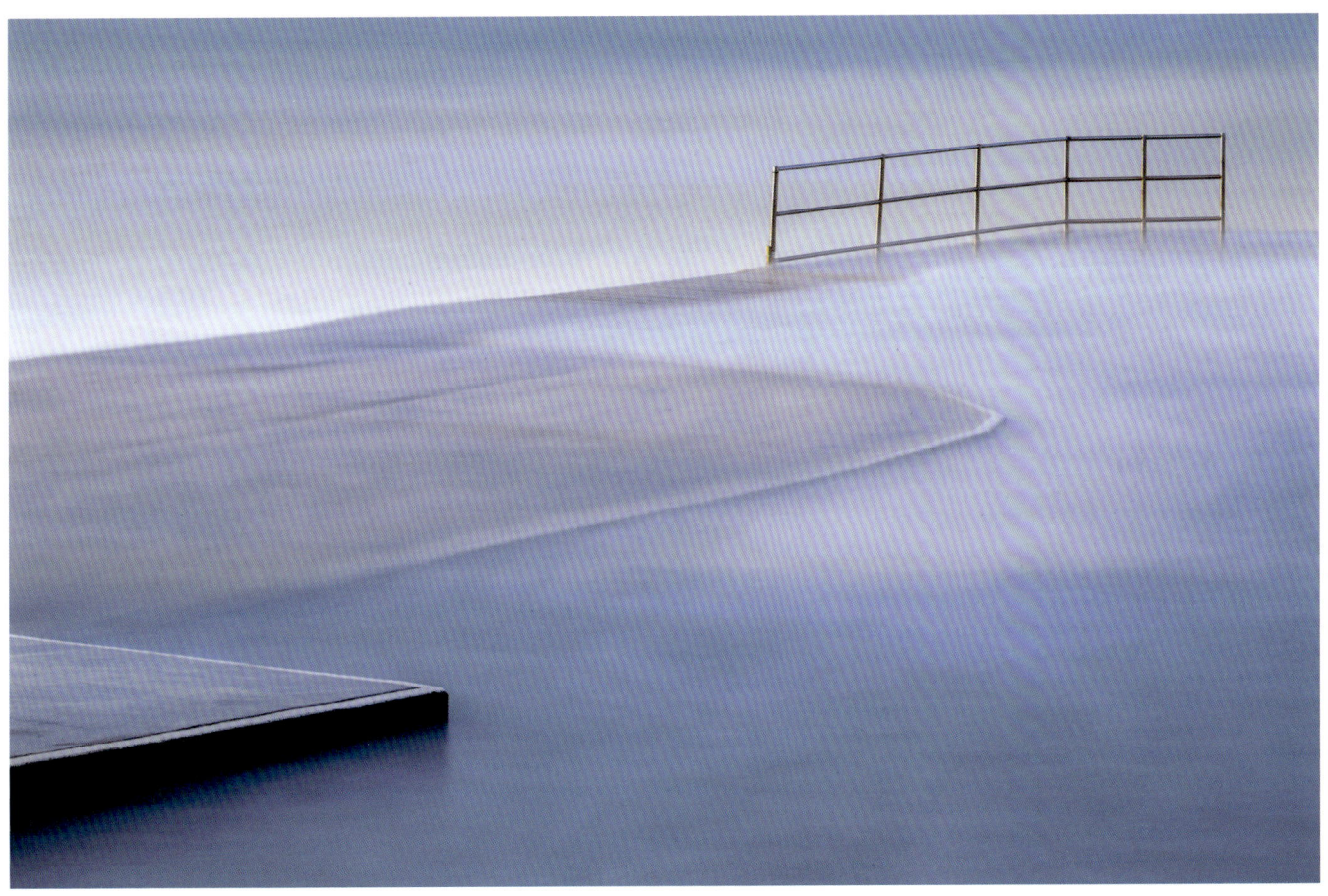

▲ BATHING POOL

With many views the temptation is to go wide-angle and capture a large, sweeping vista. However, key points of interest, shape, form, and color can get lost within the landscape with this approach. On this occasion, I opted for a longer lens instead, to simplify this view, and place emphasis on the shapes and lines of this Cornish sea pool. A lengthy exposure helped create a minimalist result.

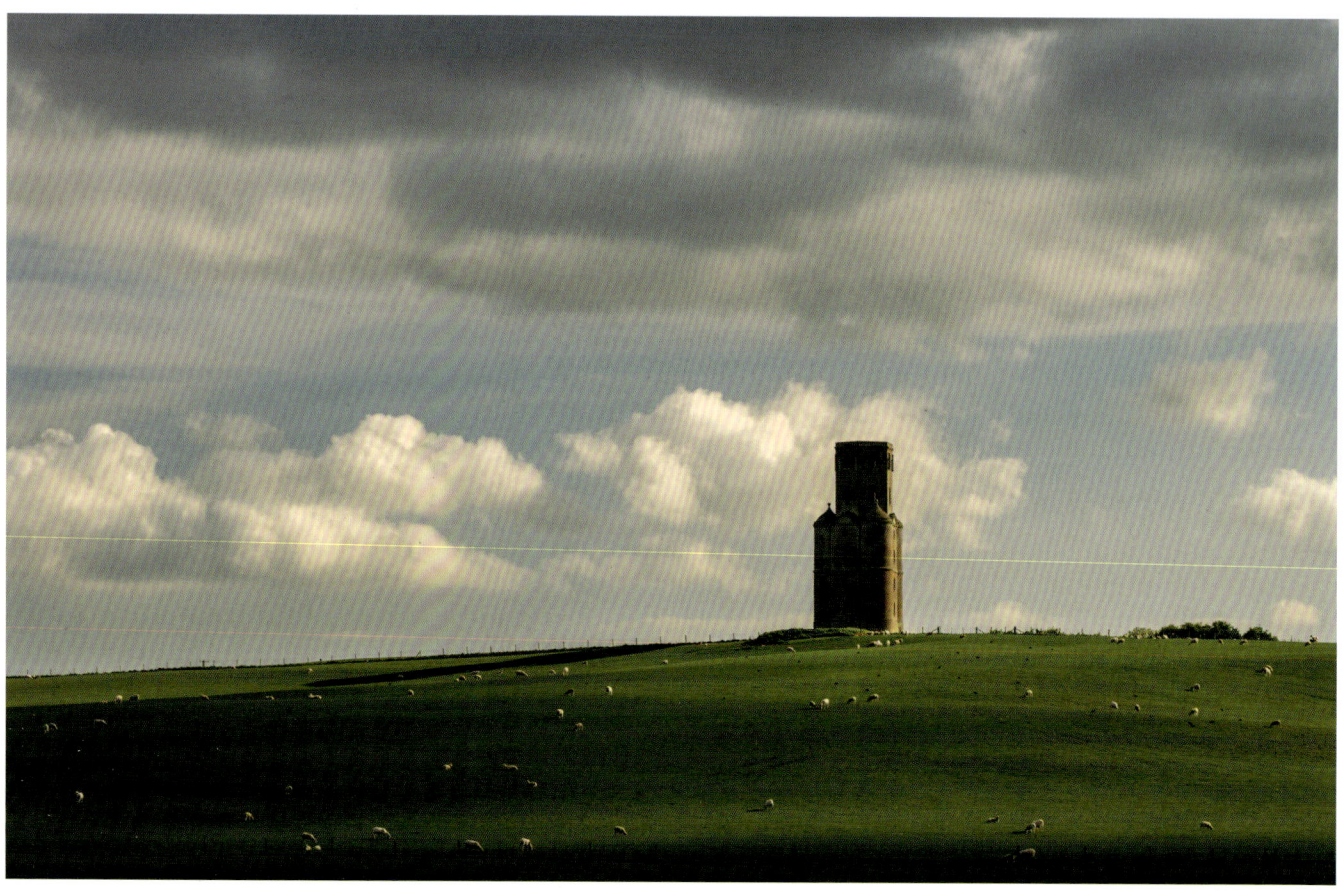

FOCUS ON...
TELEPHOTO SHARPNESS

There are several things photographers can do to ensure bitingly sharp results. For example, use a tripod (see page 22) and release the shutter remotely to eliminate any camera motion. However, when using longer focal lengths, any flaw in your technique will be exaggerated and exposed. For example, depth of field is shallower when using telephotos, so there is no leeway for error when focusing. One of the most common errors photographers make when shooting long-lens landscapes is assuming that, because they are using a tripod, sharp results are guaranteed. However, in blowy weather, long lenses are most susceptible to being caught by the wind due to their size. Therefore, always replay and review your photos, using the magnify button to enlarge key details, and closely scrutinize critical sharpness. Don't be afraid to adjust ISO sensitivity to generate a faster, more practical shutter speed in windy weather. Simply increase ISO speed incrementally until you achieve a speed that achieves sharp results. Timing is also important. In blustery weather, trigger the shutter between gusts to minimize any weather disturbance, and try using your body as a windbreak. Also, consider hanging your camera bag from the tripod using a bungee cord. The additional weight will aid stability, with the bag acting like an anchor. The bag should always sit firmly on the ground, though—if it is allowed to swing below the tripod, it is more likely to cause movement than prevent it.

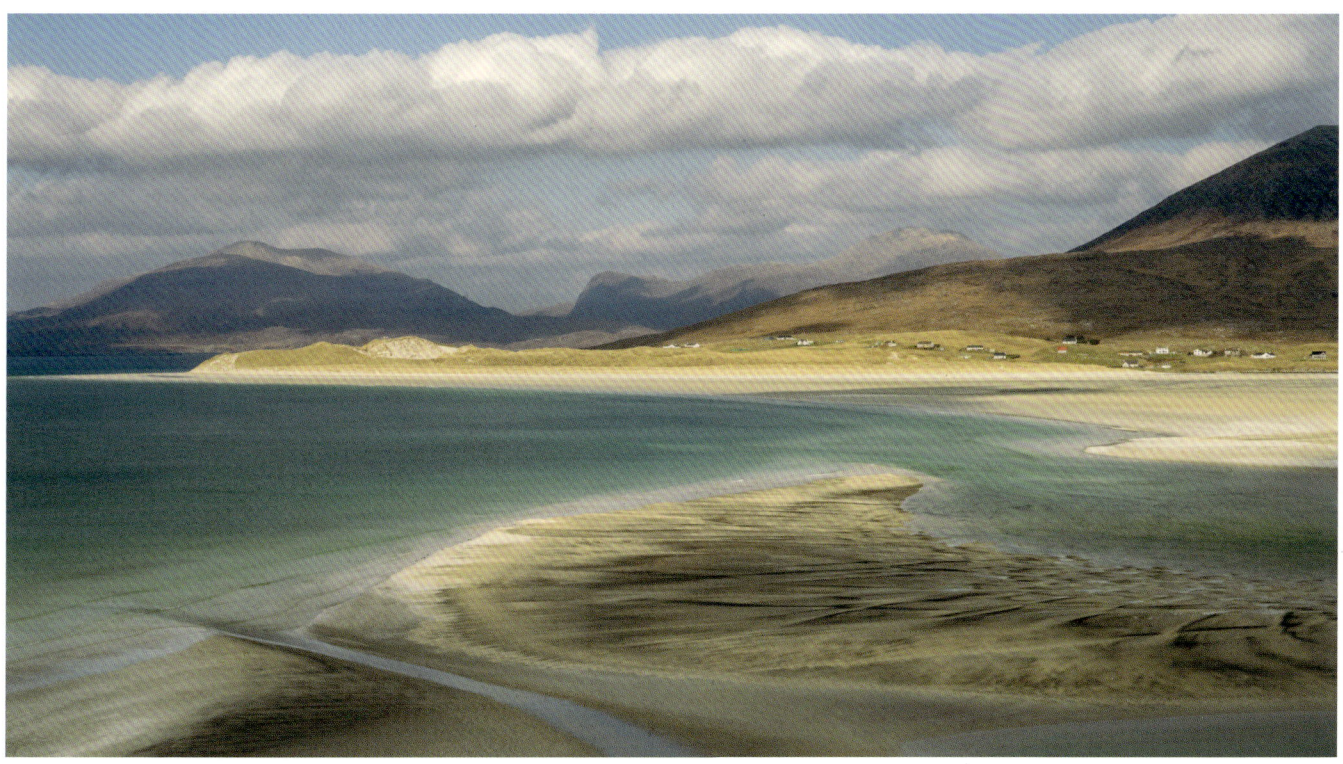

◄ HORTON TOWER

Long lens compression helps simplify the landscape, allowing you to neatly place emphasis on your focal point and the shapes, lines, and lighting within the scene.

▲ ISLE OF HARRIS

In this instance, the use of a longer focal length has helped compress this scene into a much tighter, more succinct frame, where all the elements work neatly together. A short telephoto has helped highlight the shapes and layers within the landscape. Isolating detail in this way has also helped compensate for the afternoon light, which lacked warmth and drama.

FLOWERS

We've already discussed the influence of color, and few subjects that occur naturally within the landscape provide more vibrancy than flowers. Photogenic swathes of flowers occur both naturally and due to commercial growth. Flowers—of various size, color, structure, and shape—can be found growing in meadows, along coastal cliff tops, carpeting woodland, and at altitude with a mountain backdrop. They not only add color to landscapes, but interest, depth, and texture as well. They provide an obvious entry point to wide-angle compositions and flowers can also help to convey a seasonal message.

Typically, spring and summer are when flowers are at their peak. For example, in parts of Europe, bluebells carpet ancient woodlands in their millions, while the super bloom in the deserts of California occurs once every decade. Spectacular displays of flowers can be found almost anywhere in the world. Some flowers don't open fully until the sun is high in the sky, while others will follow the sun's path to stay facing the light. Therefore, timing is essential—flowers are often close to their vibrant best in late afternoon light, for instance. Closely monitor progress by making repeat visits to landscapes where flowers are the key feature and plan your shoot for when the conditions and the blooms are at their most suitable.

A polarizing filter is essential for shooting flowers in the landscape. The filter will reduce glare radiating from petals and foliage and help you record strong, vivid colors.

COMPOSITION

Flowers can either act as an entry point to the landscape beyond, or provide the main focus for your shot. The grandeur and impact of a wildflower landscape can be greatly diluted if your composition isn't carefully structured and thought through, though. Camera height, orientation, and perspective are all important considerations, and to help you identify just the right shooting angle it can be worthwhile working handheld initially. This will give you added freedom to quickly and instinctively explore various viewpoints unhindered. Once you've tried different angles and focal lengths, you can then assess results before setting up a tripod to closely replicate—and carefully refine—the composition that you feel works best.

FOCUS ON...
WHERE TO FOCUS
WITHIN THE LANDSCAPE

When you include close-by foreground interest—for example, flowers—and wish to record them sharply, together with their background, you need to think carefully about where you focus. With such a large zone of focus, you cannot afford to waste any available depth of field. Roughly speaking, depth of field extends one third in front of your point of focus and two thirds beyond it, so if you focus too close or too far away, you are wasting some of it. However, for every focal length and aperture combination, there is one distance that will maximize the depth of field in your shot—the hyperfocal distance. There are hyperfocal distance charts or apps you can use to help you calculate the optimum distance for your camera—sensor size affects the calculation. However, while the theory is sound, in practice this mathematical formula is outdated and not always reliable.

Arguably, a better and easier method to apply is called double-distance focusing. It is a focusing technique designed to distribute the available depth of field relatively evenly throughout the image rather than prioritize foreground or background sharpness. Simply, identify the closest point within the scene that you wish to record sharply, estimate how far away this point is, double it, and focus this distance away. For example, if you have a foreground boulder in your shot that is two yards away, focus at four yards. This is a more reliable and easier to apply technique than calculating the hyperfocal distance. Admittedly, this approach still relies on a degree of guesstimation, but even if you slightly misjudge the distance, results still tend to be very good. You can apply the double distance principle regardless of the focal length and aperture in use, although there is an assumption here that you will be using mid to small f/stops to generate good depth-of-field.

If you are unable to generate sufficient depth of field through your combination of aperture and point of focus, consider focus stacking instead (see page 134).

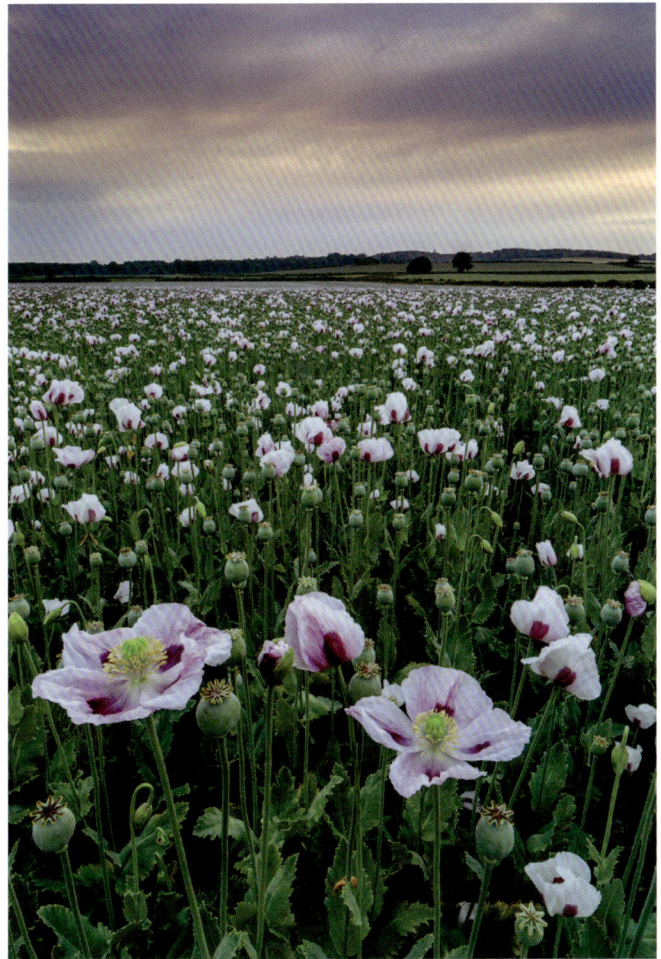

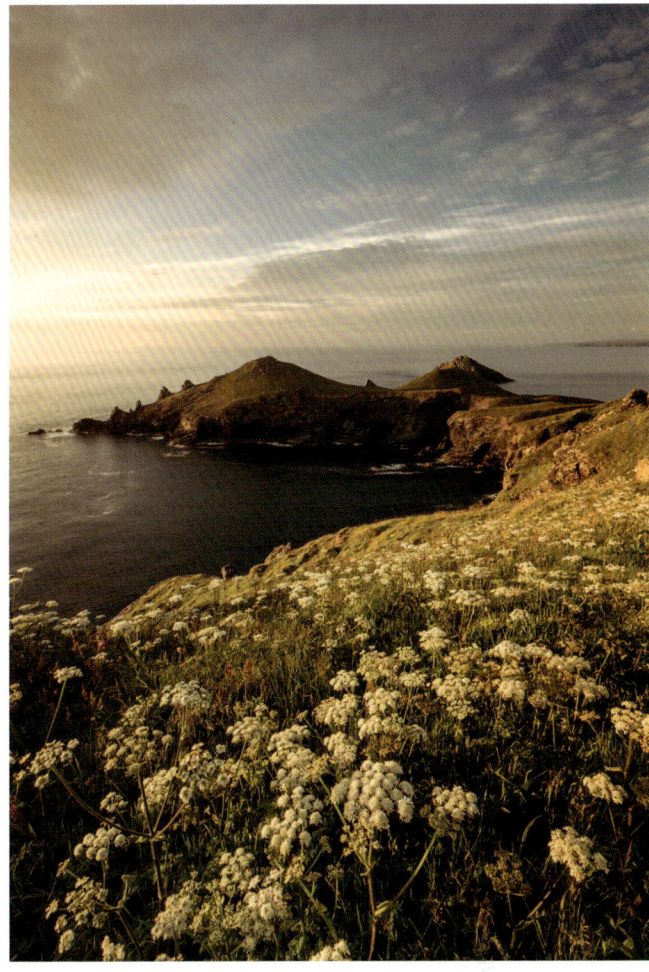

▲ OPIUM POPPIES

Flowers are fragile and delicate things and easily wind-blown. Any wind motion will grow more exaggerated the larger and more looming they are in the frame. Unless you want to creatively blur subject motion, it is best to take photos on windless days when flowers are perfectly still. Therefore, monitor the weather forecast closely and time your visit when the conditions are most suitable.

▲ COASTAL FLOWERS

Flowers can provide great foreground interest and an introduction to the landscape beyond. Wild flowers—such as thrift, bluebells, heather, and alpine flowers—not only add a splash of color to the landscape, but scale and context as well. Often, only a wide-angle view will do justice to this type of natural spectacle.

Simplicity is often best in landscape photography. Combining two or three key colors within the frame, rather than a much larger combination, will often prove more pleasing to the eye. Therefore, look to isolate areas where just one or two species of flower dominate. With smaller flowers, try getting close to them with a wide-angle lens to help make foreground blooms look larger and more impactful in relation to their surroundings. Tilting your camera slightly downward will help ensure the emphasis remains on your foreground subjects, not on the sky. Moisture will often enhance the vibrancy of flowers, helping to make colors appear more intense. Therefore, shooting after rainfall—when blooms and foliage have been washed clean—can be a good ploy.

CORE TECHNIQUE
USING POLARIZING FILTERS

As we outlined in our preparation chapter, a polarizer is a must-have filter for landscape photography. They are most useful during daytime while shooting sunlit landscapes. Therefore, afternoon shoots are as good a time as any to put the filter to use. Its ability to combat subject glare and reflections and saturate the color of clear blue skies makes it an essential piece of kit for outdoor photography. But photographers are often unsure as to how to use the filter most effectively.

Polarized light can cause ugly glare and reflections and reduce the intensity of a surface's color, diminishing a photograph's vibrancy and overall impact. The only way to reverse the effect is using a polarizing filter at the time you trigger the shutter. However, that is not to say this is a filter you should keep permanently fixed to your camera. The filter absorbs a degree of light—up to two stops—so shutter speed is lengthened when using one. While this can be desirable if you wish to blur subject motion, it is less so if you are shooting handheld. Therefore, if you wish to maintain a fast enough shutter speed to prevent camera or subject motion, it is probably best to keep the filter off.

There are other issues to consider. It is possible to over-polarize a scene. The effect is most obvious on clear, cloudless skies, particularly at higher altitudes. If you always rotate the filter to achieve maximum polarization, blues can grow too dark, saturated, and inky. When using almost any filter, the goal is normally to achieve natural-looking results—the use of a filter shouldn't be obvious. Therefore, scrutinize results and check that your skies look natural. Remember that the polarizing effect can look very seductive through the viewfinder or on your camera's monitor, but the most pronounced effect will not always produce the best results. You may find you need to reduce the level of polarization, by adjusting the filter in its mount, to achieve a natural-looking result.

Polarizers won't benefit every scene, but you will be surprised how many they do enhance. They are great for restoring natural color saturation in woodland (see page 68) and rural scenes containing lots of reflective foliage. They will remove the sheen from water, making it appear darker, deeper, and more saturated. A polarizer will also help eliminate ugly reflections and reduce the brightness of specular highlights on the water's surface.

The filter is most effective when used at a 90° angle to the sun—"Brewster's Angle"—but if your composition falls at this angle, it should be coincidental rather than a conscious choice. The effect of a polarizer can be subtle or substantial. If you are ever unsure if the filter might enhance a scene or not, simply pop it on the lens—or hold it out in front of your eye—and twist the filter to see what it does. The technique is straightforward: rotate the filter until you achieve the effect you desire—there is no great science involved.

Slimline designs—like LEE Filters' Landscape Polarizer—are a good option for wide-angle photography, as the thinner mounts reduce the risk of the filter causing vignetting. You can buy polarizing filters that either fit directly onto your lens or that are compatible with a filter holder (see page 18). We would recommend the latter, as it makes it easier to combine the filter with other filter types, such as grads or solid ND filters.

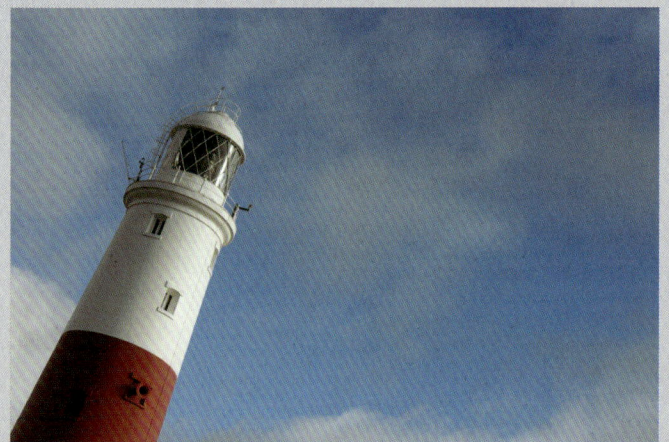

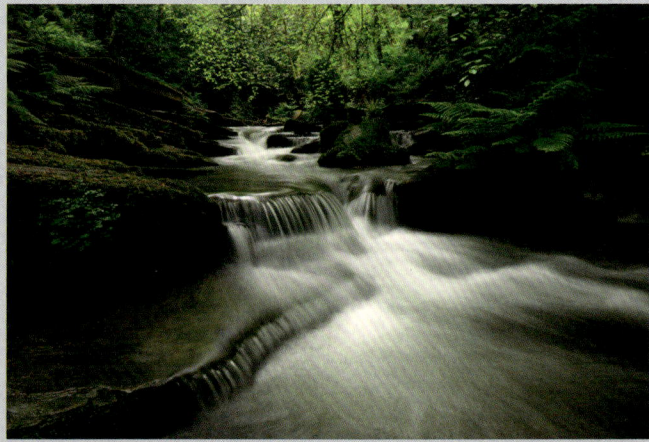

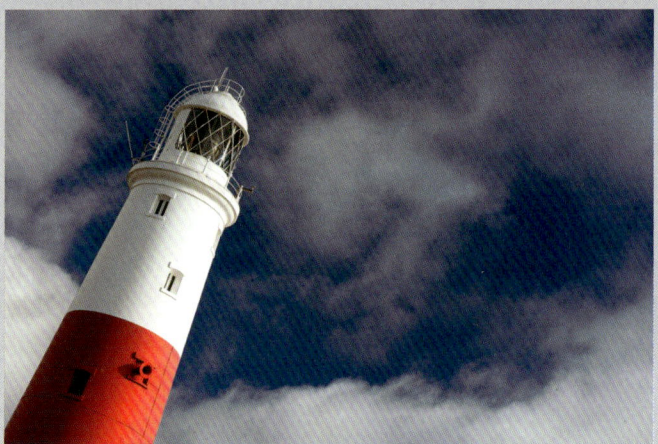

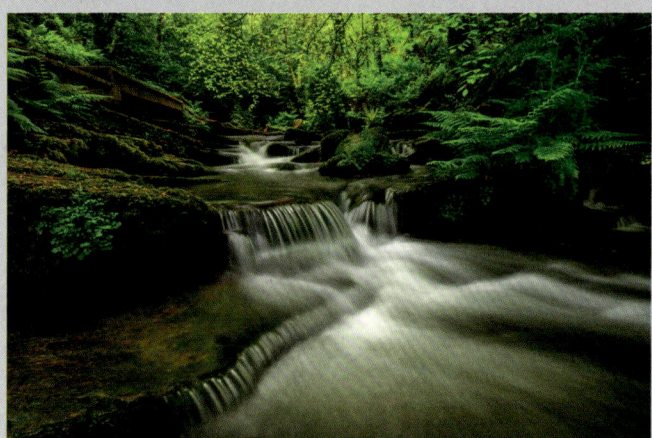

▲ POLARIZER COMPARISON

The polarizing effect can be substantial, enlivening blue skies and adding natural color saturation to landscapes. A polarizer can give images life, punch, and added depth. This simple comparison of a shot of the lighthouse without (top) and with (bottom) a polarizer helps illustrate the difference such a filter can make.

▲ SPRING WATERFALL

Many photographers will only attach a polarizer when confronted with scenes boasting blue skies or reflective water—the most obvious subjects for this filter type. However, as this comparison helps to illustrate, a polarizer's effect (bottom) on woodland scenes—or any landscape containing water or shiny, reflective foliage—can be substantial. In this instance, the filter has restored natural color saturation, increased contrast, and reduced the sheen from the foreground water.

COMPOSITION
LEAD-IN LINES

One of the best ways to give a two-dimensional image a three-dimensional feel, or depth, is to use lead-in lines—a visual trick that draws the viewer's eye into the frame and directs it through to the middle ground, or far into the distance.

You can achieve this visual illusion by using perspective creatively. Our eyes tend to instinctively look for, and follow, lines—a trait landscape photographers can consciously take advantage of by including them thoughtfully within compositions. The landscape is full of strong shapes and lines—both artificial and natural. Rivers, paths, roads, crop lines, hedges, breakwaters, jetties, and shadows are just some of the examples of lines that can be found in the landscape. Some lines are less obvious, though, and they can even be incomplete or implied. For example, if you include a person or animal within the shot, we instinctively tend to follow the direction of their gaze, while a trail of rocks or boulders can act like stepping stones, leading the eye into the photo. You will quickly begin to recognize the many potential types of lead-in lines.

Our choices of focal length and viewpoint can help to create or exaggerate lines. Wide-angle lenses will distort perspective, stretching and exaggerating the size of nearby objects, lines, and angles. Don't be afraid to go wide and get close to foreground objects to manipulate perspective creatively. However, a large depth of field is often required to do this, so select a small aperture in the region of f/11 or f/16 and focus carefully to maximise front-to-back sharpness. If this still doesn't suffice, you could consider focus-stacking (see page 134) to artificially extend the depth of field.

Lines don't have to be perfectly straight to lead you into an image or direct you to a certain focal point. Regardless of whether a line is vertical, converging, diagonal, zigzagged, wavy, curved, or S-shaped, its effect will be similar—encouraging the viewer's eye into the frame and creating the impression of depth. Diagonal lines, in particular, are considered powerful, while curved lines and arcs are gentler and more flowing. Converging vertical lines are particularly photogenic, creating a vanishing point and an almost unrivaled sense of depth.

So, examine the landscape closely and look for lines and shapes that you can include to lead the eye through your photos to convey depth and dynamism.

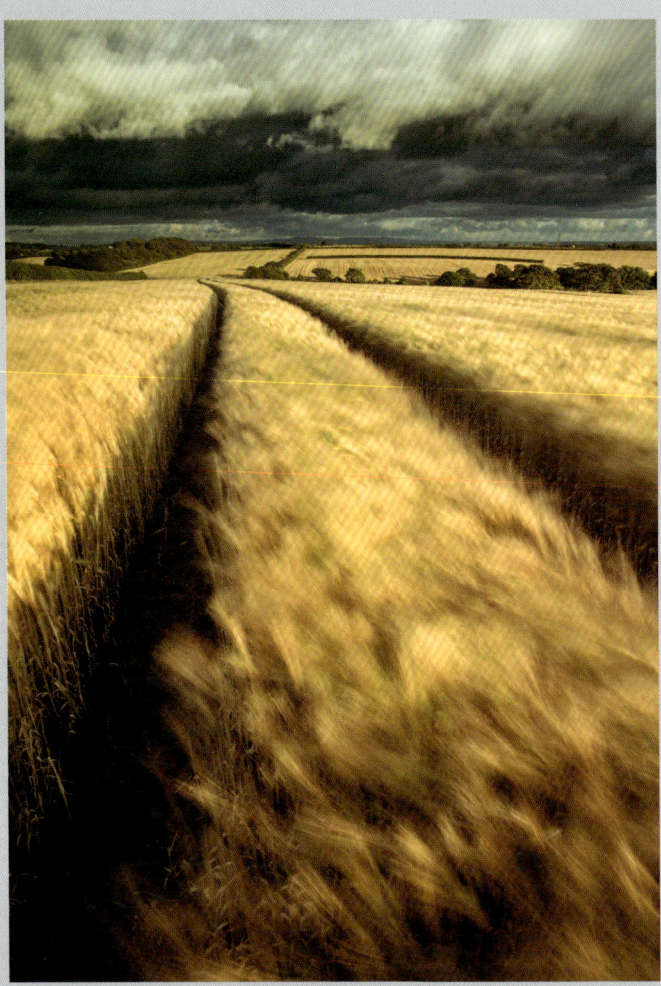

▲ **BARLEY FIELD**
The crop lines in this image provide a compelling lead-in, directing the eye through the landscape from the foreground to the middle distance and beyond. Lines leading from (or close to) the corners of a frame tend to provide added visual impact.

FOCUS ON...
VANISHING POINTS

A vanishing point occurs when elements within the scene appear to diminish in size the further away they are. The theory behind vanishing points is closely related to linear perspective and how the eye judges distance—lines and planes seem to narrow and converge as they get progressively further away. Anything with parallel lines works well. A road, railway track, bridge, walkway, river, or the plow lines in a field are examples of the type of things to look for. If you place objects like this so that they are leading away from the camera, into the distance, they will ultimately appear to converge in the photograph, even though they do in fact remain parallel. Photographers can exaggerate the effect by getting close to foreground lines and, using a wide-angle, stretch the apparent distance between nearby and distant objects. Camera height also has an influence. The lower the shooting angle, the greater the level of convergence. A vertical composition tends to emphasize lines and the feeling of depth and height. Ideally, lines receding into the distance will lead to a point of interest, like a building, figure, tree, or mountain peak.

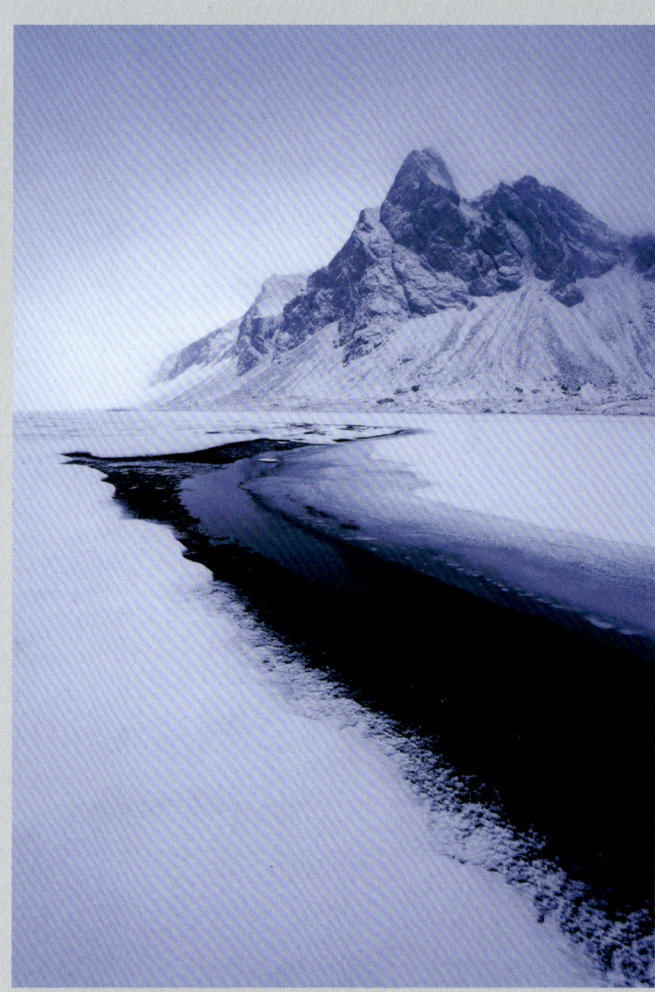

▲ EYSTRAHORN

I took this photograph in Iceland just after lunch while snow was still falling. Due to the extreme windspeed, I had to shoot handheld—a tripod would not have stayed upright. Although I had to compose my image speedily, the waterline provided a strong and obvious lead-in line with virgin snow contrasting starkly with the black beach. A wide-angle lens and vertical perspective enhanced the foreground shapes.

POST-PROCESSING STEP-BY-STEP
CONTRAST

Contrast is a term used to describe the difference in either brightness or color that defines a scene or object. Low-contrast images tend to have little or no highlight and shadow areas and will typically appear flat or soft; whereas high-contrast images display a full range of tones, from black through to white, and look more punchy, colorful, lifelike, and dramatic. Contrast is a very important ingredient—greatly influencing our perception of the landscape, texture, mood, and lighting. Contrast is particularly important to black-and-white images—without color separation, tonal contrast is the overriding method for adding impact and interest.

It is important to understand that not all photographs benefit from a full range of tones. Some scenes—for example, misty landscapes and seascapes shot in overcast conditions—are naturally low in contrast and you rarely want to add a lot of contrast to a shot if it didn't occur naturally. However, Raw files—which have no in-camera processing applied—often lack contrast straight out of the camera. Shots taken by exposing to the right (ETTR)—a technique used less frequently these days—are also light and bright (with the majority of tones skewed to the right of the histogram) and therefore lack contrast. Therefore, unless your aim is to produce a low-contrast result, your landscape shots

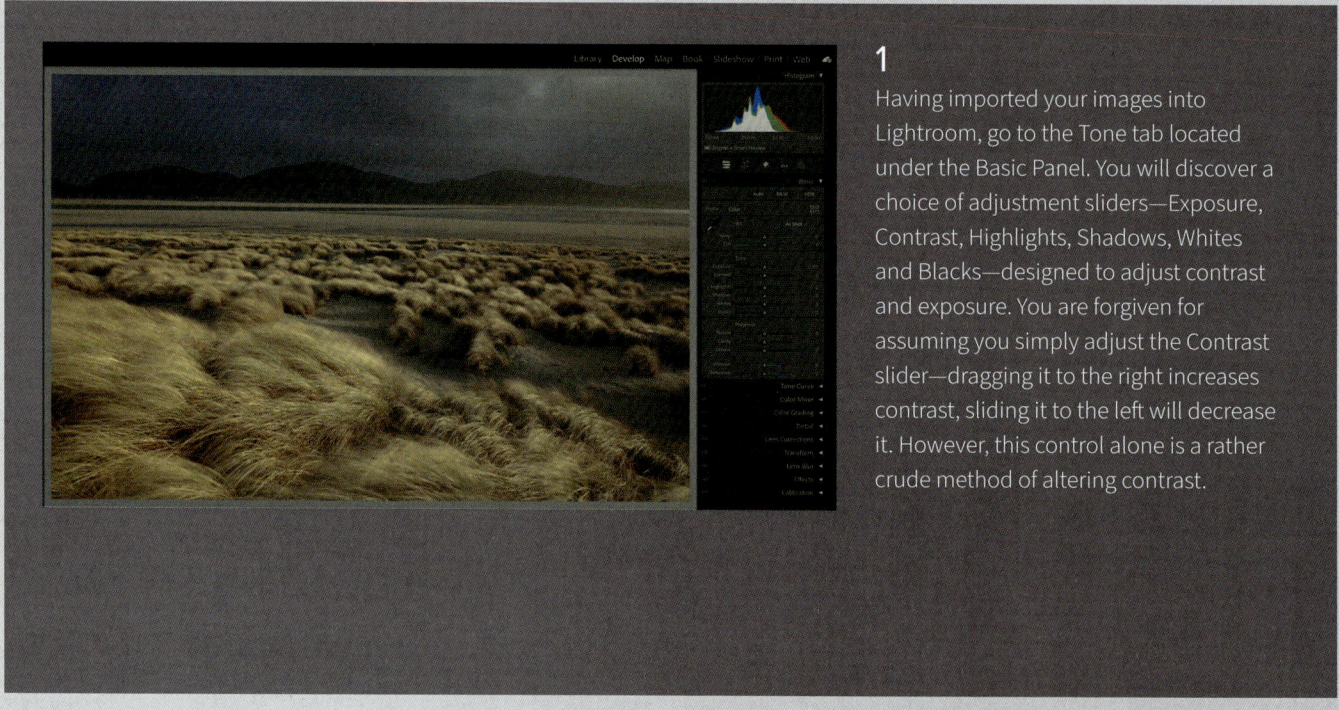

1

Having imported your images into Lightroom, go to the Tone tab located under the Basic Panel. You will discover a choice of adjustment sliders—Exposure, Contrast, Highlights, Shadows, Whites and Blacks—designed to adjust contrast and exposure. You are forgiven for assuming you simply adjust the Contrast slider—dragging it to the right increases contrast, sliding it to the left will decrease it. However, this control alone is a rather crude method of altering contrast.

will only fulfill their potential when you apply a suitable level of contrast during Raw conversion—otherwise, your images will look flat, lifeless, and desaturated instead. For this reason, one of the first things you should do when you post-process a file is set your black and white points. Doing so will apply global contrast to your images—it is one of the most fundamental steps in post-processing a landscape photograph.

Setting your black and white points to achieve a natural degree of contrast is something you should do to practically all your shots, regardless of the time of day they were captured. All Raw converters will allow you to do this, but for this demonstration

we've opted to use Adobe Lightroom. Any gaps between the right and left limits of the horizontal axis imply the shot lacks a full range of tones—as is the case with this image of Luskentyre beach, shot on a winter's afternoon.

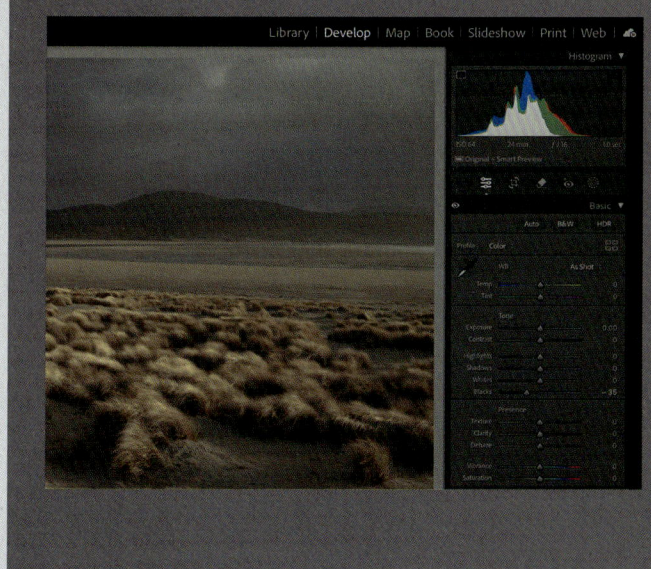

2

It is best to set your black and white points before making any other adjustments to exposure. To set the black point, move the Blacks slider to the left, close to the point just in front of the beginning of the histogram. If you hit Shift and double-click the Blacks (or Whites) slider, Lightroom will set the point automatically. However, this tends to be slightly more aggressive with the setting than if you adjust the slider manually. Instead, we recommend that you set the point intuitively on a shot-by-shot basis, increasing the Blacks as far as possible without clipping the deepest shadow.

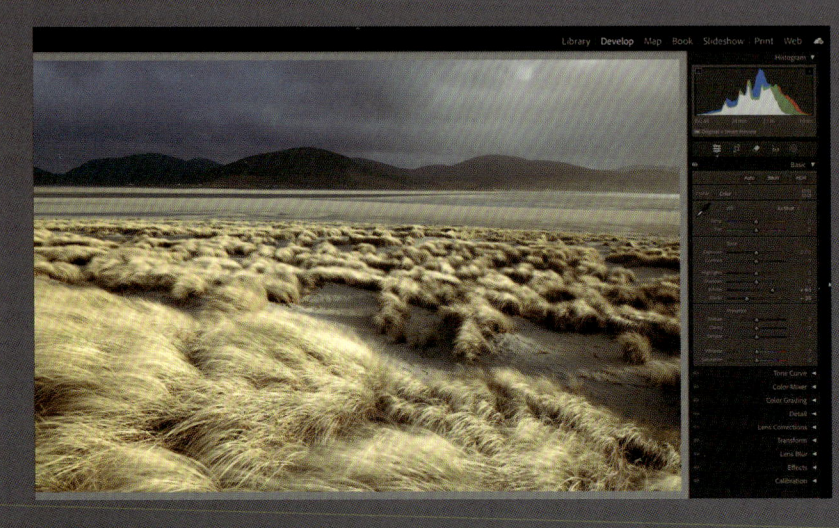

3

Now do the same with the Whites slider, dragging it to the right as far as you can without clipping highlights. You can get an onscreen preview of any clipping by pressing and holding the Option/Alt key as you drag either the Blacks or Whites slider. When adjusting Whites, the screen will turn black and any areas that start to clip will appear in white. You can also activate Lightroom's clipping warning by clicking on the triangular-shaped icon in the top corners of the histogram box. Any clipped highlights will appear overlaid on your image. When this occurs, back off slightly until any clipped areas have completely disappeared. You have now set your white point.

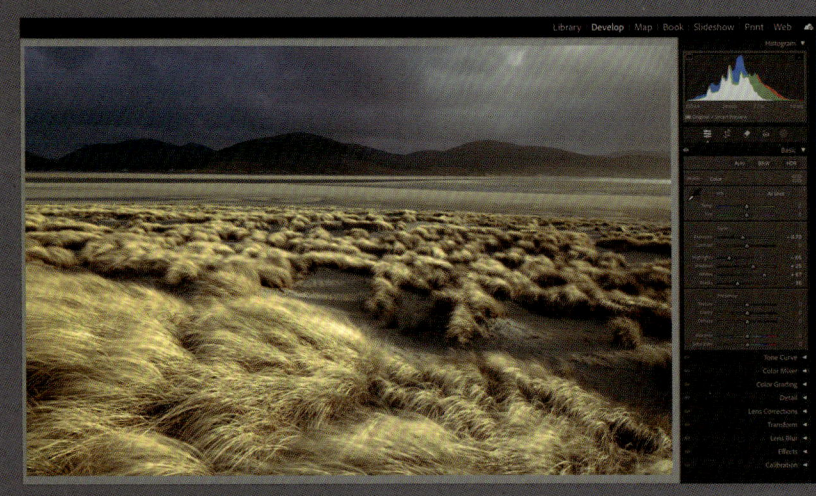

4

With some images, setting the black and white points might be all you need to do to achieve natural-looking contrast and exposure. However, in this instance, the image looks too light. You can adjust overall exposure by moving the Exposure slider, or changing the brightness of Shadows or Highlights using the appropriate sliders. In this example, I dragged back Exposure to create a darker, more authentic and dramatic result. Overall contrast is much improved compared to the original unprocessed Raw file.

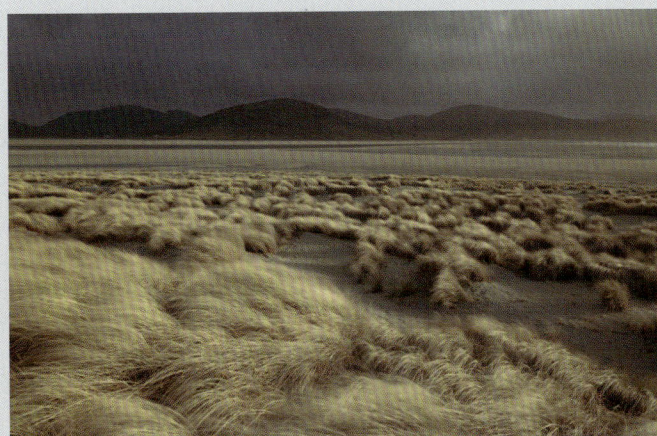

FINAL IMAGE

Having used the Tone tab to make global adjustments to contrast, you might then decide you need to apply more localized or selective adjustments to contrast—similar in principle to how photographers dodge and burn prints in a traditional darkroom. Masking, Adjustment Brush, Radial Filter Tool, and Graduated Filter Tool in Lightroom all allow you to make more precise adjustments to specific areas of the image. There are also Dodge and Burn Tools in Photoshop. You may also wish to refine color temperature and increase Vibrance or Saturation to create the more visually pleasing result.

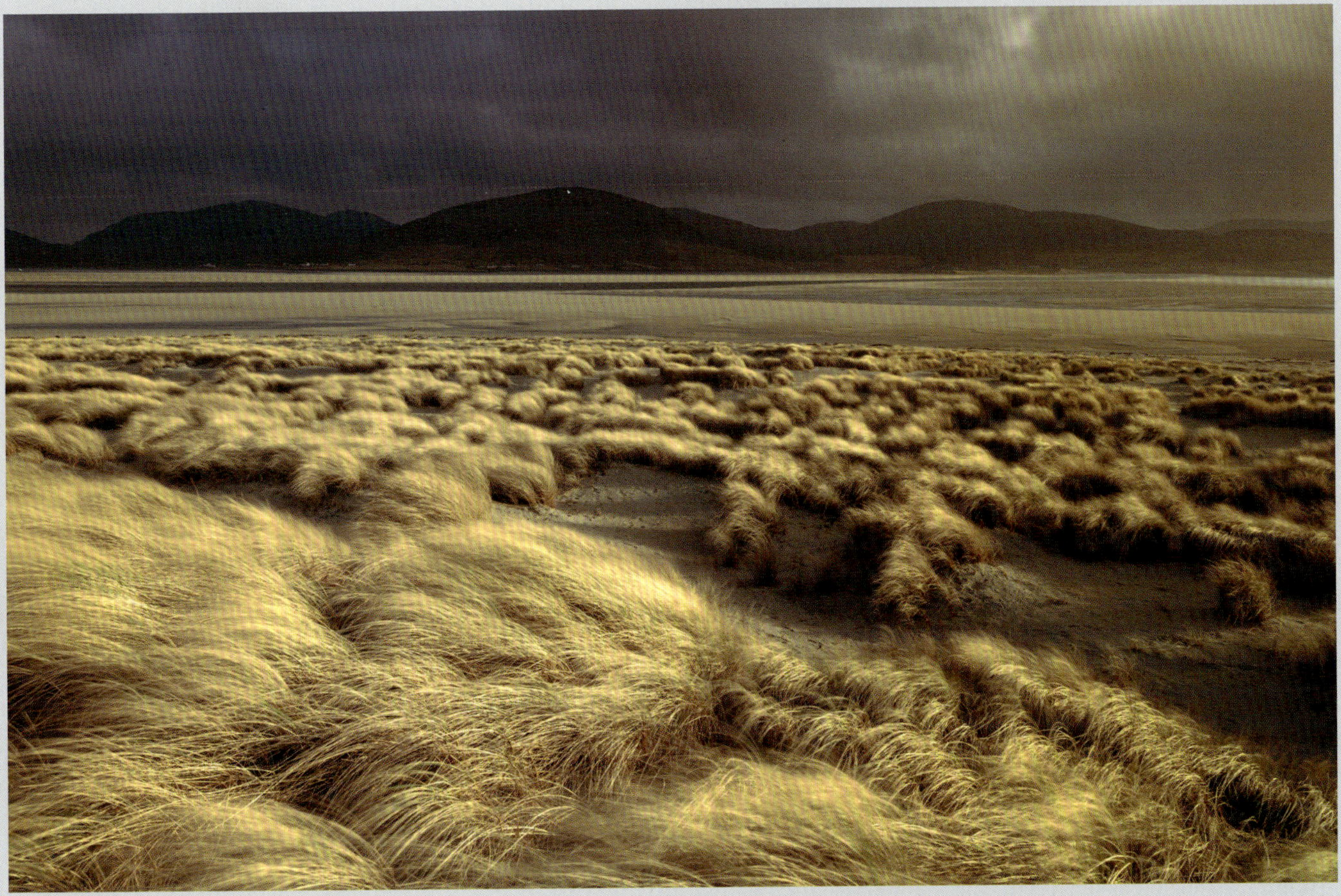

▲ FINISHED

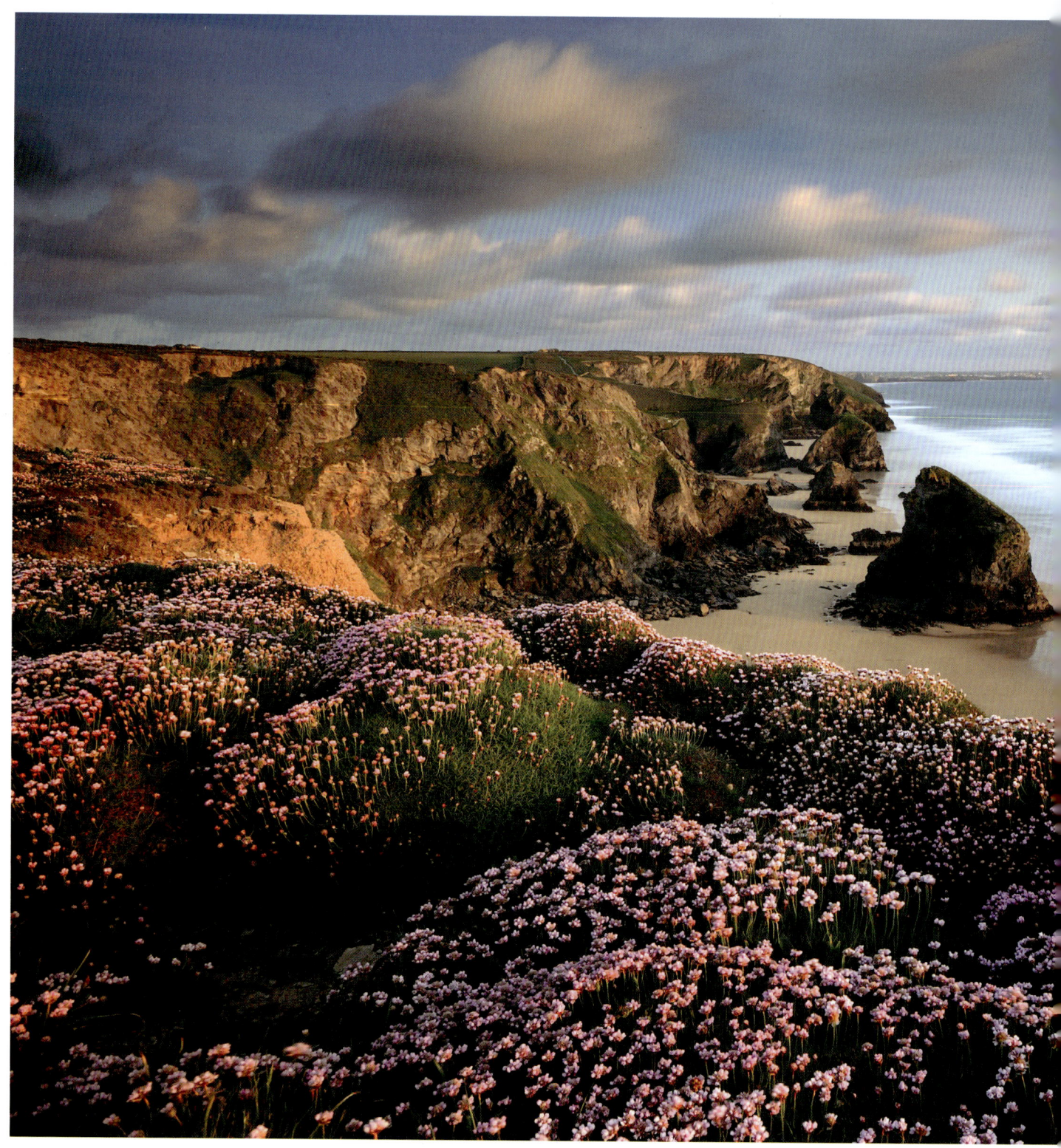

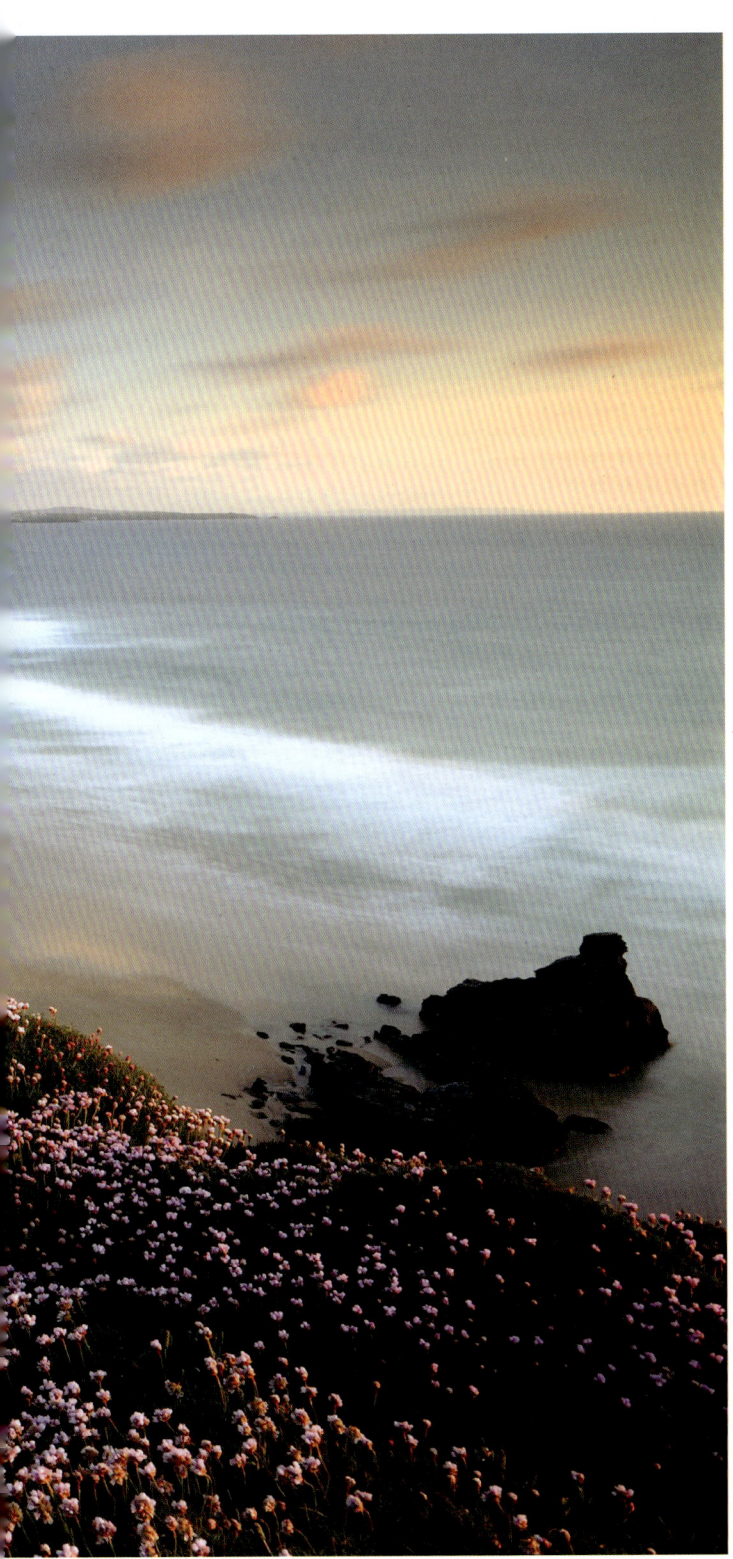

FINAL SHOT

Photographer **Ross Hoddinott**
Location **Bedruthan Steps, Cornwall, United Kingdom**
Time and date **6.38 p.m., May 13**
Camera **Nikon D700**
Lens **AF-S Nikkor 17–35mm f/2.8D IF ED (at 19mm)**
Filtration **Polarizer, 2-stop hard ND grad, 6-stop ND**
Exposure **ISO 100, 30 sec. at f/13**

THE STORY

"I live in Cornwall and know its rugged, impressive coastline well. An intimate knowledge of an area is hugely advantageous for landscape photography—it helps you make good, informed decisions on where to go, depending on the time of day, season, and also the weather. I already knew that parts of the Cornish cliff tops were covered in flowering thrift in spring. Flowers make great foreground interest and add a welcome splash of color as well. With the sun to the right of me, attractively side-lighting the cliffs, I knew a polarizing filter would have a strong, positive effect on the scene. So, I attached one with my LEE Filters system, and twisted the polarizer in its mount until the blue sky deepened in color and the passing clouds appeared more defined. I also attached a solid ND filter to extend exposure time and creatively blur the motion of the incoming waves. Although the late afternoon light wasn't yet golden, the light's quality was good. The result proved to be a vibrant, impactful shot boosting depth and interest. It was a satisfying finish to what had been a very enjoyable and productive afternoon's photography."

CHAPTER FIVE
DUSK

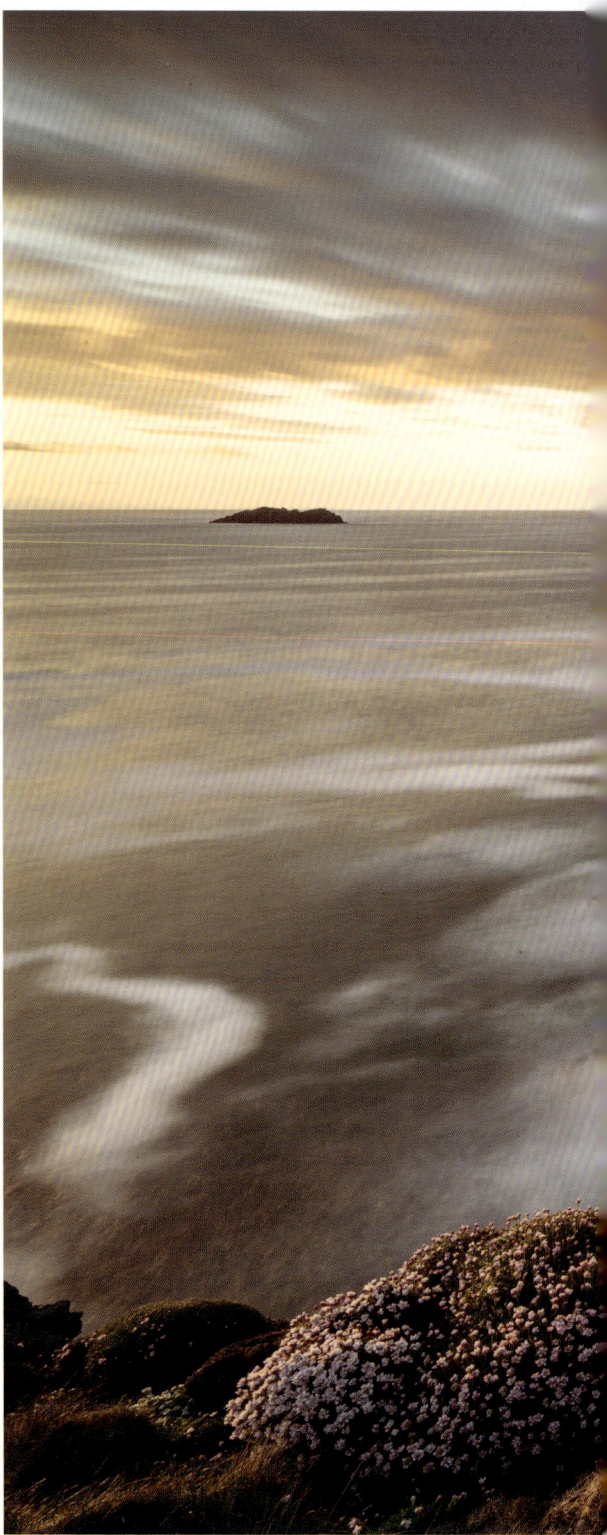

As the sun dips toward the horizon, the light's color and quality visibly improve. This is the "golden hour"—the time many landscape photographers consider to be the "business end" of the day, and those last, precious minutes of daylight are not to be wasted. Golden evening light is similar in look and quality to morning light, but many photographers prefer it—it is a more sociable time of the day for a start, and you can comfortably reach your viewpoint and set up in daylight, rather than in semidarkness.

Light quality steadily builds and improves before sunset, allowing you to identify and perfect your composition, knowing that the light is gradually getting better—not worse, as it is in the morning. In other words, there is less pressure when shooting in the evening than there is in the morning.

Late evening is often characterized by rich, gorgeous, horizontal light casting long shadows that shape and define a landscape. This light is typically warm and will illuminate and highlight clouds from below. Arguably, sunset is the pinnacle of a landscape photographer's day, so be organized, ready to react to changing light and conditions, and make the most of this golden opportunity.

▶ **LAST LIGHT**
Landscape photographers tend to be far more conscious and aware of the light's quality and warmth than non-photographers. We can feel the excitement and anticipation build as sunset approaches and the light grows warmer, softer, and more photogenic. Is there a better time of the day to take photos than the moments close to sunset?

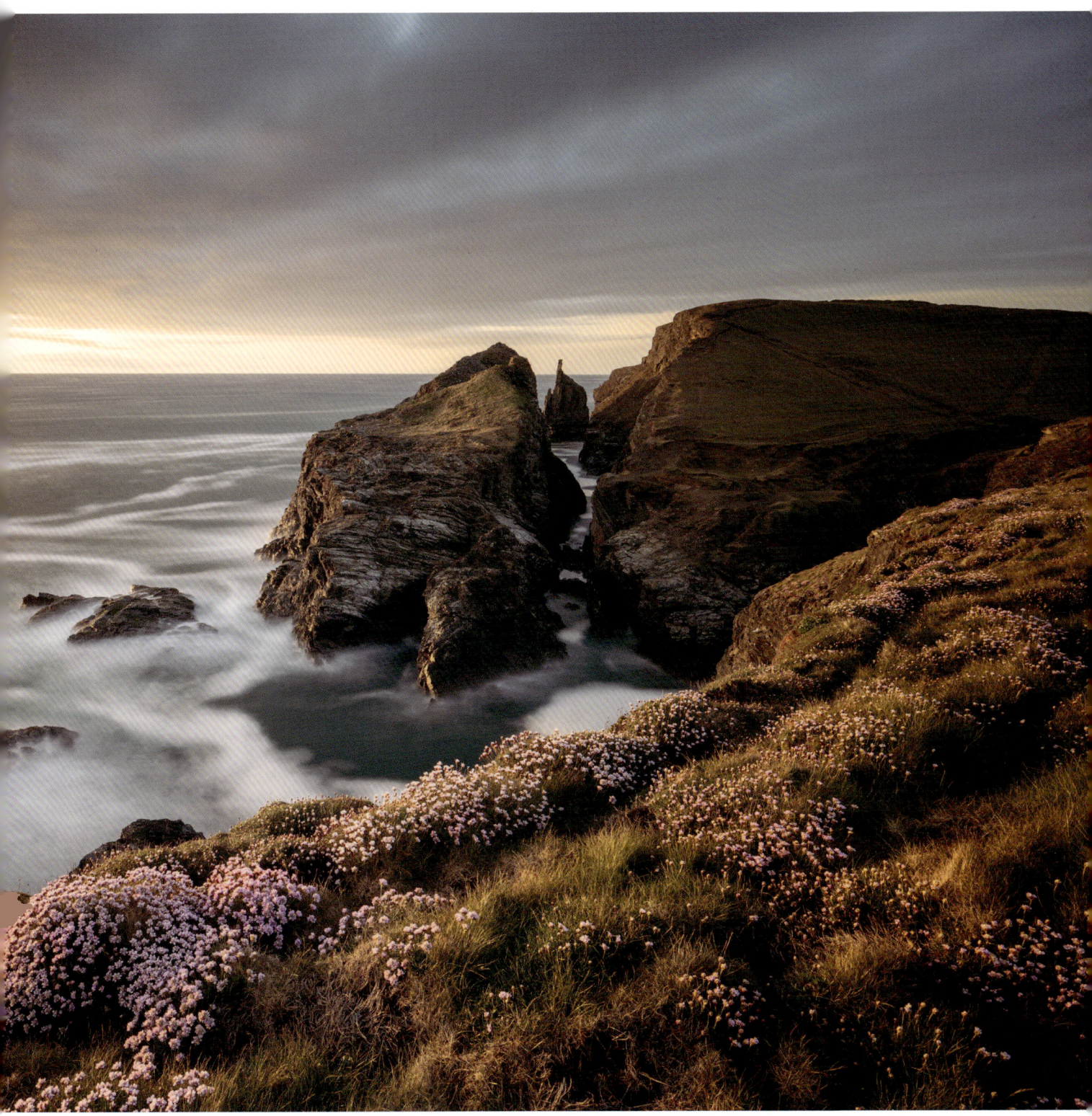

SUNSET

We've already covered "golden hour" photography in the Dawn chapter (see page 50). As the light's quality and warmth are very similar in the evening, we risk repetition if we discuss how you approach evening light in any great detail. The main difference between shooting in the evening, as opposed to in the morning, is the ability to watch and observe the light and conditions build. Therefore, as long as you give yourself sufficient time before sunset to get to the location and in position, there is generally less pressure or rush. You have some leeway for error, being able to alter your viewpoint or even location if there is any unforeseen problem—for example, maybe you've misjudged the sun's position, or another photographer has beaten you to the best spot. Not only can you set up in full daylight, but you are fully awake and alert—something that can't always be said during those early dawn shoots! This is often a very special, productive time of day. It is important you stay out late and capture those golden rays of sunlight preceding sunset. If you need reminding of the "golden rules" for golden hours, flick back to page 51.

Instead of focusing on golden light, let's skip forward to the sunset itself. Understandably, this is a favorite time for landscape photography. There is something magical about watching the sun kiss the horizon. The sun's color changes as it passes through more of the Earth's atmosphere. The bluer wavelengths of light get scattered away, typically leaving the reddest wavelengths to reach our eyes and giving the setting sun more color and glow. By the time the sun touches the horizon, it has in fact already set—it is only due to the way the atmosphere bends light (with a refraction in the region of 0.6°) that we are still able to "see" the sun. Unfortunately, many landscapes don't provide an uninterrupted path to the sun, so our view of sunset (or sunrise) is often obstructed. Photographing sunset over the ocean (see page 130) will often provide the best view and conditions.

Understandably, sunset can prove very seductive to landscape photographers. However, care needs to be taken. It would be a mistake to seriously compromise or alter an otherwise strong, well-constructed composition in an attempt to include the setting sun within your shot, or believe a red ball of fire will somehow make your shot great. Sunset images should be as equally well thought through as any other landscape—the setting sun itself should be just one contributing element to the image's success. While a stunning sunset will undoubtedly enhance an already

FOCUS ON...
REVERSE GRADUATED FILTERS

Reverse grads are more specialized and less commonly used than standard graduated ND filters, but the principle is very similar. These filters are tailored specifically for sunrise and sunset shoots. As the name suggests, reverse grads are lighter at the top of the gradient and increase in density toward the center. They typically feature a hard-edged transition to the clear part of the filter below. They are designed like this to cope with scenes where there is a very bright, intense band of light on the horizon. In situations like this, a standard ND grad can struggle to hold back the brightest highlights close to the horizon (where the sun is rising/setting), while also making the sky at the top of the frame look artificially dark. A reverse grad typically produces more natural-looking results in these types of scenarios and can prove a good addition to your kit bag. The likes of Hitech, LEE Filters, and NiSi produce them. However, with particularly challenging, high contrast scenes—where you are shooting directly toward the sun—exposure blending may well prove the better option.

▲ **REVERSE GRADUATED FILTERS**
Various manufacturers produce reverse graduated neutral density filters, which can be extremely useful for controlling the light at sunset and sunrise, when it is at its brightest near the horizon. Unlike standard grads, they are at their strongest on the horizon and fade away gradually to the top of the filter.

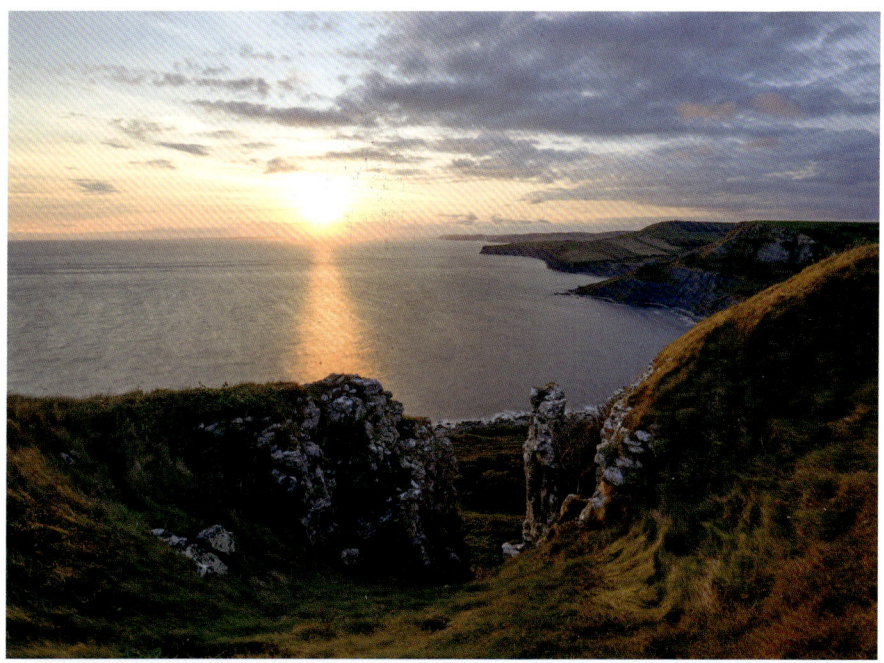

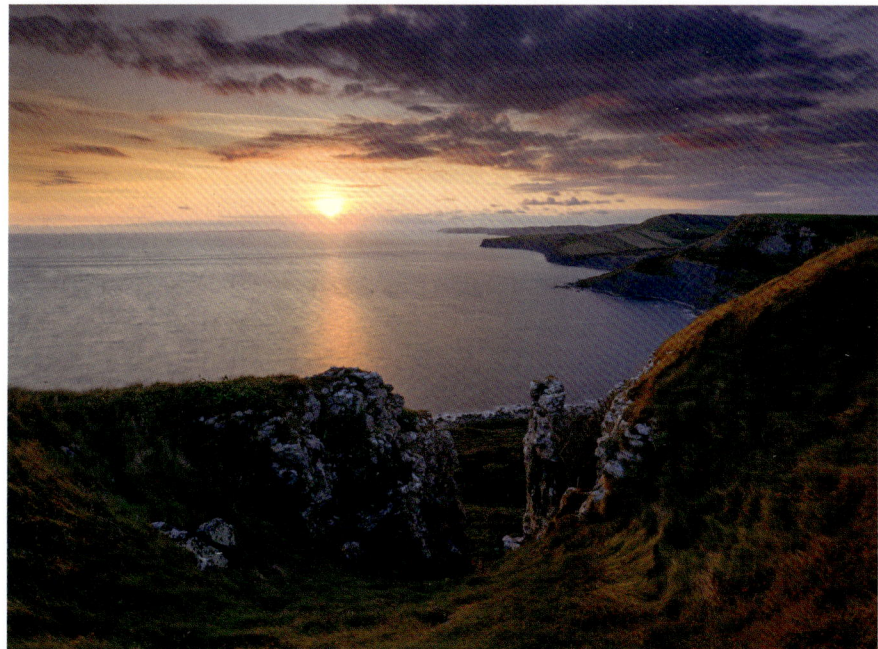

▲ REVERSE GRAD COMPARISON

In shooting situations where the horizon is particularly bright—typically just after sunrise or before sunset—a reverse graduated ND filter can be the best option (bottom). Unlike a standard ND grad, the filter is at its strongest in just the right area and it won't darken the sky toward the top of the frame artificially. The comparison illustrates just how effective these filters are.

strong scene, it won't disguise a poorly constructed shot, devoid of depth, foreground, or direction. If you wish to capture great sunset images, you need to be in the right place at just the right time, having planned and researched your viewpoint in advance, using some of the skills and apps outlined in this book. Sunset itself is brief and the color in the sky before and following may often only last for a few minutes. Therefore, if you are not set up, ready, and anticipating a great sky, you will miss the opportunity, plain and simple. In truth, a spontaneous "grab shot" of a colorful sky will rarely prove very successful. The best sunset images are the result of planning and then multiple visits to a location to find just the right conditions.

The biggest frustration with sunset photography is that it is impossible to ever truly predict a great sunset. In fact, they can be few and far between. Clear, cloudless weather will produce boring skies with little color or drama, while if there is too much cloud, the sun will vanish long before it has a chance to light up the sky. Typically, mid-level and high clouds are your friends, together with a gap toward the horizon. This is when the longer wavelengths of red and yellow light (that occur due to the sun's low angle in the sky) can illuminate the higher cloud from beneath. A forecast suggesting around 40–60% cloud cover is often promising. However, you should also check what the clouds are doing in the distance. After all, the sun won't be setting in your exact location —ideally you want clear skies a few hundred miles to the west (or east at sunrise). Air quality can also influence sunset. Clear air is very effective at scattering blue light, enhancing the likelihood of warm, colorful skies. Lower humidity tends to produce more vibrant colors too, while higher humidity tends to mute color due to the extra water content in the atmosphere.

Although, regretfully, photographers can never truly anticipate the occasions when the sky turns red and magical, by studying forecasts and weather conditions you will certainly maximize your chances. Apps are available, like SkyCandy, which are specifically designed to predict colorful skies. They certainly help, but ultimately a little luck is always involved when dealing with the unpredictability of Mother Nature. It is no coincidence, however, that the more often you place yourself in the right place at the right time, the luckier you will get!

One of the biggest technical challenges with sunset photography is contrast. While the sun is still very bright and intense, the level of contrast will often be too great, even with the aid of grads. Instead, it is better to wait for the sun to drop (or be diffused by haze or cloud), or alternatively alter your composition

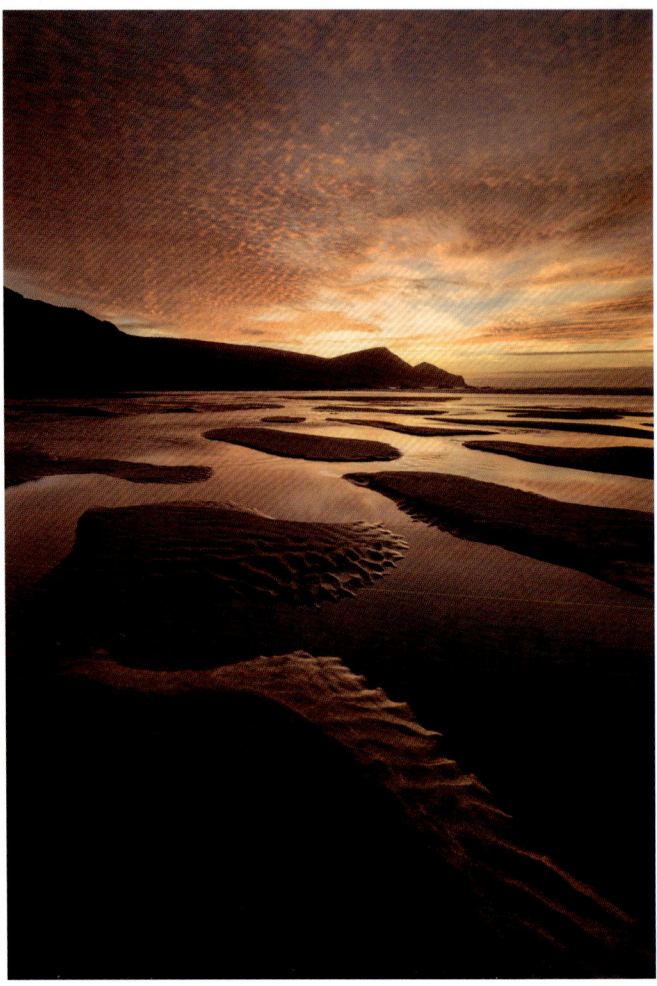

▲ DON'T PACK UP TOO EARLY
Often the best color in the sky will occur after sunset, and a good "afterglow" can linger for up to 30 minutes after the event, spreading across the sky and creating magical, moody conditions. Color can appear unexpectedly sometimes, so be patient and wait—there is nothing more frustrating than packing up too early and getting back to your vehicle just as the sky lights up.

to exclude the sun from the frame until the sun is closer to setting. During sunset, skies can be bright and colorful, but the landscape below is now in semidarkness, typically creating contrast beyond the camera's ability to capture it unaided. To achieve correct exposure throughout the scene, blend different exposures together (see page 60) or attach a graduated ND filter—typically with a density of either two or three stops. In very high-contrast

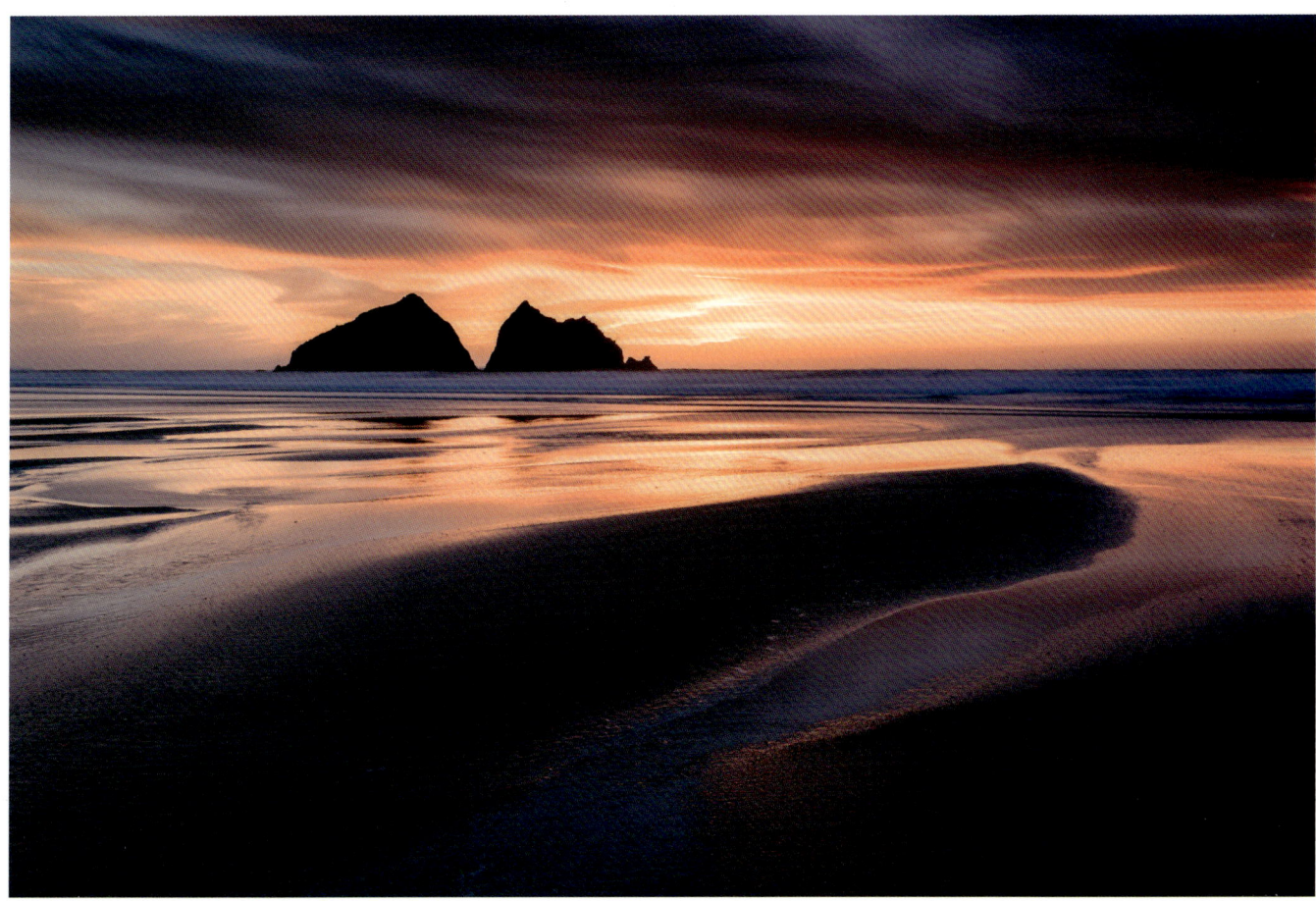

situations, you might even need to combine grads to balance the light, but this is not ideal. Soft grads will often be ineffective for sunsets, as they are at their weakest where you need the grad to be at its strongest—on the horizon. An alternative filter for sunset images is a reverse grad (see pages 126–127). Remember, colorful skies can fool Auto White Balance into neutralizing the lovely warm tones you wish to capture. Either switch to your Daylight or Cloudy preset, or correct and adjust during post-processing. Shutter speeds grow naturally long at sunset, so avoid using extreme ND filters—shutter length will grow impractically and unproductively long and you risk wasting the best of the light and conditions. Instead, consider using lower-density NDs if you still want to creatively prolong exposure, for example, three- or four-stop versions.

A colorful or dramatic sky will often provide a fitting backdrop for a strong silhouette subject and also prove a grand finale to your day's photography. Enjoy the moment.

▲ SILHOUETTE AT SUNSET

If you shoot toward sunset, you will effectively silhouette anything sandwiched between the bright sky and your camera. Silhouettes can create images with impact and appealing simplicity. Select subjects that remain instantly recognizable as an inky outline—for example, buildings, trees, landmarks, and rock stacks. To create a silhouette, expose correctly for the brighter sky and remove any graduated filter you might have been using previously.

COASTAL SUNSETS

The coast is an exhilarating place to be. It is a varied, ever-changing landscape—wild and rugged, with endless mood and motion. It provides space and opportunity to be creative. It is a seductive landscape type that—unsurprisingly—has a habit of luring photographers back time and again. But how exactly do you capture great images of the sea at this time of day?

Potentially, the coast is a great place to visit with your camera at any time, but there is something special about shooting the sun setting over the sea. Preparation is important (see page 26). Calculate the sun's position in advance to ensure you visit a coastal location that is west-facing or will benefit from the light, glow, and color of the setting sun. Remember, there can be a significant difference in the sun's position between winter and summer. Also before you go, check relevant tide times (see page 30). This is important from both a safety point of view, and also in order for you to predict how much of the beach will be exposed—some coastal views work better at either a high or low tide.

It is often easier (and safer) working with a receding tide and by doing so you also know you will always have a clean beach to photograph, free of footprints. The other advantage of a receding tide is that sand and rocks will be wet and glossy. As a result, they will reflect light and color, adding sparkle and interest to the foreground of your seascapes. Wear waterproof boots so you can work close to the water's edge, which is typically where the best action is, but always take care and avoid placing either yourself or your kit at risk in any way.

We've previously discussed the role and importance of foreground interest in landscape photography. Rocks and boulders, tidal pools, streams, groynes, sand patterns, and rockpools provide good foreground options at the coast, particularly if you favor a wide-angle approach. However, in situations where you are struggling to identify a suitably strong foreground, consider generating your own foreground interest through your choice of exposure length. On-rushing waves that get channeled between fins of rock, or that wash around rocky ledges and foreground boulders, can add texture and the impression of motion to coastal sunsets.

Length of exposure is important, with a shutter speed in the region of one second often a good option—being just long enough to look creative and intentional, without being so lengthy that detail and interest within the water are too blurred and lost. A degree of trial and error is often required, but once you identify a shutter length that works, try to maintain it. That said, at sunset, light levels are continually dropping, so shutter speeds will naturally lengthen over time. To maintain a specific exposure time, you can increase ISO sensitivity (or adjust the level of filtration). On-rushing waves can look rather messy and chaotic, so it is often better to wait for the backwash—as water drags back around any foreground objects—before you trigger the shutter. Using water motion in this way can really give your seascapes energy and an exaggerated feeling of depth. Combined with a colorful sky and light sparkling and reflecting off the water, this approach can make for truly eye-catching results.

▶ LIGHTHOUSE
To capture coastal sunsets with context, consider an elevated viewpoint from the cliff tops. This will provide a far-reaching view, where you are able to capture a better sense of place. Although it can be tempting to use a longer focal length and focus solely on the sun and color in the sky, doing so can produce rather flat, uninteresting results. Instead, use the setting sun as a compositional aid, placing it within the frame so it forms a pleasing balance with other key elements.

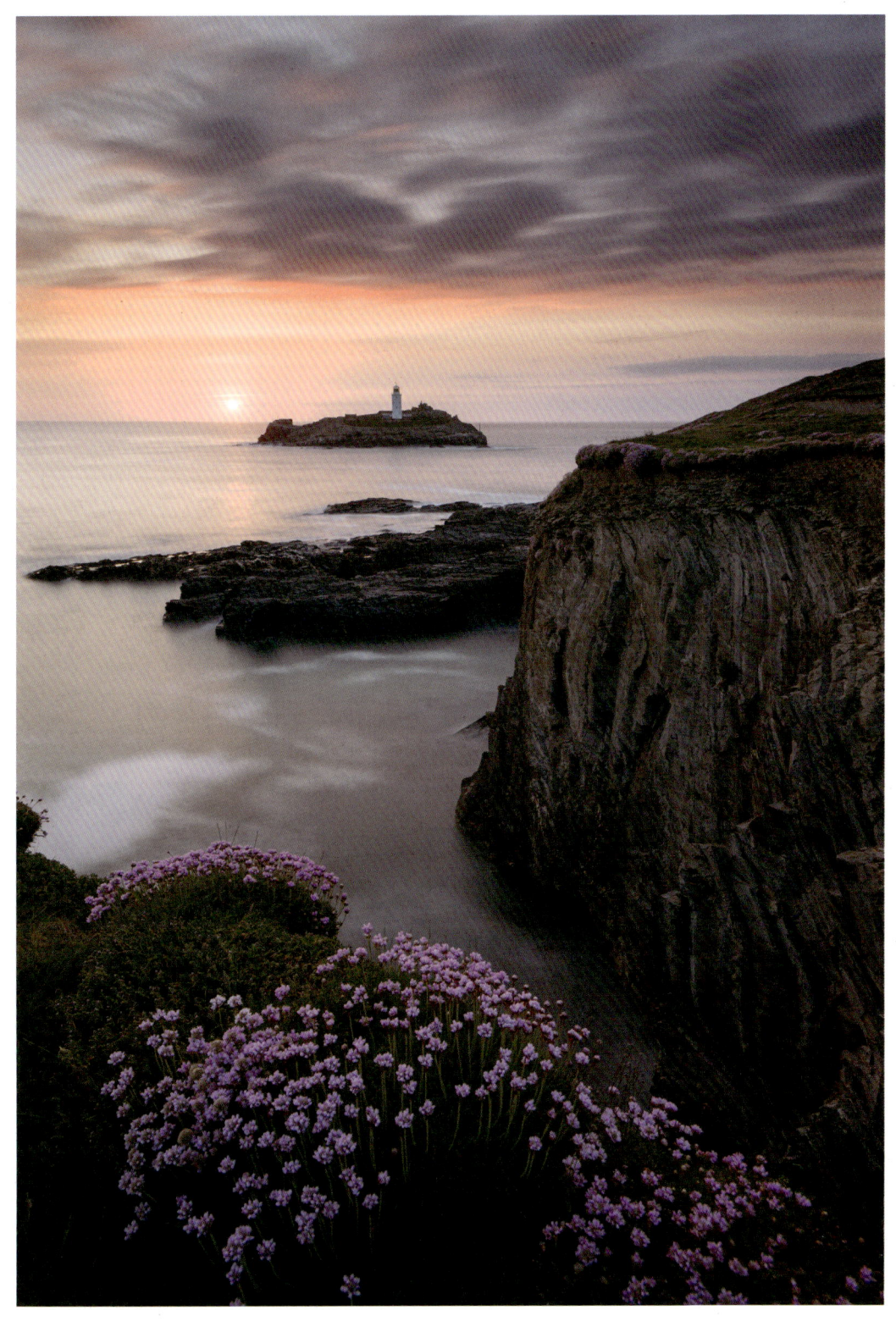

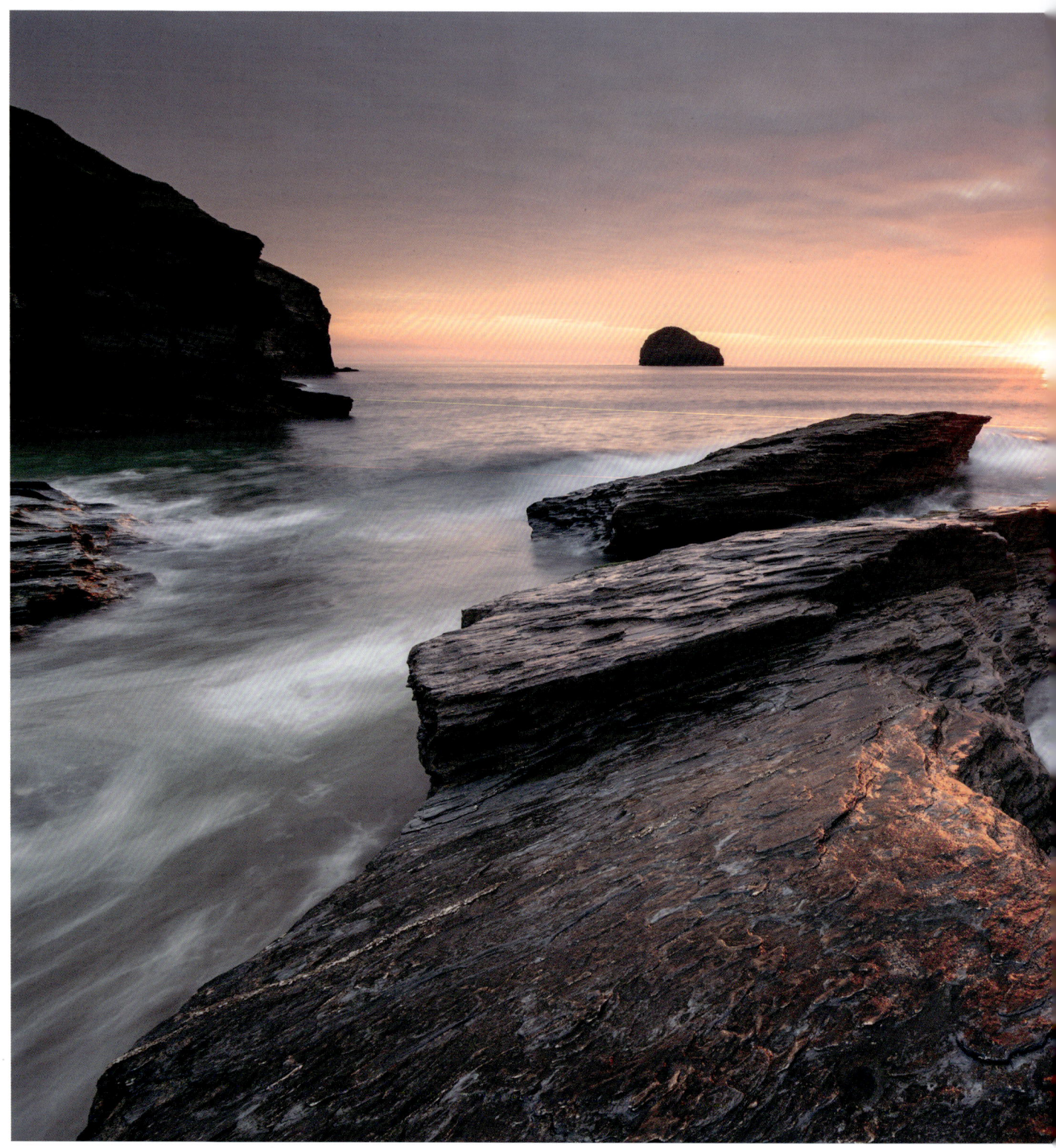

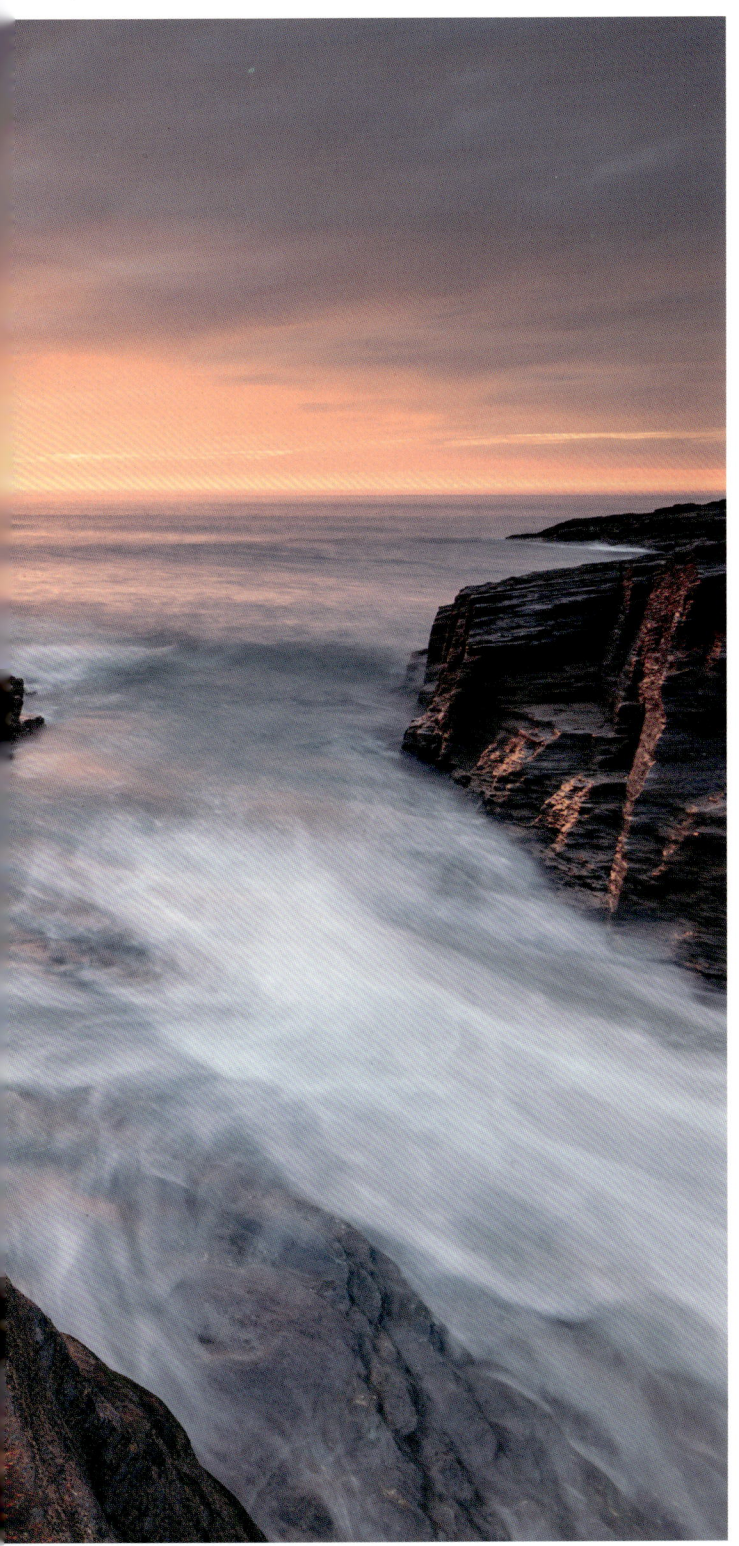

Shooting from beach level will allow you to emphasize light and color reflecting from pools and wet sand, but if you wish to capture coastal images with a greater feeling of context, you are better to shoot from an elevated viewpoint. Cliff-top views tend to be far-reaching and impressive. Once the sun is low in the sky and diffused, include it within the frame as a point of interest, but you may still need a graduated ND or reverse grad to compress the level of contrast within the scene to within the camera's capabilities and record faithful colors.

As the light fades, you may find it best to remove any solid ND filters you might have been using to prolong exposure time, as shutter speeds will grow progressively longer.

Don't pack up too soon, though—the best color can appear after the sun has set and linger in the sky for some considerable time, so you may risk missing some of the most intense, saturated colors and the best mood of the day. By the time you pack away, it can be quite dark, which is why it is important to carry a head lamp (see page 24) to help you safely navigate your way back to your vehicle.

◀ INTO THE LIGHT

There is a risk of flare when pointing your camera toward the light at sunset. When using wide-angle focal lengths and filter systems, the use of a lens hood isn't possible. Instead, when practical, try shielding the lens with your hand or body, or, if the areas of flare are fairly neat and small, you might decide to simply remove flare out of your shot during post-processing using Content Aware, Clone, or Healing tools. When shooting toward the light, any dirt, spray, or moisture on your lenses or filters will be most obvious, so ensure that all your optics are spotlessly clean before shooting.

CORE TECHNIQUE
FOCUS-STACKING

Although it is far from being established as a "rule" in landscape photography, the truth is that the majority of landscape images demonstrate extensive depth of field, being sharp from the immediate foreground through to the horizon. This is not always easy to achieve, however, and usually requires some compromise.

Sometimes, the only way to achieve sufficient depth of field is to stop the lens down to an extremely small aperture such as f/22. Unfortunately, most lenses do not perform very well at such small apertures, due to the effects of diffraction and may show quite significant softening of the image.

Setting the hyperfocal distance (see page 112) is commonly employed to maximize depth of field but the compromise here is that the background is not always critically sharp. The distances usually quoted on hyperfocal distance charts were calculated in the era before high-resolution digital sensors existed and assumed a maximum print size of 10 × 8 inches (254 × 203mm). These days, many photographers routinely print images much larger than this.

The movements available in tilt-and-shift lenses offer the ability to generate much greater depth of field than is possible with normal lenses, but they are expensive and not everyone can justify the cost of such specialist lenses that lack the versatility of autofocus zooms.

Focus-stacking is a technique that can be used with any lens and has the benefit of allowing you to shoot using your lens's "sweet spot"—the aperture (usually around f/8) at which the lens is at its sharpest. It is the blending of several shots, which have been focused at different points throughout the scene, to give a single image that consists of the sharpest parts of each shot, thus ensuring sharpness from foreground to background.

The number of shots needed to create a sharp final image will vary depending on the focal length you are shooting at, the distance from the camera of the nearest object you want to keep sharp, and the aperture you set (although for maximum sharpness this should be at the lens's sweet spot). It is important to ensure that there is no drop-off in sharpness at any point in the image, so there should be clear overlap of depth of field from one image to the next. To achieve this, follow the steps below:

1 Use live view and manual focus or back-button focus. Focus on your closest subject. Shoot.
2 Review the image and identify the point at which sharpness begins to fall off.
3 Return to live view, focus just in front of this point and then shoot again.
4 Repeat steps 1 to 3 until the depth of field reaches infinity.

Many modern cameras feature automatic focus bracketing and some, such as the Canon EOS R7, even stack the images in-camera to create a single image (albeit usually a jpeg) with extended depth of field.

POST-PROCESSING IMAGES

Having taken the images, you will need to blend them. This can be done manually in Photoshop, using layer masks, but with accurate stacking—and provided there is no movement from one image to the next—automated blending is also possible.

FOCUS ON...
SOFTWARE

Dedicated focus-stacking software is available that gives a greater degree of control and also allows you to tether your camera and automate stacking at the shooting stage. Two of the most popular applications are Helicon Focus (www.heliconsoft.com) and Zerene Stacker (www.zerenesystems.com).

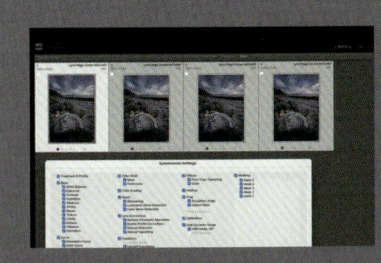

1

Process your images in Lightroom, so that exposure, white balance, etc., are the same across all images —use the Sync Settings feature. With all the images selected, right click and choose Photo > Edit In > Open as Layers in Photoshop.

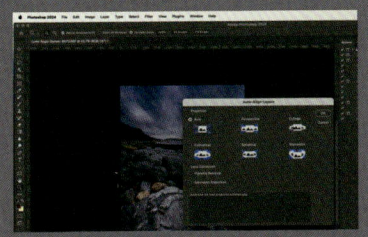

2

The files will open with each image as a separate layer. Select all the layers and click Edit > Auto-Align Layers. In the dialog box under Projection, click on Auto and wait for the layers to become aligned.

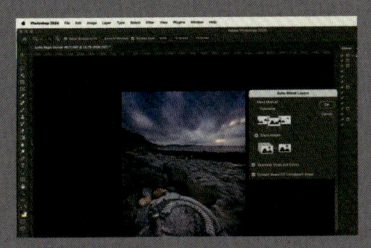

3

Click Edit > Auto-Blend Layers. Check the Stack Images box in the dialog box and click OK. Photoshop will take the sharply focused parts from each layer and blend them to produce an image with enhanced depth of field.

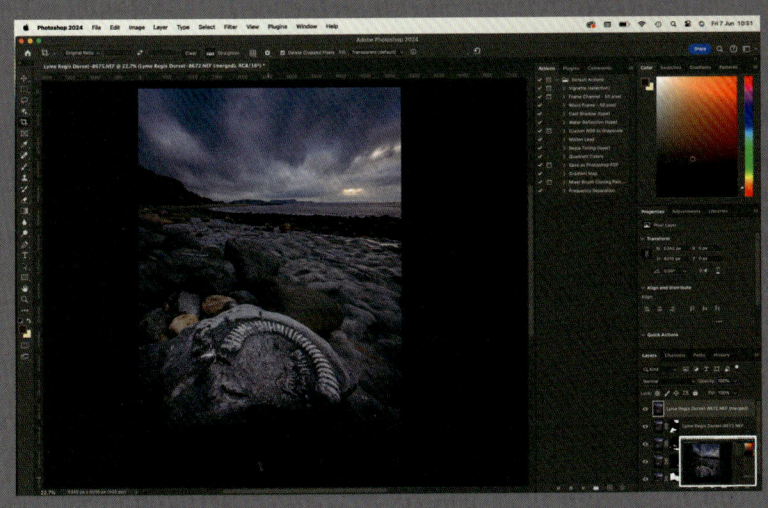

4

Check the image for sharpness throughout. If necessary, crop the image to remove blurred edges, flatten the layers, and then make further adjustments to Contrast, Color Balance, Saturation, etc., if necessary.

COMPOSITION
LENS CHOICE AND PERSPECTIVE

The focal length of a lens determines its angle of view and by how much the subject will be magnified in the frame. The human field of view is approximately the same as a 50mm lens on a full-frame camera (although, in reality, as our eyes constantly scan across scenes, we take in a lot more) and so this focal length is generally referred to as a "standard" lens. Any lens shorter than this is technically a wide-angle and anything longer is a telephoto.

It is often claimed that the focal length of a lens affects the perspective, but technically, this is untrue—the only thing that determines perspective is the distance between the camera and the subject. However, to keep a subject the same size with a telephoto and a wide-angle, you will be forced to change distance from the subject—thus changing the perspective.

The practical upshot of this is that we tend to use wide-angle lenses when we want to enhance linear perspective and telephotos to "compress" perspective. By getting in close to the nearest object in a scene with a wide-angle lens, the distance between the foreground and more distant objects will appear to be quite significant. This creates an impression of depth and enhanced perspective as objects diminish in size the further away they are. Being able to control depth of field is critical when using this technique (see page 58)—there is no point in having a shot with enhanced perspective if only part of the scene is sharp.

On the other hand, if we shoot from further away with a telephoto lens, the apparent distance between foreground and background will be reduced, creating a flatter perspective; the greater magnification of background elements will also make the background appear closer than it is. This apparent compression of the distance between planes in the image is sometimes referred to as the "stacking" effect.

Coastal sunsets are perhaps a natural fit for enhanced depth and perspective—there is usually an abundance of foreground interest and wide-open space in the distance, whereas the rolling hills of rural scenes are perhaps best suited to longer lenses, especially at the end of the day when the layering and stacking effect of telephotos is enhanced by the alternating bands of light and dark created by the low sun.

However, don't let this close your mind to other opportunities. On the coast, longer focal lengths can be used to enhance the layering of ranges of distant headlands, or to make it look as if incoming waves are stacked almost on top of each other. Inland, there is often foreground interest in the form of wild flowers, dry stone walls, and so on, as well as distinct focal points in the background, which will work well with a wide-angle approach.

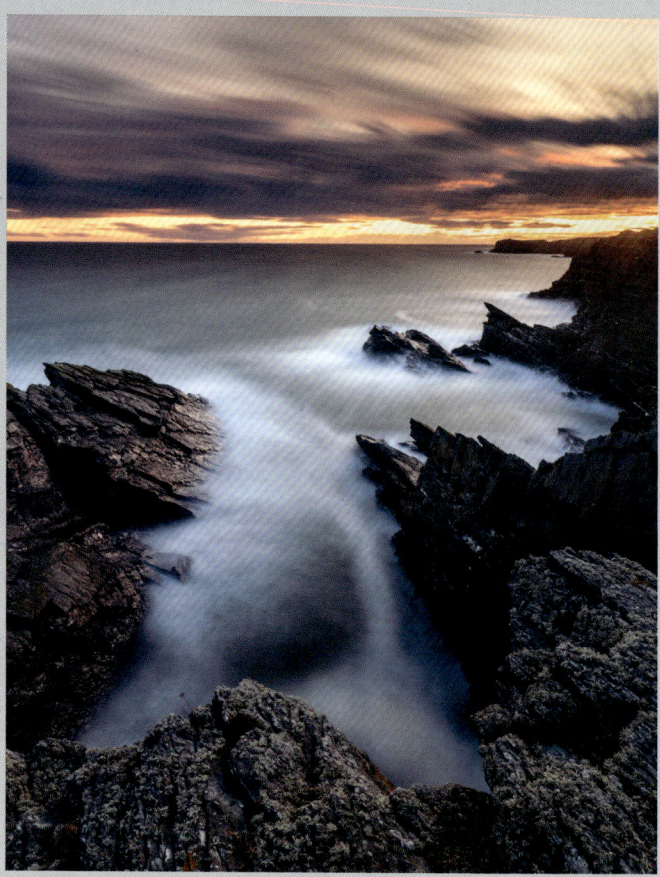

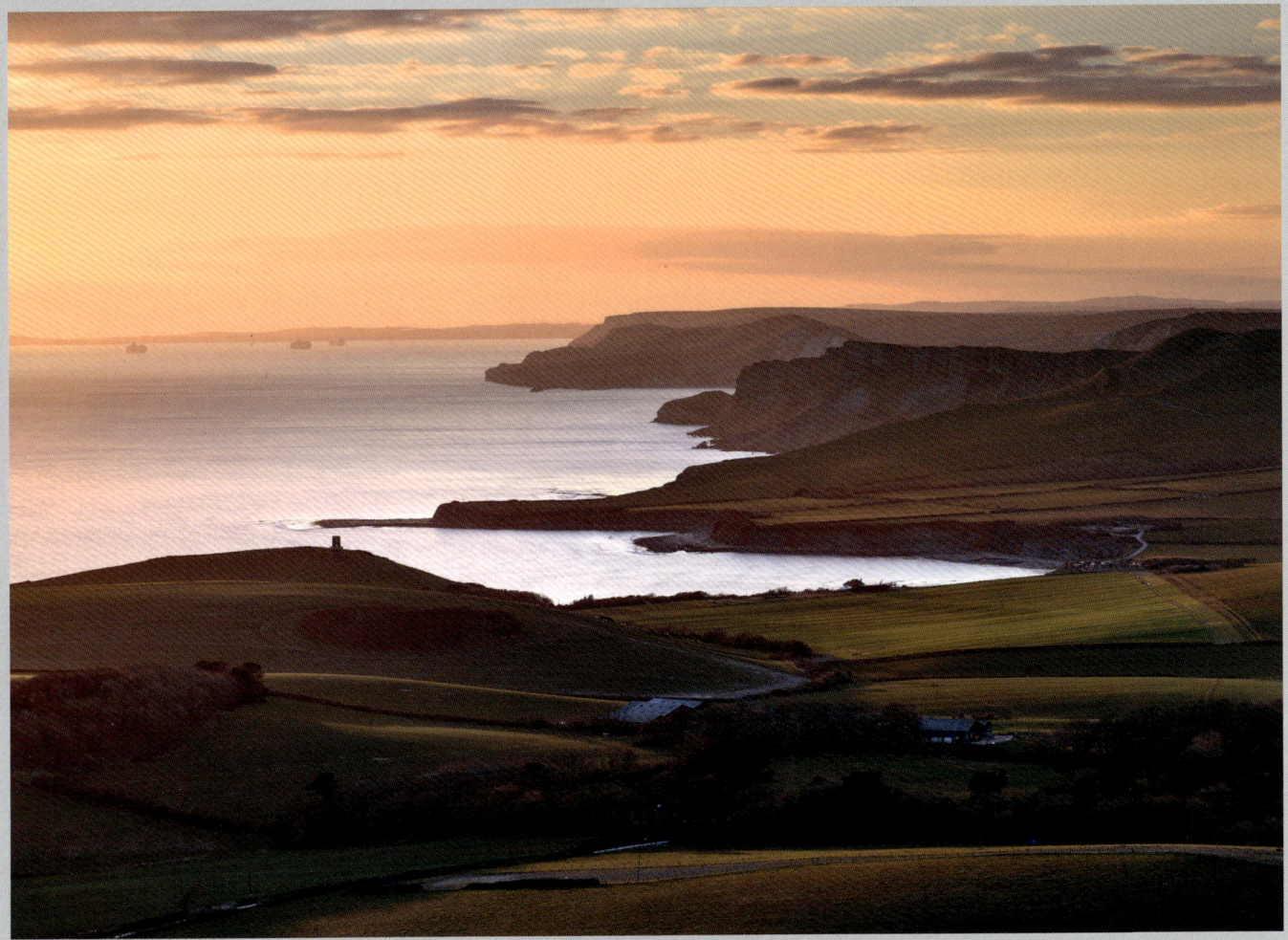

▲ **TELEPHOTO "COMPRESSION"**
Telephoto lenses do not by themselves "compress perspective"—this is a result of the greater working distances usually required when shooting with them. The apparent distance between foreground and background planes is greatly reduced in these circumstances.

◄ **WIDE-ANGLE PERSPECTIVE**
The classic use of a wide-angle lens in landscape photography is to get in close to foreground interest for enhanced linear perspective, with everything stretching out into the distance behind the foreground subject. This is a technique that works especially well with coastal scenes. Careful focusing is necessary to ensure sufficient sharpness from foreground to background; in some situations, focus-stacking (see page 134) may be necessary.

FOCUS ON... TELECONVERTERS

Telephoto lenses contain more glass than wide-angles, which makes them heavier and more expensive. If your existing lenses don't have the reach you need, a teleconverter can extend their length without adding much weight to your bag or costing as much as a new telephoto. There are compromises when using them—they are available in 1.4× or 2× magnification, with a loss of one and two stops of light, respectively. This means, that, for example, when using an f/4 lens with a 2× converter, the maximum aperture becomes f/8—this makes optical viewfinders dark and affects AF performance. Older teleconverters also reduced contrast and sharpness, but the latest models are much improved.

POST-PROCESSING STEP-BY-STEP
STITCHED PANORAMAS

The traditional photographic formats are all relatively (or completely) square: 5:4, 4:3, 1:1, even the 3:2 ratio of 35mm. However, they are quite far removed from how we experience the world, as we tend to scan across scenes, creating a panoramic impression of our location. It could therefore be argued that a panoramic format best represents how we view our surroundings.

For this reason, panoramas have always been popular, and several panoramic film cameras have been produced over the years. This trend has not continued into the digital era, however, which leaves two options: to shoot a single frame with the intention of cropping it; or to shoot a series of images, while panning across the scene, then stitch them together into a single image in post-processing. This will result in a final image that contains more detail than one cropped from a single frame, although care needs to be taken at the shooting stage in order to minimize distortion and create a set of images that will blend together seamlessly.

Specialist panoramic heads are available, but provided there is no close foreground interest in the scene, an ordinary tripod head will do the job. Make sure the camera is level and shoot in portrait orientation to reduce the effects of distortion across the frames. Use manual exposure and meter for the brightest part

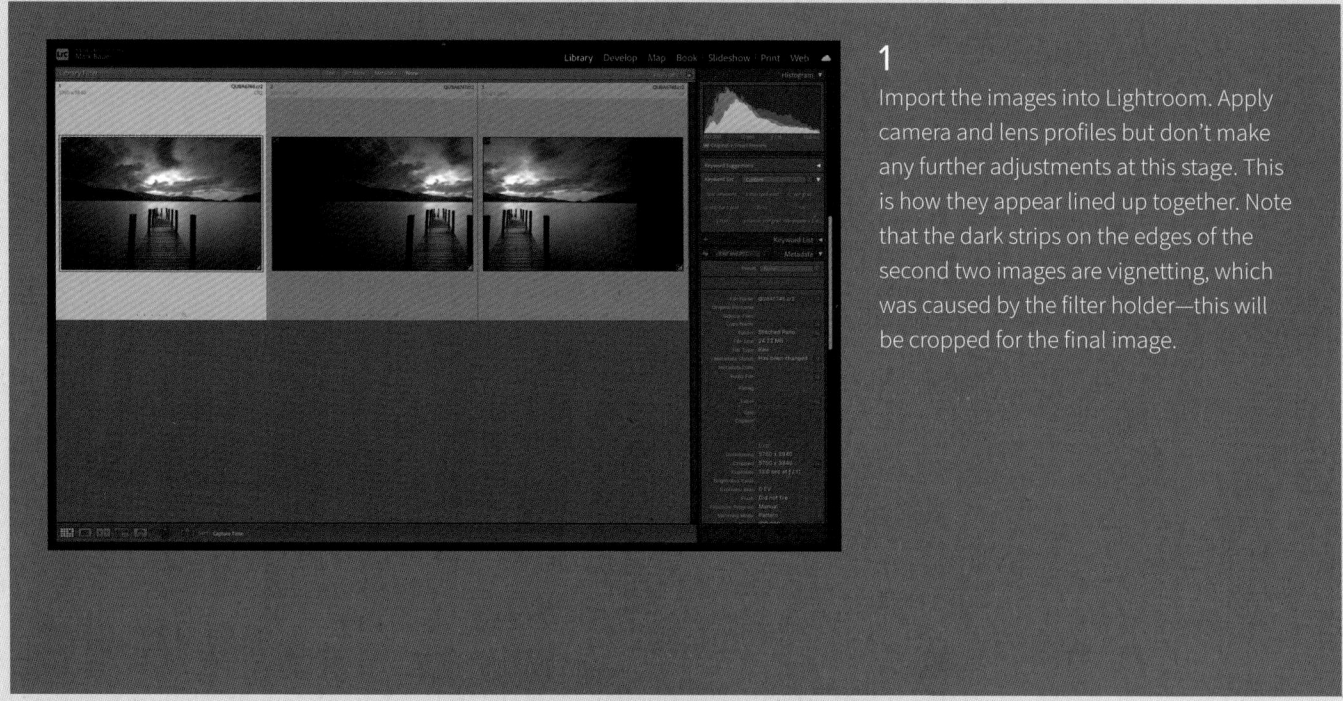

1

Import the images into Lightroom. Apply camera and lens profiles but don't make any further adjustments at this stage. This is how they appear lined up together. Note that the dark strips on the edges of the second two images are vignetting, which was caused by the filter holder—this will be cropped for the final image.

of the scene, keep white balance and focus consistent, and
avoid using polarizers, as the polarization will change as you
pan across. You should overlap each frame by at least 30% and
you will probably need to take between six and nine shots in total.
Alternatively, if you have a tilt-shift lens, you can use lateral shift
to take three horizontal frames, which will stitch together with
minimal distortion.

  When it comes to post-processing, dedicated software is
available, but there are also capable tools in Adobe Lightroom
and Photoshop. The following steps show how to create a
stitched panorama in Lightroom.

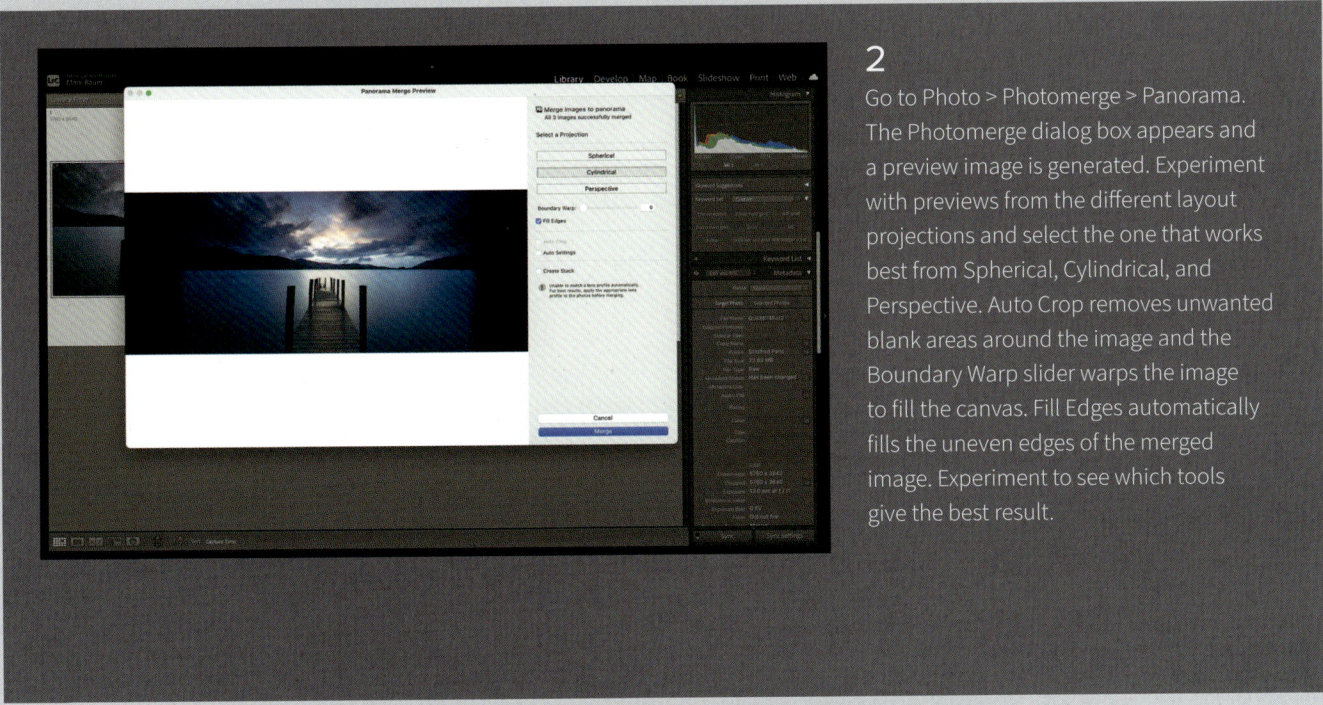

2

Go to Photo > Photomerge > Panorama.
The Photomerge dialog box appears and
a preview image is generated. Experiment
with previews from the different layout
projections and select the one that works
best from Spherical, Cylindrical, and
Perspective. Auto Crop removes unwanted
blank areas around the image and the
Boundary Warp slider warps the image
to fill the canvas. Fill Edges automatically
fills the uneven edges of the merged
image. Experiment to see which tools
give the best result.

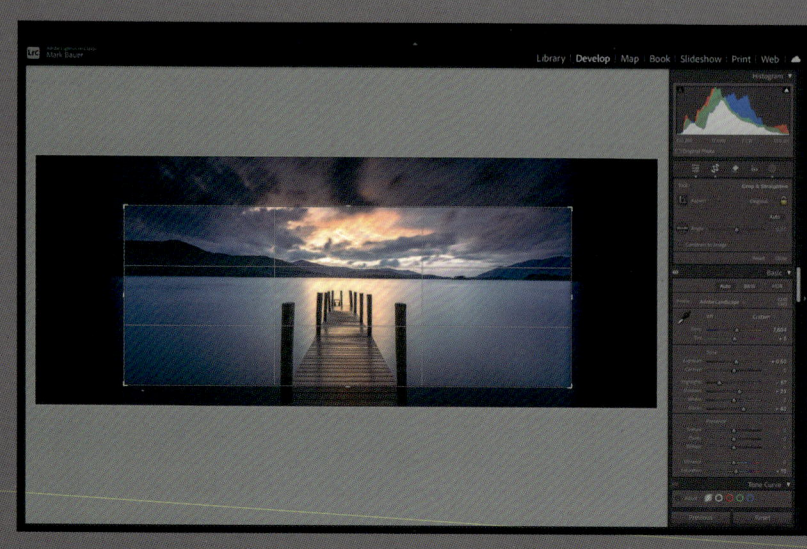

3

Once you've made your choices in the Panorama Merge dialog box, click Merge. Lightroom creates the panorama and places it in the catalog. The resulting file is a .dng file, so you can treat it as any other Raw file and continue to make all your usual adjustments: further cropping, white balance, and tonal corrections.

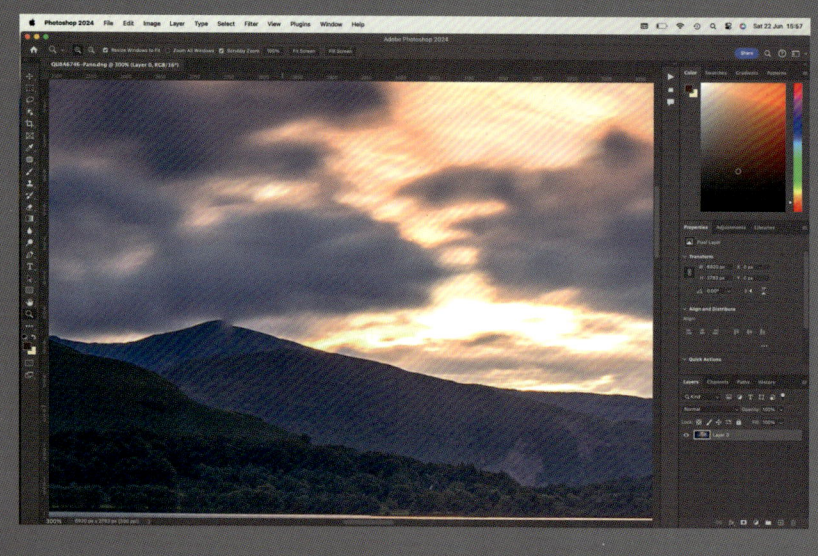

4

If necessary, you can export the image to Photoshop to make any final adjustments and correct stitching errors and distortion—although, if the original images were captured correctly in the first instance, there shouldn't be too many errors. In this image, some slight stitching errors (the distant horizon not lining up precisely) were corrected with the Clone Stamp tool.

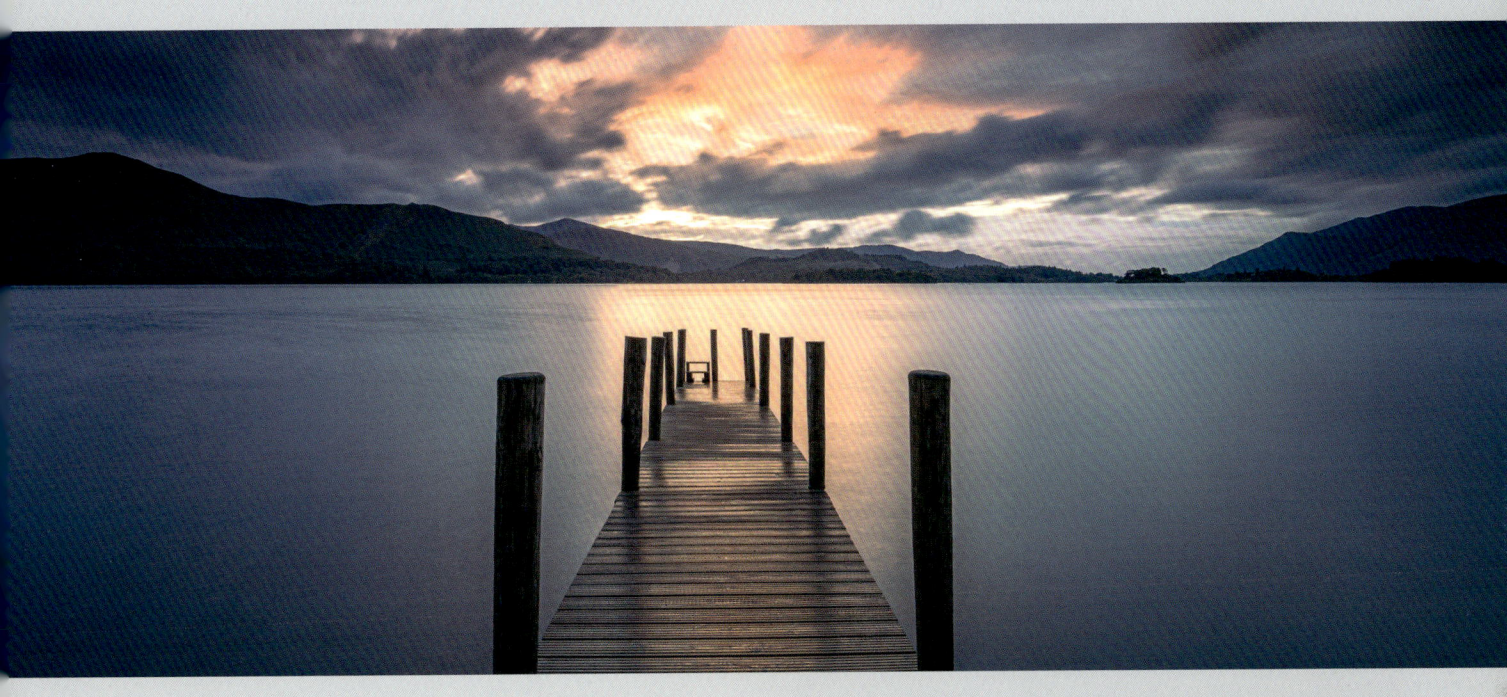

FINAL IMAGE

The final image, stitched together in Lightroom from three horizontal shots, with further corrections made in Photoshop to remove some minor stitching errors.

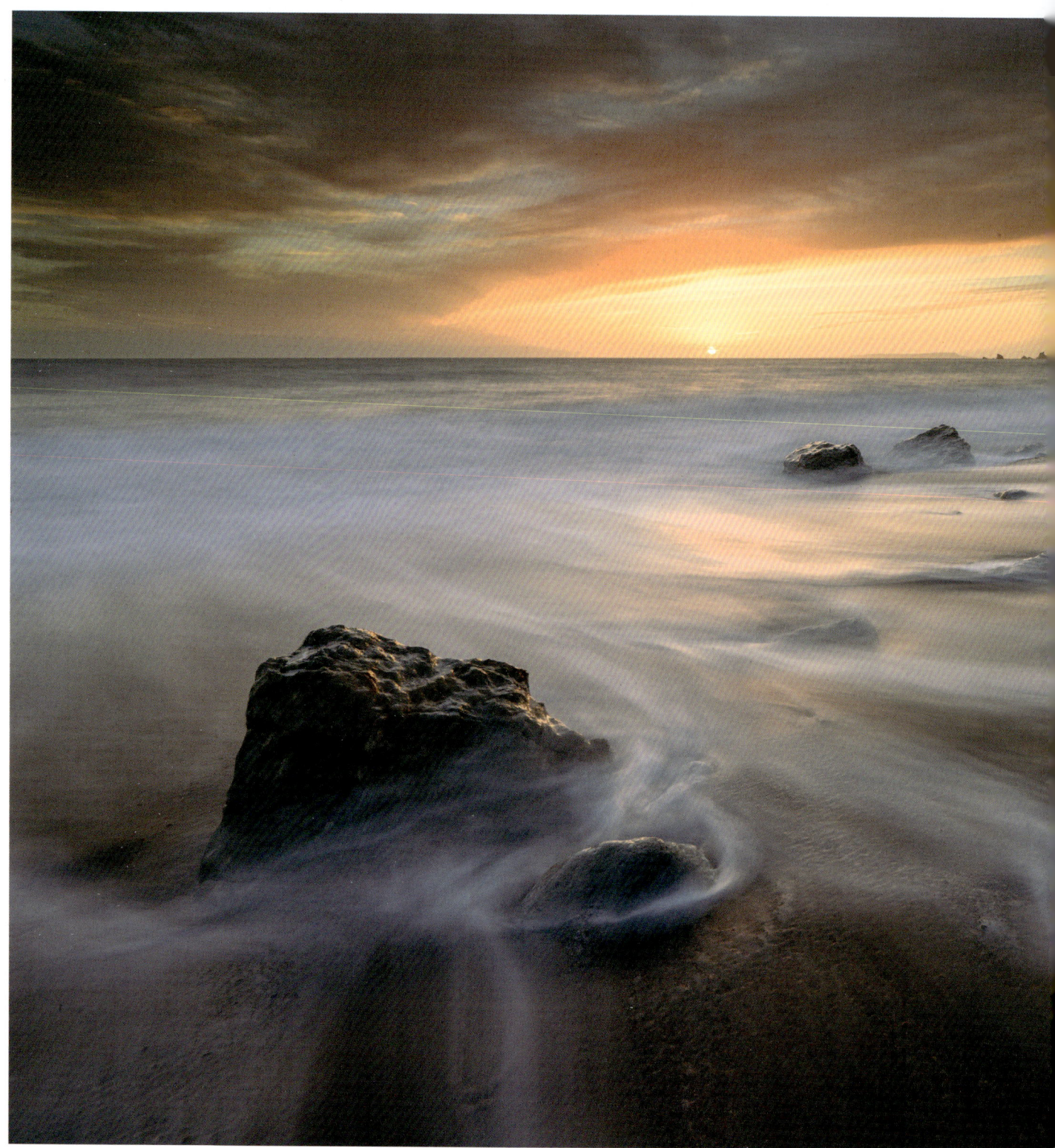

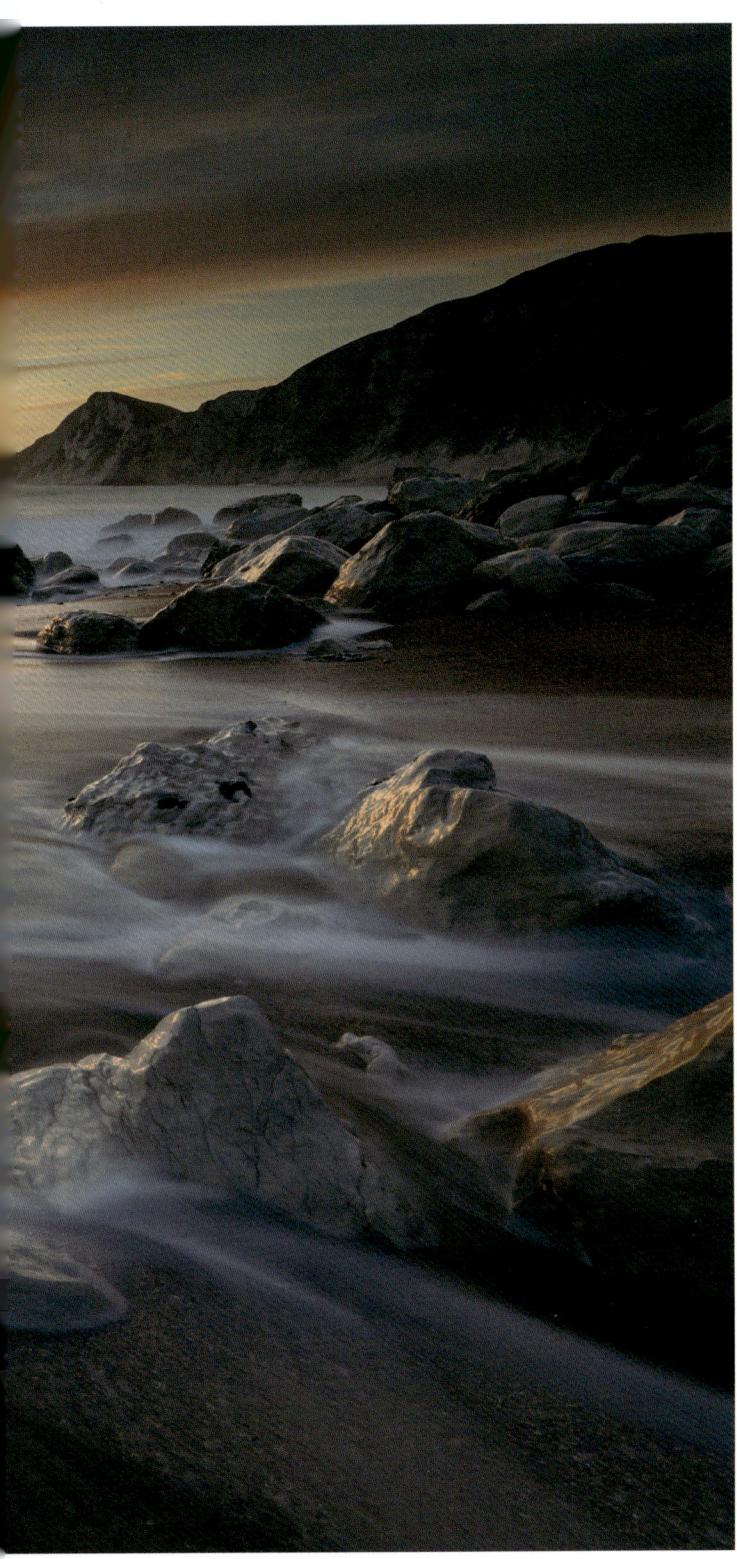

FINAL SHOT

Photographer **Mark Bauer**
Location **Worbarrow Bay, Dorset, United Kingdom**
Time and date **4.10 p.m., December 20**
Camera **Nikon Z7 II**
Lens **Nikon 14–30mm (at 14mm)**
Filtration **6-stop ND, 3-stop medium ND grad**
Exposure **ISO 64, 6 sec. at f/11**

THE STORY

"Worbarrow Bay is one of my favorite local locations, although not one I get to visit very often, due to restricted access to it as a result of it being within the Ministry of Defence firing ranges. However, the upside of this is that it is usually quiet; often, as was the case when I took this image, I'll have the bay to myself.

Capturing sunset here is tricky. As well as access being limited to weekends and vacations, the sun only sets over the sea for a few weeks in the year and this window is further narrowed by the fact that the car park closes quite early, making it challenging to shoot at sunset and then get back before the car park closes. It basically boils down to about two weeks around midwinter.

Despite the challenges, the bay is highly photogenic, with the backdrop of of the western flank of neighboring Mupe Bay and its sea stacks, and some wonderfully textured rocks scattered on the foreshore at the far end of the bay; these make great foreground interest with waves washing in between them.

Arriving about an hour before sunset, I saw that the tide was the perfect height, with waves leaving trails as they dragged back out to sea among the stones. Although the cloud cover was quite heavy, there was a gap on the horizon which the sun dipped into as it set. I composed the image with the foreground rocks pointing into the frame, having selected an ultra-wide lens to emphasize the foreground and stretch perspective. Exposure length was important: it needed to be long enough for the retreating waves to create obvious trails, but not so long that all texture in the water was lost. I experimented with filtration and found that between 5 and 10 seconds gave a good result. I took a number of shots, but this was the one where I felt all the elements came together."

CHAPTER SIX
TWILIGHT

The "blue hour" is the period of twilight each morning and evening when the residual sunlight takes on a blue hue. During this time the sun is below the horizon, but it illuminates the upper layers of the atmosphere—the longer, red wavelengths pass straight into space, while the shorter, blue wavelengths are scattered in the atmosphere. The result is a cool color temperature and saturated color.

As with dawn, there are different phases of twilight: civil twilight, when the sun's elevation is between 0° and -6°; nautical twilight, when it is between -6° to -12°; and astronomical twilight, from -12° to -18°. During civil twilight, there is still enough light to see objects clearly, and color in the sky. During nautical twilight, the sky darkens, and by astronomical twilight it is almost totally dark. The blue hour is the period of transition from civil to nautical twilight (or vice versa in the morning), although it usually lasts for between 30–40 minutes, and the peak for just a few minutes. In the morning, it normally starts about 45 minutes before sunrise, and in the evening about 15 minutes after sunset.

The cool, blue tones in this period can create an atmosphere of mystery, romance, or tranquility. So, if you like your landscapes moody, this is the time to shoot.

▶ **BRUGES**
Shooting in the blue hour can completely transform a scene, lending an air of tranquility, mystery, or romance. There can often be a pleasing contrast between the cool tones of the ambient light and the warmth of artificial light.

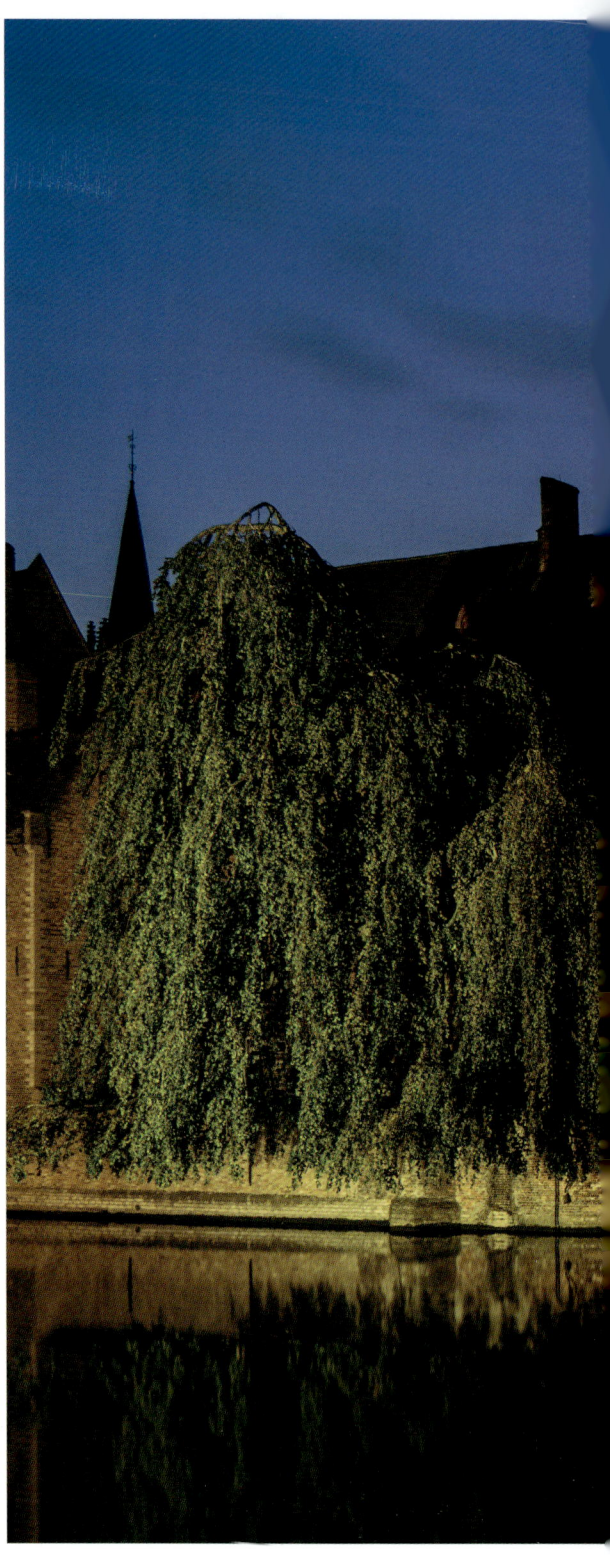

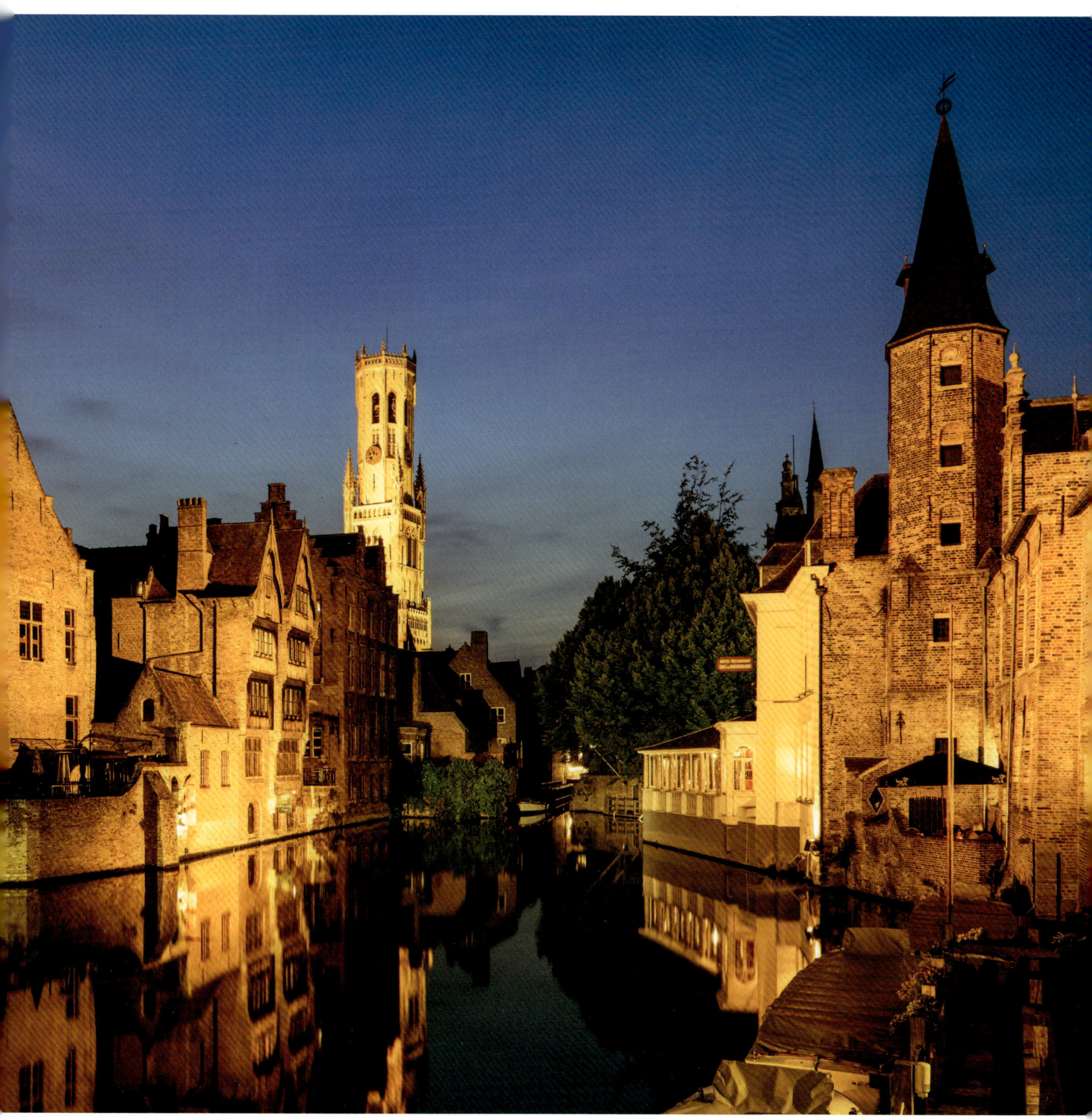

RURAL SCENES

Rural landscapes are far less associated with the blue hour than cityscapes, and it's probably fair to say that shots of the countryside and rolling hills are more suited to the golden hours. Low side-lighting reveals form and texture, adding depth to a scene, whereas the same landscape viewed without directional light will often look rather flat.

This doesn't mean, however, that when the sun sets you should pack up and make a dash for the nearest city, as there are certainly opportunities for blue-hour shots in the countryside. Silhouettes are one option (see page 147)—although these are best shot early on in the blue hour, when the sky is still relatively bright. When shooting silhouettes, choose subjects that are easily identifiable, such as trees, rocks, or recognizable landmarks. Keep the composition simple—a single isolated subject is preferable, as it will be more easily identified by the viewer. Place it low in the frame to avoid having too much dark foreground.

Mountains are an excellent twilight subject—the blue tones enhance their brooding presence and the overlapping forms of mountain ranges can be used to suggest depth where there is no light to do so. Shooting with longer lenses generally works better, as this appears to "compress" the perspective, creating a dramatic "stacking" effect where there are several ranges. If there is snow on the mountains, this creates tonal contrast with the darker blues in the scene and can also reflect color.

In a similar way, mist can transform a rural blue-hour scene. Not only does mist simplify the landscape, but it also injects tonal relief and texture when there is no direct light. The combination of low-lying mist and blue-hour lighting also creates a uniquely eerie atmosphere. For a dawn shoot, for instance, if the weather forecast suggests there may be a misty morning (see page 52), it's worth getting on location a little bit earlier than normal.

WATER

Shooting near water is another option, as reflections can be used for foreground interest, which adds depth. Lakes, rivers, and even ponds can be used as the basis for a composition. If the water is still, then objects such as trees, rocks, and hills will be reflected clearly, but even moving water will reflect the deep blue twilight colors and help to enhance depth in the image.

Out of town, however, the coast arguably provides the best subject matter in the blue hour. Coastal shots are far less dependent on the quality of light than rural shots, relying

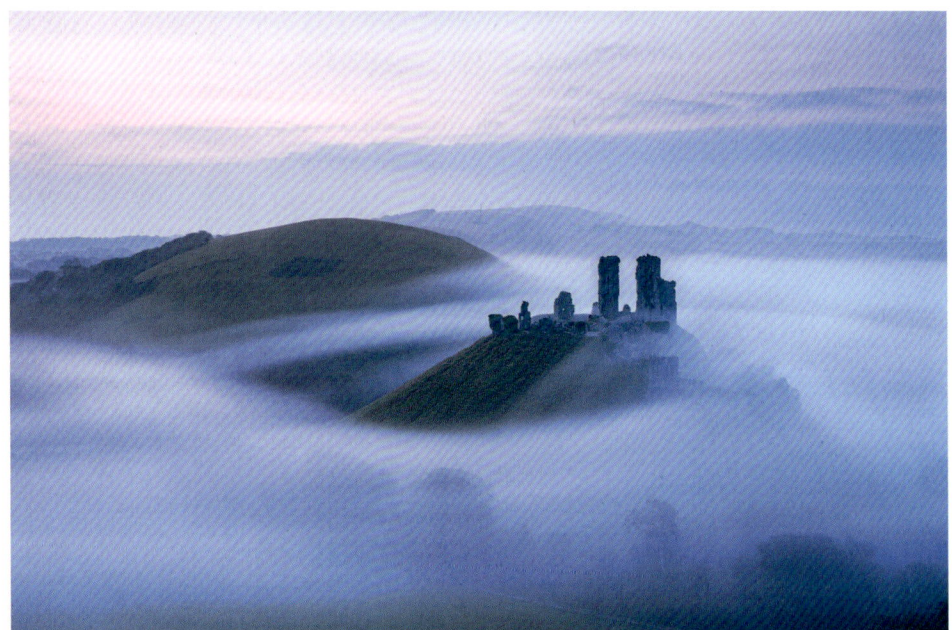

◀ BLUE-HOUR MIST
Misty landscapes shot in the blue hour have a mysterious, ethereal quality. In this instance, the beginnings of a glow on the horizon provide an attractive contrast to the cool tones.

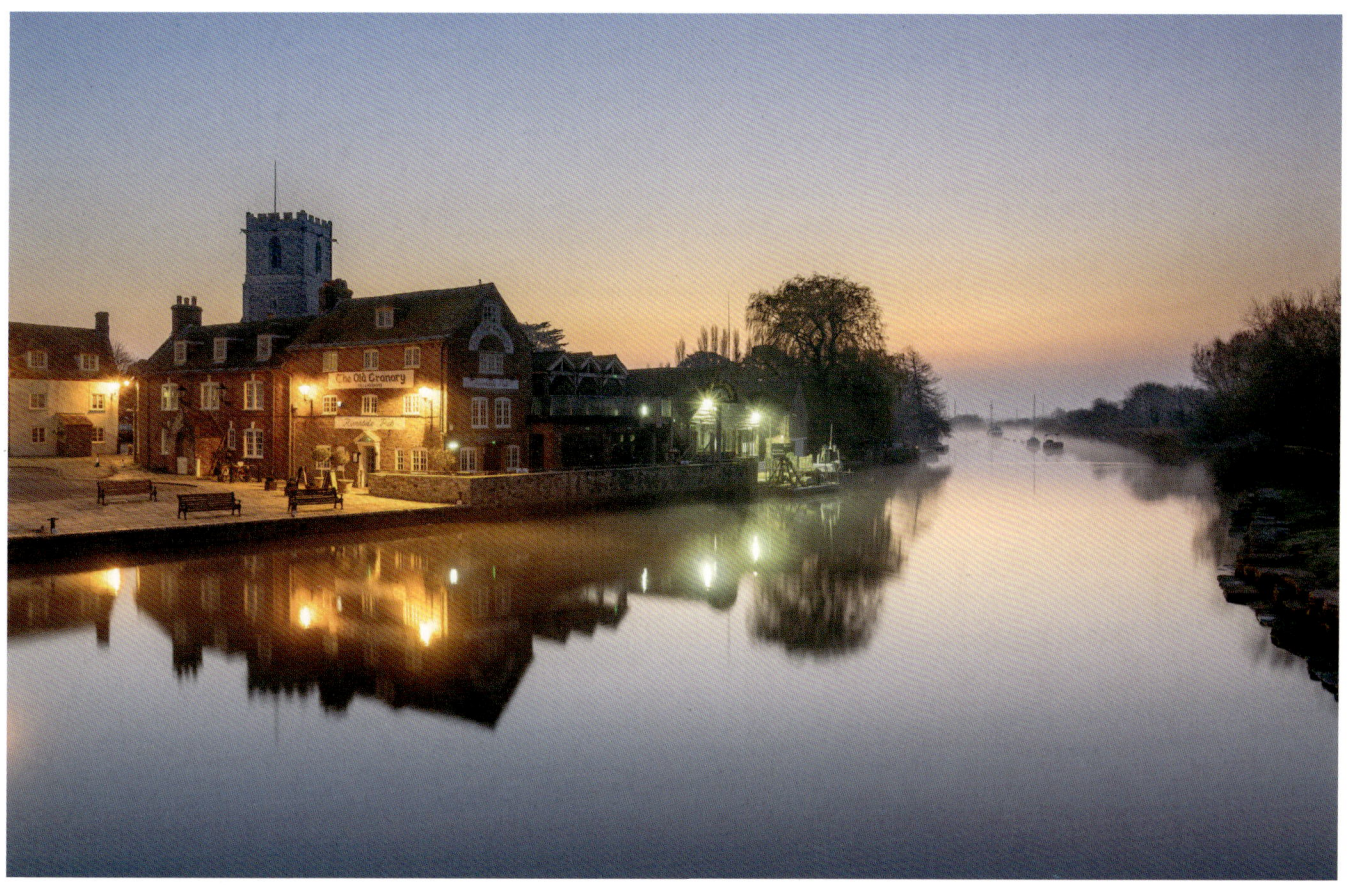

▲ BLUE HOUR REFLECTIONS

Shooting near water is one way to add depth and interest to twilight landscapes. It allows you to increase the impact of the blue hues—as well as any other color present—and reflections are an excellent way of generating foreground interest.

more on color, shape, and texture. Seascape photographers often shoot past sunset or before sunrise, hoping for some late or early color to spread across the sky, but on the coast it's worth extending shooting times into the blue hour. With so many reflective surfaces—wet rocks, wet sand, and the water itself— you can really maximize the potential of the saturated blue tones.

FOCUS ON...
EXPOSING FOR SILHOUETTES

Unlike most landscapes, where the aim is to balance the brightness difference between sky and foreground, you want to do the opposite for silhouettes. Therefore, it's best to avoid using graduated filters. Using Manual exposure mode, meter from the sky then recompose and take the shot. The resulting image will have a correctly exposed sky, with the foreground and main subject underexposed. When reviewing the image, the histogram will be bunched up on the left, which for most photos would indicate quite severe underexposure, but, in this case, the underexposure of a specific part of the scene is quite deliberate.

CITYSCAPES

Cityscapes are a popular choice for blue-hour photography, and it's easy to see why: the deep blue of the sky (often with a purple hue) provides a rich backdrop for scenes, and artificial lighting sources contrast dramatically with these blue tones. There are also many points of interest on a city skyline, including bridges, monuments, churches, and modern skyscrapers, and these often look their best under darkening evening skies, especially if they are interestingly lit. Even without any spotlighting, most buildings come into their own at twilight, with interior lighting shining through windows and the glow of street lighting warming the stonework.

Compared to shooting in the golden hours, the weather is far less important when shooting in the blue hours. Even in dull, cloudy conditions, when the light levels drop, the predominant hue is a rich blue. Cityscapes can even benefit from bad weather, as wet sidewalks will reflect street lighting, neon signs, and so on, adding to the natural vibrancy of the evening light.

Timing is crucial with city shots. There are apps and websites that give timings for the blue hour, including The Photographer's Ephemeris, PhotoPills, and www.bluehoursite.com. These are a useful guide, but the duration and intensity of the blue hour can vary. In city scenes there is always a peak time of a few minutes when the ambient and artificial light are perfectly balanced. This is a short window of opportunity, so to ensure you don't miss it, get on location early, start shooting at the beginning of the blue hour, and continue until the sky loses its blue hues. That way, you won't miss those crucial moments of perfect light.

LIGHTING

A lot of the impact of blue-hour cityscapes comes from the mixed lighting sources. Different light sources have different color temperatures. The ambient light of the blue hour is very cool, at around 10,000 Kelvin. Tungsten light and sodium street lighting are much warmer, with color temperatures of around 2,500 to 3,000 Kelvin. Photographs that include these different light sources have a very pleasing warm/cool or blue/yellow contrast.

Urban environments typically have other light sources as well. Mercury vapor lamps are also common in street lighting and floodlighting on buildings. These lamps have a "cool white" color temperature of around 7,000 Kelvin, with a blue/green tint. In cities and towns there are also car headlights and tail lights to add to the mix. It's possible to find scenes that contain all of these different light sources, creating very dynamic results.

One of the problems of shooting street scenes in the blue hour is having people in the scene, who may be recorded as blurry figures if they move during the exposure. The only way to get a fast enough shutter speed to prevent blur is to push the ISO up to a level that would generate too much noise in the image. The alternatives are to wait for a moment when nobody is in the scene (not alway possible), or to use a long enough shutter speed so that any figures moving through the scene will not be recorded at all—a moderate ND filter can help here. Another option is to take multiple shots of the same composition. Any people in the scene will likely be in different places in each frame. In Photoshop, you can use stack modes to create a composite image of the different frames in which the people are removed.

Converging verticals, caused by pointing the camera upward when shooting with a wide-angle lens, can be a problem when shooting buildings. To prevent this, try to keep the camera as level as possible. If this isn't possible, perspective correction can be carried out in post-processing. Make sure you frame the shot loosely, as the image will be cropped during the correction process. If you shoot a lot of architectural subjects, it may be worth investing in a tilt-and-shift lens (see page 17).

▶ **VENICE**
Cities and towns are popular subjects for blue-hour photography, as the contrast between the cool ambient light and warm street and flood lighting is very appealing. Paving made reflective by recent rain adds extra impact by reflecting the city lights.

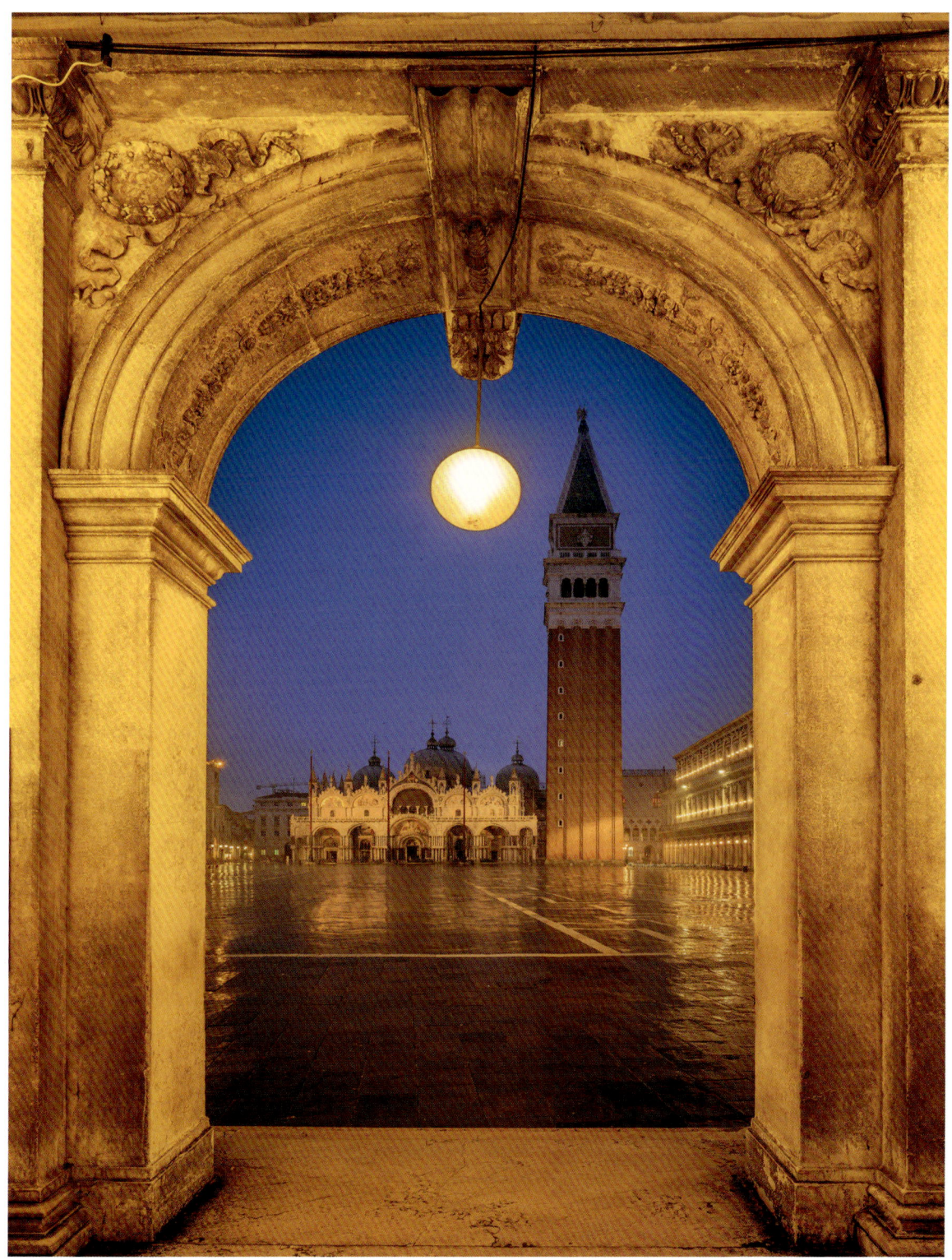

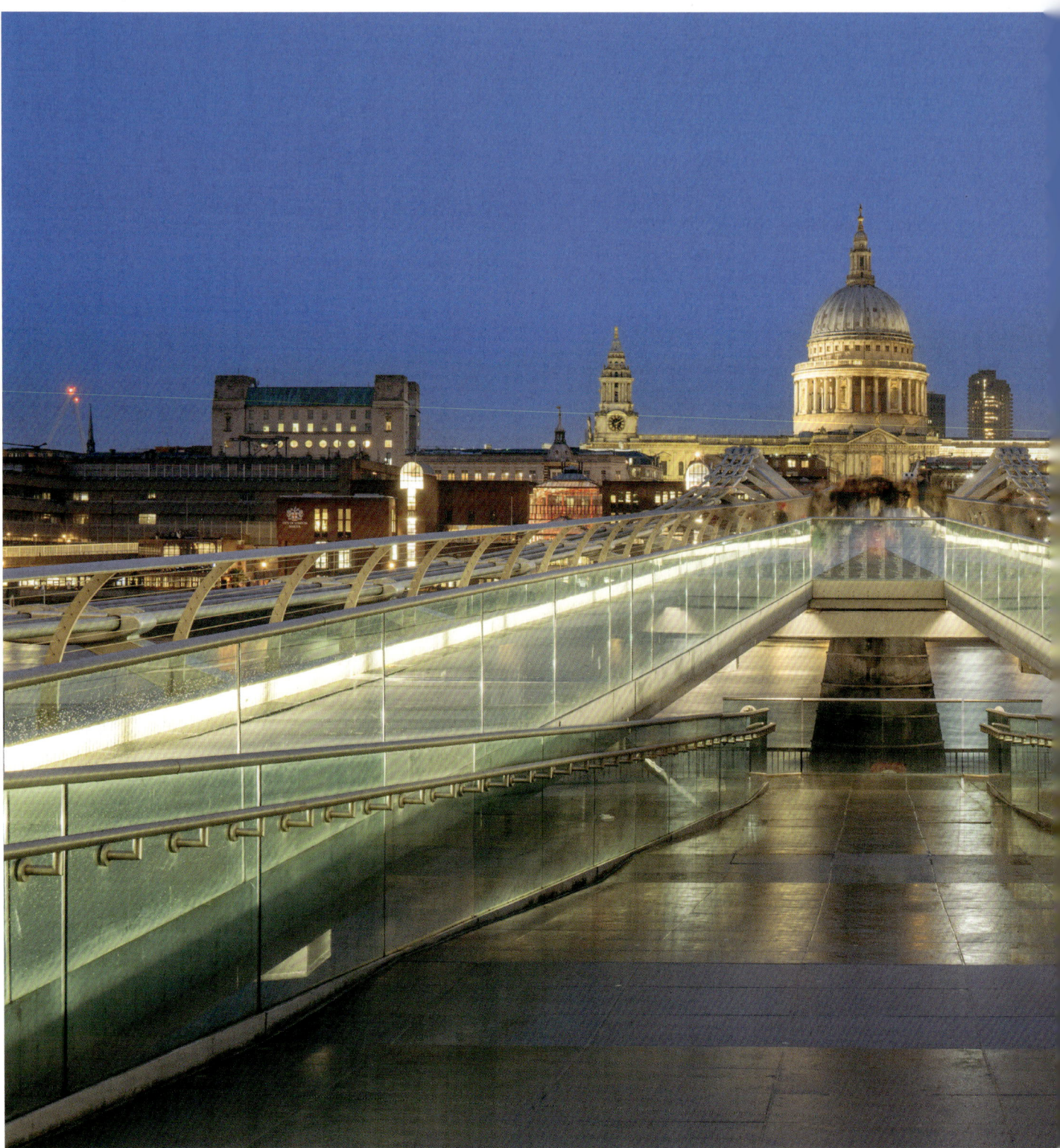

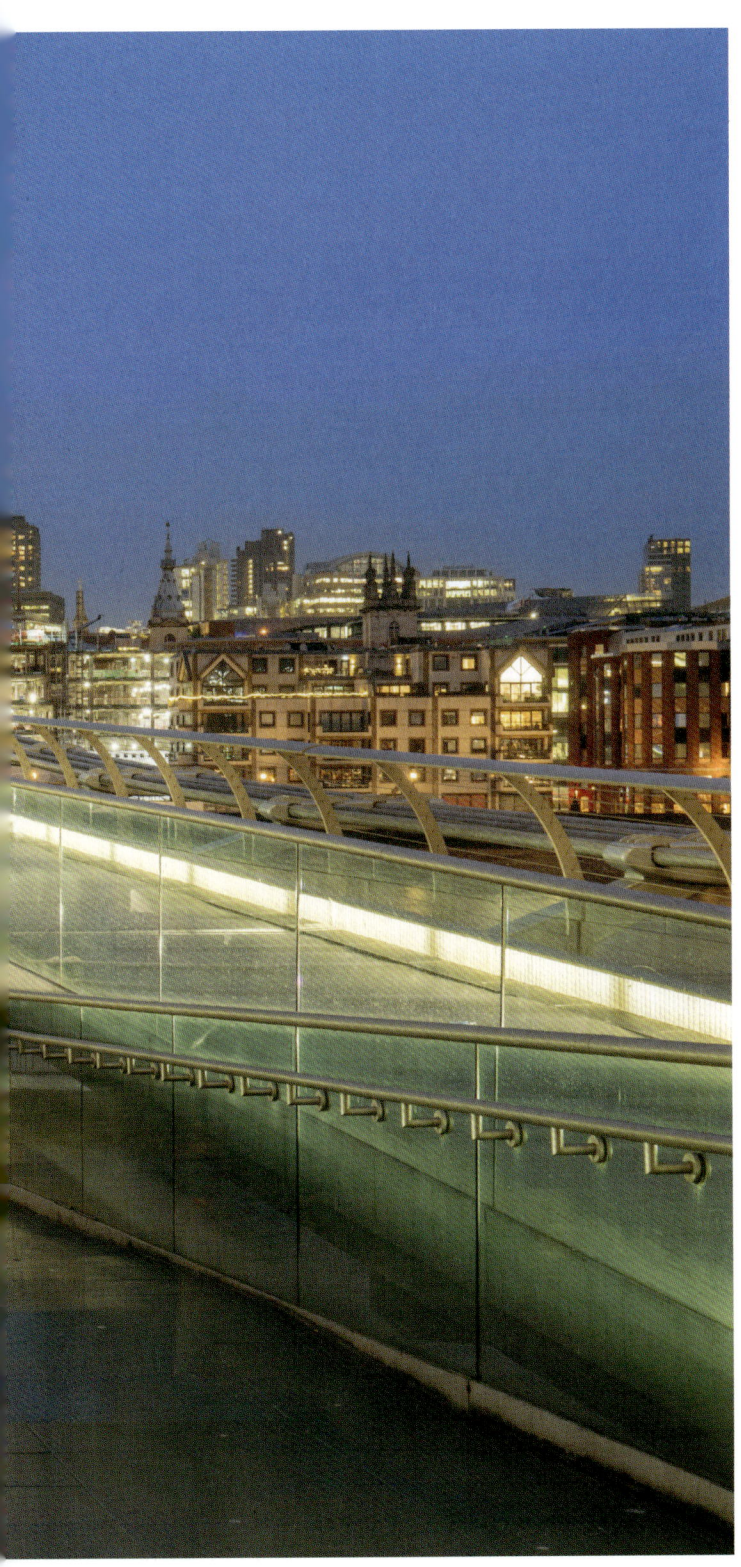

FOCUS ON...
COLOR TEMPERATURE

Different light sources have different characteristics, usually perceived as "warm" or "cool." Color temperature is measured in degrees Kelvin. Somewhat counterintuitively, the lower numbers are warm and the higher numbers are cool. Midday sun is considered to be neutral, at around 5,500K, sunrise and sunset are about 2,000K, and the "golden hour" about 3,500K. The color temperature of the blue hour is around 10,000K.

◀ CITY VISTA
The rich blues of twilight provide a wonderful backdrop for this view of St. Paul's Cathedral in London. The warm artificial lighting contrasts with the cool ambient lighting, with further contrast provided between the modern and historic architecture.

CORE TECHNIQUE
EXPOSURE

Judging exposure in low light can be tricky—not all cameras meter very accurately once the light drops to a certain level, and with longer exposures the light levels will be changing while the shutter is open. This means that there is a tendency to underexpose during the falling light in the evening blue hour, and to overexpose during the morning blue hour.

It's particularly important not to rely on the review image to judge exposure—you will be viewing the camera's LCD monitor screen in semidarkness, which can make the image seem brighter than it is. It's therefore vital to use the histogram to check that the full range of tones in the scene has been captured, with no clipping of highlights or shadows. If the scene is very contrasty, you may need to bracket images and blend them in post-processing (see page 60). Exposing to the right (ETTR), where you push the tones as far to the right of the histogram as possible, making sure not to clip them, used to be standard practice, as it captures more tonal information and keeps noise to a minimum. However, the dynamic range of modern cameras means it is a less important exposure technique than it once was.

When shooting city scenes, there will be bright highlights to consider. Keep an eye on these, and avoid overexposing them, if you can, although in very contrasty scenes this may not be possible. Using your camera's highlight alert (see page 43) will help.

FOCUS ON...
CALCULATING LONG EXPOSURES

Rather than simply guessing, use the following method to calculate long exposures. In Aperture Priority or Manual exposure mode, increase the ISO until you get a usable meter reading. Then calculate what the equivalent exposure is at base ISO, switch to Bulb mode and base ISO, and lock the shutter open for that length of time. For example, 20 sec. at ISO 400 translates to 80 sec. at ISO 100. To allow for changing light, add half a stop if shooting the evening blue hour, and take away half a stop in the morning blue hour.

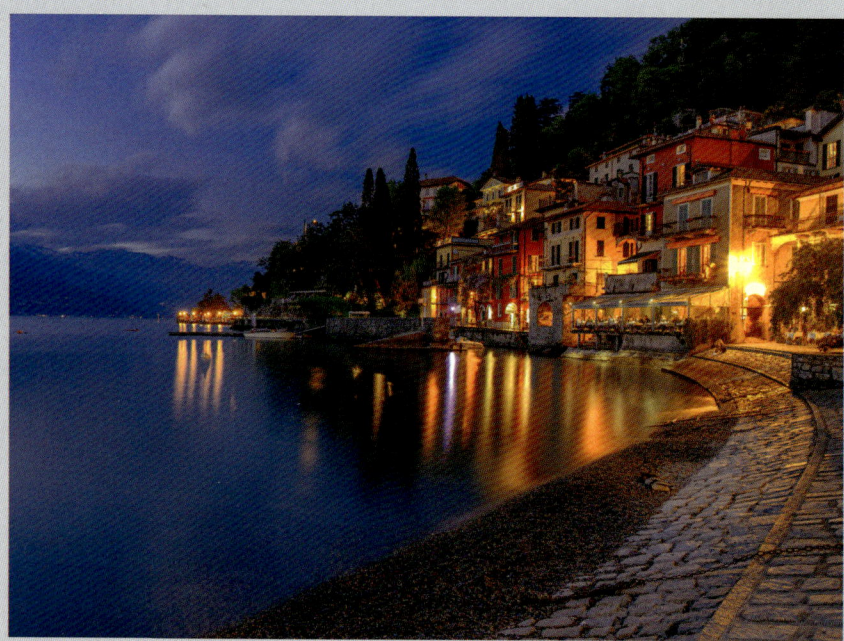

◀ BRIGHT HIGHLIGHTS
Twilight cityscapes can be very contrasty, with bright highlights, which may overexpose. If the highlights comprise just a small part of the image and are unobtrusive, such as the street lights in this image, it's acceptable to let them clip. Otherwise, you may have to bracket exposures and blend images.

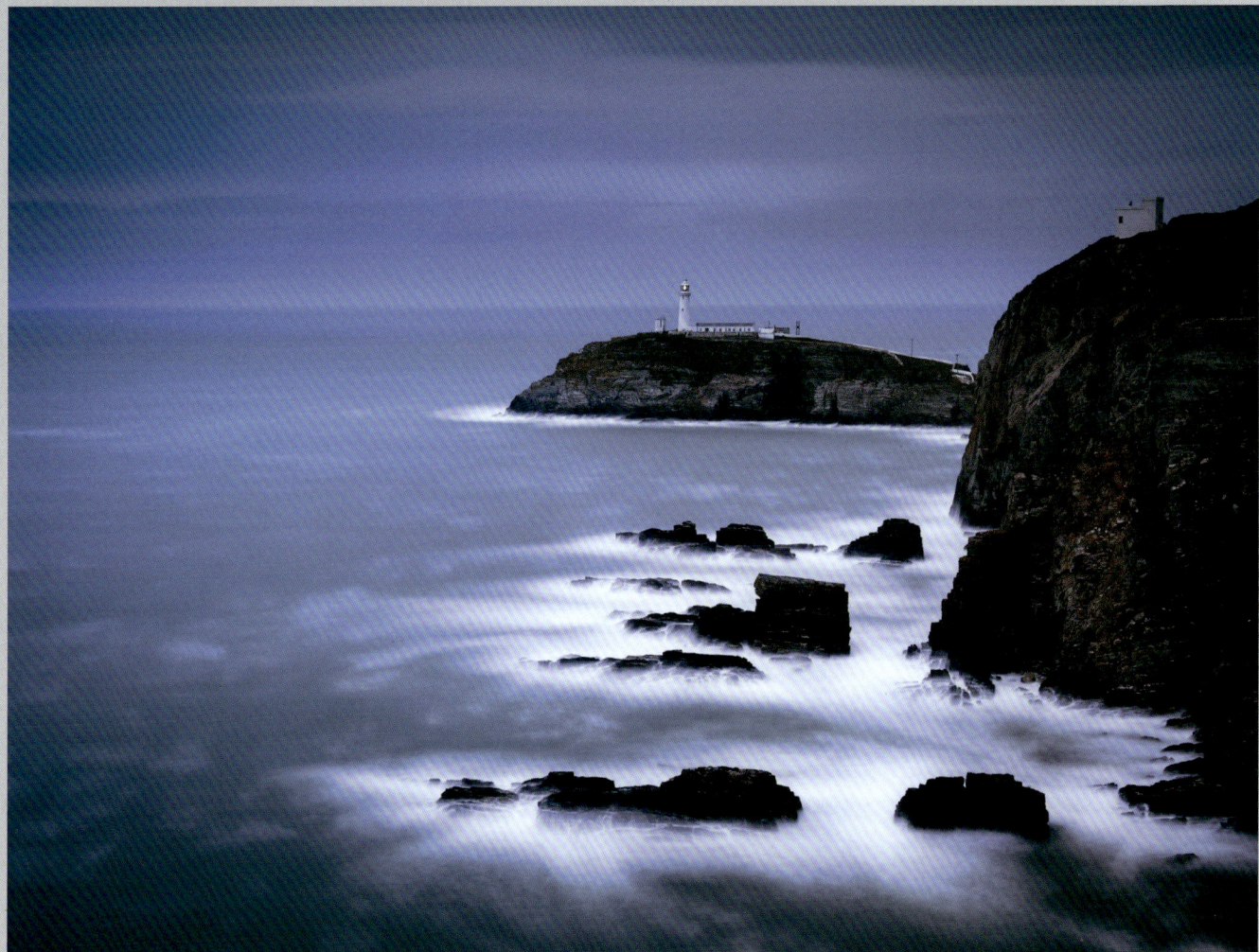

▲ SEASCAPE
When calculating long exposures, remember to allow for the fact that light levels will be changing during the exposure. This was shot at the very end of the evening blue hour, with the light falling rapidly and an additional stop of exposure time was necessary.

To maximize image quality, keep your ISO low and increase exposure times if necessary, but if they exceed 30 seconds—which is not unusual in such low light—you may need to switch to Bulb mode depending on your make of camera.

With the sky being dark, you are unlikely to need a graduated filter, but keep an eye on your histogram and highlight alerts when reviewing images and check the sky isn't overexposing.

FOCUS

Focusing accurately in low light isn't easy, but set up around half an hour before the blue hour begins and there will be enough light to focus accurately and compose your shot properly. You can focus manually or with autofocus, but once focus is achieved, make sure that your camera is set to manual focus mode so that focus is locked and the camera doesn't "hunt" in low light. Alternatively, enable back-button focusing, where focusing is assigned to one of the buttons on the rear of the camera and disengaged from the shutter, and the camera will not refocus when the shutter is released.

COMPOSITION
FOCAL POINTS

It's easy to let the moody lighting of the blue hour distract you from seeking out a powerful composition, so it's important to ensure you pay attention to this key element of photography. As with all outdoor photography, blue-hour compositions benefit from having a strong focal point. With cityscapes, this could be a prominent building, a bridge, a fountain, or similar structures. In rural scenes, you can find floodlit buildings such as churches. Alternatively, you can try "painting" an object with a flashlight to provide a focal point (see page 170).

Where you place the chosen focal point in the frame is important for the overall balance of the composition. Generally speaking, placing the focal point in the center can result in rather static images, as the eye is not encouraged to move around the frame and explore the composition. Simply offsetting the focal point encourages the eye to move around more, thus creating a more dynamic and interesting composition.

However, in order to achieve balance and harmony—arguably the main goals of composition—you will want to give a bit more thought to where you place the focal point. Arranging the elements in the frame according to the "rule of thirds" is a popular and successful way of achieving a balanced and harmonious composition. Imagine a tic-tac-toe (noughts-and-crosses) grid in your viewfinder, dividing it into thirds, horizontally and vertically. The main elements of the composition can then be arranged around the grid—for example, the horizon can be placed on one of the horizontal lines and the main focal point can be placed on an intersection of horizontal and vertical lines.

The rule of thirds is derived from a proportion known as the "golden ratio" (or "golden section" when it is applied to a rectangle), a method of harmoniously dividing the frame that has been used in art and architecture for centuries, and is also common in nature. It works like this: divide the frame into two rectangles, in which the ratio of the small rectangle to the large one is the same as that of the large one to the whole frame (expressed mathematically, the ratio is 1:1.618). The sections can then be subdivided according to the same ratio, and you end up with a grid that looks a little like a "squashed" rule of thirds grid. Again, the intersections of horizontal and vertical lines are ideal places to position focal points in the image.

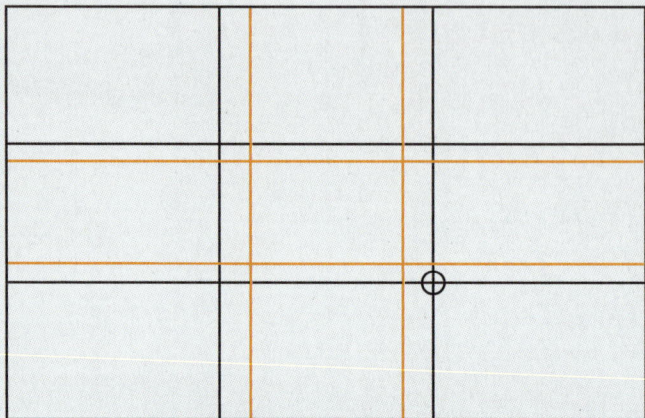

▲ **RULE OF THIRDS AND GOLDEN SECTION GRIDS**
A frame divided according to the rule of thirds (black) or golden section (gold) can be used to help organize the elements in the frame—focal points can be placed on the intersections of horizontal and vertical lines.

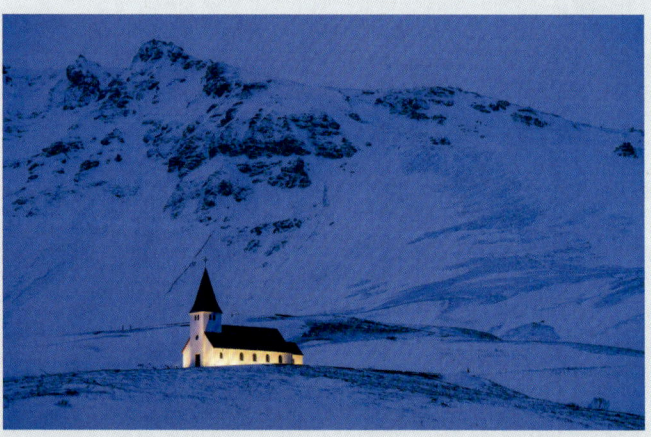

▲ **ISOLATED CHURCH**
The warm spotlighting on the church contrasts with the blue backdrop of the mountains, making it a natural focal point. I placed the church close to an intersection on the rule of thirds grid to achieve balance.

▶ **STEPS**
The steps and balustrade provide foreground interest and the street light is a strong focal point. It was placed near the edge of the frame rather than on one of the thirds, to act as a border for the view beyond.

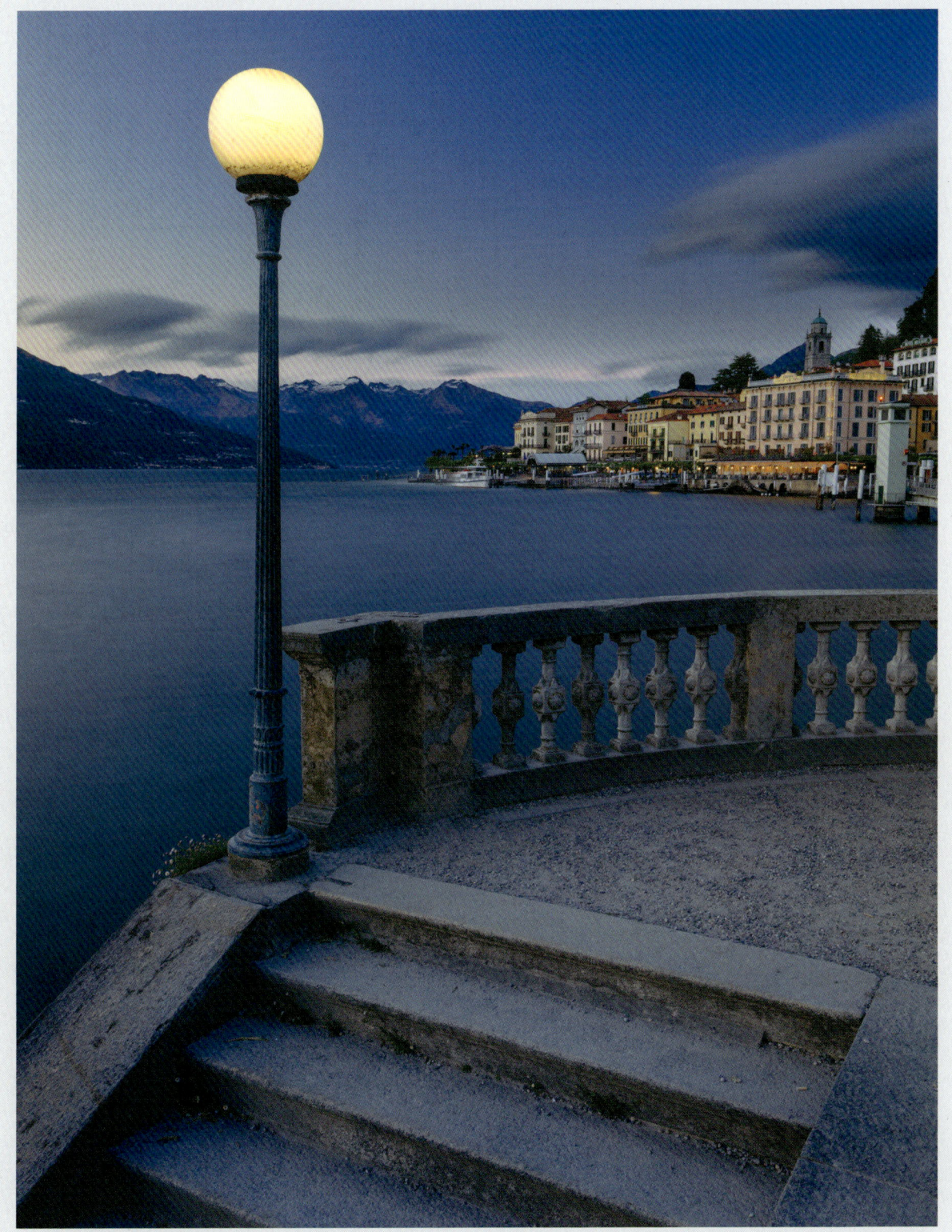

POST-PROCESSING STEP-BY-STEP
COLOR BALANCE

When it comes to processing blue-hour images, the key is achieving a suitable color balance. Firstly, you want the sky to be a rich blue—this is the whole point of shooting in the blue hour, after all—so avoid using too warm a white balance. Auto White Balance can work well with many images, but will tend to render blue-hour images on the warm side. It's best to begin with a Daylight preset and adjust to suit your taste from there.

Many blue-hour images are shot in a mixture of ambient and artificial light, which creates an attractive warm/cool contrast, especially where, for example, floodlighting on buildings gives the stonework a warm hue. When post-processing images, you need to ensure that these warm tones look right and complement the blues of the ambient light. You may, therefore, want to work on individual color channels to adjust the hue, saturation, and brightness of these colors. This can be done in Lightroom in the Color Mixer panel of the Develop module or in Photoshop, using Image > Adjustments > Hue/Saturation.

Basic tonal adjustments, such as setting black and white points, contrast, and so on, are not really different to other landscapes, and you will probably find that your usual post-processing approaches work well. The following tutorial uses Adobe Lightroom, but these or similar adjustments are possible with most good Raw converters.

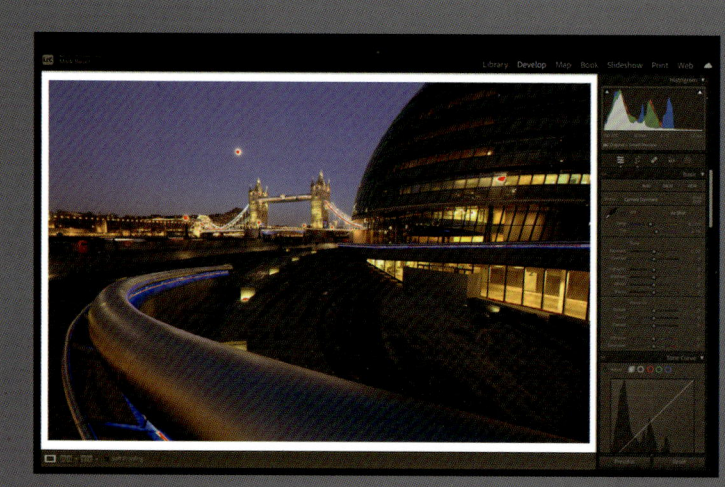

1

The unprocessed image as it appears when first imported, with the Camera Standard profile. It was shot when the artificial and natural light were nicely balanced, so looks reasonably good straight out of the camera, although the brighter highlights are just starting to clip and the shadows are slightly dark.

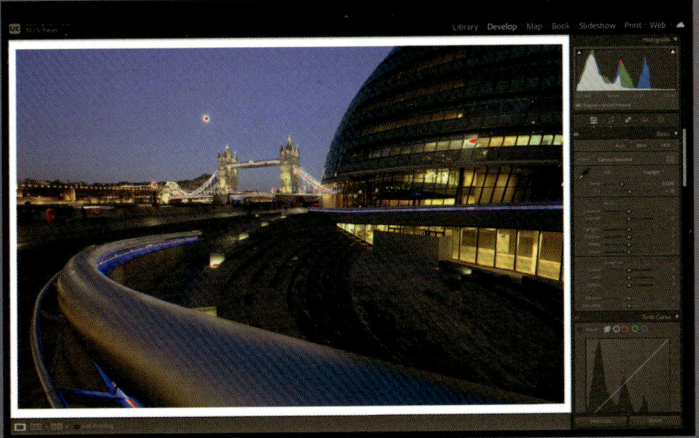

2

White balance is the key to successful post-processing with blue-hour images. It's best to start with the Daylight preset and work from there. In this instance (left), Daylight white balance is a little too cool and green. Adding +9 magenta to the Tint and increasing Temperature slightly sorts this out (below).

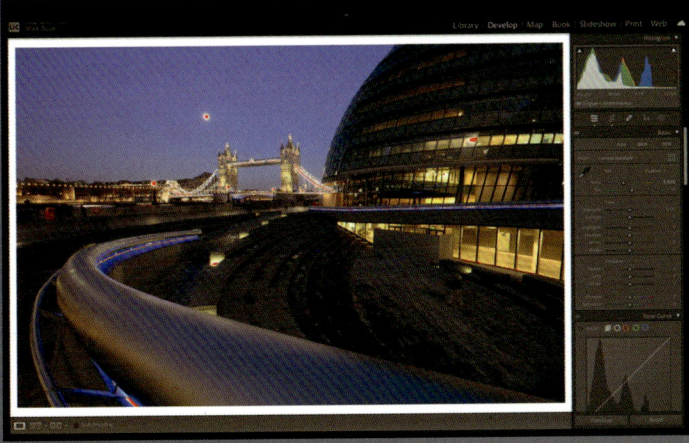

3

Make your standard tonal adjustments, i.e. set the black and white points, adjust highlights and shadows, exposure, and contrast as necessary. In this instance, pulling the Whites and Highlights sliders to the left has recovered the detail in the brighter areas and subtly darkened the sky, and boosting Shadows has lightened the darker areas. Adjust Saturation, Clarity, and Sharpening to taste.

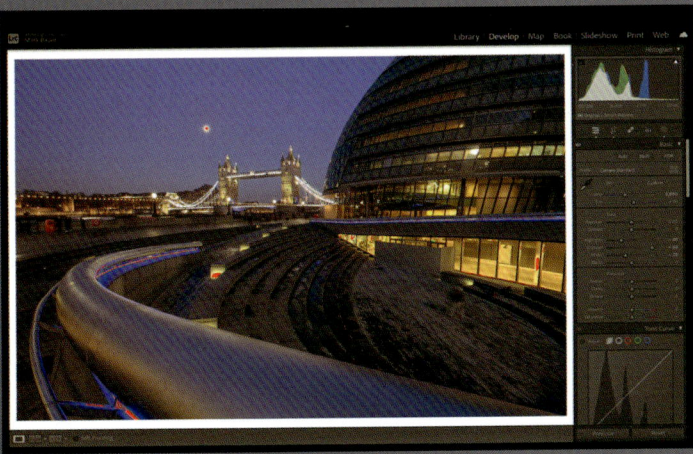

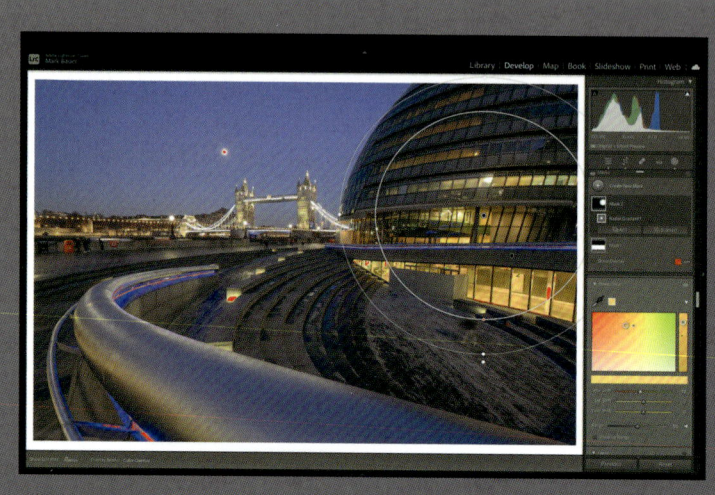

4

The lighting in the building on the right is still too green, so a rough selection is made using a Radial Gradient, and hue is adjusted using Point Color.

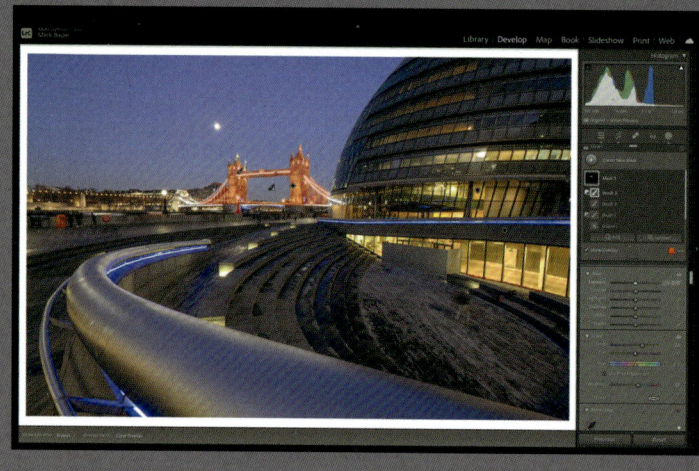

5

Tower Bridge in the background—the main focal point—needs greater emphasis. This is achieved by masking it, warming up the Color Temperature slightly, darkening it, and giving a slight boost to Saturation. Finally, the image is tidied up by cloning out some distracting elements at the bottom of the steps.

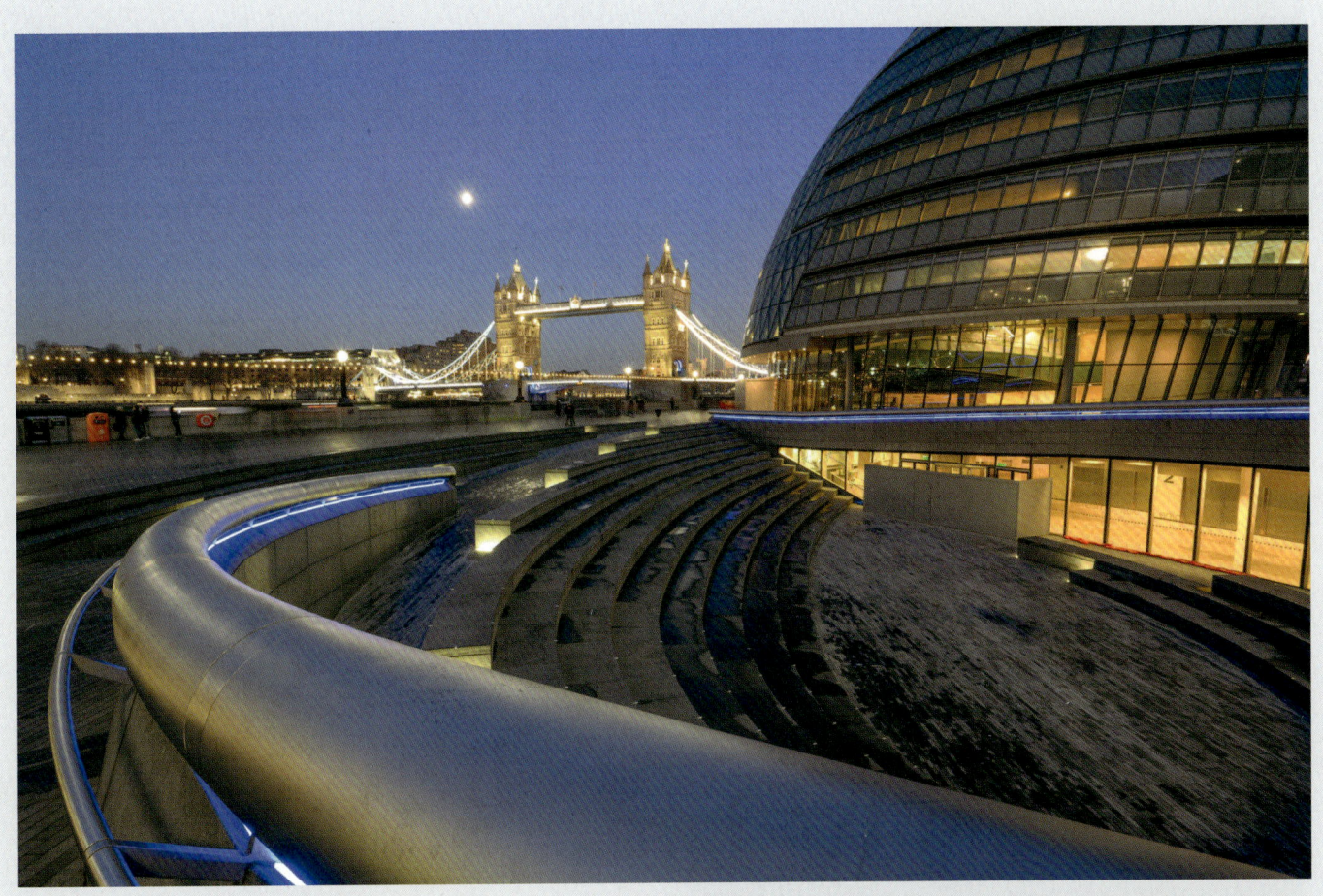

FINAL IMAGE

'The final image is nicely balanced, with a strong contrast between the warm light on Tower Bridge and other buildings in the scene, and the rich, blue tones of the sky.

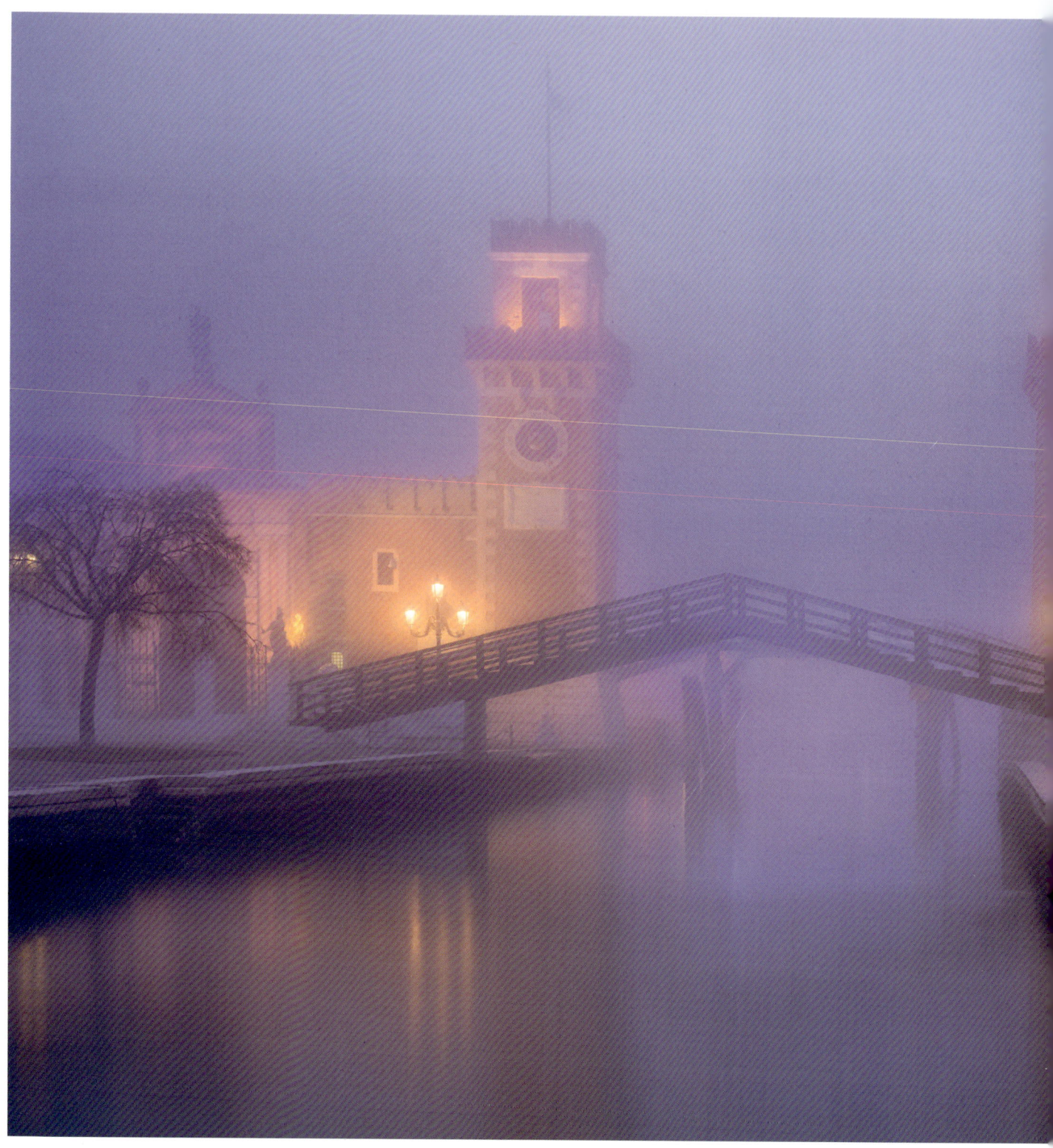

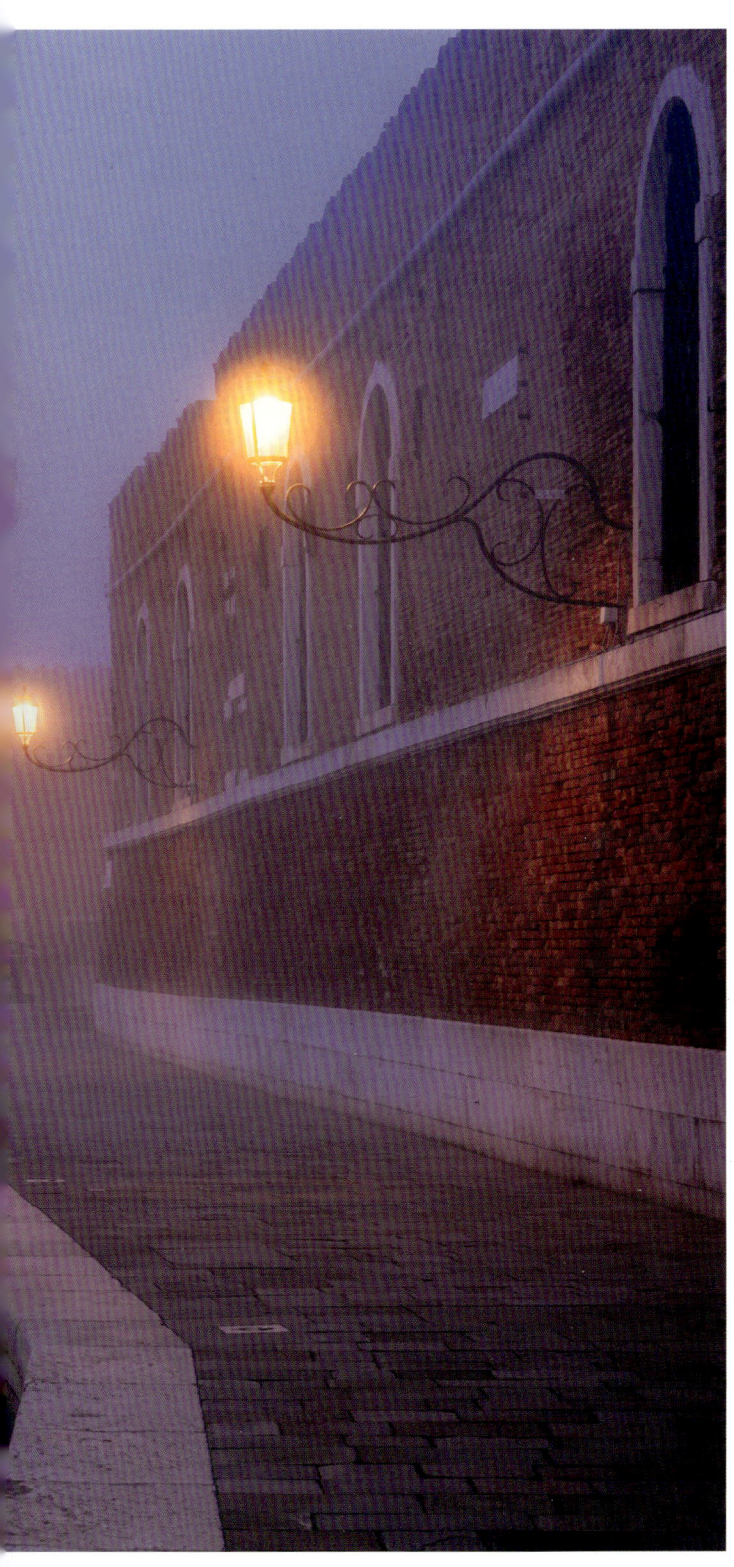

FINAL SHOT

Photographer **Mark Bauer**
Location **The Arsenale, Venice, Italy**
Time and date **4.40 p.m., December 12**
Camera **Nikon Z8**
Lens **Nikon 24–200mm f/4-6.3 (at 51mm)**
Filtration **n/a**
Exposure **ISO 200, 5 sec. at f/11**

THE STORY

"The Arsenale is one of my favorite spots in Venice. Much less photographed than the iconic viewpoints such as the view along the Grand Canal from Ponte dell'Accademia, it is nevertheless, one of the best blue hour locations in the city. Having had a day exploring the back streets of the Castello district, I was enjoying a coffee on the waterfront in the late afternoon, when I saw a bank of fog rolling in across the lagoon.

Although I'd photographed the Arsenale a number of times before, I'd never shot it in fog, and I knew that it would look even more atmospheric in these conditions. I finished my coffee, headed to the Arsenale, set up, and waited. And waited. Looking back along the canal toward the lagoon, it seemed that the fog had engulfed the waterfront and then stopped. As the sun set and it started to get dark, I was in a quandary. Should I stick where I was and hope the fog spread further or should I hurry to another location? There's really no right answer in these situations and these are the kinds of decisions that are torture for photographers.

In the end, I decided to stay put. It turned out to be the right decision, because as twilight descended, the fog finally rolled into the Arsenale. As always, there were a lot of people coming and going, crossing the bridge, often waiting at the top to admire the view or chat with a friend, so I had to grab shots in between the activity. One of the benefits of the fog was that as well as adding to the mood, it also lowered the overall contrast, diffusing the bright highlights of the streetlights and preventing them from burning out; this allowed me to shoot a little longer than perhaps I would have otherwise been able to in order to get the result I wanted."

CHAPTER SEVEN
NIGHT

●●●●●●

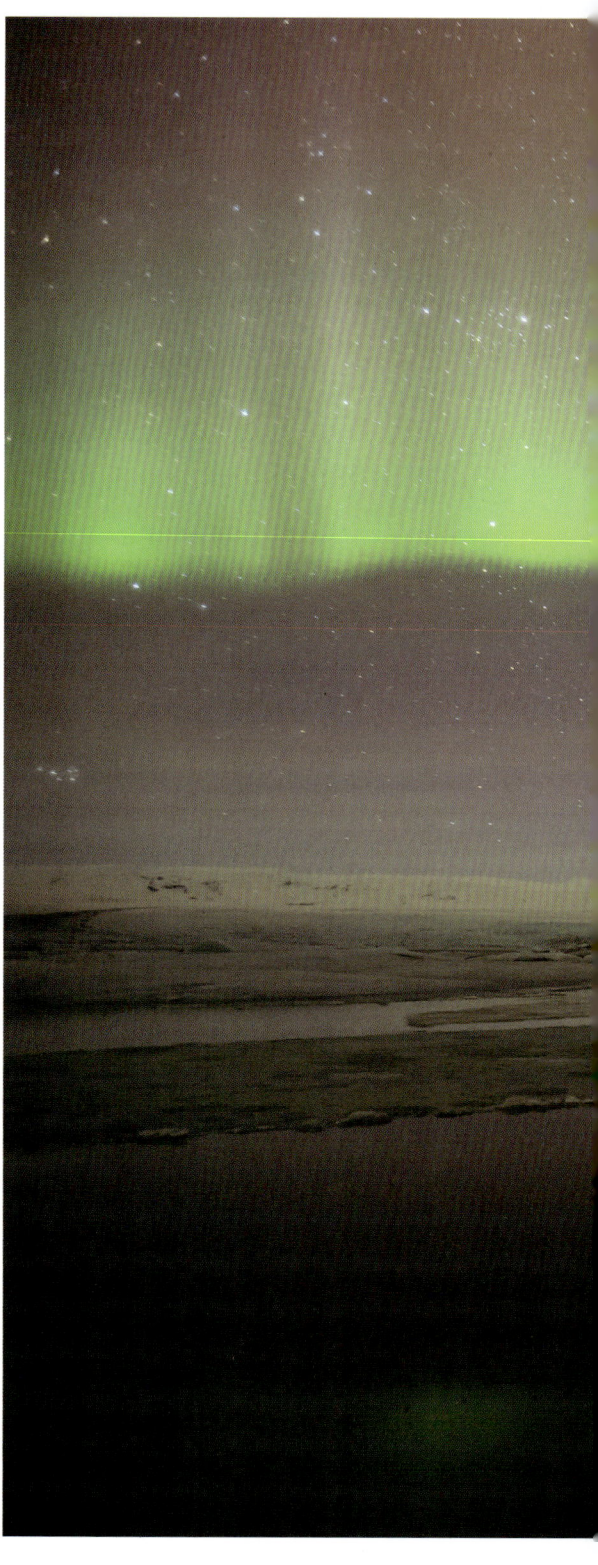

Until recently, night photography—especially astrophotography—was considered a highly specialized discipline, practiced by only a handful of photographers. However, modern equipment has made it much more accessible and it is now a very popular subgenre of landscape photography. Subjects such as the Milky Way and the Northern Lights frequently grace the pages of social media websites and the results are often stunning.

However, night photography is still far from easy. Good night shots demand excellent technique and you will be pushing your equipment to its limits, shooting at high ISO, composing and focusing in almost total darkness (often in low temperatures), and calculating exposure times when it's far too dark for your camera to meter. Added to all that is the need for thorough research and a good understanding of your subject. You also need to know the best times of the year, what conditions are likely to produce a good display, where in the sky celestial objects are most likely to appear, and much more.

In this chapter, we provide advice on all of this, together with tutorials on the techniques you will need to make the most of the special photographic opportunities at night.

▶ **NORTHERN LIGHTS**
With clear skies and an Aurora forecast of 8 on the KP index (see page 174), plans were changed at the last minute, and I and my fellow photographers headed to Jökulsárlon glacier lagoon in Iceland, hoping that the display of the Northern Lights would be as good as forecast, and that there would be enough clear water in the lagoon to pick up reflections of the lights. We weren't disappointed.

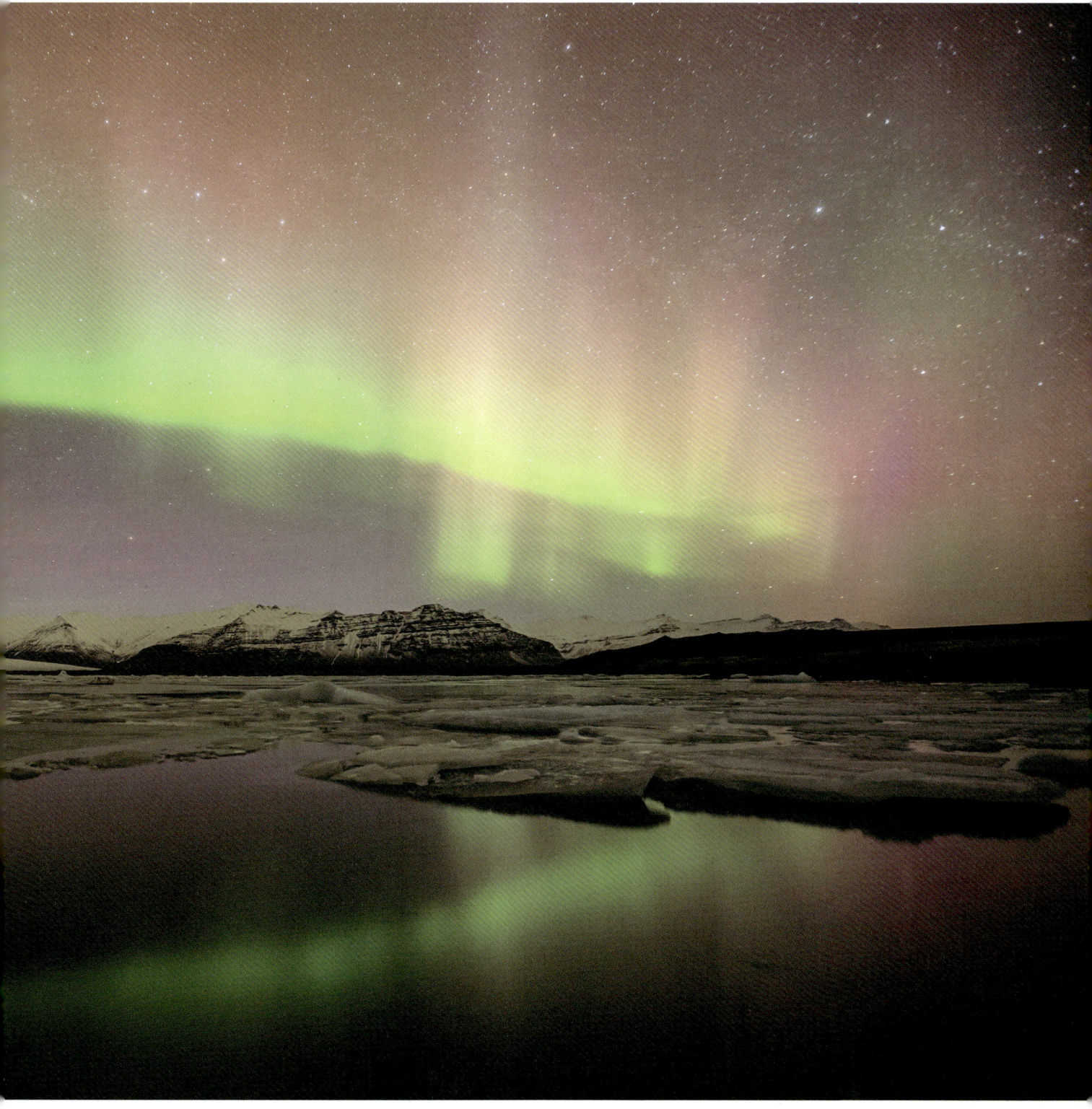

NIGHT SKY

There is something quite awe-inspiring about a clear, dark sky filled with thousands of stars. There is a lot to think about with night sky photography and it helps to break it down into three distinct elements: location, timing, and technique.

Finding somewhere with as little light pollution as possible is a crucial factor and may involve traveling quite some distance to get away from towns and dwellings. Equally importantly, you need to remember that a night shot is just like any other photograph in that a strong composition beneath the sky is key. Seek out locations that feature strong focal points such as hills or where you can use foreground interest.

The darker the sky, the more stars will be visible, so being aware of the phase of the moon is important. During a full moon, the sky will be too bright and can appear almost like daylight in photographs. Photographing around the new moon is preferable, although a little moonlight can cast some subtle light onto the foreground. Check the weather forecast carefully when planning: the clearer the sky the better, and the stiller the air the less chance there is of exposures being ruined by wind vibrating the tripod.

TECHNIQUE

You'll need a wide-angle lens to allow you to capture both the sky and the landscape below, and preferably one with a fast aperture—f/2.8 or wider—as the biggest technical challenge is getting enough light onto the sensor. A camera capable of good results at high ISO is another must, as is a sturdy tripod and head. Finally, a cable release and intervalometer (if your camera doesn't have one built in) should also be on the kit list.

To get optimum sharpness of the sky, you will need to focus manually on infinity. Finding infinity focus is not as straightforward as you'd think as most autofocus lenses are designed to focus beyond infinity. Very few are truly focused on infinity, even when the ∞ symbol is lined up with the focusing mark. If you can, set up on location before sunset, compose, and set focus then. If this isn't possible, take test shots and check critical sharpness carefully, tweaking focus if necessary until you achieve it. To further complicate matters, many modern lenses are "focus by wire," with no mechanical connection to the lens elements and no "hard stop"—the focus ring will keep turning indefinitely. If you have a mirrorless camera, you can use the electronic distance scale to guide you; if not, do your best to focus on a distant bright object. If you struggle to find true infinity focus with an autofocus zoom, consider using manual-focus primes, with which focusing on infinity is simple.

It will be too dark to meter accurately, so the best technique is to take your best guess, shoot a test image, and then check exposure. It's absolutely vital to be guided by the histogram here, as the LCD review image will be deceptive. When surrounded by total darkness, the image will appear much brighter than it is in reality. While you won't want to "expose to the right" (see pages 43 and 152) for a night shot, keeping out of the deep shadows is important, especially if you plan to reveal some detail on the land.

If you want to have detail in the landscape below, one option is to use a flashlight to "paint with light" (see page 170). Done subtly, this can resemble moonlight. An alternative is to take two images—one exposed for the night sky and one for the landscape, which should be given more overall exposure, to reveal detail. These can then be blended in post-processing (see page 60) and this often gives a more natural-looking result than painting with light. You could also take the opportunity to change the focus distance to ensure that the foreground interest is sharp, or you could try focus-stacking (see page 134).

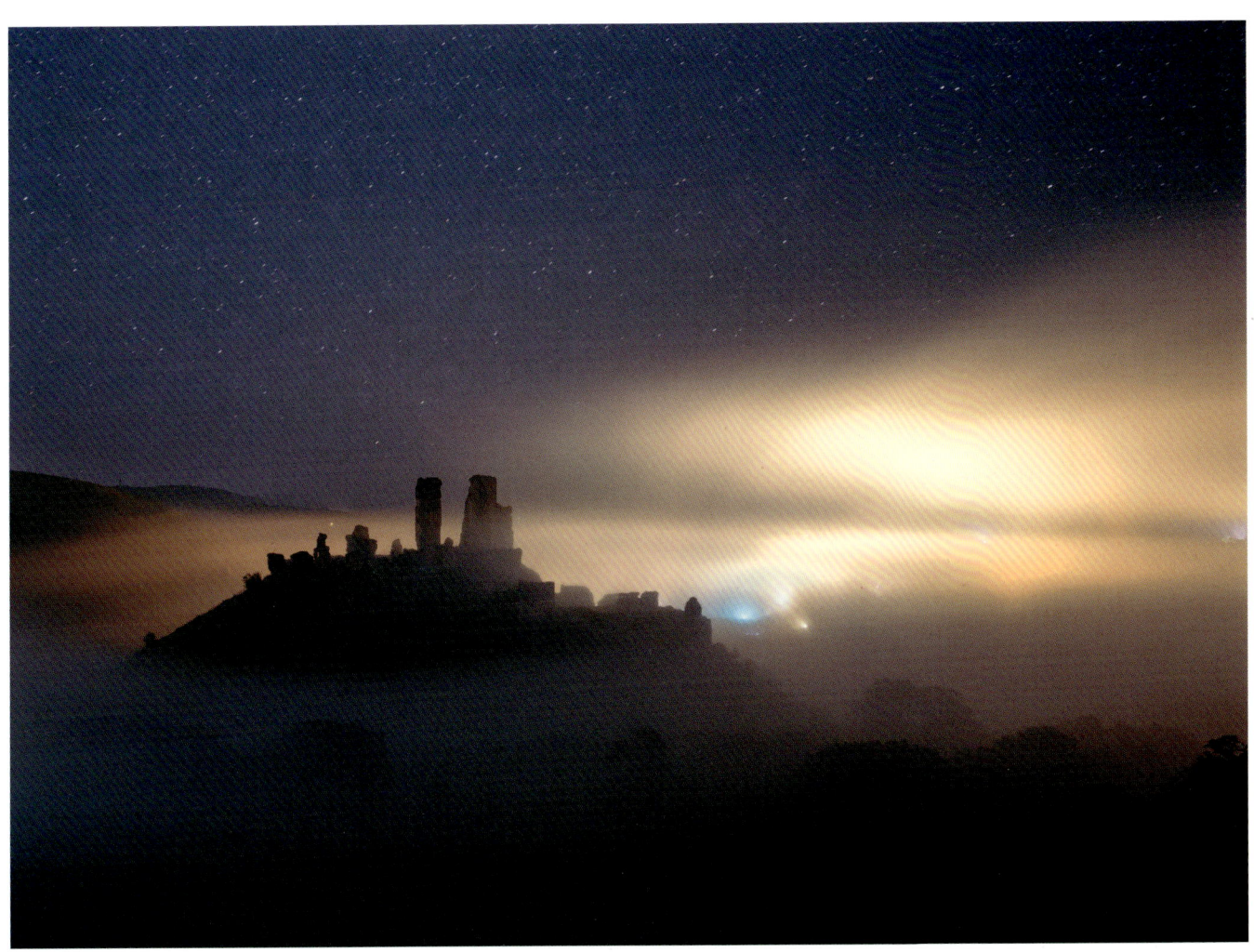

▲ NIGHT SKY

The night sky is a beautiful subject in its own right, but shots of the stars look so much better if there is a thoughtful composition beneath them; here the lighthouse makes an excellent foreground subject. As well as the stars and the Milky Way, celestial events, such as the Perseid meteor shower photographed here, are worth waiting for. (Andy Farrer)

EXPOSURE LENGTH

In terms of how you want the stars to appear, there are essentially two choices: keep them sharp, so they appear as points of light, or blur them to create star trails. To calculate the maximum exposure length that will keep stars sharp, you can use the "500 rule." Simply divide 500 by the focal length you're shooting at. So, for example, if shooting at 20mm, the maximum exposure you can shoot at before seeing star movement is 25 seconds. This calculation assumes a full-frame camera, so with crop sensors use the "300 rule" instead. Once you know the maximum exposure time, with your lens at maximum aperture, adjust the ISO until you get the correct exposure at this shutter speed. There is a bit of trial and error involved here, but, as a guideline, start at ISO 1600 and adjust from there.

STAR TRAILS

To create star trails it is possible to take one single long exposure, but better results are usually possible by taking a number of shorter exposures and combining them, using dedicated software such as StarStax (www.starstax.net). The advantages of this approach are that the sensor generates less thermal noise at shorter exposures, and you can remove the "bad" frames that include intrusive light sources. For best results, point the camera toward the North Star (or find the south celestial pole in the southern hemisphere). This will create star trails that rotate around the North Star.

Use the 500 rule to calculate the exposure time and then take test shots to establish the ISO, as above. Check and adjust focus if necessary. Set the camera's intervalometer to take shots with a delay of two seconds between them. This allows the sensor to cool down a bit and reduce thermal noise but is not long enough to leave gaps in the trails. Make sure you turn off Long Exposure Noise Reduction (see page 92) as this will double the time between shots. Shoot for two to five hours. Obviously, the longer you shoot for, the longer the trails will be in the final image.

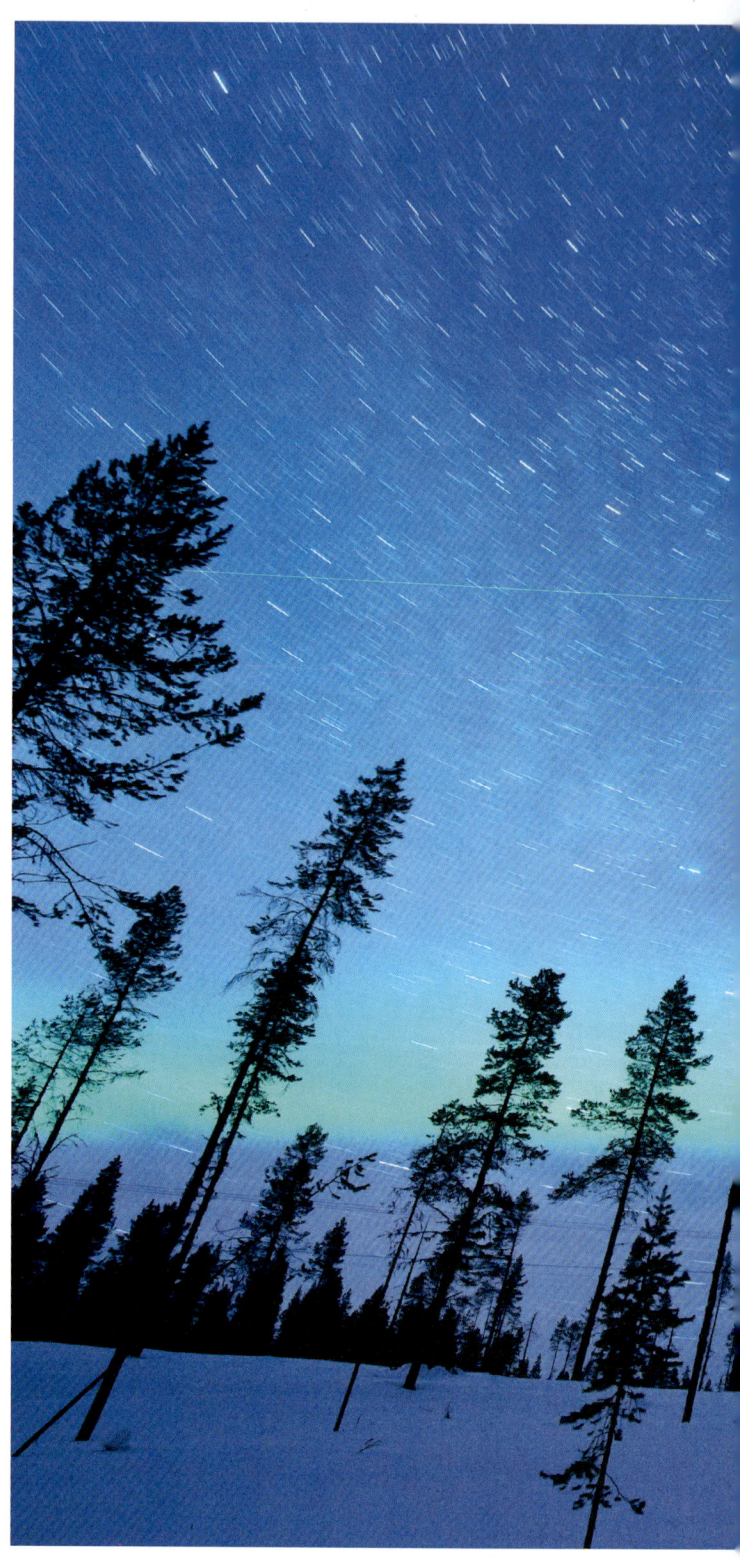

▶ STAR TRAILS
The trees make a powerful foreground for this shot of the night sky, with the central tree pointing up to the North Star. The star trails circle around it and, as a bonus, there is a faint display of the Northern Lights in the sky. (Jeremy Walker)

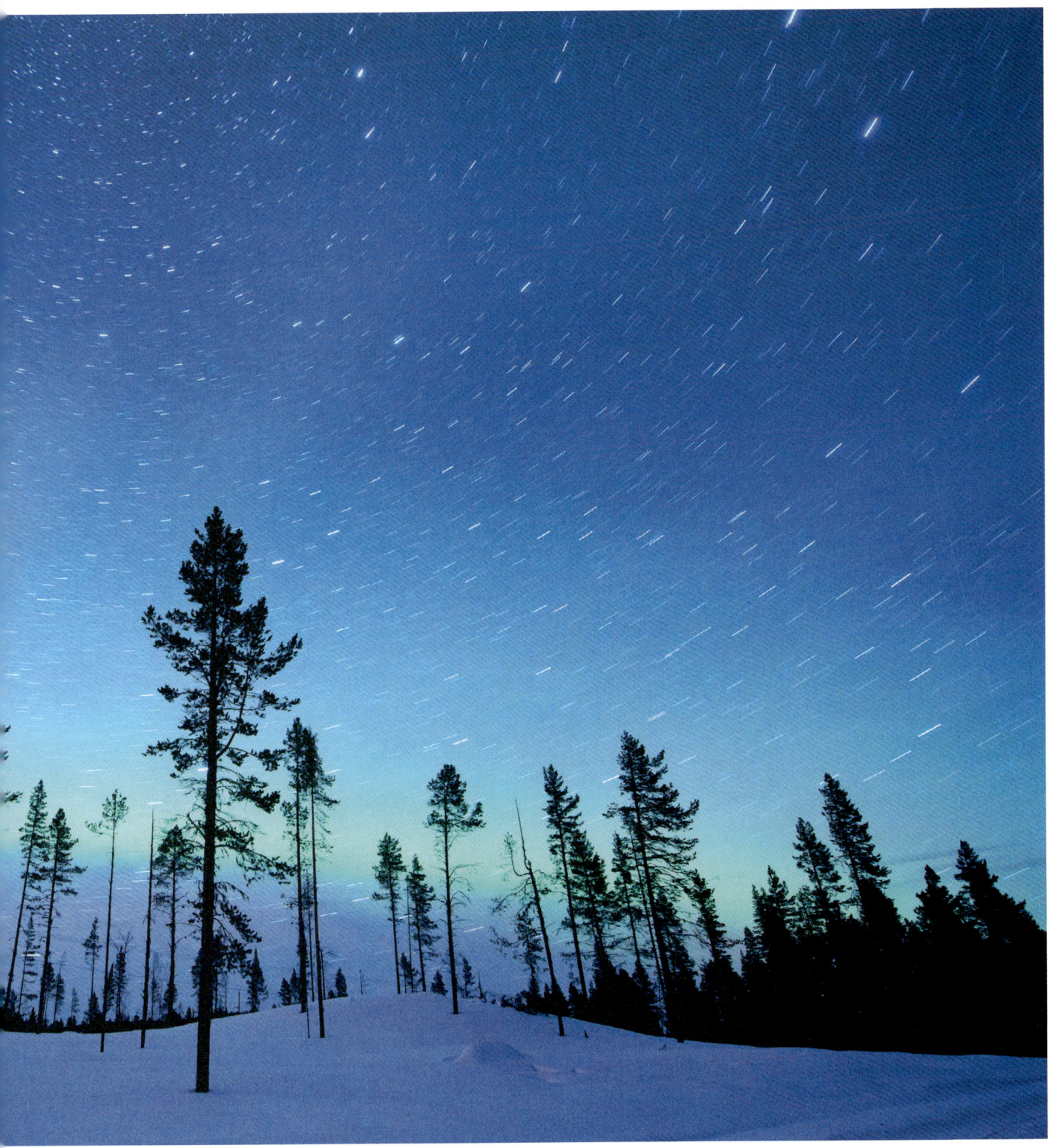

MILKY WAY

The Milky Way—the galaxy that contains our solar system—is a popular subject for astrophotographers; photographed well, it can add the same impact to a night landscape as a stormy sky or colorful sunset does to a daytime landscape.

Although the Milky Way is visible all year round, the galactic center or "core" is only visible from March to October. As this is the brightest and most colorful part of the galaxy, this is what most photographers concentrate on and the period when it is visible is sometimes referred to as the Milky Way "season."

The Milky Way changes its position and orientation throughout the season. Early on, the galactic core appears in the south east and the Milky Way is low in the sky in a horizontal orientation. Later in the season, from July to October, the galactic core appears in the south west and the Milky Way is in a more vertical orientation. In the middle of the season, the galaxy is diagonal and the galactic core is visible to the south.

Having this information will help you choose locations and plan suitable compositions for the time of year. For example, early in the season is an excellent time for shooting panoramas, with the Milky Way in an arch, low in the sky.

For the southern hemisphere, the season is the same but the core of the Milky Way is much higher in the sky, almost overhead (depending how far south you are), with the band sweeping from the south west horizon to the north east horizon.

In terms of shooting technique, the basic principles still apply. You need a strong composition, and use the 500 rule (see page 166) to calculate the maximum exposure time possible to avoid star movement. Shoot on or near the new moon and be prepared to either illuminate your foreground with some subtle light

painting (see page 170), or to shoot a separate exposure for the foreground and blend the images in post-processing (see page 60)—an exposure for the land should be two to three stops longer than the one for the sky.

(see page 170)... (see page 60)

FOCUS ON... PHOTOPILLS

The key to successful Milky Way shots is planning. Until fairly recently, this was a laborious process, requiring fairly specialist knowledge. These days, there are a number of websites and apps available to do the hard work for you. One of the most comprehensive is PhotoPills—this includes a planning app similar to The Photographer's Ephemeris, but with the addition of specific information for shooting the Milky Way.

For your chosen location, you can find out the times the galactic core becomes visible and then disappears from view for any date, as well as the moon phase, the location of the galactic core, its orientation, and more. If you are on location, you can use the Night AR (augmented reality) view to check the scene in front of you rather than trying to visualize it using the information from a two-dimensional map.

For more detail, PhotoPills has a highly informative website, with a number of useful articles, tutorials, and video tutorials: www.photopills.com

▶ MILKY WAY SHOOT PLANNING

Here is an example from a real shoot planned with PhotoPills. In this example, the red pin shows my shooting position and the secondary (black) pin is placed on the subject that I wanted under the Milky Way. The light gray line shows where the galactic core becomes visible and the dark one where it sets—timings are found by swiping right on the top information bar. The circles, thin white line, and dots are used to identify the orientation of the Milky Way. Here, with the dots close to the center, we can see that the Milky Way is in an almost vertical position—also indicated in the image top left of the screen. The elevation of the Milky Way and its galactic center are also shown and the thicker white line is the azimuth line of the core, showing its position at different times. Using this information, I was able to determine that the ideal time to get the shot I wanted was around 11 p.m. on August 22.

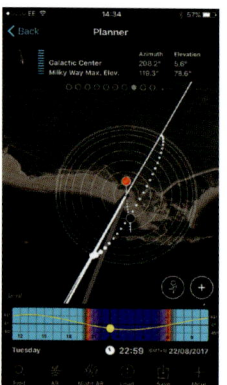

▶ MILKY WAY

This image of the Milky Way was the result of the planning described left. Two exposures were blended—one for the sky and one for the main subject.

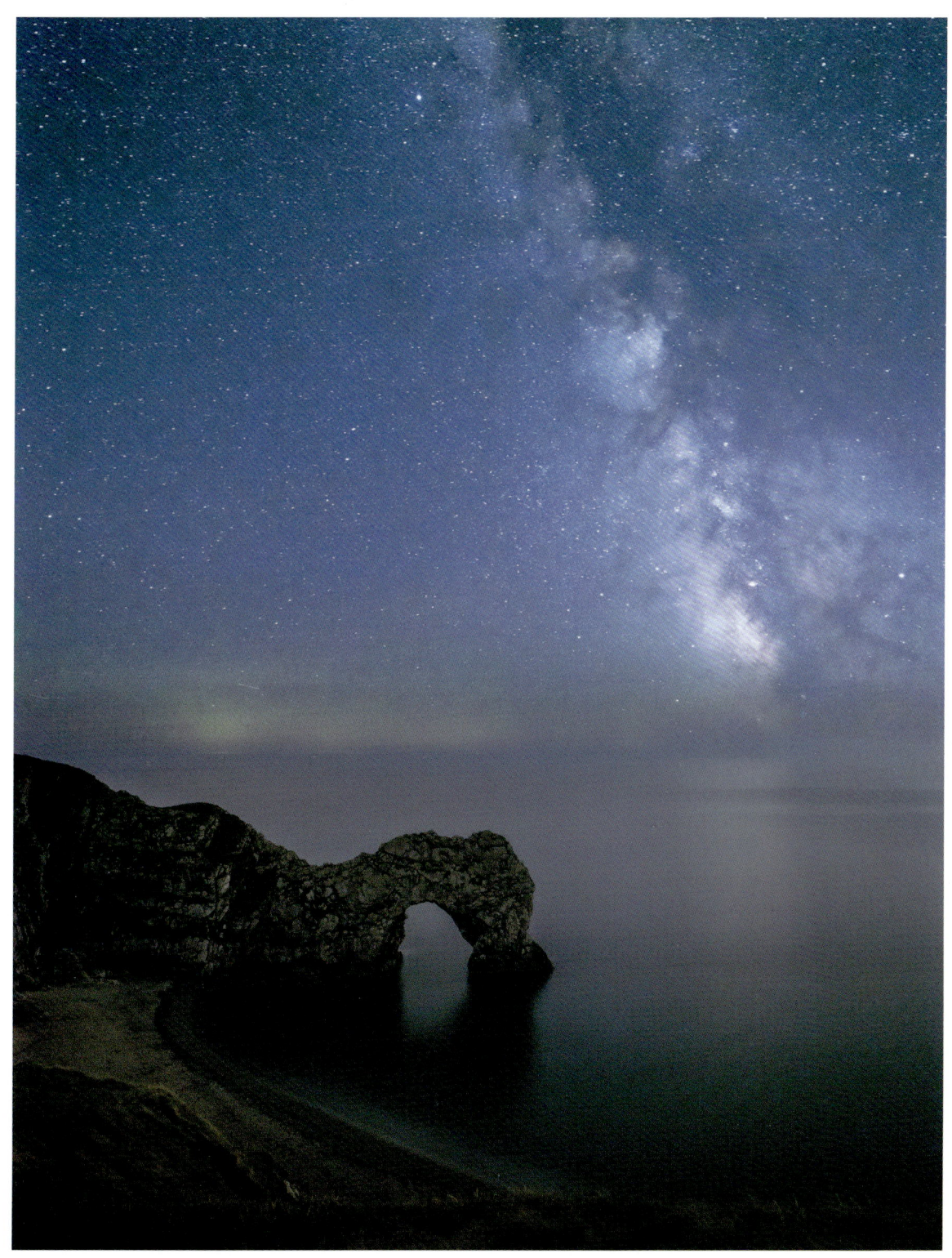

CORE TECHNIQUE
PAINTING WITH LIGHT

Apart from when shooting the Northern Lights, most night photography is best done when there is a new moon, as moonlight obscures fainter stars. However, this means that the foreground receives very little light to reveal detail. One way around this is to blend two exposures—one taken for the night sky and one for the foreground—but this isn't always practical (you can end up needing extremely long exposures for the foreground) and many photographers would prefer to keep their processing simple and work on a single image.

One approach that allows you to capture detail throughout the image in a single exposure is to use an additional light source, such as a powerful flashlight, to "paint" your foreground with light. Done subtly, this is a very effective technique. Care is necessary, however, as it is very easy to "overpaint," with the result that foregrounds appear unnaturally bright or parts of the scene are unevenly lit in your image.

Painting with light is a technique that doesn't have to be reserved for night-sky photography. With the right subjects—monuments and old buildings work well, for example—excellent results are possible on cloudy evenings as well. In certain circumstances, light pollution can even enhance shots, adding a warm, sunset-like glow to the horizon.

Most modern flashlights use LED lights and brightness is measured in lumens. There is no one "correct" brightness for light painting as the power you need depends on how distant your subject is—anything between 200 and 1000 lumens could be appropriate. LED lights tend to have a rather cool color temperature, which can give a rather harsh result, depending on the subject—you can use lighting gels to warm the light.

EXPERIMENT

It's important to keep the flashlight moving and to try to paint your subject(s) evenly. If lighting multiple parts of the scene, remember that further objects will require more light. There is no need to paint your subject for the entire duration of the exposure—if your flashlight is too bright, use it for just part of the exposure. Some experimentation may be necessary to find the ideal time. Painting from off-camera, rather than directly behind it, creates directional light that creates shadows, reveals texture, and adds depth.

When illuminating a close foreground object, the lighting could be too harsh if you paint it directly. Instead, consider diffused lighting, perhaps bouncing light off a reflector off-camera, or using off-camera objects to bounce light back into the foreground.

FOCUS ON...
LOW-LEVEL LIGHTING

An alternative to light painting is to use a constant, dim light source mounted on a tripod. LED panels are typically used for this, positioned to provide directional lighting. As there is no need to keep moving the light source, results are controllable and more predictable. The aim is to provide an additional two to three stops of light on the foreground—this is roughly equivalent to weak moonlight. Positioning the lights off-camera provides modeling light for depth, and gels can be used to warm up cool LEDs. If possible, lights should be positioned 100ft (30m) or more from the focal point, to create uniform lighting. As with light painting, the tendency is to use too much light at first—some test shots and experimentation will be necessary. Often, the light's lowest setting is best. If it is still too bright, you can try diffusing it.

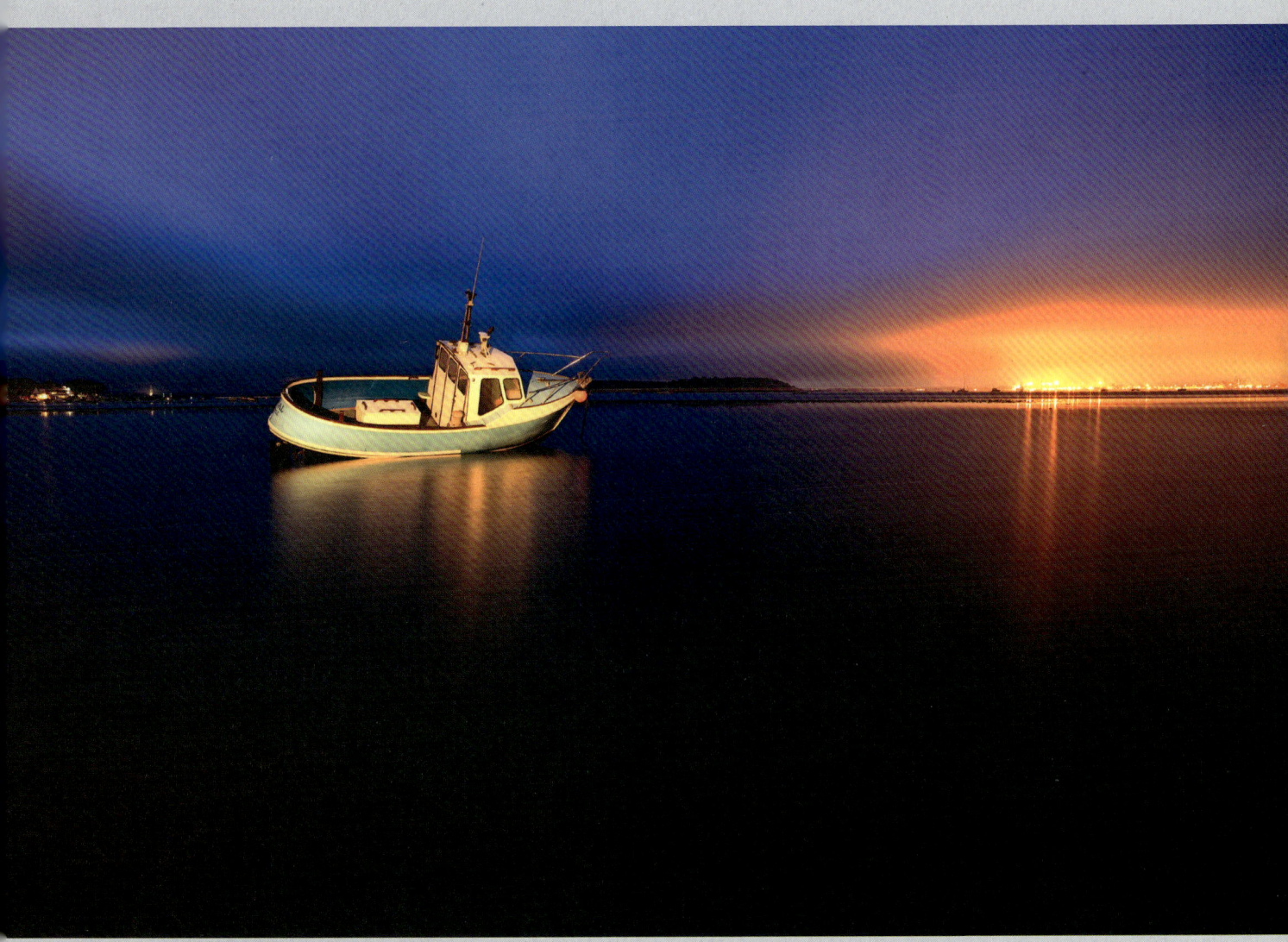

▲ BOAT WITH PAINTED LIGHT
On a cloudy evening, this boat was painted with a powerful halogen flashlight (chosen because of its attractive, warm light) for around half the duration of the exposure. What looks like the glow of a sunset on the horizon is actually light pollution from a distant town.

COMPOSITION
NORTHERN LIGHTS

The Aurora Borealis or Northern Lights are one of the most spectacular natural phenomena. The Northern Lights are becoming increasingly popular, not just with photographers, but also with general tourists, and countries such as Iceland and Norway now welcome huge numbers of visitors in winter, all hoping to see them.

The techniques for shooting the Aurora are similar to shooting the Milky Way but the main difference is that you don't need a new moon—a strong Northern Lights display can be quite bright, so moonlight is less intrusive. Many photographers, myself included, actually prefer some moonlight in the scene—even the light of the full moon—in order to illuminate the foreground and balance the exposure. Moonlight will also help you to keep exposure times to a minimum, which is important not just for avoiding star movement, but also to prevent the Aurora from losing its shape as it moves during the exposure. You should also remove all filters from lenses, including ultraviolet filters, as they can cause interference patterns in the image. As with shots of the Milky Way, location is important—the absence of light pollution is more or less essential, and ideally you should have a strong foreground and focal point.

BALANCE

Composition is just as important as with any landscape photograph. The Northern Lights really are a spectacular sight and it's easy to get caught up in the excitement of the moment and forget about the basics, especially composition. Remember that, for your images to have real impact, you need to have something interesting underneath the sky. Look for balance, and use the same compositional devices as you would for any landscape—position focal points according to the rule of thirds or the golden section, and use foreground interest to enhance linear perspective, as well as lines to guide the eye.

To a large extent, composition will be determined by the position of the Northern Lights and the shapes formed during the display, but always try to apply basic compositional principles where possible. Scouting locations and planning compositions in advance is useful, but it is also important to be able to react quickly to what is in front of you.

CONDITIONS

Obviously, you can only shoot the Northern Lights if you can see them, so what conditions should you look for? First, you need clear skies—even the strongest display will be invisible behind total cloud cover. Then you need solar activity. The Northern Lights are caused by solar storms sending out charged particles that react with the Earth's magnetic field and atmosphere. It is possible to predict the chances of Northern Lights by looking at solar activity, and there are a number of useful resources that can help (see page 174). Finally, you need patience. Inexperienced Aurora hunters will often give up too early, only to find out that there was a display a couple of hours after they went to bed; unless you are very lucky it may be necessary to wait quite a while.

▶ **NORTHERN LIGHTS IN GREENLAND**
A clear sky and interesting foreground make for an eye-catching Northern Lights shot.

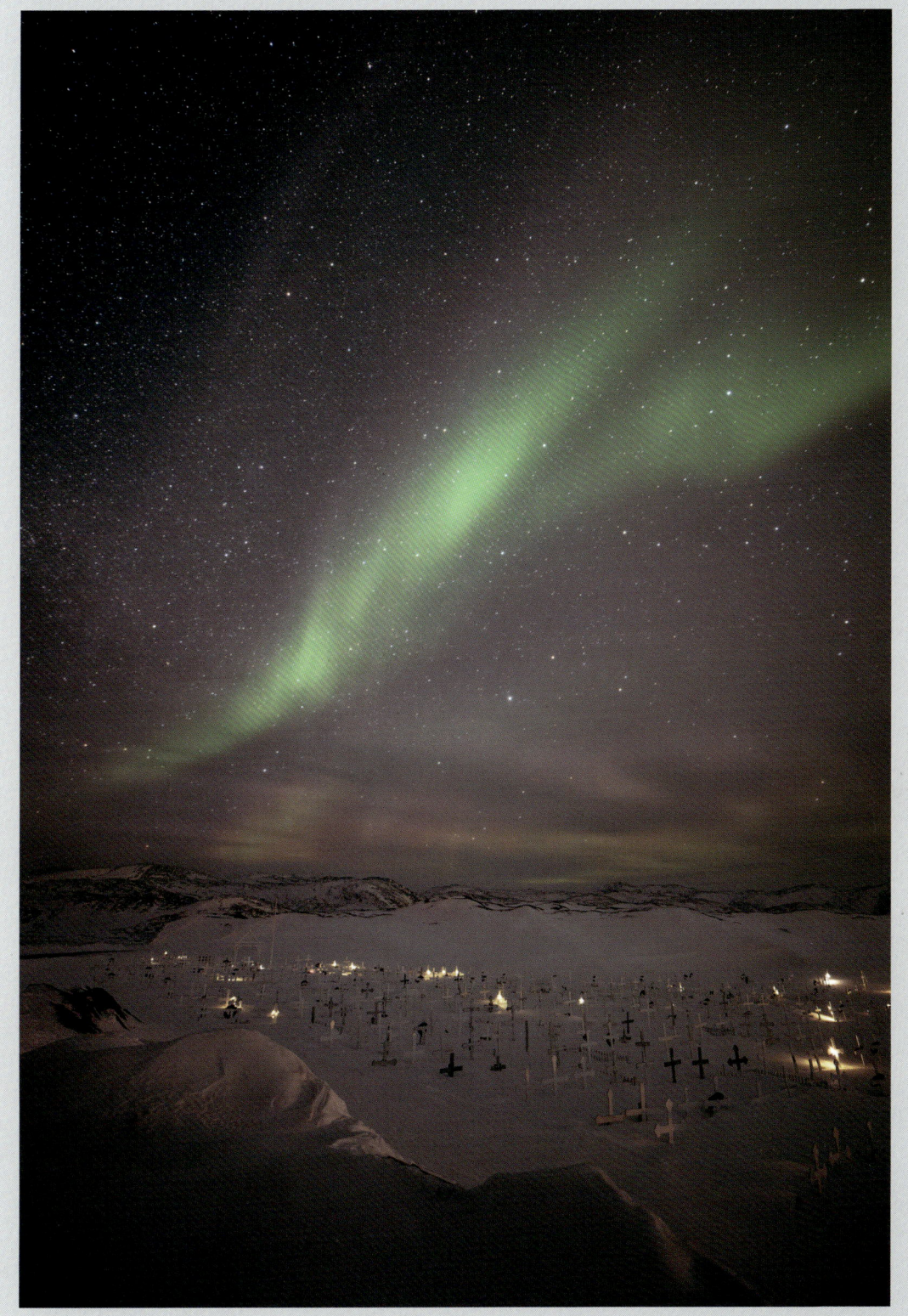

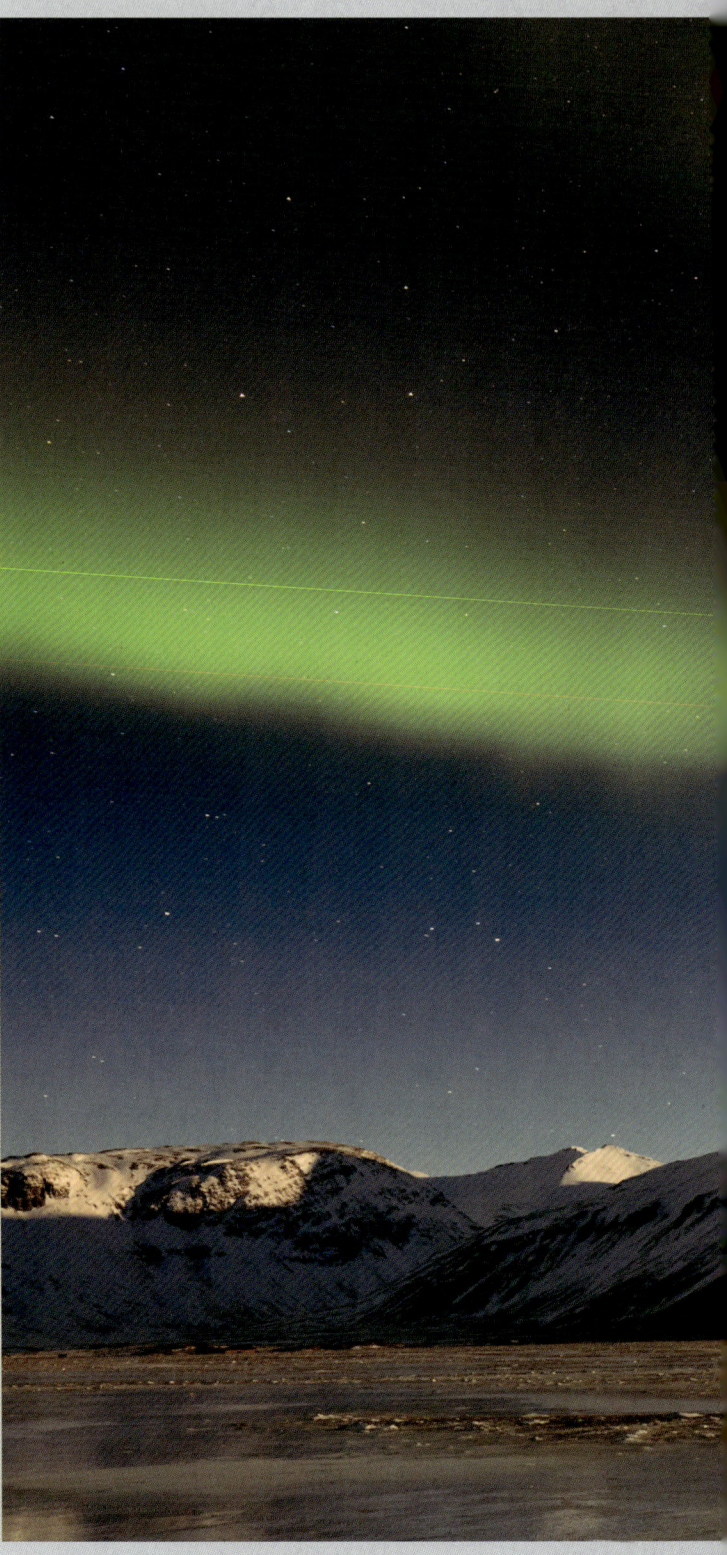

FOCUS ON...
WEBSITES FOR AURORA
PHOTOGRAPHY

Clear skies are essential for aurora photography. Many photographers swear by the detailed information given by Clear Outside: visit www.clearoutside.com or use their smartphone app.

There are many websites and apps for forecasting Aurora activity, but these are recommended: www.spaceweatherlive.com and www.softservenews.com. For smartphone apps, look at My Aurora Forecast. Remember also that local weather forecasts, such as the Icelandic Meteorological Office, can be very helpful.

The strength of an Aurora display is measured using the KP Index, which ranges from 0–9. Anything over KP 5 is considered storm level, but excellent displays can be seen with a KP index of 3 or sometimes even 2.

FOCUS ON...
CLOTHING

You may be standing for several hours in very cold conditions, so it's hard to overstress the importance of suitable clothing. Multiple layers—including good thermal base layers—are essential, as are warm gloves (with thin gloves on underneath, so you can remove the main glove to change camera settings). A thick down jacket is also recommended. You lose heat quickly if you are not moving, so wear more layers than you think you will need.

▶ **MOON-LIGHTING**
Unlike in Milky Way photography, moonlight can actually enhance shots of the Aurora. In this image, taken when it was nearly full moon, the Northern Lights are still clearly visible, but the moonlight picks out detail in the landscape below.

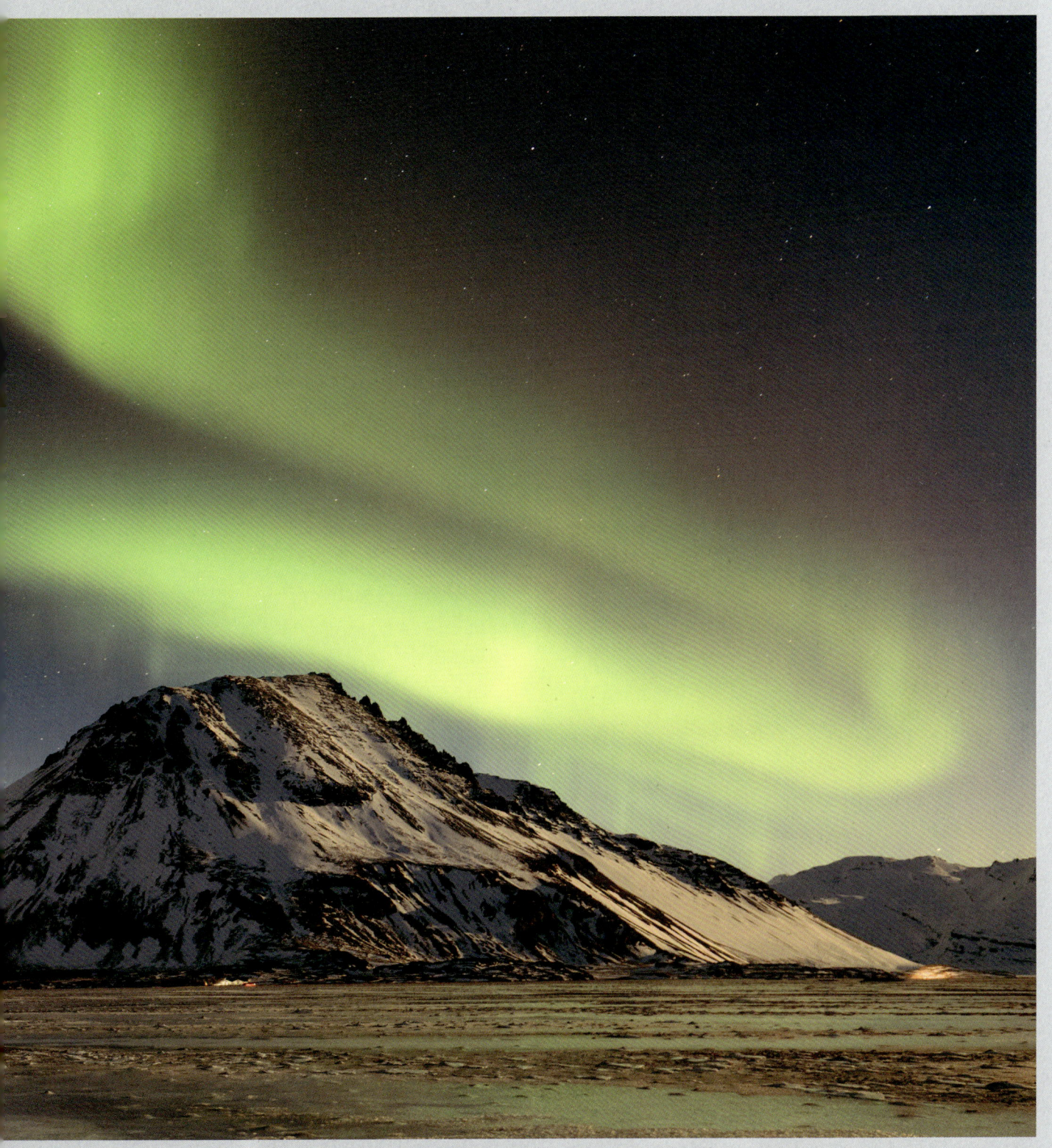

POST-PROCESSING STEP-BY-STEP
NOISE

Night photography necessitates shooting at high ISO levels, and one side-effect of this is noise. Fortunately, modern software such as Adobe Lightroom features powerful noise reduction tools.

There are essentially two types of noise. Color noise manifests itself as multicolored pixels in the areas of an image that should show flat color. Luminance noise is monochromatic and has an appearance similar to film grain.

Editing software usually provides tools for dealing with both types of noise. In Lightroom's Detail panel, for example, there are three sliders for tackling luminance noise: Luminance, Detail, and Contrast. Luminance controls the amount of noise reduction, Detail sets the noise threshold, and Contrast, as the name suggests, adjusts luminance contrast. The amount of detail and contrast retained can therefore be fine-tuned, but at the expense

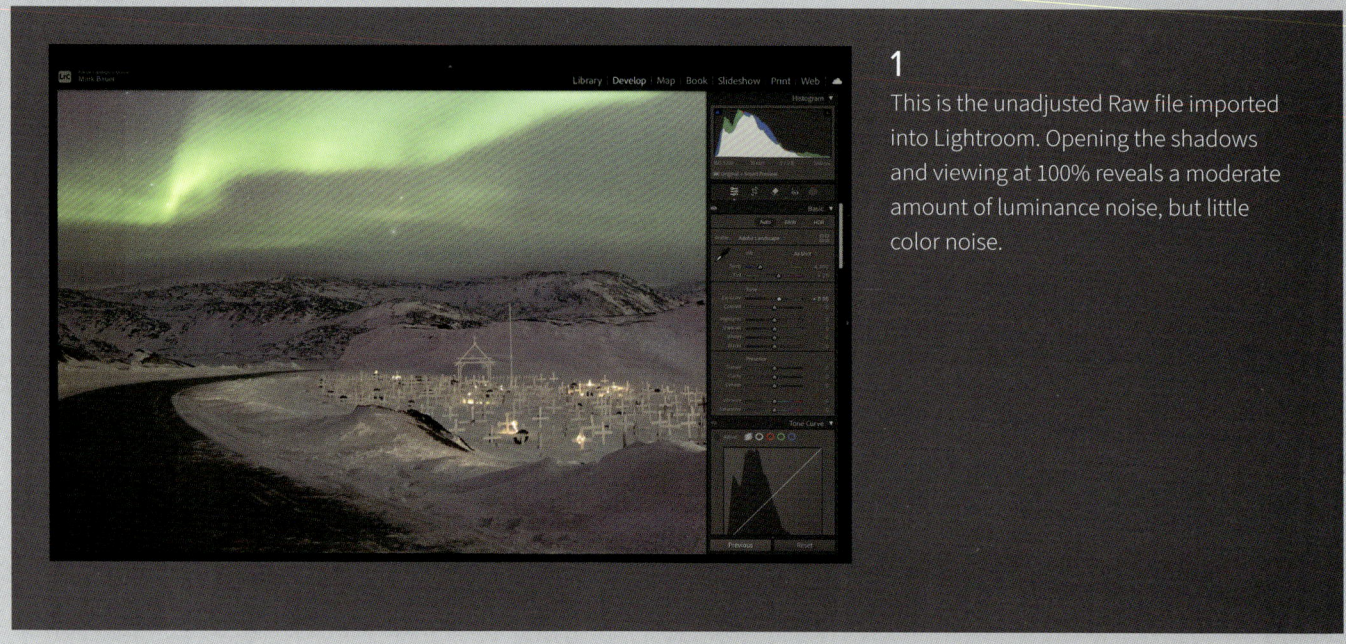

1
This is the unadjusted Raw file imported into Lightroom. Opening the shadows and viewing at 100% reveals a moderate amount of luminance noise, but little color noise.

of accentuating residual noise. For controlling color noise there are two additional sliders: the Detail slider, which controls the color noise threshold, and the Smoothness slider for reducing color mottling. It is also possible to apply local noise reduction using the masking, although you cannot fine-tune Detail and Contrast. There is also the AI-powered "Denoise" button, which provides pretty much a one-click solution and works particularly well with heavy noise. For moderately noisy images or if you prefer more control, use the tools described above.

When sharpening, you should also pay attention to the Masking slider, which allows you to mask off areas of smooth texture, so that noise is not made more prominent in these areas.

Remember that any noise reduction is a balance between removing the appearance of noise and preserving detail.

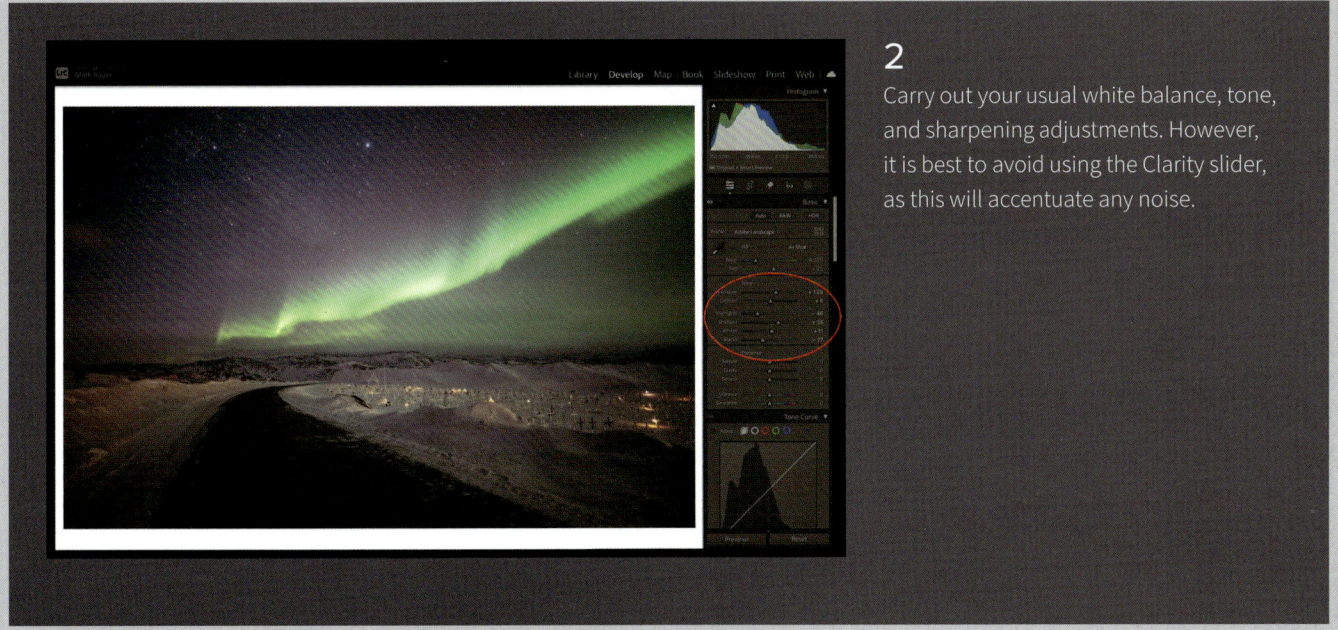

2
Carry out your usual white balance, tone, and sharpening adjustments. However, it is best to avoid using the Clarity slider, as this will accentuate any noise.

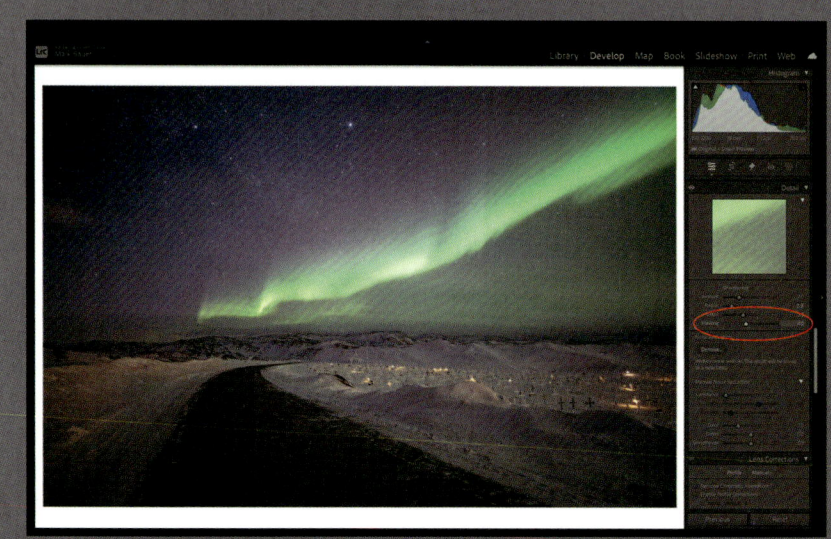

3

Apply Sharpening and then adjust Masking. Holding down the Option/Alt key and pushing the slider to the right shows which areas are masked—black is masked, white unmasked. Usually, a masking level of around 10–15 works well, but in this case, with little fine detail in the shot, it is possible to mask quite a large area.

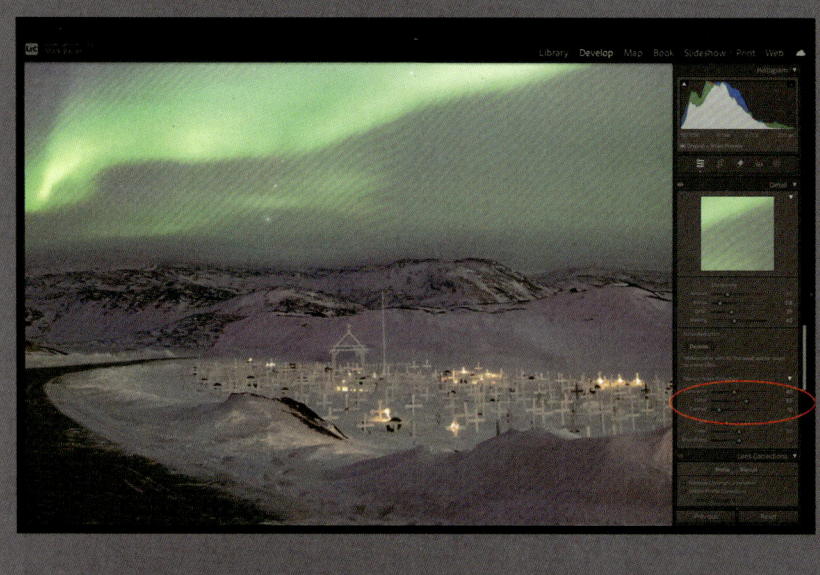

4

Adjust the Noise Reduction Luminance slider to obtain a balance between reducing noise and retaining detail. Make some further fine adjustments using the Detail and Contrast sliders if necessary. If needed, apply Color noise reduction.

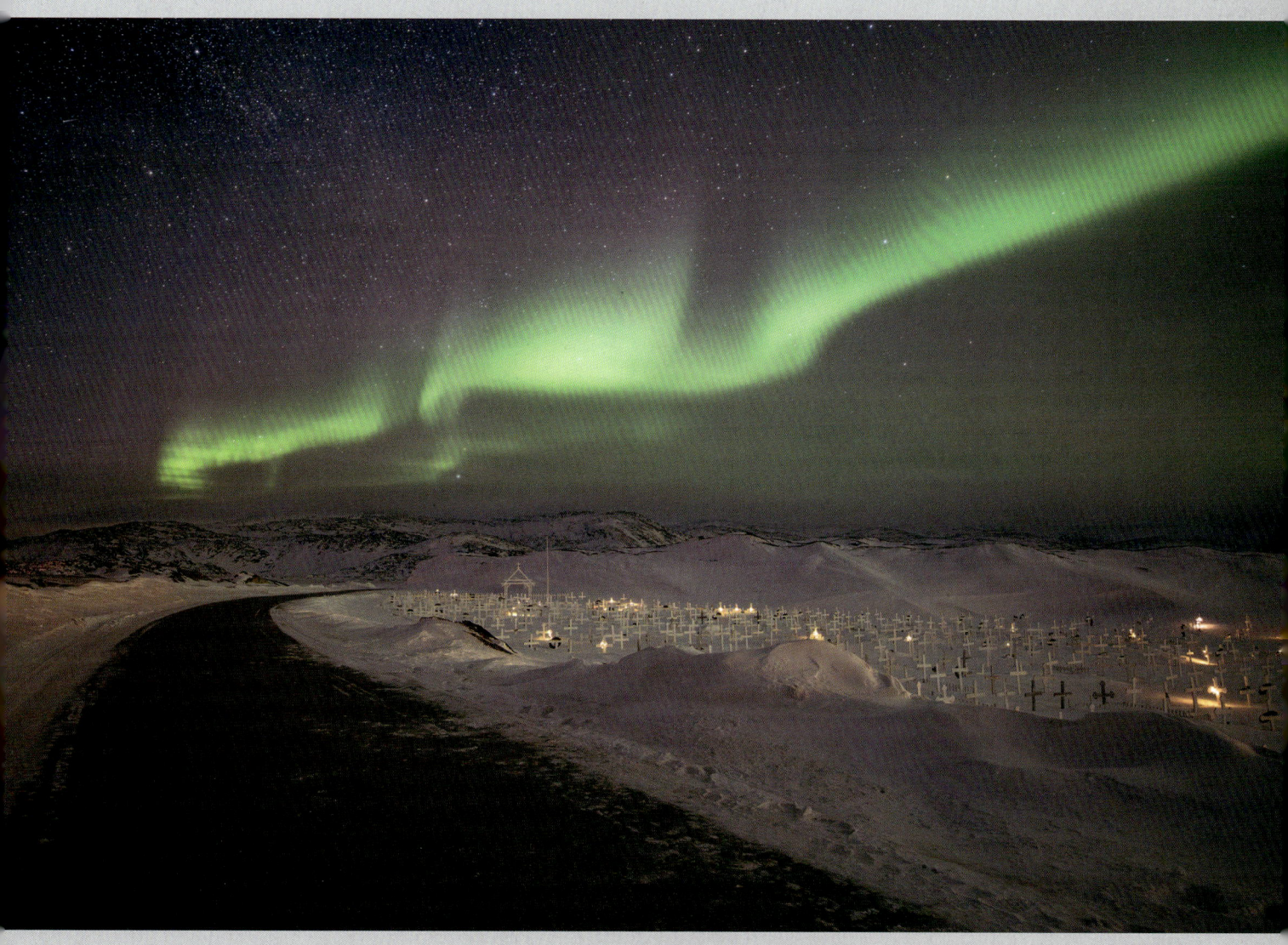

FINAL IMAGE
The final image shows excellent clarity and detail, but with minimal noise—a very large print could be made from this file.

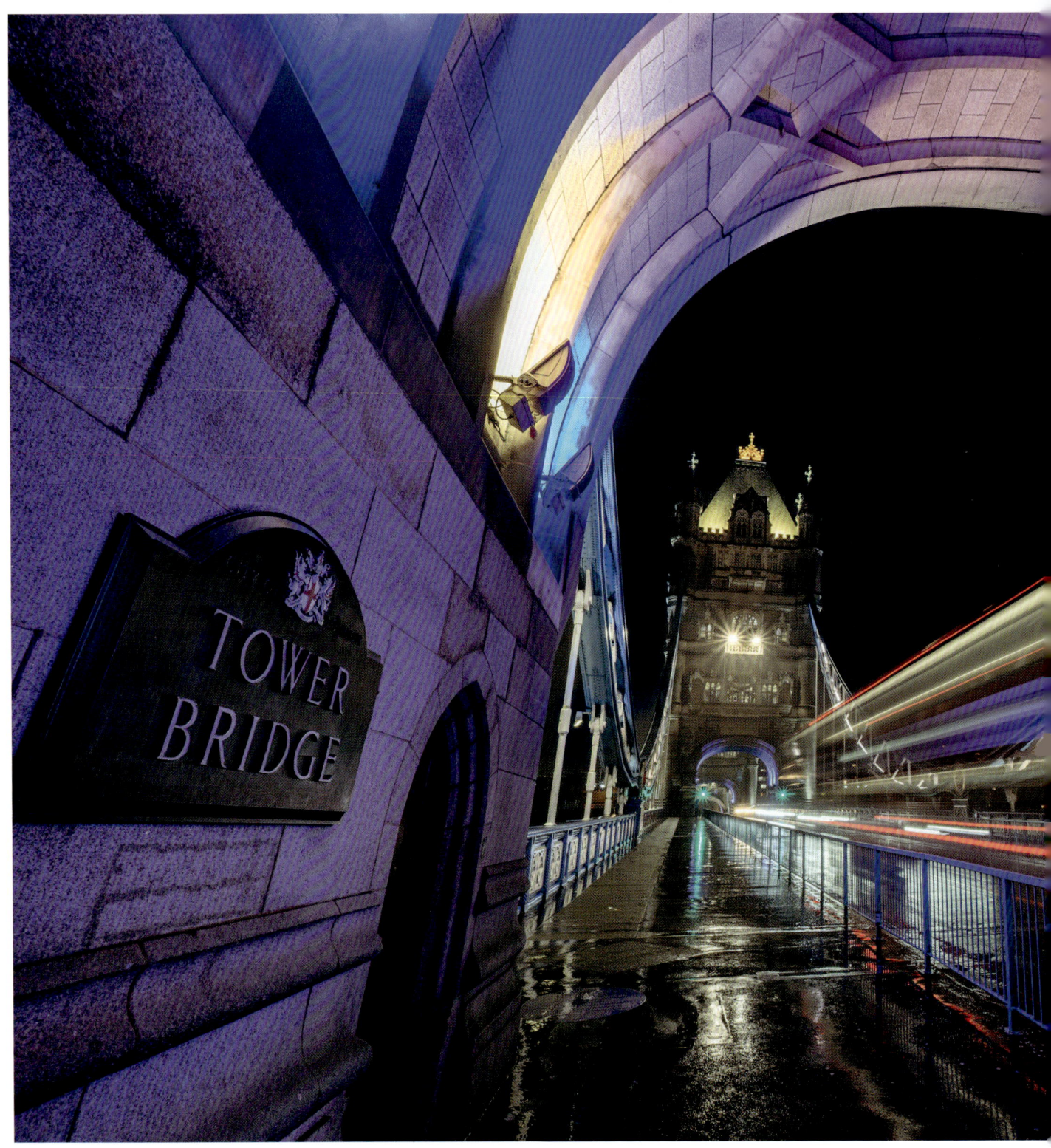

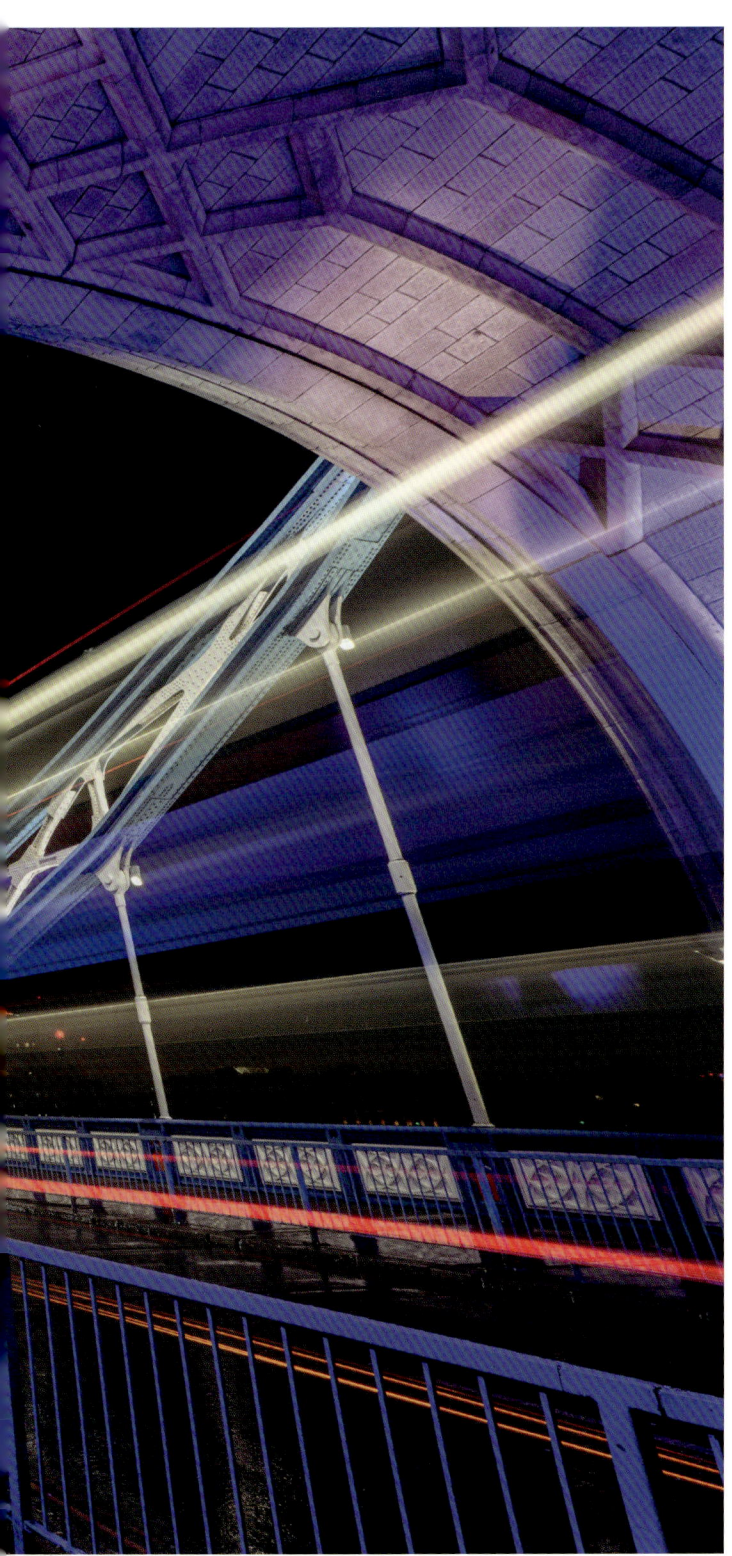

FINAL SHOT

Photographer **Mark Bauer**
Location **Tower Bridge, London, United Kingdom**
Time and date **5.50 a.m., February 18**
Camera **Nikon Z8**
Lens **14–30mm f/4 (at 14mm)**
Filtration **None**
Exposure **ISO 200, 3 sec. at f/11**

THE STORY

"The focus of this chapter has mostly been on rural—even quite remote—landscapes. However, as with twilight, nighttime can also be an excellent time to shoot cityscapes, and subjects such as traffic trails can work really well. There is more contrast when the sky is truly dark, with less detail in shadows, so scenes where there is plenty of artificial light filling in the darker areas tend to work best.

On a trip to London, I was staying at a hotel near Tower Bridge and had long wanted to photograph this iconic landmark— ideally at night, with light trails streaking through the arches. Not an original shot, but one that I thought would be fun to do. I headed out early in the morning when the streets were reasonably quiet and set up about an hour and a half before sunrise, while the sky was still completely black. The weather certainly helped here—heavy cloud meant that any pre-sunrise light would be delayed. It was also raining, which had the added benefit of making the road and sidewalk shiny and reflective, doubling the impact of the lights and color.

I set up a composition underneath one of the arches of the bridge. This provided not only a frame for the tower behind it, but also some shelter from the rain. To include the detail of the underside of the arch and the 'Tower Bridge' sign on the left, I needed my widest focal length of 14mm. I waited for a bus to pass through the arch so that there would be light trails in the top half of the frame as well as the lower part. With few vehicles on the road at such an early hour, the bus was traveling fast enough for a shutter speed of just a few seconds to be enough to create the desired effect."

GLOSSARY

Angle of view The area of a scene that a lens records, measured in degrees.

Aperture The opening in a camera lens through which light passes to expose the image sensor. The relative size of the aperture is denoted by f-numbers (f-stops).

Aspect ratio The relative horizontal and vertical measurements. For example, if an image has an aspect ratio of 2:1, it means that the width is twice the length of the height.

Autofocus (AF) A through-the-lens focusing system allowing accurate focus without the user having to manually focus the lens.

Big Stopper An extreme neutral density filter with a density equivalent to 10 stops, made by LEE Filters.

Blue hour A period of twilight in the morning and evening when the residual, indirect sunlight appears predominantly blue.

Camera shake Movement of the camera during exposure that, particularly at slow shutter speeds, can lead to blurred images. Often caused by an unsteady hold or support.

Chromatic aberration Also known as color or purple fringing, it is a lens defect that is most noticeable on high-contrast edges.

Color temperature The color of a light source expressed in degrees Kelvin (K).

Clipping When all detail in Highlights or Shadow areas of an image is lost due to incorrect exposure, a histogram is said to be clipped.

Composition The placement or arrangement of visual elements in an image. The term composition means "putting together" and can apply to any work of art. It is a term often used interchangeably with design, form, or visual ordering.

Context In composition, context refers to surroundings and placing objects so that they remain in keeping with their environment.

Contrast The range between the highlight and shadow areas of an image, or a marked difference in illumination between colors or adjacent areas.

Cropping To remove part of the image, from the left, right, top, or bottom (or any combination thereof). Normally in order to enhance composition or balance.

Dawn The period of the day when light from the sun begins to appear in the sky.

Depth of field (DOF) The amount of an image that appears acceptably sharp. This is controlled by the aperture—the smaller the aperture, the greater the depth of field.

Distortion Typically, when straight lines are not rendered perfectly straight in a photograph. Barrel and pincushion distortion are examples of types of lens distortion.

Dusk The period of partial darkness between day and night.

Dynamic range The ability of the camera's sensor to capture a full range of shadows and highlights.

Electronic viewfinder (EVF) A screen where the image captured by the lens is projected electronically.

Exposure The amount of light allowed to strike and expose the image sensor, controlled by aperture, shutter speed, and ISO sensitivity. Also the act of taking a photograph, as in "making an exposure."

Exposure compensation A control that allows intentional over- or underexposure for corrective or creative purposes.

Filter A piece of colored, or coated, glass or plastic placed in front of the lens for creative or corrective use.

Focal length The distance, usually in millimeters, from the optical center-point of a lens element to its focal point, which signifies its power.

Frame To arrange or compose. Also, purposefully using objects within the landscape to create a "frame," or frame other elements.

F-stop/F-number Number assigned to a particular lens aperture. Wide apertures are denoted by small numbers such as f/2.8, and small apertures by large numbers such as f/22.

Golden hour The time of day shortly after sunrise and before sunset when daylight adopts a warmer color temperature.

Grad Graduated filter. A filter that is half-coated, half-clear.

Highlights The brightest areas of an image.

Histogram A graph used to represent the distribution of tones in an image.

ISO (International Standards Organization) The sensitivity of the image sensor measured in terms equivalent to the ISO rating of a film.

JPEG (Joint Photographic Experts Group) A popular image file type, compressed to reduce file size.

Landscape The visible features of an area of land, including the physical elements of landforms and water bodies, such as rivers, lakes, and the sea. Can also include human elements, such as buildings and structures, and transitory elements such as lighting and weather conditions.

LCD (liquid crystal display) The flat screen on the back of a digital camera that allows the user to playback and review digital images and shooting information.

Lens The eye of the camera. The lens projects the image it sees onto the camera's imaging sensor. The size of the lens is measured and indicated as focal length.

Lightroom Raw conversion software by Adobe that is popular for archiving and post-processing files.

Little Stopper An extreme neutral density filter with a density equivalent to six stops, made by LEE Filters.

Live view A camera function where the viewfinder image is continuously and directly projected onto the screen on the back of the camera via the sensor.

Manual focus This is when focusing is achieved through manual rotation of the lens's focusing ring.

Megapixel One megapixel equals one million pixels.

Metering Using a camera or handheld lightmeter to determine the amount of light coming from a scene and then calculate the required exposure.

Metering pattern The system used by the camera to calculate the exposure.

Mirror lock-up Allows the reflex mirror of an SLR to be raised and held in the "up" position, before the exposure is made.

Monochrome Image consisting only of gray tones, from black to white.

Multiplication factor The amount the focal length of a lens will be magnified when attached to a camera with a cropped-type sensor, smaller than 35mm.

Negative space The empty space surrounding the main subject in your photograph. The subject itself is known as "positive space."

Noise Colored image interference caused by stray electrical signals.

Noise reduction A process—either in-camera or during post-processing—in which signal noise is reduced to enhance image quality and clarity.

Overexposure A condition when too much light reaches the sensor. Detail is lost in the highlights.

Perspective In the context of visual perception, it is the way in which objects appear to the eye depending on their spatial attributes, or their dimensions and the position of the eye relative to the objects.

Photoshop A graphics-editing program developed and published by Adobe Systems Incorporated. It is considered the industry standard for editing and post-processing photographs.

Pixel Abbreviation of "picture element." Pixels are the smallest bits of information that combine to form a digital image.

Post-processing The use of software to make adjustments to a digital file on a computer.

Prime lens A lens with a fixed focal length, that is, not a zoom lens.

Raw A versatile and widely used digital file format in which the shooting parameters are attached to the file.

Remote release A device used to trigger the shutter of a tripod-mounted camera to avoid camera shake.

Resolution The number of pixels used to either capture an image or display it, usually expressed in ppi (pixels per inch). The higher the resolution, the finer the detail.

RGB (red, green, blue) Computers and other digital devices understand color information as shades of red, green, and blue.

Rule of thirds A compositional device that places the key elements of a picture at points along imagined lines that divide the frame into thirds.

Saturation The intensity of the colors in an image.

Shadow areas The darkest areas of the exposure.

Shutter The mechanism that controls the amount of light reaching the sensor by opening and closing when the shutter release is activated.

Shutter speed The shutter speed determines the duration of exposure.

Silhouette The dark shape or outline of an (underexposed) object cast against a brighter background.

SLR (single lens reflex) A camera type that allows the user to view the scene through the lens, using a reflex mirror.

Spot metering A metering system that places importance on the intensity of light reflected by a very small percentage of the frame.

Standard lens A lens with a focal length similar to the vision of the human eye, typically 50mm.

Symmetry Corresponding in size, form, and arrangement on the opposite side of a plane, line, or point. Regularity of form or arrangement.

Telephoto lens A lens with a large focal length and a narrow angle of view.

TIFF (Tagged-Image File Format) A universal file format supported by virtually all image-editing applications. TIFFs are uncompressed digital files.

TTL (through-the-lens) metering A metering system built into the camera that measures light passing through the lens at the time of shooting.

Underexposure A condition in which too little light reaches the sensor. There is too much detail lost in the shadow areas of the exposure.

Vanishing point The point at which parallel lines appear to converge in the rendering of perspective, often on the horizon.

Viewfinder An optical system used for composing and sometimes focusing the subject. Also known as an optical viewfinder (OVF).

Vignetting Darkening of the corners of an image, due to an obstruction, usually caused by a filter(s) or lens hood.

White balance A function that allows the correct color balance to be recorded for any given lighting situation.

Wide-angle lens A lens with a short focal length.

Zoom lens A lens that has a focal length which can be adjusted to any length within its focal range.

IMAGE TECHNICAL DETAILS

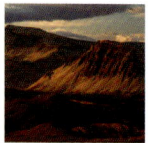

Page 6
Camera Nikon Z8
Lens 24–120mm at 83mm
ISO 64
Shutter speed 1/3 sec., tripod
Aperture f/11
Filter Landscape polarizer

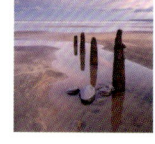

Page 19
Camera Nikon Z7 II
Lens 14–30mm at 26mm
ISO 64
Shutter speed 8 sec., tripod
Aperture f/11
Filter 2-stop med ND grad, 3-stop ND

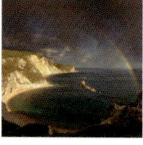

Page 31
Camera Fujifilm GFX 50S
Lens 32–64mm at 32mm
ISO 100
Shutter speed 1/25 sec., tripod
Aperture f/1
Filter Landscape polarizer

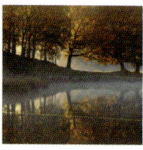

Page 7
Camera Nikon Z8
Lens 24–120mm at 120mm
ISO 64
Shutter speed 1/8 sec., tripod
Aperture f/11
Filter Landscape polarizer

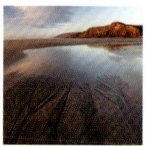

Page 21
Camera Nikon D810
Lens 17–35mm at 19mm
ISO 64
Shutter speed 6 sec., tripod
Aperture f/16
Filter Polarizing filter

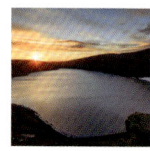

Page 32
Camera Canon EOS 5DS
Lens 16–35mm at 24mm
ISO 200
Shutter speed 5 sec., tripod
Aperture f/16
Filter 3-stop medium ND grad, 4-stop ND

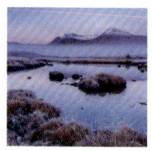

Page 9
Camera Nikon Z8
Lens 24–120mm at 38mm
ISO 64
Shutter speed 2.5 sec., tripod
Aperture f/11
Filter 2-stop med ND grad, Landscape polarizer

Page 22
Camera Nikon Z8
Lens 24-120mm at 97mm
ISO 400
Shutter speed 1/10 sec., tripod
Aperture f/8
Filter n/a

Page 33
Camera Canon EOS 5DS
Lens 70–300mm at 78mm
ISO 100
Shutter speed 1/800 sec., tripod
Aperture f/8
Filter n/a

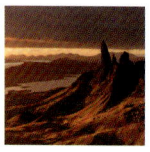

Page 11
Camera Nikon D850
Lens 24–70mm (at 35mm)
ISO 64
Shutter speed 6 sec., tripod
Aperture f/11
Filter 2-stop ND med grad

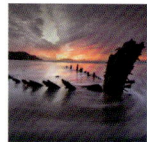

Page 27
Camera Nikon Z7 II
Lens 14–30mm at 15mm
ISO 160
Shutter speed 8 sec., tripod
Aperture f/11
Filter 4-stop ND, 2-stop medium grad

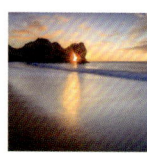

Page 34
Camera Canon EOS 5D Mark II
Lens 21mm
ISO 100
Shutter speed 6 sec., tripod
Aperture f/22
Filter 3-stop soft ND grad, 3-stop ND

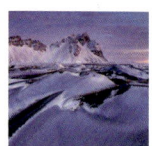

Page 12
Camera Nikon Z8
Lens 14–30mm at 18mm
ISO 64
Shutter speed 20 sec., tripod
Aperture f/13
Filter 2-stop med ND grad, Landscape polarizer

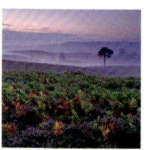

Page 28
Camera Fujifilm GFX 50S
Lens 32–64mm at 37mm
ISO 100
Shutter speed 20 sec., tripod
Aperture f/16
Filter Landscape polarizer

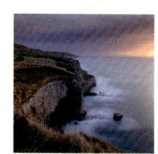

Page 35
Camera Fujifilm X-Pro2
Lens 10–24mm at 11mm
ISO ISO 200
Shutter speed 180 sec., tripod
Aperture f/11
Filter 2-stop medium ND grad, 10-stop IRND

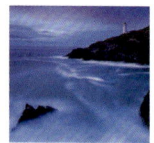

Page 15
Camera Nikon D810
Lens 50mm
ISO 100
Shutter speed 3 min., tripod
Aperture f/11
Filter 2-stop medium ND grad, 10-stop ND

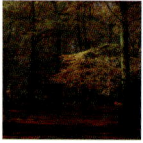

Page 29
Camera Fujifilm GFX 50R
Lens 32–64mm at 60mm
ISO 100
Shutter speed 1/3 sec., tripod
Aperture f/16
Filter Landscape polarizer

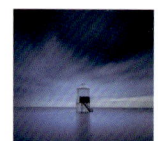

Page 36
Camera Nikon Z8
Lens 24–120mm at 39mm
ISO 64
Shutter speed 120 sec., tripod
Aperture f/8
Filter 10-stop ND

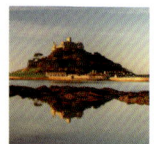

Page 16
Camera Nikon D850
Lens 24–70mm at 70mm
ISO 64
Shutter speed 4 sec., tripod
Aperture f/14
Filter Landscape polarizer, 2-stop medium ND grad

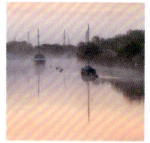

Page 30
Camera Nikon Z8
Lens 100–400mm at 175mm
ISO 800
Shutter speed 1/4 sec., tripod
Aperture f/16
Filter n/a

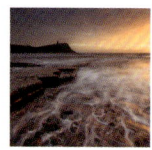

Page 37
Camera Fujifilm GFX 50R
Lens 23mm
ISO 100
Shutter speed 5 sec., tripod
Aperture f/16
Filter 4-stop ND

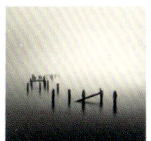

Page 38
Camera Nikon Z8
Lens 24–200mm at 30mm
ISO 64
Shutter speed 30 sec., tripod
Aperture f/11
Filter 10-stop ND

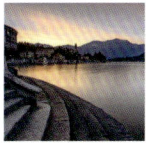

Page 39
Camera Fujifilm GFX 50S
Lens 32–54mm at 32mm
ISO 100
Shutter speed 25 sec., tripod
Aperture f/16
Filter 3-stop soft ND grad,
6-stop IRND

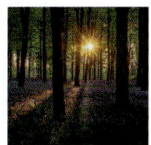

Page 41
Camera Nikon Z7 II
Lens 24-200mm at 59mm
ISO 400
Shutter speed 1/4 sec., tripod
Aperture f/16
Filter Landscape polarizer

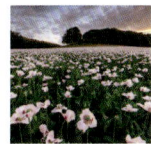

Page 42
Camera Fujifilm X-Pro2
Lens 10–24mm at 10mm
ISO 200
Shutter speed 1/6 sec., tripod
Aperture f/16
Filter 3-stop medium ND grad

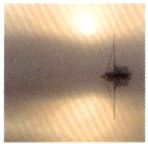

Page 45
Camera Nikon D810
Lens 24–70mm at 24mm
ISO 64
Shutter speed 1/125 sec., tripod
Aperture f/8
Filter 2-stop med ND grad

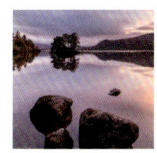

Page 47
Camera Nikon Z8
Lens 14–30mm at 15mm
ISO 64
Shutter speed 30 sec., tripod
Aperture f/11
Filter 2-stop med ND grad

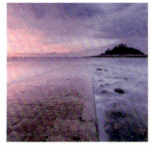

Page 49
Camera Nikon D810
Lens 17–35mm at 17mm
ISO 64
Shutter speed 15 sec., tripod
Aperture f/11
Filter 2-stop hard ND grad,
3-stop ND

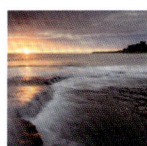

Page 50
Camera Nikon Z8
Lens 14–30mm at 24mm
ISO 64
Shutter speed 1.6 sec., tripod
Aperture f/18
Filter 3-stop med ND grad,
4-stop ND

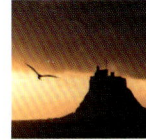

Page 51
Camera Nikon D800E
Lens 70–200mm at 110mm
ISO 100
Shutter speed 1/100 sec., tripod
Aperture f/11
Filter n/a

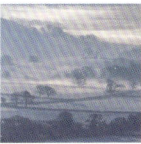

Page 52
Camera Nikon Z7 II
Lens 100–400mm at 380mm
ISO 400
Shutter speed 1/500 sec., tripod
Aperture f/8
Filter n/a

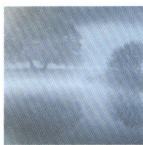

Page 53
Camera Nikon Z8
Lens 24–120mm at 110mm
ISO 64
Shutter speed 1 sec., tripod
Aperture f/11
Filter n/a

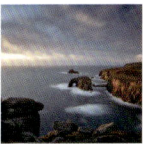

Page 55
Camera Nikon D810
Lens 17–35mm at 17mm
ISO 100
Shutter speed 30 sec., tripod
Aperture f/11
Filter 3-stop medium ND grad,
6-stop ND

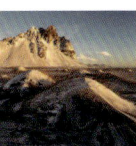

Page 57
Camera Nikon Z8
Lens 14–30mm at 25mm
ISO 64
Shutter speed 1/10 sec., tripod
Aperture f/11
Filter 2-stop soft ND grad

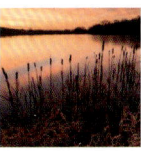

Page 59
Camera Nikon D850
Lens 17–35mm at 24mm
ISO 64
Shutter speed 13 sec., tripod
Aperture f/13
Filter 2-stop med ND grad

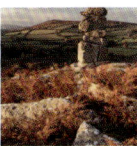

Page 59
Camera Nikon D810
Lens 24–70mm at 38mm
ISO 64
Shutter speed 1.6 sec., tripod
Aperture f/16
Filter Landscape polarizer,
2-stop medium ND grad

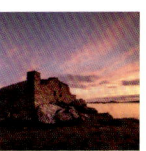

Page 61
Camera Nikon Z 8
Lens 14–30mm at 14mm
ISO 64
Shutter speed 20 sec., tripod
Aperture f/13
Filter n/a

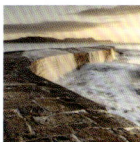

Page 62
Camera Nikon D810
Lens 17–35mm at 30mm
ISO 100
Shutter speed 0.6 sec., tripod
Aperture f/16
Filter 3-stop medium ND grad,
3-stop ND

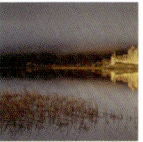

Page 65
Camera Nikon Z8
Lens 24–120mm at 27mm
ISO 64
Shutter speed 1.6 sec., tripod
Aperture f/11
Filter 2-stop med ND grad

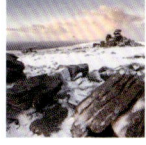

Page 67
Camera Nikon D810
Lens 17–35mm at 20mm
ISO 200
Shutter speed 1/5 sec., tripod
Aperture f/16
Filter Landscape polarizer,
2-stop hard ND grad

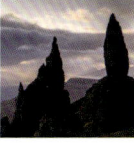

Page 67
Camera Nikon Z7
Lens 24–70mm at 60mm
ISO 64
Shutter speed 1/13 sec., tripod
Aperture f/11
Filter 3-stop soft ND grad

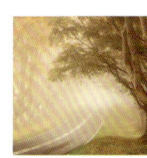

Page 68
Camera Canon EOS 5DS
Lens 70–300mm at 120mm
ISO 100
Shutter speed 1/2 sec., tripod
Aperture f/16
Filter Landscape polarizer

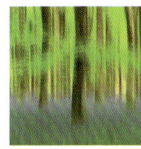

Page 70
Camera Nikon Z8
Lens 24–120mm at 120mm
ISO 64
Shutter speed 1.3 sec.
Aperture f/11
Filter Landscape polarizer

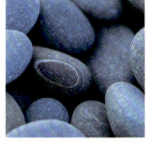

Page 72
Camera Nikon D810
Lens 105mm
ISO 200
Shutter speed 1/320 sec.
Aperture f/6.3
Filter n/a

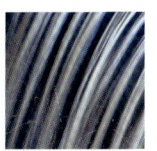

Page 73
Camera Nikon D70
Lens 70–300mm at 270mm
ISO 200
Shutter speed 1/6 sec., tripod
Aperture f/32
Filter n/a

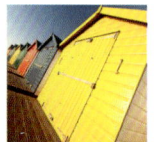
Page 74
Camera Nikon D700
Lens 17–35mm at 17mm
ISO 400
Shutter speed 1/20 sec.
Aperture f/11
Filter Landscape polarizer

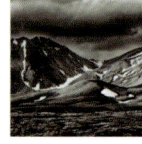
Page 89
Camera Canon EOS 5DS
Lens 70–300mm at 155mm
ISO 100
Shutter speed 1/5 sec., tripod
Aperture f/11
Filter Landscape polarizer

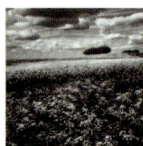
Page 101
Camera Canon EOS 5D Mark III
Lens 24–200m at 29mm
ISO 400
Shutter speed 1/125 sec., tripod
Aperture f/16
Filter Landscape polarizer

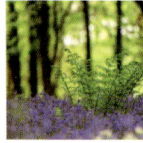
Page 75
Camera Nikon Z7 II
Lens 100–400mm at 320mm
ISO 400
Shutter speed 1/320 sec.
Aperture f/5.3
Filter Landscape polarizer

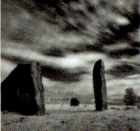
Page 91
Camera Fujifilm GFX 50S
Lens 32–64mm at 32mm
ISO 400
Shutter speed 15 sec., tripod
Aperture f/8
Filter Infrared

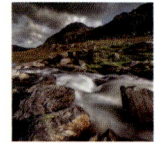
Page 102
Camera Nikon Z8
Lens 14–30mm at 14mm
ISO 64
Shutter speed 1.6 sec., tripod
Aperture f/11
Filter Landscape polarizer,
4-stop ND, 2-stop soft grad

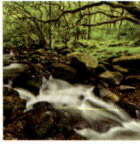
Page 76
Camera Nikon D810
Lens 17–35mm at 17mm
ISO 64
Shutter speed 1.6 sec., tripod
Aperture f/16
Filter Landscape polarizer

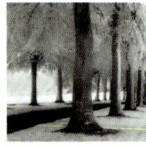
Page 91
Camera IR-converted Fujifilm X-T2
Lens 18–135mm at 52mm
ISO 1600
Shutter speed 1/300 sec., tripod
Aperture f/11
Filter n/a

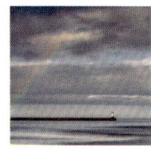
Page 105
Camera Nikon Z8
Lens 24–120mm at 73mm
ISO 32
Shutter speed 8 sec., tripod
Aperture f/16
Filter Landscape polarizer,
6-stop ND

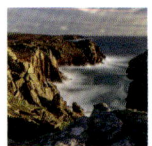
Page 77
Camera Nikon Z8
Lens 14–30mm at 26mm
ISO 64
Shutter speed 60 sec., tripod
Aperture f/13
Filter Landscape polarizer,
10-stop ND

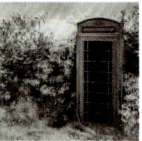
Page 91
Camera Canon EOS 1D Mark II
Lens 24–105mm at 35mm
ISO 100
Shutter speed 1/20 sec., tripod
Aperture f/11
Filter Hoya R72

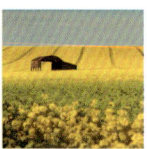
Page 106
Camera Nikon D700
Lens 70–200mm at 125mm
ISO 200
Shutter speed 1/20 sec., tripod
Aperture f/8
Filter Landscape polarizer

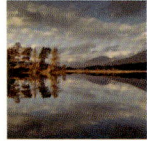
Page 81
Camera Nikon Z8
Lens 24–120mm at 24mm
ISO 64
Shutter speed 1/13 sec., tripod
Aperture f/11
Filter Landscape polarizer,
2-stop ND med grad

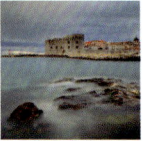
Page 93
Camera Canon EOS 7D Mark II
Lens 10–22mm at 18mm
ISO 100
Shutter speed 90 sec., tripod
Aperture f/11
Filter Landscape polarizer,
10-stop ND

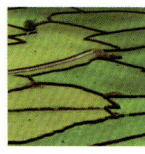
Page 107
Camera Nikon D850
Lens 70–200mm at 150mm
ISO 64
Shutter speed 1/400 sec., tripod
Aperture f/8
Filter Landscape polarizer

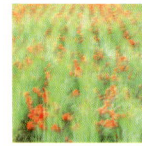
Page 82
Camera Nikon Z8
Lens 24–120mm at 84mm
ISO 64
Shutter speed 1/3 sec.
Aperture f/22
Filter n/a

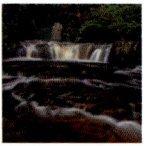
Page 95
Camera Fujifilm GFX 50R
Lens 32–64mm at 42mm
ISO 400
Shutter speed 1.5 sec., tripod
Aperture f/16
Filter 4-stop ND

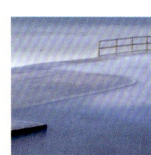
Page 109
Camera Nikon Z8
Lens 100–400mm at 120mm
ISO 64
Shutter speed 60 sec., tripod
Aperture f/11
Filter 10-stop ND

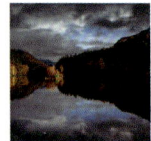
Page 85
Camera Nikon Z8
Lens 14–30mm at 26mm
ISO 64
Shutter speed 1/8 sec., tripod
Aperture f/11
Filter Polarizer

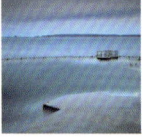
Page 96
Camera Canon 5Ds
Lens 24–70mm at 53mm
ISO 200
Shutter speed 480 sec., tripod
Aperture f/8
Filter 15-stop ND

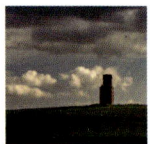
Page 110
Camera Nikon Z7 II
Lens 100–400mm at 120mm
ISO 400
Shutter speed 1/200 sec.
Aperture f/11
Filter Landscape polarizer

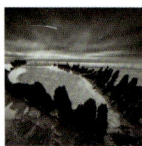
Page 87
Camera Nikon Z8
Len 14–30mm at 14mm
ISO 400
Shutter speed 1/100 sec.
Aperture f/11
Filter Landscape polarizer

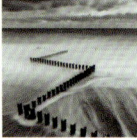
Page 97
Camera Fujifilm GFX 50R
Lens 23mm
ISO 200
Shutter speed 5 sec., tripod
Aperture f/16
Filter 6-stop ND, 2-stop ND grad

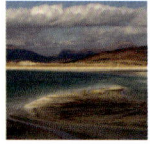
Page 111
Camera Nikon Z8
Lens 24–120mm at 75mm
ISO 400
Shutter speed 1/500 sec.
Aperture f/11
Filter Landscape polarizer

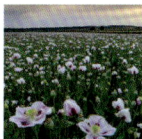

Page 113
Camera Canon EOS 5D Mark III
Lens 21mm
ISO 100
Shutter speed 1 sec., tripod
Aperture f/22
Filter 2-stop hard ND grad

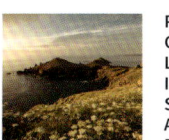

Page 113
Camera Nikon D810
Lens 17–35mm at 17mm
ISO 64
Shutter speed 1.6 sec., tripod
Aperture f/14
Filter Landscape polarizer,
2-stop hard ND grad

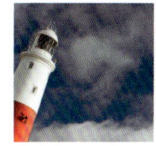

Page 115
Camera Nikon D810
Lens 24–70mm at 70mm
ISO 200
Shutter speed 1/200 sec.
Aperture f/10
Filter Landscape polarizer

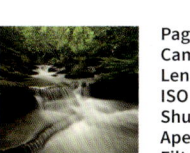

Page 115
Camera Nikon Z8
Lens 14–30mm at 20mm
ISO 64
Shutter speed 1.6 sec., tripod
Aperture f/14
Filter Landscape polarizer

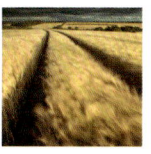

Page 116
Camera Nikon D800
Lens 17–35mm at 20mm
ISO 50
Shutter speed 1.3 sec., tripod
Aperture f/16
Filter Landscape polarizer,
2-stop hard ND grad

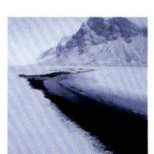

Page 117
Camera Nikon Z8
Lens 14–30mm at 14mm
ISO 400
Shutter speed 1/13 sec.
Aperture f/14
Filter n/a

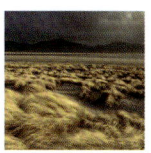

Page 121
Camera Nikon Z8
Lens 24–120mm at 24mm
ISO 64
Shutter speed 1 sec., tripod
Aperture f/16
Filter Landscape polarizer,
2-stop medium ND grad,

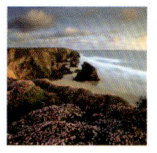

Page 122
Camera Nikon D700
Lens 17–35mm at 19mm
ISO 100
Shutter speed 30 sec., tripod
Aperture f/13
Filter Landscape polarizer,
2-stop hard ND grad, 6-stop ND

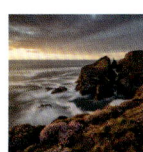

Page 125
Camera Nikon Z7 II
Lens 14–30mm at 17mm
ISO 64
Shutter speed 60 sec., tripod
Aperture f/16
Filter Landscape polarizer,
3-stop medium ND grad, 10-stop
ND

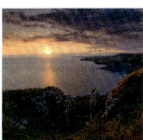

Page 127
Camera Fujifilm GFX 50S
Lens 23mm
ISO 100
Shutter speed 8 sec., tripod
Aperture f/16
Filter 3-stop reverse ND grad,
6-stop ND

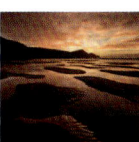

Page 128
Camera Nikon Z8
Lens 14–30mm at 14mm
ISO 64
Shutter speed 6 sec., tripod
Aperture f/14
Filter 3-stop medium ND grad

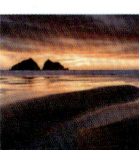

Page 129
Camera Nikon D810
Lens 17–35mm at 32mm
ISO 64
Shutter speed 5 sec., tripod
Aperture f/16
Filter 3-stop hard ND grad

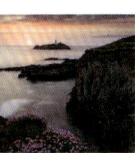

Page 131
Camera Nikon D810
Lens 17–35mm at 22mm
ISO 64
Shutter speed 30 sec., tripod
Aperture f/13
Filter Landscape polarizer,
3-stop hard ND grad, 3-stop ND

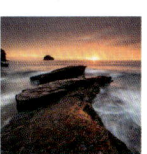

Page 132
Camera Nikon Z8
Lens 14–30mm at 14mm
ISO 64
Shutter speed 1/2 sec., tripod
Aperture f/16
Filter Landscape polarizer,
3-stop medium ND grad

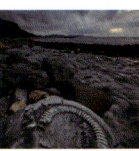

Page 135
Camera Nikon Z8
Lens 14–30mm at 14mm
ISO 64
Shutter speed 6 sec., tripod
Aperture f/11
Filter 4-stop ND,
2-stop medium grad

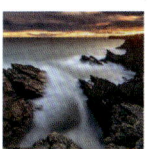

Page 136
Camera Fujifilm GFX 100
Lens 23mm
ISO 100
Shutter speed 120 sec., tripod
Aperture f/22
Filter 10-stop ND,
3-stop reverse ND grad

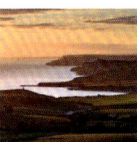

Page 137
Camera Fujifilm GFX 100S
Lens 100–200mm at 113mm
ISO 100
Shutter speed 1/3 sec., tripod
Aperture f/16
Filter Landscape polarizer

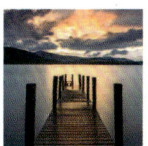

Page 141
Camera Canon EOS 5D Mark III
Lens 17mm
ISO 200
Shutter speed 13 sec., tripod
Aperture f/1
Filter 6-stop ND,
2-stop medium grad

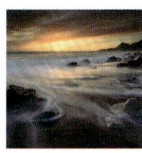

Page 142
Camera Nikon Z7 II
Lens 14–30mm at 14mm
ISO 64
Shutter speed 6 sec., tripod
Aperture f/11
Filter 6-stop ND,
3-stop medium ND grad

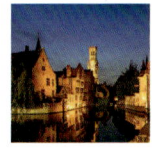

Page 145
Camera Nikon Z8
Lens 14–30mm at 24mm
ISO 64
Shutter speed 5 sec., tripod
Aperture f/8
Filter 4-stop ND

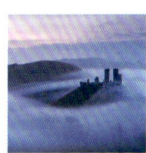

Page 146
Camera Fujifilm GFX 100S
Lens 32–64mm at 57mm
ISO 100
Shutter speed 15 sec., tripod
Aperture f/11
Filter n/a

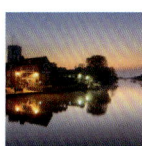

Page 147
Camera Nikon Z7 II
Lens 24–200mm at 24mm
ISO 64
Shutter speed 6 sec., tripod
Aperture f/11
Filter n/a

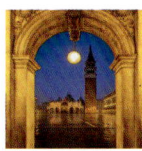

Page 149
Camera Fujifilm GFX 50R
Lens 23mm
ISO 100
Shutter speed 7 sec., tripod
Aperture f/16
Filter Landscape polarizer

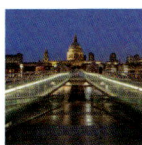

Page 150
Camera Nikon Z8
Lens 24–200mm at 38mm
ISO 64
Shutter speed 13 sec., tripod
Aperture f/11
Filter n/a

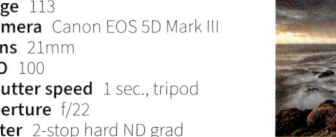
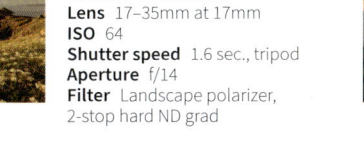

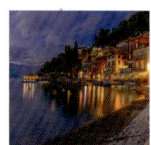

Page 152
Camera Canon EOS 5DS
Lens 16–35mm at 20mm
ISO 100
Shutter speed 3.2 sec., tripod
Aperture f/8
Filter n/a

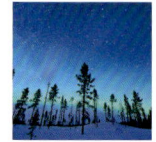

Page 166
Camera Nikon D700
Lens 14-24mm f/2.8 at 18mm
ISO 1600
Shutter speed 293 sec., tripod
Aperture f/8
Filter n/a

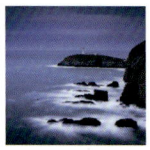

Page 153
Camera Nikon Z8
Lens 24–200mm at 44mm
ISO 100
Shutter speed 60 sec., tripod
Aperture f/11
Filter 4-stop ND

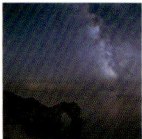

Page 169
Camera Fujifilm GFX 50S
Lens 23mm
Sky ISO 6400, 30 sec., f/4, tripod
Foreground ISO 1600, 8 min., f/4, tripod
Filter n/a

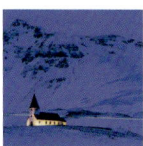

Page 154
Camera Nikon Z8
Lens 24–200mm at 135mm
ISO 200
Shutter speed 2.5 sec., tripod
Aperture f/8
Filter n/a

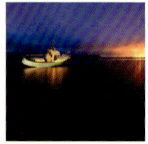

Page 171
Camera Canon EOS 5D Mark II
Lens 21mm
ISO 200
Shutter speed 180 sec., tripod
Aperture f/8
Filter n/a

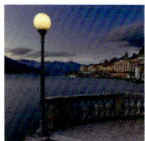

Page 155
Camera Fujifilm GFX 50S
Lens 32–64mm at 38mm
ISO 100
Shutter speed 120 sec., tripod
Aperture f/16
Filter n/a

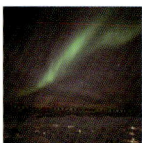

Page 173
Camera Canon EOS 5DS
Lens 16–35mm at 16mm
ISO 3200
Shutter speed 30 sec., tripod
Aperture f/2.8
Filter n/a

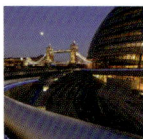

Page 159
Camera Nikon Z7II
Lens 14–30mm at 16mm
ISO 200
Shutter speed 5 sec., tripod
Aperture f/11
Filter n/a

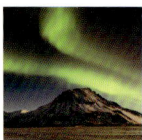

Page 175
Camera Canon EOS 5DS
Lens 16–35mm at 28mm
ISO 2000
Shutter speed 20 sec., tripod
Aperture f/4
Filter n/a

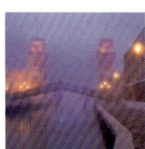

Page 160
Camera Nikon Z8
Lens 24–200mm at 51mm
ISO 200
Shutter speed 5 sec., tripod
Aperture f/11
Filter n/a

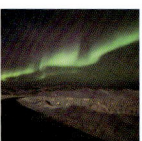

Page 179
Camera Canon EOS 5DS
Lens 16–35mm at 18mm
ISO 3200
Shutter speed 20 sec., tripod
Aperture f/2.8
Filter n/a

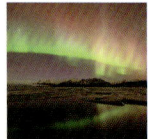

Page 162
Camera Canon EOS 5D Mark III
Lens 16–35mm at 16mm
ISO 3200
Shutter speed 30 sec., tripod
Aperture f/2.8
Filter n/a

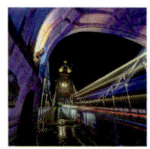

Page 180
Camera Nikon Z8
Lens 14–30mm at 14mm
ISO 200
Shutter speed 3 sec., tripod
Aperture f/11
Filter n/a

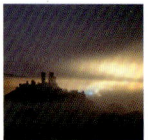

Page 165
Camera Fujifilm GFX 50S
Lens 32–64mm at 44mm
Sky ISO 1600, 30 sec., f/2.8, tripod
Foreground ISO 1600, 240 sec., f/4, tripod
Filter n/a

USEFUL WEBSITES

OUTDOOR EQUIPMENT AND CLOTHING

Brasher www.brasher.co.uk
Bridgedale www.bridgedale.com
Mammut www.mammut.com
Meindl www.meindl.de
Paramo www.paramo-clothing.com
Patagonia www.patagonia.com
Petzl www.petzl.com
Rab www.rab.equipment
Salomon www.salomon.com
Scarpa www.scarpa.com
Sealskinz www.sealskinz.com

PHOTOGRAPHIC EQUIPMENT

Canon www.canon.com
Fujifilm www.fujifilm.com
Fstop gear www.fstopgear.com
Gitzo www.gitzo.com
Hoodman www.hoodmanusa.com
LEE Filters www.leefilters.com
Manfrotto www.manfrotto.com
Nikon www.nikon.com
Olympus www.olympus.com
Pentax www.pentaximaging.com
Really Right Stuff www.reallyrightstuff.com
Samyang www.samyanglensglobal.com
Sandisk www.sandisk.com
Sigma www.sigma-photo.com
Sony www.sony.com
Tamron www.tamron.com

PHOTOGRAPHY AND ONE-TO-ONE TUITION

Mark Bauer www.markbauerphotography.com
Ross Hoddinott www.rosshoddinott.co.uk

PHOTOGRAPHY WORKSHOPS

Dawn 2 Dusk Photography www.dawn2duskphotography.co.uk

PLANNING

Google Maps maps.google.com
Ordnance Survey www.ordnancesurvey.co.uk
PhotoPills www.photopills.com
The Photographer's Ephemeris www.photoephemeris.com

PUBLISHER

Ammonite Press www.ammonitepress.com

SOFTWARE

Adobe www.adobe.com
Helicon Focus www.heliconsoft.com
Photomatix Pro www.hdrsoft.com
Zerene Stacker www.zerenesystems.com

TIDE TIMES

Ayetides www.ayetides.com
Tide-Forecast www.tide-forecast.com

WEATHER

AccuWeather www.accuweather.com
MeteoEarth www.meteoearth.com
The Met Office www.metoffice.gov.uk
Yr www.yr.no

INDEX

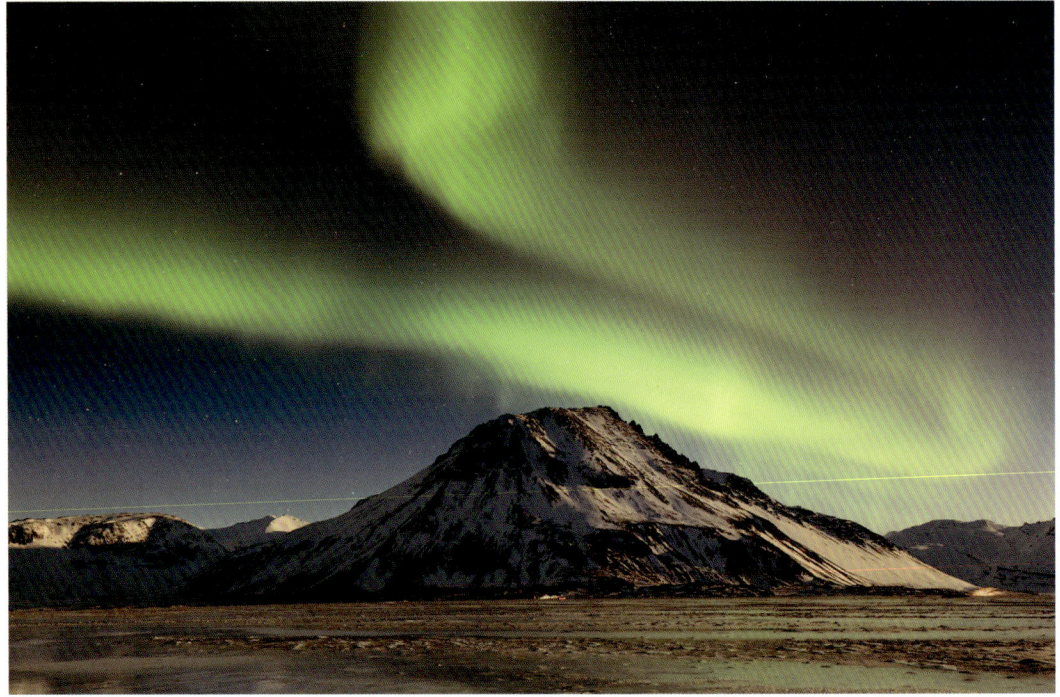

ACKNOWLEDGMENTS

I'm sure it is no surprise that the first and biggest thank you of all is reserved for our long suffering families—Mark's wife Julie and son Harry; and Ross's wife Felicity and children Evie, Maya, and Jude. To capture the best light, landscape photographers work long and often unsociable, inconsistent, and unpredictable hours. We are regularly working away from home and constantly under pressure to hit deadlines or capture a particular shot! We couldn't do what we do without our families' endless support, belief, and understanding. Quite simply—thank you and love you!

However, this book wouldn't have been possible without the encouragement (and patience!) of Publisher Jason Hook at Ammonite Press—thank you. We thank Robin Shields for the book's clean, stylish design, while editor Rob Yarham has yet again done a fantastic job of knocking our material into shape! They are a fantastic team to work with—thank you! Thank you also to photographers Jeremy Walker and Andy Farrer for allowing us to pinch a couple of your superb night shots, and also F-stop Gear, Fujifilm, Hoodman, LEE Filters, and Nikon.

Lastly, a big shout out to all our workshop participants. Over the years, they have encouraged us to share our knowledge and experience with a wider audience. And if you enjoyed From *Dawn to Dusk—Mastering the Light in Landscape Photography*, why not join us on one of our popular Dawn 2 Dusk Photography workshops? We hope to meet you in person soon...

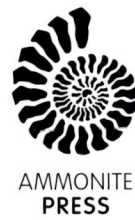

AMMONITE
PRESS

www.ammonitepress.com